Readings in

Child Abuse

Special Learning Corporation

42 Boston Post Rd. Guilford, Connecticut 06437

Special Learning Corporation

Publisher's Message:

The Special Education Series is the first comprehensive series designed for special education courses of study. It is also the first series to offer such a wide variety of high quality books. In addition, the series will be expanded and up-dated each year. No other publications in the area of special education can equal this. We stress high quality content, a superb advisory and consulting group, and special features that help in understanding the course of study. In addition we believe we must also publish in very small enrollment areas in order to establish the credibility and strength of our series. We realize the enrollments in courses of study such as Autism, Visually Handicapped Education, or Diagnosis and Placement are not large. Nevertheless, we believe there is a need for course books in these areas and books that are kept up-to-date on an annual basis! Special Learning Corporation's goal is to publish the highest quality materials for the college and university courses of study. With your comments and support we will continue to do this.

John P. Quirk

First Edition

1 2 3 4 5

ISBN 0-89568-103-X

SPECIAL EDUCATION SERIES

* ● Abnormal Psychology: The Problems of
        Disordered Emotional and Behavioral
        Development
  ● Administration of Special Education
  ● Autism
* ● Behavior Modification
     Biological Bases of Learning Disabilities
     Brain Impairments
  ● Career and Vocational Education for the
        Handicapped
  ● Child Abuse
* ● Child Psychology
  ● Classroom Teacher and the Special Child
* ● Counseling Parents of Exceptional Children
     Creative Arts
  ● Curriculum Development for the Gifted
     Curriculum and Materials
* ● Deaf Education
     Developmental Disabilities
* ● Developmental Psychology: The Problems of
        Disordered Mental Development
* ● Diagnosis and Placement
  ● Down's Syndrome
  ● Dyslexia
* ● Early Childhood Education
  ● Educable Mentally Handicapped
* ● Emotional and Behavioral Disorders
     Exceptional Parents
  ● Foundations of Gifted Education
* ● Gifted Education
* ● Human Growth and Development of the
     Exceptional Individual

● Hyperactivity
* ● Individualized Education Programs
  ● Instructional Media and Special Education
  ● Language and Writing Disorders
  ● Law and the Exceptional Child: Due Process
* ● Learning Disabilities
  ● Learning Theory
* ● Mainstreaming
* ● Mental Retardation
  ● Motor Disorders
     Multiple Handicapped Education
     Occupational Therapy
  ● Perception and Memory Disorders
* ● Physically Handicapped Education
* ● Pre-School Education for the Handicapped
* ● Psychology of Exceptional Children
  ● Reading Disorders
     Reading Skill Development
     Research and Development
* ● Severely and Profoundly Handicapped
        Social Learning
* ● Special Education
  ● Special Olympics
* ● Speech and Hearing
     Testing and Diagnosis
  ● Three Models of Learning Disabilities
  ● Trainable Mentally Handicapped
  ● Visually Handicapped Education
  ● Vocational Training for the Mentally Retarded

● Published Titles   *Major Course Areas

TOPIC MATRIX

Readings in Child Abuse provides the reader with a comprehensive overview of the subject. This book is designed to follow a basic college course of study, or supplement courses in child welfare, pediatrics, primary care, psychiatry, law, psychology, sociology, nursing, counseling, education, administration and public health.

COURSE OUTLINE:

Child Abuse

I. Introduction to Child Abuse and Neglect
  a. legal definition
  b. incidence

II. Character Analysis
  a. abusing parents
  b. abused children

III. Sexual Abuse
  a. types of sexual abuse
  b. assistance for victim and legal implications

IV. Abuse Outside the Home and Community Assistance
  a. Schools
    1. educator's responsibility
    2. corporal punishment
  b. institutional abuse
  c. intervention by non-professionals

V. Professional Prevention and Intervention
  a. multidisciplinary approach
  b. legislative approach

Readings in Child Abuse

I. Understanding Child Abuse and Neglect

II. The Parent and Child

III. Sexual Child Abuse

IV. Schools, Institutions and the Community

V. The Professionals: Help for Troubled Families

Related Special Learning Corporation Readers

I. Readings in Counseling Parents of Exceptional Children

II. Child Psychology

III. Emotional and Behavioral Disorders

CONTENTS

3. Sexual Child Abuse

4. Schools, Institutions and the Community

5. Help for Troubled Families

GLOSSARY OF TERMS

abandonment Parent* leaving a child without adequate supervision or provision for an excessive period of time.

adjudication hearing Court hearing that decides whether or not charges against a parent are substantiated by admissible evidence.

advocacy Interventive strategy in which a helping person assumes an active roll in assisting or supporting a specific child and/or family, or a cause on behalf of children and/or families.

anomie Breakdown or failure of standards, rules, norms, and values in the family.

apathy-futility syndrome Immature personality type characterized by inability to feel and find any significant meaning in life.

assessment 1) Determination of the validity of a reported case through investigatory interviews with persons involved. 2) Determination of treatment potential and treatment plan for confirmed cases.

assault Intentional or reckless threat of physical injury to a person.

best interest of the child Standard for deciding among alternative plans for care, usually assumes that the home provides the best care, provided the parents can respond to treatment.

child abuse and neglect "The physical or mental injury, sexual abuse, negligent treatment or maltreatment of a child under the age of eighteen by a person who is responsible for the child's welfare under circum-

---

★Parents in all cases refer to "parent or caretaker."

stances which indicate that the child's health or welfare is harmed or threatened thereby." (Child Abuse Prevention and Treatment Act, 1974)

child development Pattern of sequential stages of interrelated physical, psychological, and social development in the process of maturation.

child health visitor Professional or paraprofessional who visits a home shortly after the birth of a baby and periodically thereafter to identify current and potential child health and development, and family stress problems.

child protective service or child protective services A specialized child welfare service, legally responsible in most states for investigation and intervention.

children's rights Rights of children as individuals to the protection provided in the Constitution as well as the care and protection necessary for normal growth and development.

civil proceeding Juvenile, family court cases and any lawsuit other than criminal prosecutions.

commissions, acts of Overt acts by a parent toward a child resulting in physical or mental injury.

community awareness A community's level of understanding of child abuse and neglect.

community neglect Failure of a community to provide adequate support and social services for families and children, or lack of community control over illegal or discriminatory activities with respect to families and children.

confidentiality Professional practice of not sharing with others information entrusted by a client or patient.

corporal punishment Physical punishment inflicted directly upon the body. In a 1977 Supreme Court ruling, corporal punishment in the schools, under certain circumstances was upheld.

discipline Training that develops self-control, self-sufficiency, and orderly conduct, is often confused with punishment.

due process The rights of persons involved in legal proceedings to be treated with fairness.

early intervention Programs and services focusing on prevention by relieving family stress before child abuse and neglect occur.

educational neglect Failure to provide for a child's cognitive development. May include failure to conform to state legal requirements regarding school attendance.

emotional abuse Occurs when a parent refuses to recognize or obtain help for a child's identified emotional disturbance.

exploitation of children 1) Involving a child in illegal or immoral activities for the benefit of a parent or caretaker. 2) Forcing workloads on a child in or outside the home so as to interfere with the health, education and well-being of the child.

families-at-risk Refers to families evidencing high potential for abuse or neglect because of risk factors which may not always be conspicuous and are often multiple.

family dynamics Interrelationship between and among individual family members.

foster care A form of substitute care for children who need to be removed from their own homes.

Glossary adapted from "Interdisciplinary Glossary on Child Abuse and Neglect: Legal, Medical and Social Work Terms," prepared by the Midwest Parent-Child Welfare Resource Center, now Region V Child Abuse and Neglect Resource Center, ©1978, U.S. Department of Health, Education and Welfare, (OHDS) 7 8-30137

guardian ad litem (GAL) Adult appointed by the court to represent the child in a judicial proceeding.

incest Sexual intercourse between persons who are closely related by blood.

institutional child abuse and neglect 1) Abuse and neglect as a result of social or institutional policies, practices, or conditions. 2) Child abuse and neglect committed by an employee of a public or private institution or group home against a child resident.

liability for failure to report State statutes which require certain categories of persons to report cases of suspected child abuse and/or neglect are often enforced by the imposition of a penalty, fine, and/or imprisonment, for those who fail to report.

maltreatment Actions that are abusive, neglectful, or otherwise threatening to a child's welfare.

medical neglect Failure to seek medical or dental treatment for a health problem or condition which, if untreated, could become severe enough to represent a danger to the child.

mental inury Injury to the intellectual or psychological capacity of a child as evidenced by observable and substantial impairment in his/her ability to function within a normal range of performance and behavior, with due regard to his/her culture.

multidisciplinary team Group of professionals and paraprofessionals representing a variety of disciplines who interact and coordinate their efforts for diagnosis and treatment.

parens patriae "The power of the sovereign." Refers to the state's power to act for or on behalf of minors.

parents' rights Society accords parents the right to custody and supervision of their own children. This plus parents' rights to privacy may complicate investigations and treatment of suspected cases of child abuse and neglect.

passive abuser Parent or caretaker who does not intervene to prevent abuse by another person in the home.

physical abuse Child abuse which results in physical injury.

physical neglect Failure to provide for a child's basic survival needs.

psychological/emotional abuse Child abuse which results in impaired psychological growth and development.

punishment Infliction of pain, loss or suffering on a child because he/she has disobeyed or otherwise antagonized a parent or caretaker, sometimes confused with discipline.

recidivism Recurrence of child abuse and neglect.

regional resource centers Funded as demonstration project in the ten HEW regions under the 1974 Child Abuse Prevention and Treatment Act, and function in some degree as extensions of the National Center to help fulfill its aims. (see appendix)

reporting laws Requires specified categories of persons, such as professionals, and allows other persons, to notify public authorities of cases of suspected child abuse and, sometimes, neglect.

role reversal Process whereby a parent seeks nurturance and/or protection from a child rather than providing this for the child, who frequently complies.

self-help group Persons with similar, often stigmatized, problems who share concerns and experiences in an effort to provide mutual help to one another. (Parents Anonymous)

sexual abuse Child abuse which results in any act of a sexual nature upon or with a child.

situational child abuse and neglect Cases where the major causative factors cannot be readily eliminated because they relate to problems over which the parents have little control.

staff burnout Apathy and frustration felt by protective service workers who are overworked, undertrained, and lacking agency or supervisory support.

supportive services Human services which provide assistance to families or individuals to help them fulfill their potential for positive growth and behavior.

suspected child abuse and neglect Reason to believe that child abuse or neglect has or is occurring in a given family. Anyone can, in good faith, report to the local mandated agency.

termination of parental rights Legal proceedings freeing a child from his/her parents' claims making him/her free for adoption without parents' written consent.

verbal abuse Form of psychological/emotional abuse characterized by constant verbal harassment and denigration of a child.

world of abnormal rearing (WAR) Generational cycle of development in which abused or neglected children tend to grow up to be abusive or neglectful parents unless intervention occurs to break the cycle.

The glossary was made possible by Grant No. 90-C-600 from the National Center on Child Abuse and Neglect, Children's Bureau, Administration for Children, Youth, and Families, Office of Human Development Services, U.S. Department of Health, Education and Welfare. Its contents should not be construed as official policy of the National Center on Child Abuse and Neglect or any other agency of the Federal Government.

HELP DESTROY A FAMILY TRADITION.

Although few people talk about it, child abuse is almost as American as apple pie. In many cases it's a family tradition in which helpless parents inflict beatings, neglect, emotional strain or sexual abuse on their helpless children.

Abused children grow up learning abuse as a way of life. When they become parents, they pass that learning on to their children.

It is estimated that there are at least one million cases of child abuse in America each year. Over 2,000 of those children die from abuse.

Most people erroneously believe that child abusers cannot be helped. They can be helped. But, since abused children so often grow up to be abusive parents, the only way to destroy that tradition is to prevent abuse before it occurs. Get more information on how you can help.

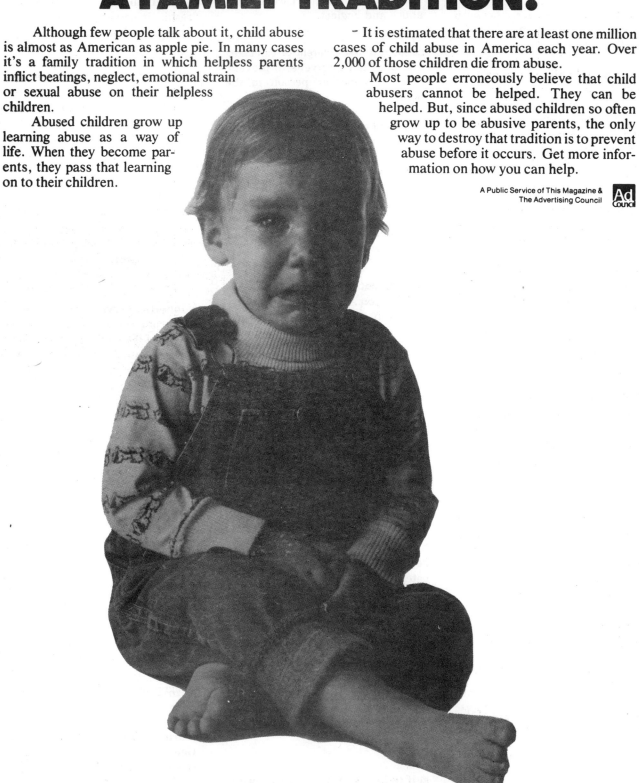

PREVENT CHILD ABUSE. WRITE:
National Committee for Prevention of Child Abuse, Box 2866, Chicago, Ill. 60690.

PREFACE

Informed estimates on the number of child abuse and neglect cases per year run from 600,000 to one million. Many feel that the actual number is significantly higher. *Readings in Child Abuse* presents an overview of the problem, emphasizing that it is not restricted to class but a societal illness. Child maltreatment takes place in all forms, in all neighborhoods.

The purpose of this reader is to provide realistic alternatives for prevention and assistance. Examples of programs that are working and suggestions for future legislation are offered. Designed to follow a course of study, it provides an organized source book not only for the student, but the helping professional, the physician, public health and school nurse, social worker, counselor, lawyer, legislator, teacher, parent and others interested in guaranteeing equal rights for children.

It is impossible to include all of the studies and programs that are now providing services in the United States. An effort has been made to include a representative selection. We would like to emphasize the importance of the role of the individual, the "lay therapist" or "community volunteer" in understanding, prevention and intervention. It is to their work we dedicate this reader.

Understanding Child Abuse

The first section is directed towards an increased understanding of child abuse and maltreatment. A basic definition is taken from the American Humane Association's pamphlet "Understanding Child Neglect and Abuse." This provides the basis for questions asked throughout the text.

Laurie Beckelman, a freelance writer, finds that the two major obstacles in helping the abused child are the sanctity of familial privacy and the value of physical force as discipline. She quotes Dr. Eli Newberger, director of the Family Development Study at Children's Hospital in Boston, as saying "Children's rights have never been defined because we believe in the inviolability of the family and feel that we shouldn't wrest control from parents who have the right to discipline their children." She points to social inequities and acceptance of violence by society as the root of the problem. This theory is supported by the research of Dr. Richard J. Gelles, a noted sociologist. To date, there has been little reliable data on incidence and prevalence in parental use of violence and aggression. Using sophisticated techniques and a large cross section of the population, he found that between 84 and 97 percent of parents use some sort of physical violence. Gelles feels even these high statistics are probably an underestimate.

At the Second National Conference on Child Abuse and Neglect (April, 1977) a professor of social work at the University of Wisconsin, Alfred Kadushin, called attention to the lack of study and intervention in cases of neglect. It is estimated that cases of neglect are at least four to five times more common that cases of abuse. Yet, the time and money has not been available for further studies. He poses questions and ideas as to why

The United Kingdom has found similar patterns to those reported in the U.S. studies. In a paper presented at the same conference, Raymond L. Castle, Executive Director of the National Advisory Center on the Battered Child, United Kingdom, describes the study of child abuse and organization of alternative delivery systems.

The section closes with questions posed by the National Alliance for the Prevention and Treatment of Child Abuse and Maltreatment. "Should punishment be used to deter child abuse or neglect?" "Should society intervene in a family because of the likelihood a child will be harmed?" "Should an expectant mother be held responsible for the health of an unborn child?" "Should childrearing values be imposed on others?" The National Alliance encourages community seminars for discussion of these and other questions. A problem cannot be solved without understanding the total community involvement.

Understanding Child Neglect and Abuse

Wayne M. Holder

Patricia Schene

THE DEFINITION OF CHILD NEGLECT AND ABUSE

Child maltreatment within the family unit or care situation takes many forms and is defined in legal terms (sometimes rather generally) and in non-technical terms. The legal definitions help determine the perimeters of intervention by the child protective service agency and the courts. Legal definitions are a part of law and vary by state. Less technical definitions are useful in helping the public understand this social malady, and therefore, be in a better position to identify the problem and report it.

Because of the wide variation of state laws defining child neglect or abuse, it seems more practical to refer to the model Child Protective Services Act. This model is not presented as the only acceptable statement but does demonstrate to the reader one sort of legal definition.

Excerpts:

a.   "child" means a person under the age of 18.

b.   an "abused or neglected child" means a child whose physical or mental health or welfare is harmed or threatened with harm by the acts or omissions of his parent or other persons responsible for his welfare.

c.   "harm" to a child's health and welfare can occur when the parent or other person responsible for his welfare:

    i.   inflicts or allows to be inflicted, upon the child, physical or mental harm, injury, including injuries sustained as a result of excessive corporal punishment, or

    ii.   commits or allows to be committed, against the child, a sexual offense, as defined by state law, or

    iii.   fails to supply the child with adequate food, clothing, shelter, education, or health care, though financially able to do so or offered financial or other reasonable means to do so . . . or

    iv.   abandons the child . . . or,

    v.   fails to provide the child with adequate care, supervision, or guardianship by specific acts or omissions of a similarly serious nature requiring the intervention of child protective service or a court.

"Understanding Child Neglect and Abuse," Wayne M. Holder and Patricia Schene, from Understanding Child Neglect and Abuse, ©1978 by the American Humane Association.

d.   "threatened harm" means a substantial risk of harm.

e.   "a person responsible for a child's welfare" includes the child's parent; guardian; foster parent; an employee of a public or private residential home, institution or agency, or other person legally responsible for the child's welfare in a residential setting.

f.   "physical injury" means death, or permanent or temporary disfigurement, or impairment of any bodily organ.

g.   "mental injury" means an injury to the intellectual or psychological capacity of the child as evidenced by an observable and substantial impairment in his ability to function within a normal range of performance and behavior, with due regard to his culture.

Vincent De Francis, former director of American Humane, Child Protection and a true pioneer in the child protection field, succinctly answered the question of what is child neglect and abuse in a paper presented at the National Symposium on Child Abuse in 1971:

1.   It is a violation of the rights of children through failure to meet the needs of children; their right to have their needs met is violated in some fashion;

2.   It results from dereliction of parental duty, i.e., failure on the part of a parent to carry out parental obligations; and

3.   It results from a combination of the first two elements.

Neglect or abuse may well be said to be an act of omission on the part of the parent or an act of commission. All neglect and abuse falls into one or the other of these categories. It is either an omission or a commission on the part of the parents.

1. UNDERSTANDING

But neglect and abuse cover a variety of conditions relating to child care. I catalog eight types of neglect and abuse. Very briefly, let me enumerate what they are:

    a.   Children are physically neglected when their needs in terms of food, shelter and clothing are neglected.

    b.   Children are morally neglected when they are subjected to influences which have corrupted or which pose present danger of corrupting the child.

    c.   Children are emotionally neglected when their mental health is affected by failure to provide for a child the nurturing qualities which are so necessary for the development of a sound personality.

    d.   Children are medically neglected when their need for diagnosis or treatment of a medical condition may be ignored.

    e.   Children are educationally neglected when there is a failure to provide the education required by state law.

    f.   Children are physically abused when they are on the receiving end of acts of commission.

    g.   Children are sexually abused. This is the child about whom too little is known in most communities. Even our most sophisticated persons coming into contact with children—the social work community—know very little about the extent, the incidence and the intensity of damage to children arising out of the problem of sexual abuse.

    h.   Children are victims of community neglect. Community failure through acts of omission or acts of commission results in much neglect of children.[1]

Before leaving the issue of definition, it is important to make some distinction between abuse and other things. First, consider discipline. Where does discipline leave off and abuse begin? This question is only relevant if you consider discipline to be punishment, and the answer can then be very evasive and laden with values.

Discipline, in terms of an appropriate conception, is not in the same continuum with abuse. *Discipline is teaching.* It is part of a socialization process which enables us all to know what the rules are, what is right and wrong, what is acceptable, what is safe or dangerous and what consequences can be expected from various behaviors. Discipline involves a positive approach to providing external controls which, if done effectively, will become internalized controls for the child. Setting physical limits, providing alternatives, discussion, rewards and withholding rewards, rule setting and so on are appropriate means of discipline. Physical punishment or verbal abuse are clearly not the only alternatives and should not be the last ones. In simple terms, *discipline is an act of love and concern; abuse is an act of violence and disregard.*

A second distinction is the difference between abuse and an abusive act. Probably all parents have been abusive toward their children, usually resulting in minimal damage, like hurt feelings or some bruising. Abusive acts are the same as abuse when specific actions, such as losing your temper and shaking your child, are taken. The difference is abuse becomes apparent when abusive acts are constant, continual and a part of the child's daily life. Seriousness of the act also is a determinant, such as broken bones, black eyes, and so on. Child abuse is a pattern involving results (the child's condition), based on the parent's emotional capacity, stress, behavior, economics and a wide range of interacting variables.

Figure 1 shows schematically the distinction between abuse and abusive acts. The notion suggested is that even a superior parent may have a slip and perform an abusive act. This, of course, does not give allowance for abusive acts. Parents should always be on guard against losing control of their behavior. However, recognizing parents are human, we must accept that a parent, in a moment of frustration, calling his child "dummy" is not a child abuser. The critical question relies on the pervasive quality of the parent-child relationship. *Is it fear, distance and anger or is it love, nurturance and concern?*

Figure 1
Abusive Acts vs Abuse

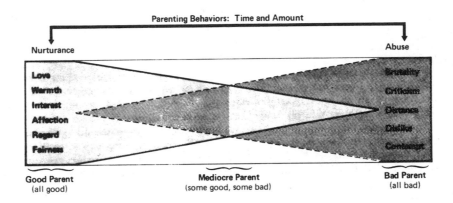

Judy Glasser

WHY THE CRY OF THE BEATEN CHILD GOES UNHEARD

Laurie Beckelman

Laurie Beckelman is a freelance writer with a special interest in behavioral subjects.

A mother told me in confidence that her husband was beating their son. She made me promise not to say anything because she was afraid of ruining the marriage. But the kid was a real behavior problem. I was afraid to report it because, if I broke her confidence, I'd sever the only link I had with the family. I also feared that the father would retaliate by beating the kid even more. I talked to our school psychologist who agreed that I should continue trying to work through the mother. He also suggested that I pray and use lots of Band-Aids with Vaseline.

—FOURTH-GRADE TEACHER.

A neighbor, a very young divorcee, asked me to watch her baby for an evening. When I got the infant it was all bruised. There were even cigarette burns on its arms and back. I felt sick. I wanted to call the police but my husband said no. He said to just give the

baby back and never take it again, that if we reported it they'd think we'd done it and we'd be sued. So I gave the baby back without saying a word.

—A HOUSEWIFE.

From the neighbor who overhears a young child's screams to the doctor who treats the bruises and lesions on his battered body, more often than not, adults who are in a position to help abused children don't. They are stymied by concerns as raw as the fear of personal harm or of lawsuits; as subtle as subconscious sympathy with the abuser. They are deterred by societal ethics that warn against involvement in another man's affairs, and halted by their own uncertainty as to what does or does not constitute abuse. Factors twist together like the fibers of a rope and keep the helping adult from the hurting child. As a result, less than a third of the estimated one million American children abused each year ever reach the attention of child-protective agencies. If a greater amount of violent mistreatment is to

be prevented, more must be understood about the dynamics of intervening, about why people don't come to the aid of such children.

A fundamental barrier confronting the would-be intervener is the fact that society doesn't really support intervention. The clichés that glibly capsulize societal attitudes tell the story. A man's home is his castle. Curiosity killed the cat. Spare the rod; spoil the child. Whip him into shape. Two deeply entrenched beliefs—one in the sanctity of familial privacy, the other in the value of physical force as discipline—conspire against the abused child's receiving help. "Our society upholds a tradition of family autonomy," says Dr. Eli Newberger, director of the Family Development Study at Children's Hospital Medical Center in Boston. "Children's rights have never been defined because we believe in the inviolability of the family and feel that we shouldn't wrest control from parents who have the right to discipline their children." Public sentiment on this issue is so strong that involvement rather than noninvolvement is

often seen as pathological. One forensic psychiatrist who has petitioned the courts for removal to foster care of 320 abused children says that each time he goes into court someone makes him feel "like a hit man who has taken out a contract on the part of the kids to get the parents." And in a well-publicized Chicago case, a woman who had nursed an abused child back to health and then fought to gain custody of him said of her dealings with the police: ". . . two policewomen arrived, from the youth division. They questioned us as if *we* were the offenders. They kept referring to the fact that we had no doctor's report to substantiate our 'claims.' "

Anticipation of such situations stops many people from involving themselves. Others are deterred by their own reluctance to pry, to seem nosy. For still others, the taboos against interfering are so strong that the possibility is never considered. A Stanford University graduate recalls: "There was an abused child on our housing court at Stanford University. We knew it, but there was this feeling that we terred by societal ethics that warn against involvement in another man's affairs, and halted by their own uncertainty as to what does or does not constitute abuse. Factors twist together like the fibers of a rope and keep the helping adult from the hurting child. As a result, less than a third of the estimated one million American children abused each year ever reach the attention of child-protective agencies. If a greater amount of violent mistreatment is to be prevented, more must be understood about the dynamics of intervening, about why people don't come to the aid of such children.

A fundamental barrier confronting the would-be intervener is the fact that society doesn't really support intervention. The clichés that glibly capsulize societal attitudes tell the story. A man's home is his castle. Curiosity killed the cat. Spare the rod; spoil the child. Whip him into shape. Two deeply entrenched beliefs—one in the sanctity of familial privacy, the other in the value of physical force as discipline—conspire against the abused child's receiving help. "Our society upholds a tradition of family autonomy," says Dr. Eli Newberger, director of the Family Development Study at Children's Hospital Medical Center in Boston. "Children's rights have never been defined because we believe in the inviolability of the family and feel that we shouldn't wrest control from parents who have the right to discipline their children." Public sentiment on this issue is so strong that involvement rather than noninvolvement is often seen as pathological. One forensic psychiatrist who has petitioned the courts for removal to foster care of 320 abused children says that each time he goes into court someone makes him feel "like a hit man who has taken out a contract on the part of the kids to get the parents." And in a well-publicized Chicago case, a woman who had nursed an abused child back to health and then fought to gain custody of him said of her dealings with the police: ". . . two

policewomen arrived, from the youth division. They questioned us as if *we* were the offenders. They kept referring to the fact that we had no doctor's report to substantiate our 'claims.' "

Anticipation of such situations stops many people from involving themselves. Others are deterred by their own reluctance to pry, to seem nosy. For still others, the taboos against interfering are so strong that the possibility is never considered. A Stanford University graduate recalls: "There was an abused child on our housing court at Stanford University. We knew it, but there was this feeling that we shouldn't interfere; somehow it was a private matter." The only thing that did happen, he

says, was that people avoided the child.

Americans protect the family's right to privacy as fiercely as a lioness protects her den. The assumption is that parents know what they're doing by virtue of their parenthood. Mother has the "mothering instinct" and father, after all, "knows best." Confronting an abusive parent is doubly discomforting: Not only is the intervener stepping into private territory, but he or she is also questioning the unquestionable—the parent's ability to perform his role.

Complicating matters further is the generally healthy reputation enjoyed by physical force as a valid mode of resolving conflict—even if that con-

flict involves children. At the same time that the Federal Government is providing money for child-abuse hot lines, establishing mother-child shelters and starting parenting education in the delivering-mother's hospital room, the Supreme Court has ruled that teachers can hit children to maintain order in the classroom. Their decision wasn't based on an incident of mild paddling, but on cases in which one child was injured badly enough to remain out of school for 11 days, and another lost the use of one arm for a week. The mixed message is nothing new: John Wayne and Charles Bronson epitomize it. Americans want an orderly, nonviolent world, but, if need be, will use violence to get it. That goes for keeping children in line as well as for keeping peace on the streets of Carson City. The difference between discipline and abuse is more often one of quantity than of quality. Most adults agree that a good spanking never hurt any child, and are reticent to claim that another man's hickory stick has turned into a whip. Often, they fear that their personal biases about discipline, rather than an objective appraisal of the situation, are firing their desire to intervene. "You have to discern between true abuse and discipline that might seem overly severe to you, but perhaps is not abusive," says one pediatrician. "You can hit a child." The ramification is that people usually won't step in unless behavior is way out of bounds. "You assume an adult knows what he's doing," says Brandeis University sociologist David Gil, "The basic assumption is that the way to rear a child is by setting limits through physical force. Also, we have a great belief in experts. When the Supreme Court says it's O.K. to beat kids, people are likely to believe it."

The caution surrounding intervention also stems from honest confusion about whether a child has been abused. The vast majority of cases are not clear-cut. As with one healthy-looking child whose back was covered with

1. UNDERSTANDING

the half-moon marks left by an electric cord, the injuries are often concealed, and often the child is intimidated into silence. The nebulous area of emotional abuse, and the inevitably hidden incidents of sexual abuse are even harder to ferret out. Endless questions beset concerned adults. If a child is always sleepy and his clothes are shabby, does that mean he's being neglected? What if a child needs psychiatric care and his parents refuse to get it for him? What about the subtle signs that are unaccompanied by apparent physical injury—flinching; fear or distrust of adults; overly disruptive or withdrawn behavior; enormous aggression? What might they signify?

Sometimes those who do see the more subtle effects of violence on children hesitate to act because of mitigating circumstances. One inner-city teacher reflects that the children she teaches always resolve problems in the physical mode. "It's cultural," she says. "There's a macho element . . . . Except in extreme cases, I feel I have to respect that." Also, there's the chance that what looks like abuse really isn't. In one recent case, an infant with multiple bone fractures was removed from his parents and later discovered to have a fatal, congenital bone disease. He was returned home for the remaining few years of his life. Mistakes like this are rare, but so are the sensational cases, the headliners that complicate intervention.

Another difficulty is that misconceptions about the nature of child abuse still blind people to its existence. Vincent Fontana, chairman of a mayoral task force on child abuse in New York, says many still believe either that child abuse is rare, that it's low income or that abusers are insane. These misconceptions result in an it-can't-happen-in-this-neighborhood mentality. One woman still shakes her head in amazement a full year after a neighbor's child was placed in foster care: "We just couldn't believe it. I'd read about child abuse in the

papers, but here? Down the block? The mother must have been a closet alcoholic or something."

Many people simply cannot imagine parents as being out of control, and, therefore, assume that the abuser deliberately hurts the child—a possibility is so unthinkable that they, consciously or unconsciously, seek alternative ways of explaining the injuries. "You're in a position of needing to make Dracula look like Bambi," explains one psychiatrist. "People will often say that the mother 'accidentally' burned the kid with a cigarette, or that the beatings are 'necessary' to discipline a rowdy child."

The misconceptions persist despite efforts at public education by such research and information groups as the National Committee for the Prevention of Child Abuse, despite considerable media coverage—even the integration of child abuse into afternoon soap operas. Experts speculate that to some extent the misconceptions themselves are psychologically important to the nonabuser. "Individual families can take comfort in knowing that those are the bad parents who abuse their kids over there. What we do in our home is O.K.," said Dr. Eli Newberger in testimony before Senate hearings. "This helps us not to think about, for example, our acceptance of corporal punishment and the emotional poverty of so many of our lives."

It also helps many adults not to confront their own psychological identification with violence against children. There's barely a parent who hasn't at some time threatened a child with "if you don't stop doing that I'll kill you." Robert Brooks, a psychologist with McLean Hospital's children's center in Belmont, Mass., says, "It's not only that children make us angry, but we often unconsciously assume they're going to gratify our wishes. When they don't, we want to strike back." Most parents have enough ego control to harness their angry reactions, but all have the potential for abuse, and this frightens them badly. Experts speculate that adults who label recognized abusers as malevolent, crazy or of another class help deny the potential in themselves. But that process too often results in hatred of the abuser, shuts off the compassion needed if he is to be helped.

Some specialists go so far as to suggest that people not only unconsciously identify with the abuser, but to some degree need him. The argument runs that abusers live out ag-

gressive impulses for nonabusers as well as for themselves. People respond to them with anger rather than compassion because helping the abuser would mean eliminating a necessary psychological foil. The abuser may provide the nonabuser with an outlet for guilt. David Gil points out that, while aggressive impulses are common during childrearing, they're in conflict with the ideal of constant parental love. Many parents may deny and repress such feelings. Their outrage against parents who succumb to aggressive impulses may be a "convenient mechanism for relieving their own sense of guilt."

☐

Despite this snare of social and psychological attitudes, many people do recognize and seek to help the abused child. But even they have to overcome some fears. One teacher relates a meeting she had with her principal and the father of a child she suspected was abused. She felt that the father was "glaring" at her throughout the meeting. For days afterward, she had a friend pick her up at work rather than travel home alone. She now says that her fears were "silly," but the anxiety was real and she wonders whether she'd be willing to go through it again. There is also the fear of harassment. Forensic psychiatrist Stephen Cronin says that this really can

be a problem for social-service professionals or others who might intervene in the case of problem parents who can afford lawyers. "Lawyers can do a job on you. They go for defamation of character. They'll dig out things from your past. Knock on your door, when you're with another patient. They can harass you so that your credibility and your practice are impaired. If it happens once, chances are you won't report again."

☐

Harassment to that degree, however, isn't common, especially considering the small number of cases that go to court. The bigger problem for the intervening adult is frustration with the child-protective agencies themselves. "It's a waste of time to report something unless it's very well documented. You really have to build your case or it's never investigated," says a New York City schoolteacher.

10

"People who've been here for eight, 10 years don't try anymore. It's not incompetence or disinterest, but a beaten feeling of helplessness. You watch whole families come up and nothing changes."

"Only about 5 percent of child abusers are handled properly," says Cronin. Caseworkers are overworked, have inflexible loads and can't do their jobs correctly. Reports aren't followed up. In one case he cites, police answered what they assumed was a routine call and found a young boy with blood running down the back of his legs. The father claimed that the child had backed into a hot wire screen in front of the fireplace, but there was no flesh on the screen, nor burn imprints on the boy's legs. The case was reported but, even with this clear inconsistency, never investigated.

The lack of follow-up is widespread and largely due to the lack of money and sufficient staff. The average caseworker handles a load of 20 to 25 cases and cannot cope with them all. The pressure is often so overwhelming that turnover rates are high, and families don't receive the consistent care and support they need. According to Douglas Besharov, director of H.E.W.'s National Center on Child Abuse and Neglect in Washington—which helps support state programs and has assisted in developing the new service techniques—this is true of most communities in the country. Though still only 30 percent of all suspected child-abuse cases are ever reported, this is a dramatic increase over the number reported 10 years ago. Funding, training and supervision have not kept up with demand for services. In Massachusetts, the Children's Protective Services must turn away two out of three referrals for continuing service and often have to close cases prematurely. Because of staff shortages, many clients wait several months before assignment.

Needless to say, this situation deters many people, who have once reported a case of child abuse, from reporting again. "The amount of report-ing is directly proportionate to the amount of services received," says Kathern Bond of the American Humane Association, in Englewood, Colo. "This is especially true for professionals. If a doctor calls a couple of times, and no one gets to him and he knows the child is still being abused, he's not going to call back. Why waste his time?"

A cycle evolves. Poor services discourage callers. But increased demand is the only thing that will get more money pumped into the system and force it to operate more efficiently. Indeed, there is some evidence that, despite the continued problems, this is slowly happening. "I have no doubt that the child-protective programs have become more effective because more is expected of them," says Besharov. He points out that heightened demand has led to important legislation, such as the Federal Child Abuse Prevention and Treatment Act, which encourages each state to implement clear-cut procedures for reporting and managing child-abuse cases. Agencies "are now able to provide some immediate service, and are becoming more capable of following up on crisis intervention," he says. "The weakness now is in delivering long-term support."

Another inherent difficulty is the reliance that is generally placed on foster care in this country—a damned-if-you-do, damned-if-you-don't solution. The stated goal of child-protective services is to preserve the family unit by strengthening parental capacity and ability to provide good child care. Unfortunately, the support needed to do so is long-term, time-consuming and expensive. Optimally, it ought to help parents find jobs, in some cases, or better housing or day care for the child; it should provide counseling, parenting education and homemaking help. But few agencies have the resources. As a result, many rely heavily on foster care, and only suggest that a child be left at its own home when the risk of his being hurt again seems low. As Besharov points out, "unfortunately there's no machine you can put a family through to find out whether or not the child will be abused again," and many children are. The double bind is obvious. Foster care abandons the goal of preserving the family unit. It is also potentially damaging to the child, who often interprets removal from his parents as meaning he's been so bad that they completely reject him. Both situations—taking a child out of its own home or leaving it there to be further abused—arouse public outrage; both deter people from reporting cases of abuse.

According to Eli Newberger, the problem could be partially alleviated if foster care were used only temporarily, to expedite the situation while help was given to the parents, and if money already in the human-services system were rechanneled. Most states spend a great deal more on foster homes than they do on keeping families intact. Newberger says the overreliance reflects psychological barriers faced by the care giver as much as it does a lack of resources. "It's hard work to work with families that are crisis ridden. We're much more willing to remove the child to a foster home. In many ways it's easier. . . . One cannot but wonder whether society is really willing to offer a helping hand to abusing parents, or whether we just want to control the problem through coercive means like the threat of removing the child."

□

A helping hand must be extended both on the societal and individual levels if more children are to be saved and more families enabled to function. Actions and attitudes must change so that the social mores, personal fears and practical concerns that now inhibit adults from reaching out are more easily overcome. A first step toward this goal, suggest the experts, is recognizing that help, not accusation, is at the base of intervention. "One of the biggest problems we have," says Newberger, "is that the terms 'child abuse' and 'neglect' are

1. UNDERSTANDING

explicitly accusatory. They say a parent is a bad parent. We have to abandon these labels of blame that make it so hard for us to respond compassionately."

Eliminating the assumption of blame would go a long way toward helping would-be interveners overcome the social discomfort they feel at approaching the abuser: Telling a neighbor how to bake his cake is one thing, but *lending* him a cup of sugar is another. "We must recognize that abuse is a plea for help," says John J. Hagenbuch Jr., of the Children's Protective Services in Massachusetts. "What the abuser needs is you as a neighbor, someone who will offer support. Call. Say, "I'm concerned about you and your child." If you see a mother overburdened with packages at the supermarket about to smack a bratty kid, go over and say, "Can I help you?' "

Intervening in this way isn't likely to put the abusive parent on the defensive and doesn't necessitate that the intervener be certain that abuse is taking place. It does, however, put the helping adult in a position to learn more about the family's situation and to ascertain whether further help is needed. Determining whether or not abuse is taking place remains a sticky problem, but there are some generally accepted guidelines that can help concerned adults recognize abused children.

By law, child abuse and neglect are defined as acts of "commission" or "omission" on the part of the child's parents or guardians that results in serious physical or mental injury, malnutrition, sexual abuse, drug addiction at birth, or lack of proper clothing, shelter, medical care, supervision, or education. Some of the most common warning signs include repeated injuries; neglected appearance; parents who are overly critical; families that are extremely isolated. No one of these factors alone necessarily signals child abuse, but when they occur repeatedly or in conjunction with one another, there is cause for concern.

Specialists suggest that it is

'We assume children are going to gratify our wishes. When they don't, we want to strike back. Most parents have enough ego control to harness this reaction, but all have the potential for abuse.'

also helpful for adults to recognize some of the traits that characterize abusive parents. Abusive parents are usually under stress. Unemployment, inadequate housing, alcoholism, drug addiction, single-parent families, unpreparedness for parenting (due to age or intelligence level), marital or other family tensions, are common factors. Often abusers were abused children themselves. When under stress they replay their parents' patterns. Many share certain psychological traits. They often distrust others, are isolated and lonely. They tend to expect rejection and act in ways that bring it on, thus cutting themselves off from the social support needed during parenthood. People need to use caution and good sense in identifying child abuse—every parent makes errors in judgment and action sometimes. But if there is a confluence of the above symptoms and, most importantly, if they occur *repeatedly*, then it's time for help.

There are some steps interveners can take short of filing official reports of child abuse. If they have befriended the family, they might suggest medical or social services, or self-help groups like Parents Anonymous that can offer support. If they are less involved with the family, but don't feel comfortable calling a child-protective agency, they might consider getting in touch with the child's teacher, a school nurse or counselor. If these measures don't result in the family's receiving help, however, the adult has a moral responsibility to file a report.

While some of the concerns people have about the child-protective services remain unfortunately real (i.e., the reliance on foster care), many are dissolved by an understanding of how the system works.

Acting on a case of suspected child abuse means calling the police, or a local private child-protective service, usually listed in the yellow pages under social services, or calling the local welfare department. All 50 states now have child-abuse reporting laws that protect the caller from a lawsuit if his report is inaccurate, so long as it's made in good faith. Furthermore, the law stipulates only that the abuse be "suspected"—the onus of substantiating the case lies with the social-service agency. While most agencies caution people against jumping to conclusions, they also encourage calling if fears seem well-founded. ☐

The situation is a little different for professionals working with children. While they are protected under the reporting laws, they are also legally required to file written reports documenting suspected cases of abuse. The specific professionals so mandated differ from state to state, but those named are liable if they *don't* report. A California physician was recently sued on these grounds.

Placing the initial report is often the extent of the caller's involvement. Both John Hagenbuch and Walter Wright Jr., executive director of children's protective services for the Ohio Humane Association

say they will even accept anonymous calls. "We assure people that they're not going to be revealed if they don't want to be," says Wright, "but we almost always encourage them to give their names, to be available."

When the call comes in, it's the job of the agency worker to determine whether it is a valid referral for services. He will ask the caller for as much specific information as possible. It might help individuals who consider reporting cases of child abuse to keep a written record of the occasions on which they have suspected abuse, of the parental behavior, of the child's appearance or injuries responsible for their suspicions and of any other relevant facts. If a caller is concerned about his own role in the case, there's no reason he shouldn't voice these concerns. "Part of the intake person's job is to allay fears callers might have about their own involvement," says Kathern Bond. "The worker should also be able to ascertain whether or not the case is really child abuse or neglect. If not, he should be able to refer the caller to an agency that might be able to help with the particular problem."

Once an agency has assigned a social worker to investigate the case, there are only a limited number of ways in which the caller can continue to be involved. He's encouraged to report any futher incidence and, if willing, to tell the family that he's filed the report. This, Hagenbuch explains, helps pave the way for the social worker.

There is also the outside chance that an adult who has intervened will be called to testify if the case goes to court. Approximately 10 percent of all reported child abuse cases do go to court. Most often, the court process involves only the family and the social-service agency. However, a third party can be subpoenaed if it's felt that testimony is essential. It's unlikely that a relative or neighbor would ever be asked to testify—Wright says that, in his years with the Ohio Humane Association, it's never happened—but medical or school personnel sometimes are. While the law can protect against suit, it can't protect against lost time in the courts.

Perhaps the biggest question people have once they have reported a case is what to do if they fear no action has been taken and have reason to suspect that the child is still being abused. Professionals interviewed suggest that the reporter call again. It is possible that after investigating the agency decided the case was not really child abuse or neglect, or that services are being provided of which the caller is unaware. It is possible, too, that the case has fallen between the cracks. If a second or third call doesn't bring results, one should call a second agency; a private child-protective service if the welfare department was originally contacted, or perhaps a hospital that has a special child-abuse unit.

□

In the last analysis, there can be no guarantees that the family will receive help. But if no one reports that help is needed, it almost certainly will not be forthcoming. Reporting alone will not eliminate the problem; the social inequities and acceptance of violence that are at the root of the matter remain untouched. Vincent Fontana writes that "child abuse is a symptom of the violence running rampant in our society today. . . . It is inextricably linked with unbearable stress, impossible living conditions, material or spiritual poverty, distorted values, disrespect for human life, drug addiction, alcoholism, assaults, armed robberies, murders and other ills in the midst of which we live—and for which we must find massive healing."

As long as children are abused, every individual is obligated to intervene. But the greater challenge lies in finding the healing necessary to eliminate abuse, in recognizing that what is involved is not primarily strategic but rather philosophical or political, not isolated but part of a larger social dynamic. "The question each individual must ask," says David Gil, "is do I wish, through what I do, to support the status quo, or do I support equal rights for children?"

VIOLENCE TOWARD CHILDREN IN THE UNITED STATES

Richard J. Gelles, P.h.D.

This paper reports results of a survey of a representative sample of 2143 American families, designed to examine the incidence, modes, and patterns of parent-to-child violence. Findings suggest that violence, well beyond ordinary physical punishment, is an extensive and patterned phenomenon in parent-child relations. Implications are discussed, and directions for further research are indicated.

This paper reports on the incidence, modes, and patterns of parent to child violence in the United States. Despite the considerable attention that has been focused on the issue of child abuse and neglect, and the significant and lengthy discussions concerning the physical punishment of children, valid and reliable data on the incidence and prevalence of the use of violence and aggression on children by their parents are almost nonexistent. The statistics that are available on child abuse and physical punishment do not report on the numerous violent acts that are neither routine physical punishment nor abusive. The wide range of acts between spankings and grievous assault have largely gone unnoticed and unresearched by social scientists.

Available data are often flawed by conceptual, definitional, sampling, and measurement problems. Moreover, the available statistics are usually general estimates of incidence which do not give even the crudest breakdown by age, sex, or demographic characteristics of the children or parents. Nevertheless, the figures on violence and aggression between parents and children do shed *some* light on the scope of the phenomenon.

Physical Punishment

The most comprehensive research on the use of physical force on children are the studies of physical punishment. Between 84% and 97% of all parents use some form of physical punishment on their children.[3, 9, 23] The advantage of these data is that they are typically based on nationally representative surveys. The disadvantages are that they do not provide age specific rates nor do they examine specific acts of force.

Child Abuse

A variety of research strategies have been employed to investigate the incidence of child abuse in America.

Official statistics. Investigations of official reports of child abuse provide varying degrees of the yearly incidence of abuse. Gil's 1968 survey yielded a figure of 6000 abused children.[16] One problem with the Gil survey is that all fifty states did not have mandatory reporting laws for the period Gil studied. The Children's Division of the American Humane Society documented 35,642 cases of child abuse in 1974, which were reported to its clearinghouse for child abuse and neglect reports.[1] However, only 29 states reported to the clearinghouse.

Estimates derived from official reports suffer from various problems. First, official reports do not cover all possible states and localities. Second, states and localities do not employ uniform definitions of "child abuse." Third, official reports represent only a fraction of the total number of children who are abused and battered by their parents.

Household surveys. In 1965, the National Opinion Research Corporation and David Gil collaborated on a household survey of attitudes, knowledge and opinions about child abuse. Of a nationally representative sample of 1520 individuals, 45, or three percent of the sample, reported knowledge of 48 different incidents of child abuse. Extrapolating this finding to the national population, Gil estimated that between 2.53 and 4.07 million adults knew of families involved in incidents of child abuse.[16] Light,[20] by applying corrective adjust-

ments to Gil's data and considering possible overlap of public knowledge of incidents, revised the estimate to be approximately 500,000 abused children in the United States during the survey year.

Survey of community agencies. Nagi[21] attempted to compensate for the shortcoming of estimates of child abuse based on official records by surveying a national sample of community agencies and agency personnel to ascertain how many cases of child abuse they encountered annually. Nagi's estimate of child abuse was arrived at by extrapolating from reporting rates which would be expected on a national basis using presumed "full reporting rates" found in Florida. Nagi's estimate is that 167,000 cases of abuse are reported annually, while an additional 91,000 cases go unreported.[21]

Statistical projection. Estimates of the incidence of child abuse have also been based on projections from regional, state, city, or single agency samples. The range of these estimates is quite wide. DeFrancis estimated that there are between 30,000 and 40,000 instances of "truely battered children" each year.[28] Fontana[10] proposed that there may be as many as 1.5 million cases of child abuse each year. Kempe[19] set the figure closer to 60,000 cases. Cohen and Sussman[8] used data on reported child abuse from the ten most populous states and projected 41,104 confirmed cases of child abuse in 1973.

Deaths of Children by Violence

Just as estimates of the incidence of child abuse vary, so do estimates of the number of children killed each year by parents or guardians. Fontana[10] provided a conservative estimate of 700

"Violence Toward Children in the United States," Richard J. Gelles, *American Journal of Orthopsychiatry*, 48 (4), October 1978. © 1978 American Journal of Orthopsychiatry.

children killed each year. Helfer[28] has stated that, if steps are not taken to curb child abuse, there will be over 5000 deaths a year over the next ten years. *Pediatric News*[22] reported that one child dies each day from abuse—a yearly incidence of 365. Gil[16] cited data from the U.S. Public Health Service, which reported 686 children under fifteen died from attacks by parents in 1967.

Summary of Research

Perhaps the most accurate summary of the research on the incidence and extent of child abuse is provided by Cohen and Sussman,[8] who concluded that:

the only conclusion which can be made fairly is that information indicating the incidence of child abuse in the United States simply does not exist.

It is evident that most projections of the incidence of child abuse are "educated guesses." Information gleaned from official statistics must be qualified by the fact that they represent only "caught" cases of abuse, which become cases through varied reporting and confirmation procedures.[13] In addition, information on child abuse is difficult to interpret because the term "child abuse" is as much a political concept (designed to draw attention to a social problem) as it is a scientific concept that can be used to measure a specific phenomenon. In other words, child abuse can be broadly and loosely defined in order to magnify concern about this social problem. While some social scientists use the term to cover a wide spectrum of phenomena that hinder the proper development of a child's potential,[17] others use the term to focus attention on the specific case of severely physically injured children.[18]

The lack of valid and reliable data on the incidence of child abuse in the United States led to the inclusion of a clause in the Child Abuse Prevention and Treatment Act of 1974 (PL-93-237) calling for a full and complete study on the incidence of child abuse and neglect. Such a study has already been contracted by the National Center of Child Abuse and Neglect. As an indication of the major problems that arise when one tries to measure the abuse and neglect of children, the contracted study has moved into the third quarter of its two-year existence and no decisions have been made on appropriate definitions of abuse or what research design should be employed in the study.

A Note on Trend Data

It should be pointed out that the problems involved in estimating the incidence of child abuse make the task of interpreting trend data almost hopeless. First, it is impossible to determine if rates of reported abuse are rising due to an actual increase in the true rate of abuse or due to increased sensitivity on the part or professionals who see children and families. Second, the constant change in the definition of abuse and the constant revisions of state child abuse and neglect laws, tend to broaden the definition of child abuse. This means that more families and children are vulnerable to being identified as abusers and abused.

The Need for a Study of Parental Violence

It was after evaluating the available evidence on the extent of force and violence between parents and children that we embarked on a national study of parental and family violence. While physical punishment of children appears to be almost a universal aspect of parent-child relations, and while child abuse seems to be a major social problem, we know very little about the modes and patterns of violence toward children in our society. We know almost nothing about the kinds of force and violence children experience. Are mothers more likely than fathers to hit their children? Who employs the most serious forms of violence? Which age group is most vulnerable to being spanked, slapped, hit with a fist, or "beaten up" by parents? Although answers to these questions will not completely fill in the gaps in our knowledge about child abuse, we see the information we generate in this study as providing an important insight into the extent of force and violence children experience and the numbers of children who are vulnerable to injury from serious violence.

METHOD

One of the most difficult techniques of studying the extent of parental violence is to employ a household interview that involves the self-reporting of violent acts. Although this technique is difficult and creates the problem of underreporting, we felt that, because of the shortcomings of previous research on child abuse,[14] this was the only research design

we could employ to assess the extent and causes of intrafamily violence.

Sample and Procedures

Response Analysis (Princeton, N.J.) was contracted to draw a national probability sample. A national sample of 103 primary areas (counties or groups of counties) stratified by geographic region, type of community, and other population characteristics was generated. Within these primary areas, 300 interviewing locations (census districts or block groups) were selected. Each location was divided into ten to 25 housing units by the trained interviewers. Sample segments from each interviewing location were selected. The last step involved randomly selecting an eligible person to be interviewed in each designated household.

Eligible families consisted of a couple who identified themselves as married or being a "couple" (man and woman living together in a conjugal unit). A random procedure was used so that the sample would be approximately half male and half female.

The final national probability sample produced 2143 completed interviews.* Interviews were conducted with 960 men and 1183 women. In each family where there was at least one child living at home between the ages of three and seventeen, a "referent child" was selected using a random procedure. Of the 2143 families interviewed, 1146 had children between the age of three and seventeen living at home. Our data on **parent-to-child violence are based on the analysis of these 1146 parent-child relationships.**

The interviews were conducted between January and April 1976. The interview protocol took 60 minutes to complete. The questions on parent-to-child violence were one part of an extensive protocol designed to measure the extent of family violence and the factors associated with violence between family members.

Violence: Defined and Operationalized

For the purposes of this study, violence is nominally defined as "an act carried out with the intention, or perceived intention, of physically injuring another person." The injury can range from slight pain, as in a slap, to murder. The motivation may range from a con-

---

* The completion rate for the entire sample was 65%, varying from a low of 60% in metropolitan areas to a high of 72.3% in other areas.

1. UNDERSTANDING

Table 1   TYPES OF PARENT-TO-CHILD VIOLENCE (N=1146) [a]

| | OCCURRENCE IN PAST YEAR | | | | |
INCIDENT	ONCE	TWICE	MORE THAN TWICE	TOTAL	OCCURRENCE EVER
Threw Something	1.3%	1.8%	2.3%	5.4%	9.6%
Pushed/Grabbed/Shoved	4.3	9.0	27.2	40.5	46.4
Slapped or Spanked	5.2	9.4	43.6	58.2	71.0
Kicked/Bit/Hit with Fist	0.7	0.8	1.7	3.2	7.7
Hit with Something	1.0	2.6	9.8	13.4	20.0
Beat Up	0.4	0.3	0.6	1.3	4.2
Threatened with Knife/Gun	0.1	0.0	0.0	0.1	2.8
Used Knife or Gun	0.1	0.0	0.0	0.1	2.9

[a] On some items, there were a few responses omitted, but figures for all incidents represent at least 1140 families.

nearly three parents in 100 said they had ever threatened their child with such weapons. The same statistics were found for parents admitting actually using a gun or knife—one-tenth of a percent for the year, almost three percent ever.*

One can extrapolate these frequencies to estimate how many children were victims of these serious modes of violence in 1975 and how many ever faced these types of violence. There were nearly 46 million children between the ages of three and seventeen years old who lived with both parents in 1975.[7] Of these children, between 3.1 and 4.0 million have been kicked, bitten, or punched by parents at some time in their lives, while between 1.0 and 1.9 million were kicked, bitten, or punched in 1975. Between 1.4 and 2.3 million children have been "beat up" while growing up, and between 275,000 and 750,000 three- to-seventeen-year-olds were "beat up" in 1975. Lastly, our data suggest that between 900,000 and 1.8 million American children between the ages of three and seventeen have ever had their parents use a gun or a knife on them. Our figures do not allow for a reliable extrapolation of how many children faced parents using guns and knives in 1975, but our estimate would be something close to 46,000 children (based on an incidence of one in 1000 children).

An examination of the data on violence used on children in 1975 indicates that violence typically represents a *pattern* of parent-child relations rather than an isolated event. Only in the case of using a gun or knife was the violent episode likely to be a one-time affair. While it is generally accepted that slaps, spankings, and shoves are frequently used techniques of child rearing, we find that even bites, kicks, punches, and using

objects to hit children occur frequently in the families where they are employed.

Children at Risk

As stated earlier, our examination of violent acts without information on the consequences of those acts prevents us from accurately estimating how many children incurred physical harm from violence during any one year. Our problem is compounded by the fact that we rely on the subject's own definition of what is meant by "beating up" a child. In addition, we do not know what objects were used to hit the child (a pipe or a paddle?), and we do not know how the guns or knives were deployed. Nevertheless, we felt it was important to generate an estimate of children-at-risk. We chose to compile an "at-risk" index which combined the items we felt produced the highest probability of injuring or damaging the child (kicked, bit, or hit with a fist; hit with something; beat up; threatened with a knife or a gun; used a knife or a gun). Using this index, we found that 3.6% of the parents admitted to using at least one of these modes of violence at least once in 1975. Assuming the acts we indexed have a high potential of causing harm to the intended victim, between 1.4 million and 1.9 million children were vulnerable to physical injury from violence in 1975.

A Note on the Incidence Data and Extrapolations

The data on the incidence of physical violence between parents and children, and the extrapolations which produced estimates of the number of children who experienced violence and who are at risk of physical injury, ought to be considered *low estimates of violence to-*

ward children. First, we are dealing with self-reports of violence. Although subjects who reported spanking or slapping their children may constitute an accurate estimate of incidence, the desire to give socially acceptable responses is likely to have caused many people to underreport the more serious modes of violence. If one subject in a thousand answered that he used a gun or knife, it might be reasonable to assume that at least another one in a thousand used these weapons and did not admit to it in the interview. Second, we interviewed only "intact" families, where both adult males and females were in the household. If, as some believe, parental violence is more common in single-parent families, then our data will underestimate the number of children experiencing potentially damaging acts from their parents. Third, we examined violence used by only one of the two parents on the referent child. Lastly, our lower than expected response rate might mean that some highly violent families refused to be interviewed; if so, our incidence statistics might again be low estimates of violence toward children.

As a result of the sampling frame used and the methodological problems involved in using self-reports of violence, we see our statistics, although they may seem high to some, as being quite conservative and low estimates of the true level of violence toward children in the United States.

Violence Toward Children by Sex of Parent

Sixty-eight percent of the mothers and 58% of the fathers in our sample reported at least one violent act toward their child during the survey year. Seventy-six percent of the mothers and 71% of the fathers indicated at least one violent episode in the course of rearing their referent child. Our data on violence in the survey year indicate a small but significant difference between mothers and fathers using violence on their children. It has been frequently argued that mothers are more prone to use violence because they spend more time with their children. We hypothesize that the explanation for mothers' greater likelihood of using violence goes beyond the simple justification that they spend more time with the children. Our future analyses of the information gathered in our survey of violence in the family will examine this relationship from a number of points of view, including family

---

* We do not know exactly what is meant by *using* a gun or knife. It could mean a parent threw a knife at the child, or it could mean attempting to stab or actually stabbing the child; a gun could have been fired without the child being wounded. However, the fact is that these parents admit using the weapon, not just threatening its use.

cern for a child's safety (as when a child is spanked for going into the street) to hostility so intense that the death of the child is desired.[15]

We chose a broad definition of violence (which includes spankings as violent behavior) because we want to draw attention to the issue of people hitting one another in families; we have defined this behavior as "violent" in order to raise controversy and call the behavior into question. In addition, our previous research [12] indicated that almost all acts, from spankings to murder, could somehow be justified and neutralized by someone as being in the best interests of the victim. Indeed, one thing that influenced our final choice of a concept was that acts parents carry out on their children in the name of corporal punishment or acceptable force, could, if done to strangers or adults, be considered criminal assault.

Violence was operationalized in our study through the use of a Conflict Tactics Technique scale. First developed at the University of New Hampshire in 1971, this technique has been used and modified extensively since then in numerous studies of family violence.[2, 6, 25] The Conflict Tactics Technique scales were designed to measure intrafamily conflict in terms of the means used to resolve conflicts of interest.[26] The scale used contains eighteen items in three groups: 1) use of rational discussion and argument (discussed the issue calmly; got information to back up your side; brought in/tried to bring in someone to help settle things), 2) use of verbal and nonverbal expressions of hostility (insulted or swore at the other; sulked or refused to talk about it; stomped out of room or house; cried; did or said something to spite the other; threatened to hit or throw something at other; threw, smashed, hit, or kicked something), and 3) use of physical force or violence as a means of managing the conflict (threw something at the other; pushed, grabbed, shoved the other; slapped or spanked; kicked, bit, or hit with a fist; hit or tried to hit with something; beat up the other; threatened with a knife or gun; used knife or gun).*

Administration of the Conflict Tactics Technique involves presenting the subjects with the list of eighteen items,

in the order enumerated above, and asking them to indicate what they did when they had a disagreement with the referent child in the past year and in the course of their relationship.

Reliability and validity. The reliability and validity of the Conflict Tactics Technique has been assessed over the five-year period of its development and modification. Pretests on more than 300 college students indicated that the indices have an adequate level of internal consistency reliability.[26] Bulcroft and Straus [6] provided evidence of concurrent validity. In addition, evidence of "construct validity" exists, in that data compiled in the pretests of the scale are in accord with previous empirical findings and theories.[26]

Advantages and disadvantages of the violence scale. An advantage of the violence scale, aside from previous evidence of its reliability, "concurrent" validity, and "construct" validity, is that the mode of administration increased the likelihood of the interviewer establishing rapport with the subject. The eight force and violence items came at the end of the list of conflict tactics. Presumably, this enhanced the likelihood that the subject would become committed to the interview and continue answering questions. Our analysis of the responses to the items indicates that there was no noticeable drop in the completion rate of items as the list moved from the rational scale questions to the most violent modes of conflict management.

Two disadvantages of the scale are that it focuses on conflict situations and does not allow for the measurement of the use of violence in situations where there was no "conflict of interest," and that it deals with the *commission* of acts only. We have no idea of the *consequences* of those acts, and thus have only a limited basis for projecting these statistics to the extent of the phenomenon "child abuse," since child abuse normally is thought to have injurious consequences for a child. While we may learn that a parent used a gun or a knife, and we can presume that this has negative consequences for a child, even if the child was not injured, we do not know what the actual consequences were.

RESULTS

As proposed at the outset of this

paper, "ordinary" physical punishment and "child abuse" are but two ends of a single continuum of violence toward children. In between are millions of parents whose use of physical force goes beyond mild punishment, but for various reasons does not get identified and labeled as child abuse.

Sixty-three percent of the respondents who had children between the ages of three and seventeen living at home mentioned at least one violent episode during the survey year (1975). The proportion of our sample reporting at least one violent occurrence in the course of raising the child was 73%.

As expected, and reported in TABLE 1, the milder forms of violence were more common. Slaps or spankings were mentioned by 58% of the respondents as having occurred in the previous year and by 71% of the parents as having ever taken place. Forty-one percent of the parents admitted pushing or shoving the referent child during 1975, while 46% stated that pushes or shoves had occurred some time in the past. Hitting with something was reported by thirteen percent of the parents for the last year and by twenty percent for the duration of their raising the referent child. Throwing an object was less common—approximately five percent of the parents did this in the survey year, while fewer than ten percent had ever thrown something at their referent child.

The more dangerous types of violence were the least frequent. However, extrapolating the data to the population of children three to seventeen years of age living with both parents produces an astoundingly large number of children who were kicked, bitten, punched, beat up, threatened with a gun or a knife, or had a gun or a knife actually used on them. First, looking at the number of parents who reported each type of violence, approximately three percent of the parents reported kicking, biting, or hitting the referent child with a fist in 1975; nearly eight percent stated that these acts had occurred at some point in the raising of the child. Slightly more than one percent of the respondents reported "beating up" (operationally defined as more than a single punch) the randomly selected referent child in the last year, and four percent stated that they had ever done this. One-tenth of one percent, or one in a thousand parents, admitted to threatening their child with a gun or a knife in 1975, while

---

* Copies of the scale used, containing questionnaire items and response categories, are available from the author on request.

1. UNDERSTANDING

Table 2   PARENT-TO-CHILD VIOLENCE BY SEX OF PARENT[a]

INCIDENT	IN PAST YEAR		EVER	
	FATHER	MOTHER	FATHER	MOTHER
Threw Something	3.6%	6.8%*	7.5%	11.3%*
Pushed/Grabbed/Shoved	29.8	33.4	35.6	39.5
Slapped or Spanked	53.3	62.5**	67.7	73.6*
Kicked/Bit/Hit with Fist	2.5	4.0	6.7	8.7
Hit with Something	9.4	16.7**	15.7	23.6**
Beat Up	0.6	1.8	4.0	4.2
Threatened with Knife/Gun	0.2	0.0	3.1	2.6
Used Knife or Gun	0.2	0.0	3.1	2.7

[a] Reports of 523 fathers and 623 mothers; figures for all incidents represent at least 520 fathers and 619 mothers.
* $\chi^2 \leqslant .05$.
** $\chi^2 \leqslant .01$.

power, coping ability, resources, and personality traits.

Examining the relationship between sex of the parent and various modes of violence used on children (see TABLE 2), we find that, for both the survey year and the duration of the relationship, mothers are more likely to throw something at the child, slap or spank the child, or hit the child with something. There are no significant differences between mothers and fathers with respect to any of the other forms of violence. It is interesting to note that even for the most serious forms of violence (beating up; kicking, biting, punching; using guns or knives), men and women are approximately equal in their disposition to use of these modes of violence on their children. This is important because it suggests that the management of children is one of the only situations in which women are as likely as men to resort to violence.

Violence Toward Children by Sex of the Child

While females are more likely to use violence in parent-child relations, male children are slightly more likely to be victims. Sixty-six percent of the sons and 61% of the daughters were struck at least once in the survey year, while 76% of the male children and 71% of the females were ever hit by their parents.

Why sons are slightly more likely than daughters to be victims of parental violence is open for debate. Some might argue that boys are more difficult to raise and commit more "punishable offenses" then daughters. Another hypothesis is that our society accepts and often values boys experiencing violence because it serves to "toughen them up." The data from the 1968 National Commission on the Causes and Prevention of Violence Survey seem to bear this out

in that seven in ten people interviewed believed that it is good for a boy to have a few fist fights while he is growing up.[23] Thus, experiencing violence might be considered part of the socialization process for boys and a less important "character builder" for girls.[24]

Data on violence in the survey year (TABLE 3) show that the only significant difference between boys and girls was whether they were pushed, grabbed, or shoved. The other forms of violence showed no significant differences between the sexes. In the course of growing up, boys are more likely to be pushed, grabbed, shoved, spanked, or slapped.

Violence Towards Children by Age of the Child

The literature on physical punishment and abuse of children presents various hypotheses and findings on the relationship between age and being punished or abused. A number of researchers and clinicians have proposed that the most dangerous period in a child's life is from three months to three years of age.[10, 11, 18] Bronfenbrenner[4] proposed that the highest rates of child abuse and battering occur among adolescents. Gil[6] discovered that half of the confirmed cases of child abuse were children over six years of age, while nearly one-fifth of the confirmed reports were children in their teens.

Our survey excluded parental relations with children three years of age or younger, since we also studied child-to-parent violence in the interview. Thus, our data cannot be used to infer the rate of violence used on infants.

During the survey year, younger children were most likely to be victims of some form of physical force. Eighty-six percent of children three and four years old had some mode of force used on them in 1975; 82% of the children five

to nine had been hit; 54% of preteens and early teenage children (ten to fourteen years of age) were struck; and 33% of the referent children fifteen to seventeen years old were hit by their parents ($\chi^2 \leqslant .01$).

It appears that younger children are vulnerable to a wide range of forceful and violent acts. As shown in TABLE 4, preschoolers and children under nine years old were more likely to be pushed, grabbed, shoved, slapped, spanked, and hit with an object. The older children seemed more vulnerable to the severest types of violence, including being beaten up and having a gun or a knife used on them, although the differences are not statistically significant.

Again, there are a number of reasons why younger children are more frequent victims of parental violence. Parents may perceive difficulties in using reason to punish their younger children. A second reason might be that younger children interfere with their parents' activities more than do older children. Our future analyses of the data will focus on the factors associated with young children's susceptibility to being struck.

DISCUSSION AND CONCLUSIONS

These data on the incidence of parent-to-child violence only begin to scratch the surface of this very important topic. Our results indicate that violence toward children involves acts that go well beyond ordinary physical punishment and is an extensive and patterned phenomenon in parent-child relations. In addition, we see that mothers are the most likely users of violence, while sons and younger children are the more common victims.

A number of controversial points arise from our presentation. First, disagreement over our nominal and operational definitions of violence may lead some to disagee with our conclusion that violence is widespread in families. If someone views slaps and spankings as acceptable punishment, then they might dispute our statistics as being based on a too broadly constructed definition of violence. Although we believe there are many salient reasons for considering spankings and slaps violent, we would counter this argument by pointing to the statistics for beating up children or using a gun or a knife on a child. If a million or more children had guns or knives used on them in school, we would consider that a problem of epidemic pro-

Table 3   PARENT-TO-CHILD VIOLENCE BY SEX OF CHILD [a]

INCIDENT	IN PAST YEAR		EVER	
	SONS	DAUGHTERS	SONS	DAUGHTERS
Threw Something	5.9%	4.4%	10.1%	8.8%
Pushed/Grabbed/Shoved	38.1	24.9**	43.9	30.7**
Slapped or Spanked	60.1	56.1	73.9	67.8*
Kicked/Bit/Hit with Fist	3.8	2.6	8.0	7.3
Hit with Something	14.9	11.2	21.5	18.1
Beat Up	1.6	0.7	4.2	4.0
Threatened with Knife/Gun	0.2	0.0	2.4	3.3
Used Knife or Gun	0.2	0.0	2.6	3.3

[a] Reports on 578 sons (responses reported for at least 574) and 547 daughters (responses for at least 545).
* $\chi^2 \leq .05$.
** $\chi^2 \leq .01$.

portions. The fact that these acts occur in the home tends to lessen concern about the impact and consequences. However, the impact and consequences are potentially dramatic, since the child is experiencing violence from those who claim love and affection for him.

A second point that will be raised about our findings is the question of bias and whether our respondents actually told the truth. We have spent seven years developing and testing the instruments used in this study. However, we do not know the actual validity of our findings or whether our subjects "told the truth." The major bias in this study of family violence is likely to be one of underreporting. We doubt that many subjects will report beating up their children or using a gun or a knife on them when they did not. Thus, our statistics are probably underestimates of the true level of parent-child violence in the United States. If one considers the possibility that, for every subject who admitted using a knife or a gun, an additional subject used these weapons but did not admit it, then our estimates of risk could be doubled to produce a true estimate of risk of physical violence.

Another issue that will be pursued after examining our data, and an issue we will pursue in later analyses, is the fact that people actually admitted using severe and dangerous forms of physical violence. Our tentative explanation of this is that many of our subjects did not consider kicking, biting, punching, beating up, shooting, or stabbing their chil-

dren deviant. In other words, they may have admitted to these acts because they felt they were acceptable or tolerable ways of bringing up children. Thus, it may be that one major factor contributing to the high level of parent-child violence we have found is the normative acceptability of hitting one's children.

Despite the methodological problems, this is the first survey of parent-to-child violence based on a true cross-section of American families. Thus, the data presented here probably come closer to describing the real situation of violence toward children in America than anything available until now.

REFERENCES

1. AMERICAN HUMANE ASSOCIATION. 1974. Highlights of the 1974 National Data. American Humane Association, Denver. (mimeo)
2. ALLEN, C. AND STRAUS, M. 1975. Resources, power, and husband-wife violence. Presented to the National Council on Family Relations, in Salt Lake City.
3. BLUMBERG, M. 1964. When parents hit out. Twentieth Century 173(Winter):39–44.
4. BRONFENBRENNER, U. 1958. Socialization and social class throughout time and space. In Readings in Social Psychology, E. Maccoby, T. Newcomb, and E. Hartley, eds. Holt, New York.
5. BRONFENBRENNER, U. 1974. The origins of alienation. Scientif. Amer. 231:53.
6. BULCROFT, R. AND STRAUS, M. 1975. Validity of husband, wife, and child reports of conjugal violence and power. Presented to the National Council on Family Relations, Salt Lake City.
7. BUREAU OF THE CENSUS. 1975. Estimates of the population of the United States by age, sex, and race: 1970–1975. Current Population Reports, Series P-25, No. 614, Government Printing Office, Washington, D.C.
8. COHEN, S. AND SUSSMAN, A. 1975. The incidence of child abuse in the United States. (unpublished)
9. ERLANGER, H. 1974. Social class and corporal punishment in childrearing: a reassessment. Amer. Sociol. Rev. 39(Feb.): 68–85.
10. FONTANA, V. 1973. Somewhere a Child is Crying: Maltreatment—Causes and Prevention. Macmillan, New York.
11. GALDSTON, R. 1965. Observations of children who have been physically abused by their parents. Amer. J. Psychiat. 122(4): 440–443.
12. GELLES, R. 1974. The Violent Home: A Study of Physical Aggression Between Husbands and Wives. Sage Publications, Beverly Hills, Calif.
13. GELLES, R. 1975. The social construction of child abuse. Amer. J. Orthopsychiat. 45 (April):363–371.
14. GELLES, R. 1978. Methods for studying sensitive family topics. Amer. J. Orthopsychiat. 48(3):408–424.
15. GELLES, R. AND STRAUS, M. 1978. Determinants of violence in the family: toward a theoretical integration. In Contemporary Theories About the Family, W. Burr et al, eds. Free Press, New York.
16. GIL, D. 1970. Violence Against Children: Physical Child Abuse in the United States. Harvard University Press, Cambridge, Mass.
17. GIL, D. 1975. Unraveling child abuse. Amer. J. Orthopsychiat. 45(April):364–358.
18. KEMPE, C. ET AL. 1962. The battered child syndrome. JAMA 181(July 7):17–24.
19. KEMPE, C. 1971. Pediatric implications of the battered baby syndrome. Arch. Dis. Children 46:28–37.
20. LIGHT, R. 1974. Abused and neglected children in America: a study of alternative policies. Harvard Ed. Rev. 43(Nov.): 556–598.
21. NAGI, R. 1975. Child abuse and neglect programs: a national overview. Children Today 4(May–June):13–17.
22. PEDIATRIC NEWS. 1975. One child dies daily from abuse: parent probably was abuser. Pediat. News 9(April):3.
23. STARK, R. AND MC EVOY, J. 1970. Middle class violence. Psychol. Today 4(Nov.): 52–65.
24. STRAUS, M. 1971. Some social antecedents of physical punishment: a linkage theory interpretation. J. Marr. Fam. 33(Nov.): 658–663.
25. STRAUS, M. 1974. Leveling, civility, and violence in the family. J. Marr. Fam. 36 (Feb.):13–30.
26. STRAUS, M. 1978. Measuring intrafamily conflict and violence: the conflict tactics (CT) scales. J. Marr. Fam. (in press).
27. STRAUS, M., GELLES, R. AND STEINMETZ, S. 1976. Violence in the family: an assessment of knowledge and research needs. Presented to the American Association for the Advancement of Science, in Boston.
28. UNITED STATES SENATE. 1973. Hearing Before the Subcommittee on Children and Youth of the Committee on Labor and Public Welfare. United States Senate, 93rd Congress First Session, on S.1191 Child Abuse Prevention Act, U.S. Government Printing Office, Washington, D.C.

Table 4   PARENT-TO-CHILD VIOLENCE IN PAST YEAR BY AGE OF CHILD

INCIDENT	3–4 YEARS	5–9 YEARS	10–14 YEARS	15–17 YEARS
Threw Something	5.1%	7.0%	3.6%	5.1%
Pushed/Grabbed/Shoved	39.0	39.1	27.9	20.8*
Slapped or Spanked	84.1	79.9	47.9	23.0*
Kicked/Bit/Hit with Fist	6.2	3.2	2.2	2.5
Hit with Something	19.2	19.7	9.6	4.3*
Beat Up	1.1	0.9	1.1	1.7
Threatened with Knife/Gun	0.0	0.0	0.3	0.0
Used Knife or Gun	0.0	0.0	0.3	0.0
	(N=177)[a]	(N=346)[a]	(N=365)[a]	N=236)[a]

[a] No more than three responses omitted on any category.
* $\chi^2 \leq .01$.

Neglect--Is It Neglected Too Often?

Alfred Kadushin, PhD, Professor
School of Social Work
University of Wisconsin
Madison, Wisconsin

This is the question with which we will deal: "Is neglect neglected too often?" This is similar to the man who was asked, "How is your wife?" and answered, "Compared with what?" The logical comparison for neglect is with "abuse," and the question can be reformulated, "Is neglect neglected too often as compared with abuse?"

As I see it, a review of the relevant material results in a resounding and unequivocal answer: yes, neglect is neglected far too often as compared with the attention and focus given to abuse.

State abuse and neglect reporting laws reflect this: for many years every state required the reporting of abuse. For a long time, however, many states did not require the reporting of neglect, and as of April, 1977, three states still do not require neglect to be reported.

The literature which reflects what is being studied, discussed, researched, and practiced overwhelmingly reflects this. A conscientious tally of publications over the last 10 years shows 19 books published on child abuse. By contrast, only three books were written on child neglect-- and all by the same authors, Norman Polansky and his colleagues. This is roughly a 6:1 ratio in favor of child abuse.

Periodical literature is even more heavily weighed in favor of abuse as compared with indifference to neglect. The *Journal of Clinical Child Psychology,* for example, offered a special issue on child abuse (Spring, 1975) but not on neglect. In special issues of *Children Today* (May, June, 1975) devoted to child abuse and neglect, six of 10 articles exclusively focused on abuse. The other four are concerned primarily with abuse although they devote some consideration to neglect. As a consequence of the preponderant concern with abuse as compared with neglect, the Library of Congress has a special entry for abuse but not for neglect.

A review of the latest available Child Abuse and Neglect Research Projects and Publications (May, 1976) also shows an equally unbalanced listing of projects and publications concerned with abuse.

There is, in recapitulation, no index which one sensibly can employ to assess the time, energy, and resources devoted to abuse and neglect, and which does not confirm that abuse receives the overwhelming share of such time, energy, and resources.

The present conference program, once again, reaffirms the preponderant concern with abuse. Twenty-two different panels or workshops are concerned exclusively with abuse in one form or another. Only two workshops or panels are concerned exclusively with neglect--a 11:1 ratio in favor of abuse.

It might be argued that this unbalanced, lopsided state of affairs is justified--justified on the basis of the number of children affected by abuse as compared with neglect, and by the greater seriousness of the problem of abuse. However, the argument can be proven incorrect.

"Neglect--Is it Neglected Too Often?" Alfred Kadushin, Ph.D., *Child Abuse and Neglect: Issues on Innovation and Implementation,* ©1978 U.S. Department of Health, Education and Welfare.

Every statistic we have available shows many more children are affected by neglect. Our most recent comprehensive national statistics are published by the National Clearinghouse on Child Abuse and Neglect which collates reporting statistics from each state. "Highlights of 1975 National Data," made available by the Clearinghouse in February, 1977, showed twice as many cases of neglect were reported as compared to abuse. The report says this 2:1 ratio in favor of neglect is biased to show a lower than true ratio because many states do not require neglect to be reported. It also shows that New York has a 5:1 ratio for neglect vs. abuse, and a 6:1 ratio in Michigan.

A 1976 report by the Standing Committee on Health, Welfare, and Social Affairs to the Canadian House of Commons shows a 7:1 ratio in favor of neglect.

It is difficult to demonstrate that neglect is a more serious problem than abuse considering the severity of harm inflicted. If one considers the number of fatalities as the most severe manifestation of harm, then an attempt can be made to demonstrate the severity of neglect. The National Clearinghouse Report published in October, 1976, shows that 631 children died in 1974 due to abuse; no comparable figures are given in the 1975 reports. By contrast, nobody has tallied the number of children who died due to lack of proper medical care, or who fell out of windows or down stairs, or ingested poisonous substances, or were hit by cars—all because parents neglected to take reasonable precaution and care.

In contrast with the 631 child abuse fatalities reported by the National Clearinghouse in 1974, one could list the unnecessary fatalities caused by community neglect of infant needs. Our national infant mortality rate is higher than many other countries, and varies from state to state within the United States. In 1975, a U.S. Public Health Service report, "Reducing Infant Mortality: Are We Doing Enough?" noted that, "If every state in the nation had achieved the infant mortality rate as reported by the best states in the period 1968-1970, 53,000 infant deaths in that two-year period could have been prevented." About 26,500 preventable deaths occurred each year, not because of deliberate abuse but by community neglect to provide mother and child with necessary nutritional and medical care; 26,500 neglect fatalities as compared to 631 abuse fatalities. If countered by the well-worn "tip of the iceberg" argument, the argument is applied equally to possible statistics on neglect. In both cases, this may be the tip of the iceberg. The neglect iceberg is likely to be, however, considerably larger than the abuse iceberg when both are uncovered fully.

If a greater number of children are affected more severely by neglect while more time, energy, and resources are devoted to abuse, this raises another question./ Since we are concerned with the sociology of social problems, why, and at what point in time do some conditions achieve community concern? /

Durkeim once said, "An action shocks the community conscience not because it is criminal but rather it is criminal because it shocks the community conscience." We do not reprove it because it is a crime, but it is a crime because we deplore it. The objective situation may not have changed, only our perception of it—the subjective condition—changed.

Anyone who worked in the ghetto areas in the 1930s knew that drug use, particularly of marijuana (then called reefers), was frequent. Anybody working in these areas in the late 1940s and early 1950s knows poverty was a problem. Both "drugs" and "poverty" were "discovered" by the general community in the 1960s and only then became "social problems."

The objective reality regarding child abuse did not change much before the discovery of the "battered child syndrome" in the early 1960s. Child abuse was "discovered" before the late 19th century, and a whole network of child protective agencies were concerned with this problem long before the "battered child syndrome" emerged. The Children's Division of the American Humane Society published pamphlet after pamphlet and books were written about child abuse, but nobody appeared to listen. No fewer children were battered in the 1930s-1950s than in the 1960s and 1970s. Why the recent surge of interest in abuse?

It seems many factors fortuitously converged to supplement and reinforce each other, and helped explain the emergence of child abuse as a social issue of importance in the late 1960s and 1970s. Some of these factors are:

1. While child abuse and neglect was previously the primary concern of social workers, child abuse was rediscovered by the medical profession in the "battered child syndrome." The problem of child abuse, separated from neglect, then received sponsorship of a much more prestigous and politically powerful profession. Child abuse has medical implications and components; to a far less degree, so does child neglect;

2. Child abuse is more dramatic, more easily identified, and more easily defined than child neglect. The justification for community intervention is easier to defend in the case of child abuse, and opposition to such intervention is less intense.

1. UNDERSTANDING

We are both repelled and fascinated by violence. We oppose it yet the mass media believe it provides the most compellingly interesting news. As contrasted with neglect, abuse involves much greater public affect and reaction;

3. The "battered child syndrome" emerged about the same time the children's rights movement began growing in strength. Support for child abuse legislation and programs also increased since such activity is interrelated with the ideology of the children's rights movements;

4. Child abuse provides an issue about which the community feels it accomplishes something significant for children at low cost to the community budget. Accurate cost estimates involved are difficult to obtain. It is estimated, however, that all child abuse problems funded by federal money has involved the expenditure of about $20 million. A serious attack on child neglect, which frequently involves problems resulting from inadequate family income and resources would involve, in all likelihood, much higher public expenditures;

5. No vested interest group opposes child abuse legislation and activity. Nobody opposes taking action against child abuse.

Emerging under the auspices of prestigous professional groups and being low cost, dramatic, and without vested interest group opposition, child abuse legislation has what can be described as an amazing atypical career. Within one 10-year period, legislation which had not previously existed in any state was adopted by all states-- namely child abuse reporting laws. A federal child abuse prevention and treatment act also was passed.

Contrast this with the bitterly fought campaign to get federal legislation against child labor--which adversely affected many more children than child abuse, or with the struggle to obtain passage of other socially progressive policy changes-- mother's pensions, unemployment insurance, workman's compensation, or the current efforts to obtain passage of the Equal Rights Amendment. It is difficult to think of any social policy change which was adopted so widely so quickly as was child abuse legislation; and

6. There is an additional, more speculative, and more politically sensitive and converging consideration which must be noted. This is the need for the reorganized Children's Bureau to have a clearly acceptable and understandable function. The government was initially interested in child abuse through the activities of the old Children's Bureau, which sponsored a conference on the problem in 1962. When the Children's Bureau was reorganized in 1969 to become the Office of Child Development (OCD), most significant functions were reallocated to other units within the federal government. The newly established OCD needed a rationale for its existence, and child abuse became an issue which the office could develop. As a consequence of the need for and interest in a legitimate function and concern, the OCD, supported by appropriations from the Child Abuse Prevention and Treatment Act, sponsored much of the activity which gave visibility to the child abuse movement. The demonstration projects, research, training programs and materials, resource centers, and this conference are, to a considerable extent, offspring of the OCD. Support for these speculations can be found, for those interested, in the recent analysis of the history of the OCD in the Brookings Institution Report, *The Children's Cause* by Gilbert Steiner.

In recapitulation, it is true neglect is neglected when compared to abuse. This is true even though the relative number of children affected and the relative seriousness of the two forms of maltreatment do not justify such neglect. There are reasons which help explain the discrepancy between the high concern with abuse and lesser concern with neglect.

Child Abuse:
The United Kingdom—
Another Country,
Another Perspective

Raymond L. Castle, Executive Director
National Advisory Center on the Battered Child
National Society for the Prevention of Cruelty to Children
London, England

The child shall enjoy special protection and shall be given opportunities and facilities, by law and by other means, to enable him to develop physically, mentally, morally, spiritually, and socially in a healthy and normal manner and in conditions of freedom and dignity. In the enactment of laws for this purpose, the best interests of the child shall be the paramount consideration (United Nations Charter, Principle 2, Declaration of the Rights of the Child).

INTRODUCTION

The United Nations Declaration of Human Rights sets out a clear mandate for children. Unfortunately, resolutions, however well intentioned, do not take into account the perversities of human nature, and child abuse continues to present a major problem, both nationally and internationally.

In the past few years an increasing number of countries have become particularly concerned at the numbers of children who receive nonaccidental injuries at the hands of their parents or guardians. Many of these children suffer trauma that will affect them for the rest of their lives, while others die as the result of their injuries. The tragedy is that a large number of these families could have been helped and the suffering of these children prevented had those responsible for providing service been attuned to the real needs of the families concerned and understood what they have to tell us.

More and more we have recognized that this is a phenomenon that crosses all national frontiers and is one in which we can all learn from each other's experiences to the ultimate benefit of those we serve. On the international scene, events have transpired quite rapidly. The first International Congress on Child Abuse took place in Geneva in September 1976. The second is to be held in London at the Imperial College from the 12th to the 15th September. 1978.

The following is a discussion of some of the developments that have taken place within the United Kingdom that have relevance to any consideration of present service delivery systems and their effectiveness.

HISTORICAL TRENDS

If one studies the historic beginnings of services to protect children, it becomes immediately apparent that there have always been strong links of cooperation between the United Kingdom and the United States. For example, the story of Mary Ellen, whose suffering in 1874 affected American legislation and brought about the founding of the New York Society for the Prevention of Cruelty to Children, had an indirect but significant bearing on what followed in England. As the movement in America gained momentum, numerous people were becoming growingly concerned about the number of children who appeared to be suffering needlessly in Great Britain, and many letters were written to the press, urging that some action be taken.

"Child Abuse: The United Kingdom--Another Country Another Perspective," Raymond L. Castle, *Child Abuse and Neglect: Issues on Innovation and Implementation,* 1978 U.S. Department of Health, Education and Welfare.

1. UNDERSTANDING

In 1881, following these events, a Liverpool businessman, Mr. Agnew, visiting New York, saw the title Society for the Prevention of Cruelty to Children. He got an introduction to its president, Mr. Elbridge T. Gerry, who, together with a Mr. F. T. Jenkins, the superintendent of the Society's Children's Shelter, did all they could to help him in his quest for information (Morton, n.d.). This resulted in the promotion of a similar organization in Liverpool which was swiftly followed by the setting up of the National Society for the Prevention of Cruelty to Children (NSPCC) with branches all over the country and a headquarters in London. That organization is now the oldest and most experienced independent child protection agency in the United Kingdom, undoubtedly owing its existence to the courtesy, patience, and cooperation shown by our American colleagues back in those early days.

PROBLEMS OF STATUTORY PROVISION

Although statutory welfare services are provided as a right in the United Kingdom, it is a misconception to think that the state alone can provide all services necessary to adequately meet the needs of deprived children.

Too often social services departments find themselves short staffed with the added problem of very high generic caseloads to deal with a situation which frequently precludes them from being able to provide the on-demand availability so necessary for many of the families we see.

One has only to examine the statistics of the NSPCC to see that this agency alone was called upon to provide service to 52,200 children during last year and of these, 34,850 were potentially at risk of abuse (NSPCC, 1976).

THE NSPCC RESEARCH-TREATMENT PROGRAM

By 1967, the National Society for the Prevention of Cruelty to Children, together with a number of eminent members of the medical and legal profession, was becoming increasingly concerned at the number of very young children coming to notice with serious physical injuries for which there appeared to be no adequate explanation. NSPCC undertook a study seeking to find ways of effectively intervening in family situations where children under the age of four had suffered, or were in danger of suffering, nonaccidental injury and to create an informed body of knowledge about the syndrome (NSPCC, 1976). By contrast with some other studies, the NSPCC project was primarily social work orientated and community based; a consultant psychiatrist and psychologist were available to the team for consultation and assessment purposes.

The department was established in October, 1968 and in 1974 was expanded to become the NSPCC's National Advisory Center on the Battered Child. As part of its clinical treatment program, a 24-hour on-call service is provided to the hospitals and communities of four London boroughs. Families are referred for help at any time of the day or night, and self-referrals are encouraged. Facilities include a therapeutic day nursery, play therapy for the children, and group therapy for parents. Appropriate psychological and psychiatric services are also available. Current research, assisted by a grant from the Department of Health and Social Security, involves two projects. The first is concerned with the analysis of video recordings of mother-infant interaction. Its purpose is to discover and demonstrate to workers in the field essential behavioral differences between parents who physically injure their infants and those who do not. A second project is aimed at devising a method of investigating subsequent health and educational development in children who have suffered nonaccidental injury.

Over the years, the department has published a number of articles and research reports, the latest of which are *At Risk,* an account of the work of the Battered Child Research Department (NSPCC, 1976), and "Case Conferences—a Cause for Concern" (1976).

Proposals put forward by the department have led to the setting up of seven special treatment units by the NSPCC. These units are linked to the National Advisory Center for research purposes and have responsibility for administering and monitoring registers of suspected nonaccidental injury in their regions.

The informed body of knowledge accumulated from its work over the last eight years has enabled the center to provide educational and consultative facilities to many agencies and bodies, both nationally and internationally. There are also strong links between the National Advisory Center in the United Kingdom and that headed by Professor Henry Kempe in the United States.

RESEARCH FACTORS HIGHLIGHTED IN THE BRITISH STUDIES
Family Psychopathology: The Children
Two earlier studies showed that the greatest number of children coming to attention were in the five month or under category and that the younger the child, the more likely it is to be injured and the more serious the injury is likely to be (Skinner and Castle, 1969; Castle and Kerr, 1972).

This has subsequently been supported in other reports (Rose et al, 1976; Oliver et al, 1974).

Trauma to the soft tissues of the face and mouth appeared in 43.5 percent of all cases notified, and it became clear that bruises and injuries that might appear to be of a minor nature could signify the beginnings of increasingly violent forms of injury. It has been pointed out that the high incidence of trauma to the face may, like bruising, be an aid to early diagnosis of a nurturing problem that, if modified, may avert serious injury to a child.

In families where a firstborn child has been injured, records showed that there was a 13 to 1 chance that a subsequent child would be injured. The high risk in these families is a finding of particular importance to all those who take responsibility of weighing up the risks of supervised home care for the nonaccidentally injured child against an alternative protective course of action.

Low birth weight is a consistent factor, and in both the studies mentioned there was a significantly high rate, 13 percent and 14.5 percent respectively, more than twice the average nationally for that period. Of the most important factors, feeding difficulties and continual crying present as those causing parents most distress as illustrated by the following statement from a mother.

> I felt no love for the child when it arrived, and on getting home from the hospital, felt very distressed by a feeling of fear and inadequacy. This was accentuated when the baby cried to the point of almost uncontrollable rage and revulsion. The need to stop the noise was as overwhelming as that of a drowning person to clutch at something solid.

Family Psychopathology: The Parents

A number of suppositions are prevalent concerning the parents involved. Some suggest that the majority are of psychopathic personality and cannot be helped; others say they are individuals of low intelligence. Psychological and social work studies carried out at the National Advisory Center with the cooperation of parents do not support these propositions. Tests (Wechsler Adult Intelligence Scale and Cattell Sixteen Personality Factor Test) of a group of battering parents matched with a control group for parental and child age, ordinal position of the child, social class, educational level, type of living accommodation, and nationality, showed that the mean IQ's of both groups fell within the normal range. The majority are neither mentally subnormal nor frankly psychotic, although personality problems of long standing are more common among battering parents than the general population.

The tests did show that parents who injured their children were relatively less able in their command of verbal concepts than in their practical abilities, which suggests a rather concrete style of thinking, consistent with relative difficulty in seeing the consequences of actions and in controlling impulses to act. The integration of these findings with those of the social work research confirm an implication of immaturity, impracticality, and a tendency to flee into fantasy in the face of real problems.

Our report points out that "there is no support in this investigation for the idea that battering (as it is more widely known), is undertaken by the mother while the father passively looks on, nor for the reverse situation". Test results concur in showing abnormalities in both parents. The main contributions of the fathers are their own specifically introverted schizoid personalities. They present an abnormally introverted group.

Close contact with these families reveals that in many cases the parents themselves have from early childhood been consistently subjected to experiences of disapproval and rejection. Dr. Steele (1970), the eminent American psychiatrist, in his studies of families in which children have been abused, writes that "throughout life they (the parents) have pathetically yearned for good mothering, returning again and again to their mother, seeking for it but not finding it and ending up with disappointment, lowered self-esteem, and anger." Our own experience very much supports this view and, indeed, we have been struck by the similarity of patterns between those families being worked with here in the United States and those that we are working with in the United Kingdom. In many instances, if the names and details of residence were excluded you would be unable to tell which of our countries they actually came from.

Depression and anxiety are common, although hostility may mask the symptoms. While we know that nonaccidental injury occurs in all strata of society, we are seeing the greatest number of cases from the lower socioeconomic groups. This is not surprising when one considers that families in these groups are generally under much greater social stress and have fewer avenues of relief.

A question raised of late concerns the possible correlation between abused children and battered wives. The initial country-wide NSPCC study identified a group characterized by their essentially antisocial behavior of the predominantly aggressive type (Skinner and Castle). There were indications that these adults were habitually aggressive and that their behavior tended to be

1. UNDERSTANDING

released against any source of irritation. In our latest study, nine mothers describe their husbands as having been physically violent towards them at some time.

In these families, the main lines of tension, aggression, and violence flowed between the parents rather than between parent and child. Children were more likely to be injured by accident rather than design. In three cases, the violence was serious, frequent, and associated with drink. The three men involved often resorted to violence in other situations. Although there was occasional violence towards the children, the disorder in the family was based primarily in the psychopathology of the father and, thus, in the marital relationship rather than in the parent-child relationship. The majority of nonaccidentally injured children do not appear to come from families in which the wife is also injured. There is, however, some overlap, and we will always see a number of parents who are habitually aggressive. These particular cases make special demands on those who, while attempting to protect a defenseless child, are confronted with the possibility of increasing hostility and tension that might further endanger life.

PROBLEMS OF PROVIDING SERVICE

At present, it is estimated that approximately 3,500 to 4,000 children under the age of four suffer nonaccidental injury at the hands of their parents or guardians annually in Great Britain (Rose et al). Over the last few years, there has been a growing recognition of the problem and, understandably, medical diagnosis, particularly in the field of pediatrics, is now much better than it was at the time we started our research. If, however, we accept that this is essentially a sociomedical problem that, in a large number of instances, could be prevented, we must also recognize that growing awareness and better medical diagnosis alone cannot resolve the problem. It will greatly assist in our understanding if those concerned with diagnosis, treatment, and, ultimately, prevention, are able to accept that in the majority of cases coming to our notice, the parents, due to those factors already discussed, are to a great degree captives of their own childhood experiences and have no conscious desire to harm their children.

Henry Kempe (1976) makes the point successfully when he says "with the exception of a relatively few sadistic parents, who are child torturers in the Dickens sense of the word, child abusers are, themselves, in very deep pain." In our attempts to offer effective support, it may also be helpful to remind ourselves that angry, aggressive feelings towards those we love are perfectly normal emotions. There are probably very few people with children who have not, at one time or another, been pushed to the limit of their endurance and have felt like doing the child an injury, using such expressions as "If that child doesn't stop, I'll kill him," or "Take that baby out of my sight before I strangle her." Many will recall instances when this kind of situation has arisen. How much worse must it be for young parents often living with children in social isolation, facing numerous pressures and stresses, and unable to cope because of their own limited experience of nurturing. These are adults who have very low points of tolerance and who do need a considerable amount of reaching out to, in a supportive, nonauthoritarian manner. If prevention of injury or reinjury is the aim, the main objectives must be this difficult task of demonstrating, within the context of the professional relationship, to parents who are often hostile and highly suspicious, a genuine concern and desire to help.

This must not blind us to the fact that we are going to see some adults who have been so badly damaged in their own childhood that they are never likely to be able to provide the relationship that is so important in a child's development, and where we will have to act using what legislation is necessary to secure the ongoing welfare and healthy emotional development of the child concerned.

Following the tragic Maria Colwell case, in which a child under the supervision of the local authorities died, the Department of Health and Social Security issued a memorandum, in which it said: "Recent events have left us in no doubt of the need to repeat the professional guidance about the diagnosis, care, prevention, and local organization necessary for the management of cases involving non-accidental injury to children" (DHSS, 1974), and went on to recommend the setting up of area review committees in all regions. While these committees are doing much to ensure better management of cases involving nonaccidental injury to children, tragedies continue to occur.

The following is a headline and extract from one of our national newspapers dated 26 November, 1976.

Boy 2, Died After False Assumption by Authorities
In Birmingham, a social worker erroneously assumed a health visitor was checking on a two year old boy who later died after a violent attack by his mother.

The enquiry, formally conducted by the district council and the area health authority, found that "the full picture of events was not known to any one agency involved in the case." The child concerned died from abdominal injuries three months after his older brother was taken into care as the result of nonaccidental injury. It was assumed that the older child was scapegoated and therefore the younger child was not at risk. Two months after intensive visiting commenced, the case was transferred from the Parent and Child Center to the local health visitor, who then became the primary worker.

"It is doubtful whether she realized the real risks that were inherent and she had not the time to give adequate support," says the enquiry. "Perhaps the most crucial aspect of decision-making in relation to the younger child was the lack of consideration and assessment, both at the case conference and the following month at the Juvenile Court."

A number of problems that could arise anywhere are highlighted by this case: lack of communication, changes of worker during the early stages of treatment, a primary worker overburdened and not sure of her role, inadequacy of the case conference, and inadequacy of the juvenile court. These are situations that all of us will come across from time to time, and it may be helpful to look at some of the lessons we can learn from them.

First, it must be recognized that our prime responsibility in cases of nonaccidental injury to children must be the protection and ongoing welfare of those children.

In many of the cases coming to the notice of the center, it has been found necessary to implement juvenile court proceedings at a very early stage; in a large number of instances, after assessment, a period of separation between parent and child has been seen as in the best interest of the family as a whole, while initial relationships are being established between worker and client. The initiation of juvenile court action as a coordinated part of a casework plan can often not only protect the child but also has the effect of protecting the parents from their own actions.

One cannot overemphasize the importance of coordination and cooperation, the free-flowing interchange of information between all concerned and a recognition of each other's professionalism. Often in practice it is quite difficult to get people from different backgrounds and professions to truly coordinate and cooperate in a way that would be of the greatest benefit. It lays a responsibility on all to do much more in the way of reaching out to other colleagues, both professional and voluntary.

Case conferences should and can be the most effective way of sharing information. They need not take a lot of time, providing the conference is structured with an experienced chairperson and participants take the time to prepare reports on their involvement rather than trying to extract information from bulky files at the meeting. In the initial stages of contact with these families, there is a need for a high degree of skill and sensitivity on the part of the worker involved. As was pointed out earlier, a multiplicity of workers can increase family stress, and a type of supervision that is limited to an anxious watchfulness without specific treatment goals is not in the child's best interest (Skinner and Castle).

In some instances, shortage of qualified and experienced personnel has led to trainees being given these cases to handle; in others, because of frequent staff changes, families have had as many as three different social workers in six months. Quite often the parents involved see this as a reenactment of their earlier life experiences and feel completely rejected and bitter. This can have very serious repercussions for any future therapy, particularly if a change takes place when, for the first time in their lives, they are just beginning to respond in a positive manner.

Our work with these families leads us to believe that the first few months of contact and how they are handled are crucial to any positive movement that might be achieved. It is also a period when the parents will test out the relationship in a variety of ways and be at their most demanding. A considerable amount of reaching out on the part of the worker and a great amount of time are required. It is, however, the period when the parents, if they are at all amenable to help, will begin to respond.

In circumstances where work is progressing with a family and a change of worker must take place, it is of great help to all concerned if the parents can be forewarned and prepared for the change by the outgoing worker, allowing them time to ventilate their feelings and, when possible, to be introduced to the new worker prior to departure. Frequently, the only notice families have received is a short letter saying that their social worker is leaving, or has left, and another will visit in due course, occasionally followed by a long delay before anyone is actually able to visit. The buildup of tension created for the family by this situation can be a potentially dangerous one for the child. Those of us having administrative responsibilities should also recognize that adequate support and consultation must be readily available for the social workers involved.

One other aspect that requires our consideration is the effect these families can have on those of us who are providing a service. Families of this nature have an uncanny knack of highlighting our own inadequacies, and continually confront us with situations geared to raising

1. UNDERSTANDING

our anxiety levels. For the inexperienced, this can produce a state of immobility at a time when clear objective thinking is imperative.

Richard Galson (1970) succinctly grasps the problem when he says "the anxiety produced by anger which is unassimilated is highly contagious. It lies about like a time bomb waiting to go off and it intimidates others to flee, to put distance between themselves and source either directly or through the use of one of the many administrative devices available to any clinic or agency." One of the most important resources called upon by any therapist involved in this kind of situation is a capacity to bear the anxiety. Just as we accept that there are going to be a small number of families unable to respond to treatment, we must also accept and recognize those few instances when the social worker is unable to respond.

ALTERNATIVE DELIVERY SYSTEMS
Most research programs into the treatment of abused children and their families stress the need to provide a number of services that would not be available under normal delivery systems. In the United Kingdom there is particular concern at the lack of specialized treatment facilities for very young children who may have suffered severe emotional damage (Attention was drawn to this in a recent report (NSPCC, 1976). There are, however, a number of models now in use that have been of benefit to the family as a whole and are generally adaptable to most countries' settings. Some of those being used in the United Kingdom are described below.

CRISIS NURSERIES AND DROP-IN FOSTER MOTHERS
In setting up a serivce for families in which child abuse had occurred, we were concerned that we should learn from the experience of those parents who felt that available services did not meet their particular needs. One of the most pressing of the requirements voiced was for some form of nursery facilities where a parent under stress and frightened of injuring his or her child might leave him for a while without fear or remonstration. It became apparent that many parents had suffered quite traumatic experiences when seeking this kind of help and had consistently met with rebuffs of one kind or another. Some even felt they had been forced into a tragic situation where they had actually injured their child because they could not get the various authorities to recognize or understand the urgency of the matter or danger involved. The following is a graphic example of this situation.

> I got to the point where I seemed to have been to (sic) everyone! Things were getting worse and worse, but no-one (sic) would listen! In the end, I nearly killed my baby and then they said it was my fault.

Taking these points into consideration, there are two alternatives available. First, a nursery where the staff are geared to cope with children being brought in for varying periods and at any time. Our own experience has shown that a nursery of this kind has a particular therapeutic value if it is seen to incorporate facilities for the parents. At all times it is essential that they are made to feel welcome and have a room in which they can relax without the children. We have found that one of the results tends to be the development, quite spontaneously, of a self-help group, and many of the newly referred parents respond much earlier to treatment because of the help given them in this manner.

A vital feature of this service is the provision of a transport that goes out in the morning to all the homes of the families, brings the children and any parent who wants to come back to the nursery and returns them again at night. A member of the nursery staff accompanies the driver who, if necessary, can dress the child and ensure that he or she attends if the parent is ill.

Another extension of this can be in the form of a preschool playgroup. In both circumstances play therapy is of great assistance to the children in preparing them for later life and providing some of the outlets they have not perhaps enjoyed at home.

The nursery nurses are very much part of the therapeutic team and attention has to be given in these circumstances to ensuring that they receive adequate orientation toward their widened role, since they will find themselves as involved with the parents as they are with the children.

The second alternative, which is of particular value in areas where nursery provisions are poor, is to set up a system of drop-in foster mothers. These volunteers are paid a small retainer and provide short-stay emergency placements for children at times of crisis. For example, quite often mothers will telephone when they are going through a particularly difficult period saying that they cannot cope and asking if the baby or child can be taken out of the home and looked after for a short time. In most instances, an overnight stay is all that is needed, but it is possible to extend this for any period up to a week. As with most provisions in this field, the key factor is flexibility, and drop-in foster mothers have to be prepared to accept children at any time of the day or night. Again, when selecting suitable people, emphasis is placed on personality rather than any professional skill.

We have also tried to recruit from as wide a variety of social backgrounds as possible, since we have that found many abusing parents find it much easier to respond to someone whom they feel has had the same kind of problems to contend with. Some of our earlier referred parents who responded to treatment are helping as part of this network.

FAMILY DEVELOPMENTAL CENTERS

In a few enlightened areas, attempts have been made to set up treatment programs that will provide residential facilities for the whole of a family where significant child abuse has occurred. There is, for instance, a unit operating at the Park Hospital for Children, Oxford, England, where over the last 10 years 230 families have been successfully treated. In essence, these families are received into a small family unit within the hospital grounds for a period of 28 days and then followed up with supportive services. During this period all the family members experience the rare combination of practical help, medical treatment, and applied psychology.

CONCLUSION

While we can never hope to completely prevent child abuse, there are a number of ways in which we can reduce it drastically. Research in the United Kingdom has shown similar patterns to those reported in the United States, in particular, the very young age of many of the children involved and the low points of tolerance shown by their parents.

For any program of preventive treatment to succeed, parents should be able to seek help without being made to feel guilty and afraid. The provision of such a service requires a team approach involving both availability and flexibility on the part of those operating it. Cooperation and coordination between all concerned, (both professional and lay personnel), are vital, and they can only be achieved if we are prepared to remove some of the artificial barriers that sometimes prevent them from occurring.

Finally, we cannot consider any program of service to abused and neglected children adequate unless we are able to meet some of the very specialized treatment needs of the children, many of whom survive physically but are severely damaged emotionally and some of whom may have to be removed from their natural parents to a more conducive and nurturing environment before this can be effected.

Raymond L. Castle, Executive Director
National Advisory Center on the Battered Child
National Society for the Prevention of Cruelty to Children
London, England

Child Maltreatment:

A New Approach In Educational Programs

by Perry Duryea, Vincent J. Fontana and Jose D. Alfaro

Hon. Perry Duryea, founder of the New York State Assembly Select Committee on Child Abuse, is the author of New York State's Child Protective Services Act of 1973. Vincent J. Fontana, M.D., is medical director of the New York Foundling Hospital and chairman of the Mayor's Task Force on Child Abuse and Neglect, New York City. Jose D. Alfaro is project director, National Alliance for the Prevention and Treatment of Child Abuse and Maltreatment, Inc.

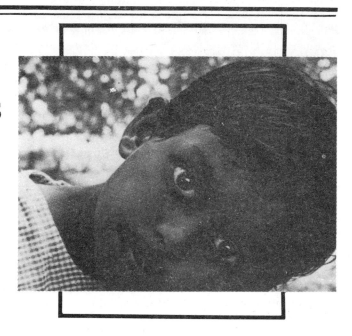

Professionals and the public have become increasingly aware of child abuse and neglect in recent years.

The now general recognition that child maltreatment exists in our society is a significant achievement. Various educational programs have undoubtedly helped to make all of us more aware of the problems of child maltreatment but until now such programs concentrated on conveying basic or technical information to the public and to various professional groups. This article describes a new kind of educational program now being conducted by the National Alliance for the Prevention and Treatment of Child Abuse and Maltreatment.

Child protective systems, and whatever public policy exists on child maltreatment, developed under the leadership of a small group of doctors, social workers and lawyers, who had no choice except to act alone. At the time, the general public, and many other professionals, did not recognize or accept the reality of child maltreatment as a widespread problem. But the times have changed and professionals are now beginning to confront the large questions inherent in efforts to prevent and treat child abuse or neglect. In doing so, they must grapple with previously unexamined values and assumptions.

In order to help those concerned begin to examine some of these unresolved issues, the National Alliance was awarded a grant from the New York Council for the Humanities to hold a series of special educational symposia in 10 communities in New York State during 1977. The National Alliance felt, and the New York Council for the Humanities agreed, that the time had come to apply a humanistic perspective to the problems of child maltreatment. Men and women educated in the traditional disciplines of the humanities have devoted their lives to studying some fundamental questions about the nature of human life, the rights and responsibilities of individuals in society, and the role of the state in regulating the lives of its citizens. Many of these concerns are relevant to the basic issues involved in child abuse and neglect and our society's response to them.

Each symposium was designed to help citizens and professionals alike expand their awareness of the profound social and human problems involved in child maltreatment. They attracted a surprisingly large number of people. In Buffalo, 200 people attended, despite a partial travel ban, the result of the worst blizzard in the city's history. More than 300 people attended each meeting in Hauppauge, Rochester and New York City, while 400 people, including some from Canada, came to the discussion in Plattsburgh. Additional programs were held in rural St. Lawrence county, Poughkeepsie, Riverhead, Schenectady and Syracuse. The Syracuse program was broadcast, and then rebroadcast, by the local educational television station as a 2-hour special.

In each of the locations, one or more community groups shared sponsorship of the symposium with the National Alliance. Their participation, which included making the local arrangements and promoting the program, was an indispensable contribution to the success of the meetings. The co-sponsoring groups, many of whom were becoming involved with the issues of child abuse and neglect for the first time, included the Junior League, the League of Women Voters, the YMCA, the

"Child Maltreatment: A New Approach in Educational Programs," Perry Duryea, Vincent J. Fontana, Jose D. Alfaro, *Children Today,* Vol. 7, No. 5, September-October, 1978. ©1978 Children's Bureau, Office of Child Development, Washington, D.C.

Girl Scouts, a mental health association, a Human Services Planning Council, a Community Council, a Cooperative Extension group, Child Abuse Task Forces and local departments of social services.

At each symposium a panel of humanists and professionals examined one of four issues identified at the beginning of the project. These were embodied in the following four questions:

Should punishment be used to deter child abuse or neglect?

Should society intervene in a family because of the likelihood a child will be harmed?

Should an expectant mother be held responsible for the health of an unborn child?

Should childrearing values be imposed on others?

The humanists included scholars of history, philosophy, literature, anthropology and jurisprudence. Family Court judges, administrative officials and workers from child protective agencies, law guardians, psychiatrists, psychologists, social workers, health and mental health department commissioners and other staff members of local public and private social service agencies represented the viewpoints of various professional groups.

To illustrate some of the issues being discussed, a film was used as a point of departure for each question.[1]

Should punishment be used to deter child abuse or neglect?

Child abuse is a crime in all states, but parents are rarely punished through criminal sanctions. Instead, society responds through the rehabilitative techniques of social casework, mental health services and social services, such as homemaking and day care. Though most professionals are committed to this rehabilitative model, there is far less agreement on it among the general public, which has not been involved in the formulation of public policy and legislation on child maltreatment. Indeed, the public often reacts to a well-publicized case of child abuse by asking, "Why are the parents allowed to get away with it instead of being punished?"

Punishment and rehabilitation represent conflicting approaches to the same goal: to change or stop behavior that is socially unacceptable or harmful to others. Punishment is the more traditional method; the rehabilitation model was developed more recently and is considered to be the more humane and practical approach. But arguments for and against each one persist, and each approach has its supporters. A philosopher asked a pertinent question during one meeting: "Does the state have a right not only to punish its citizens but also to attempt their rehabilitation?" Any discussion of child abuse, he said, would be far richer if those engaged in it understood the classical debates and current analysis of such questions.

A large, formerly unquestioned assumption behind the rehabilitative concept is that it is always a more humane approach. However, this is not necessarily so. Some who

have considered the rehabilitative treatment of mentally ill people accused of crimes claim that it may actually be less desirable than punishment: it lasts longer, it usually removes the right of legal redress and challenge, and it is often ineffective. Analogous statements have been made about efforts of the child protective process. Moreover, there is increasing doubt that placement of children in foster homes or residential institutions represents an improvement over the care many abused and neglected children receive from their own parents. If child abuse were prosecuted as a crime, far fewer parents would lose their children, or be subjected to intervention efforts, because the available proof would often be insufficient to support a criminal conviction. However, the risks to unprotected children would probably be greater.

The justness of punishing someone for actions beyond his or her control is also open to question, and it is true that child abuse and neglect are related to personal and social problems often beyond the control of parents. Yet there may be other considerations. As one philosopher asked: "If child abuse is morally wrong rather than a psychological ailment, should child abusers be punished in an appropriate way either as a deterrence to others or as simply righting a wrong?"

When punishment is discussed, it should be noted that incarceration is not the only possible form of punishment society can impose. Fining people for various infractions is a common form of punishment. Would fining parents for improper childrearing practices be effective? In England, for example, a country whose social welfare system is generally acknowledged to be advanced, parents are sometimes fined for mistreating their children. One could argue that, in some situations, fining parents might be more effective than threatening to take away their children.

Should society intervene in a family because of the likelihood a child will be harmed?

The desire to prevent child abuse is a natural result of attempts to treat it. The efforts and interest of anyone involved in treating child abuse eventually focus on the question of prevention. The concern is already reflected in the laws of half the states, which include threatened harm to a child among the situations that must or can be reported under child abuse laws. The federal Child Abuse Prevention and Treatment Act will probably complete this process; it, too, includes threatened harm and more states will adopt this provision to become eligible for funds under the federal law.

Some professionals are working to develop tools to predict the possibility that a parent will abuse a child. Pilot programs are testing the feasibility of early intervention through various means. As a result, more and more professionals are advocating prevention through early identification of high risk families, followed by intervention before abuse can occur. But, as one symposium participant asked: "What are good and sufficient reasons to justify state intrusion into the

1. UNDERSTANDING

family?"

Intervention in response to a perceived, potential harm does raise crucial ethical considerations. As one participant pointed out, civil liberty questions are involved in denoting "high risk" families and in what he called the threat of preemptive intervention. There are questions and doubts about whether the use of an "expanding net of predicators of abuse would itself be abused."

The right of the state to intervene in the lives of individual citizens has always been questioned in our society. Preventing child abuse or saving the life of an endangered child seem to be sufficient justification for intervention, but most Americans would probably oppose using predicators to identify individuals with a "high risk" of committing a crime and then using one means or another to stop them from doing something illegal before they have actually done anything, or even attempted to do it. Early intervention, in this context, does not fit well with many American traditions and values.

Knowledge about potential child abuse, however, poses a special dilemma. When harm to a child seems likely to occur, it may be unrealistic and inhuman to expect society, and its institutions, to stand aside and wait to see what happens to a child. If we know that abuse or neglect are most likely going to happen, can inaction be condoned? Perhaps it would be more humane, and more effective, to help a family before its situation has worsened. It is not easy to decide whether the claims of parental rights are stronger than the humane duty to prevent suffering.

There are various laws protecting adults, and children, from threatened or potential harm. No one would question these. Safety laws, fire regulations, negligence laws and laws against endangering the public safety all offer protection from harmful situations that might occur if these laws were disobeyed. Such laws, moreover, go even further in protecting adults. Under the penal law governing adults, a threat, coupled with the ability to carry it out, constitutes an assault. If an adult holding a large stick, for example, threatens to beat another adult, he may be guilty of assault. Yet, this is a fairly common experience for many children. Should we give to children the same protection we give to adults, who are presumably more able to defend themselves?

Should an expectant mother be held responsible for the health of an unborn child?

It is common knowledge that prenatal care of an unborn child can have a lasting effect on the human life that follows birth. An expectant mother's improper diet, inadequate medical care, alcoholism, drug addiction or even over-medication can irreparably damage a child mentally and physically. A child born to an addicted mother comes into the world suffering in pain. Everyone who has seen it knows that a child born in withdrawal from heroin or methadone suffers horribly.

In response to such situations, there is a movement to include the care of an unborn child under the child abuse and neglect laws of the states. Under present law, even though a doctor or nurse knows with absolute certainty that an unborn child will be born mentally or physically deformed because of the expectant mother's behavior, nothing can be done. Child protective service agencies are sometimes asked to intervene, but they do not have the authority to do so until after a child has been born. The concerned professional can only watch helplessly as the inevitable happens.

To hold an expectant mother responsible for the health of an unborn child would be a new concept in our society. It would mean establishing a new societal standard or norm—that an expectant mother has the same moral and legal obligation to care for an unborn child as she has for a child after its birth.

Of course, such a standard would apply only to those unborn children that mothers plan to bear; if the expectant mother planned an abortion, the situation would be different. Such a standard would clash with the belief that a woman has an absolute right to do as she pleases with her own body. Society, or the state, would be limiting that right. Even without such a general standard, however, it should be noted that most expectant mothers act as if they hold themselves responsible for the health of their unborn children.

Should childrearing values be imposed on others?

America celebrates its ethnic, religious and racial diversity. Yet child abuse and neglect laws impose a uniform, though minimal, standard of parental care and treatment of children that can conflict with the cultural background of many American families. As adults, parents are generally considered to have a constitutionally protected freedom to live their own lives and to exercise their own beliefs. But in doing so, parents can run afoul of child abuse and neglect laws when someone questions whether a child may be harmed by the parent's way of life. There are, for example, laws in every state which require parents to provide medical care and education for their children. These requirements conflict with the precepts of some religions practiced in the United States. But courts can order that children be given medical treatment against the wishes of the parents, or that they be sent to school under threat of being taken away from the parents. Sometimes the issues involved in these controversies are seen to be the parents' non-conformity rather than the safety or welfare of the child.

There are a wide variety of childrearing practices used in this country—and there has been debate about the effectiveness of every one of them. Corporal punishment is an obvious example. Many people feel it is proper and necessary, and that experiencing it as a child did not have any harmful consequences for them; others feel that any form of corporal punishment is child abuse. On the other hand, the adherents of corporal punishment sometimes say that not disciplining a child physically is a way of neglecting the development of his character.

Every region of the country has groups whose backgrounds and characteristics pose a challenge to child protective professionals trying to help children who appear to be in danger. As one participant said: "Almost all societies and cultures express love for children and profess to cherish them, but this may express itself in different ways, and many different practices may be tolerated or condemned."

Any definition of child maltreatment that establishes a standard or criterion for childrearing can favor one individual's or group's values above another's. Creating a law or social custom that can accommodate cultural diversity while meeting the constitutional requirement of uniform application to everyone equally is not as easy as it may seem to be. Because of the difficulties involved, some would advocate the necessity of ignoring this question. But doing so puts personal convenience ahead of the lives of children and of parents affected by the unacknowledged imposition of childrearing values.

As can be seen, the symposium series sought to increase awareness of some basic issues in child maltreatment, to begin a cooperative exploration of these issues and to heighten public and professional understanding of them. The response has indicated that the four issues discussed are on people's minds. Professionals have said that they have been troubled by these questions but have not had time to think about them, while members of the general public are often being exposed to them for the first time. These reactions are worth noting since the public and professionals do not always agree on the significance of these underlying issues.

After the program, some skeptics reported that they now understood the need to raise these questions and to broaden the range of discussion about them. Some of the humanists who participated in the symposia have indicated a desire to remain involved in these issues, and some have gone ahead and done more on their own. One philosopher borrowed some of the symposia materials to use in a discussion of violence in the family and an historian raised two of the issues on a popular radio talk show.

Many of the local co-sponsoring groups are looking for ways to go from talk to action; they want to do something helpful and constructive. Some are working to set up task forces or to establish volunteer programs. Most have the potential to become strong and effective community advocates.

In 1978, the National Alliance received a follow-up grant from the New York Council for the Humanities to commission eight humanists who had participated in the symposia to write essays on the issues discussed. These es-says will be presented during two conferences to be held in November 1978 in Syracuse and New York City. Humanists and professionals will discuss the subjects of the essays, which will then be revised in response to these discussions and edited for book publication.

The eight authors and their disciplines are:

Stephen Berk, Union College, Schnectady and John Demos, Brandeis University (history); Natalie Abrams, New York University, Joseph DiGiovanna, State University of New York at Pottsdam and Newton Garver, State University of New York at Buffalo (philosophy); Leslie Fiedler, State University of New York at Buffalo, and William Wasserstrom, Syracuse University (literature); and Erwin Johnson, State University of New York at Buffalo (anthropology).

The preparation and publication of such a book of humanistic essays on child abuse and neglect could be an important addition to the scholarship of the disciplines represented by the authors, as well as to the growing body of literature on child maltreatment. The National Alliance believes that professionals and citizens should be exposed to humanistic discussion of the problems of child abuse and neglect.

The symposia were presented as community programs, not as an end in themselves but to initiate community thought and action.[2] The collaboration between humanists and professionals has reinforced the idea that child abuse and neglect are no longer problems for the professional alone; they are everyone's problems. Unless a community as a whole responds to these problems, professionals will have to continue to struggle with limited means and circumscribed alternatives. The National Alliance hopes that broadened understanding will give communities more choices and involve more citizens and professionals in exercising those choices.

---

[1] The four films used and their producers are: *Fragile: Handle With Care* (Independent Order of Foresters, Florence Hallum Prevention of Child Abuse Fund, 100 Border Avenue, Ste. B., Solana Beach, Calif. 92075); *Parent-Child Interaction* (Mike Williams Associates, P.O. Box 564, Manhattan Beach, Calif. 90266); *Four Families*, narrated by Dr. Margaret Mead, (McGraw-Hill Films, McGraw-Hill Book Company, P.O. Box 404, Hightstown, N.J. 08520); and *The Littlest Junkie* (WABC-TV, 1330 Avenue of the Americas, New York, N.Y. 10019).

The first three films were edited by the National Alliance, with permission of the producers, to highlight the issues under discussion. These edited versions are available from the National Alliance for use in similar public discussions centered on humanistic concerns relating to child maltreatment.

[2] More information on the National Alliance and its education program may be obtained by writing to the National Alliance for the Prevention and Treatment of Child Abuse and Maltreatment, Inc., 41-27 169 Street, Flushing, N.Y. 11358.

The Parent
and
The Child

The Parent and the Child offers an examination of the characteristics of the abusing parents and the abused child, prevention and intervention suggestions. Kempe and Helfer (1972) identified three major factors causing abuse: 1) the parent with potential for abuse (psychological problems, often abused as children), 2) the role of the child in provoking the abuse, for example the hyperactive or unwanted child, and 3) societal and environmental stresses. Two articles offer views on neglect outside the home.

The opening article "Seeking Help as a Parent" offers a dialogue with the family in stress. The focus then turns to the parent or child. "Characteristics of the Abused/Neglected Child" is from a study by the National Institute of Mental Health and summarizes the literature and field experience. It calls for family therapy that concentrates on the kinds of interaction that may be causing the abuse.

Echoing previous research, Selwyn Smith's "Psychiatric Characteristics of Abusing Parents" cites emotional immaturity and dependence as a constant characteristic of abusing parents. A study conducted through emergency rooms in the United Kingdom supports class-related indicators of early studies. The other side of the question, a Battering Parent describes his struggle, and a model social service system that would help those who can't help themselves.

There is much confusion between discipline and abuse. "Spare the rod, spoil the child" has dictated much parental behavior. How does one discipline a child without violence? Dr. Thomas Gordon offers suggestions on how "You can Change Unacceptable Behavior Without Using Punishment." With the right approach and honesty, children can be taught to respect their parent's need and rights.

A question raised by the National Alliance for the Prevention and Treatment of Child Abuse and Neglect regards the mother's responsibility to the unborn child. The first reported association of maternal alcoholism and birth defects was in 1973. Current research data supports the theory of the adverse effects that alcohol, drugs, cigarettes and poor diet have on the fetus. "Maternal Alcoholism and the Fetal Alcohol Syndrome" describes known symptoms and lists a proper diet for the expectant mother to follow.

"The Predicament of Abused Children" and "The Phenomenon of the Abused Adolescent" concentrates on the disruption of the child's normal developmental stages because of child abuse and neglect. The first, an overview of a number of studies shows that the abused child exhibits behavior often attributed to abusing adults, such as poor self concept, psychiatric symptoms and pseudo-mature behavior. Dr. Ira. S. Lourie, through a study sponsored by the National Institute of Mental Health, finds abused adolescents have developmental problems in separation and control. While they comprise 25 to 30 percent of social services caseloads, little has been written about their special problems.

What happens to the child when the courts decide, or family abandons them to a foster home? Foster children are politically and economically dependent on agencies and the courts for their welfare. Seventeen-year-old Mike Mulligan, a foster child, learned to communicate and work with the system. He was the inspiration for the Illinois Foster Children's Association. A group composed primarily of foster children have learned to speak out for their rights, and the rights of children everywhere.

Seeking Help as a Parent

This was written by Carol A. Johnston, former director of
the Parental Stress Center of Oakland, California. It was designed
to serve as a companion to the documentary, "Raised In Anger,"
produced by WQED/Pittsburgh, with a grant from the 3M Company.

Seeking Help as a Parent

A mother has put clean training pants on her two-year-old for the fourth time. After sitting on the potty chair for 20 minutes, the child promises to stay dry. Three minutes later, she discovers the pants are wet and messed again. The mother is sure that the child is soiling the pants deliberately.

A father has told his four-year-old for the third time not to touch anything on his workbench. The child reaches for a wrench and knocks off cans of nuts and bolts which the father has just finished sorting according to size. The father is convinced that the child is deliberately disobeying his orders.

A husband has just stomped out of the house after a quarrel with his wife because she couldn't make the baby stop crying. The baby continues to scream, making her even more upset. She is furious with both the baby and her husband, but only the baby is around.

Yes, being a parent is difficult.

> **At times, when things become so difficult that we**
> > **become frustrated**
> > **lose control of ourselves**
> > **take it out on the children**
> **it's important that we ask for help.**

"Yes, it's OK to ask for help."

"Yes, other parents feel the same way."

"No you're not a bad parent if you feel like you can't stand it anymore."

"Yes, there is someone who wants to hear from you if you feel overwhelmed with the job of being a parent."

"No, it doesn't mean you're weak."

> **It takes courage to reach out,**
> > **to pick up the phone,**
> > **to talk to someone,**
> > **to tell how you feel.**

Other parents have called for help. They too found that being a parent isn't easy. They too have had moments of rage at a child.

Being a parent is one of the most demanding and most difficult jobs in the world.

The good feelings and satisfaction from being a parent can be fantastic.

Yet, the demands and frustrations never seem to end.

That's why asking for help is so important.

A Change in Routine

Every parent needs to feel good about being a parent. But the constant hard work, demands for time and attention, and pressures of being a parent can be frustrating.

Being a parent with the same old routine day after day can create

"Seeking Help as a Parent," Carol A. Johnston, from the pamphlet *Families in Stress* 1978 United States Department of Health, Education and Welfare.

a lot of stress. Often we begin to feel the children are getting in our way.

STRESS BUILDS UP when we feel overwhelmed by the demands on us, and it can cause us to react in exaggerated ways.

We'll always have some stress because just being a parent is difficult. However, we can learn to let off steam in safe ways and to keep the stress of being a parent under control.

CHANGING THE ROUTINE can be refreshing and rewarding. We can get refreshed from a walk on a spring day, a bath on a hot day, a cup of hot chocolate on a winter day, or just by talking to someone else.

It's important for parents *(and for children, too)* to make changes in the daily demands of being a parent. It's important to be refreshed by talking to someone about the frustrations of being a parent.

We feel better.
We help everyone near us feel better too.

Losing Control

No one likes to be attacked or abused.

Lashing out creates more stress, whether we do the attacking or whether we feel that someone is attacking us.

Usually, striking out at others is not really intentional. It just happens when stress builds up and when we can't handle it. As a result, we can lose control of ourselves.

When it happens, it's painful for everyone near us.

When we strike out at a child, we abuse the child.

It's painful for the child.
It's painful and scary for the parent.

It's important for every parent to get some relief, some change in routine, some help in the demanding job of being a parent.
No one should be expected to be able to do it all alone.

No one can do it all alone. There are people who can provide help.

One of the quickest and easiest ways to get help is to reach for your telephone.

Talking About It

"What good will that do? What can I get to help me out?"

"Who will find out that I called?"

"Won't the police or some social worker come knocking on my door?"

"Sometimes I wish I'd never had my child, but I don't want my child taken away and put into a foster home."

It's important that you know that help is available *before* things get out of hand.

The purpose of talking about it now is to prevent the need to separate you and your children.

It's so much better for you and for the children if help comes before, not after.

Some programs don't even ask for your name.

Some ask for your first name only, just so they can talk to you more easily.

They want to make the job of being a parent a little easier for you. And, they want to provide you a safe place to talk.

Mainly, talking about it by telephone will provide you with someone who will really listen to you.

Someone who will be able to listen without judging or putting anything on you.
Someone who will be listening to what you say without cutting you off or shutting you out.
Someone who can really hear how you are feeling and what you are thinking.

They can be real friends, helping you talk out your frustration and anger.

Your problems won't disappear, but you will be given some help—the type of help that is needed to keep the problems under control.

Why Listen to Me?

"Who would be willing to do all that? What makes me worth that kind of attention?"

"No one has offered to help me before—unless they wanted something from me."

Sometimes—when we don't get the kind of attention that makes us feel good about ourselves—we begin to think we aren't worth it.

When you feel good about yourself, you can do a lot for yourself and for others.

You've got a lot going for you—when you put it all together. And because you're unique, you're a special person who's worth the attention of other people.

In most communities, there are professionals and volunteers committed and trained to help parents and children in stress.

Who Will Talk with Me?

"Who will be listening to me and talking with me at the other end of the telephone?"

"What will they say to me?"

The people who will be listening to you and talking with you know how hard it can be at times to be a parent.

They've had *someone*—either in their own families or a special friend—who has helped them when things became difficult.

Some are staff members, others are volunteers.

Some are parents who have had similar problems and who received help when they needed it.

They want to pass that help on to someone else.

They are people who have had some special training so that they can be better listeners as well as better helpers to you.

They also have information that they can pass on to you, such as some answers about why children act the way they do, how children grow up, what you might try when things get difficult, and what kinds of help are available to you in your community.

What if I Do Call?

"Is real help always available?"

"When I've got a problem, I need help immediately—not tomorrow."

Yes, there may be some problems when you call. Programs are made up of people, and things don't always go smoothly with all calls.

For example, there may be times when someone is not available to help you the instant you call.

An operator may take too long to answer, or you may be put on hold.

The number may even have been changed.

**The most important thing is
DON'T GIVE UP!**

If you feel things aren't going too smoothly with your call:

Please stay on the line.

If you were told they would call you back, but they don't call when you expected them to:

Call them back.

If the helping process seems too slow, remember the program is just people.

But people help people best.

Some Stress and Tension Relievers

1. Count to 10, put the child in a safe area (crib, playpen, child-proof room) and go to another room or outside for a few minutes.

2. Go into another room, close the door, and cry or scream. Then take 10 minutes to read, knit or do whatever relaxes you best.

3. Lie on the floor with your feet up on a chair; place a cool wash cloth on your face; and think of the most peaceful scene you can imagine. Stay there for 5 minutes.

4. Tell your child exactly what is making you feel angry. Be really specific about what behavior needs to be changed in order to reduce your anger level.

5. After you've put the children down for a nap, forget what you "should" be doing. Take some time for yourself to relax—sleep, read, listen to music, take a bath—whatever makes you feel fresh again.

6. Designate a corner, chair or some quiet spot as a "time-out" place where you can go when you feel like losing your temper. Designate a separate one for your child. It gives both of you a few minutes to calm down, *and* it tells the other person that you are getting angry.

7. Save a special, quiet plaything to be used only at certain times. It will be a treat for your child, and will provide some quiet time for you.

Bonus Points

When things are going well, pass out rewards.

1. Compliment and reward the children for the good things, such as being quiet, not fighting, not whining, cleaning up.

2. Let the children know when their behavior is making you happy.

3. Hug the children and say "I love you."

4. Say "thanks" for small favors.

5. Treat the children and yourself to something special for doing so well.

CHILD ABUSE AND NEGLECT PROGRAMS:
Practice and Theory
Characteristics of the Abused/Neglected Child

INTRODUCTION

This chapter summarizes the literature and field experience with respect to the children of abuse and neglect.

Covered in this summary are:

- Demographic characteristics, i.e., age, sex, birth order, multiple v. singular abuse
- Child-specific precursors to abuse
- Disabilities and deficiencies resulting from abuse

DEMOGRAPHIC CHARACTERISTICS

Age of the Child

Although many abuse laws apply to children as old as 18 and no one denies that children of all ages are abused, most literature focuses on those children believed to be most often or most seriously abused: children under 3 or 4 years of age.[1] Children of this age are more vulnerable to serious physical damage and less able to defend themselves than are older children. In addition, infants are not able to communicate meaningfully with their parents who, often unskilled in child care and themselves replete with unmet needs, become frustrated. The mere presence of a small infant can lead to stress if the birth was neither planned nor wanted.

Many of the studies which conclude that very young children are more likely to be abused are hospital-based studies of emergency room and pediatric inpatient populations.[2] By definition, children included in these studies are the more severely abused children, i.e., those who need medical attention. Gil (1970) opines that these studies overrepresent the younger children. In his nationwide study of every incident reported through legal channels in 1967/68, he found that over three-quarters of the children were over age 2, and that almost one-half were older

than 6 years. His two samples, 5,993 children in 1967 and 6,617 children in 1968, also revealed nearly one-fifth to be teenagers. However, in his 1967 analysis, Gil (1970) did find that the younger children were the more seriously injured. Several other studies of reported incidents known to social service agencies[3] found between one-quarter and one-half of their sample children to be over 6 years of age.

As discussed in part I, among the programs visited, the two hospital-based programs report a large majority of children to be under 3 years of age; the social service-based programs in one case report 22 percent of abused children to be over 7 years of age; in another case 61.1 percent of the abused and neglected children were 6 and over, and children 10-18 years old represented the largest single group or 33.5 percent. The other programs visited either do not maintain these data or the data were unavailable.

It seems clear that the age of abused, and particularly of neglected, children is a function of the reporting source with hospitals reporting more of the really young children. Age of reported children is also related to definitional problems. As discussed in chapter V, what is classified as abuse in very young children is much more likely to pass as discipline when related to older children. Moreover, it is possible that suspicion levels in terms of age create the epidemiology in that a reporter who is in doubt and who has been told that abuse is more common in young children may be more likely to decide in favor of reporting a very young suspected abuse case and to decide against the reporting of an older child.

Sex of the Child

In most studies, sex differences seem to be not statistically significant. Although there may appear to be a greater number of abused children of one particular sex, the samples are so small as to preclude any general statements to this effect. Two studies (Ebbin et al. 1969; Elmer 1967c), with samples of 50 and 33, respectively, compared an abuse sample with a normal clinic population and found no significant difference in relative proportions of male and female children. In Gil's (1970) large sample there were sex differences which he related to the age of the sample. In the total study cohort, boys outnumbered girls only slightly (53 percent in 1967, 51 percent in 1968); among teenagers only, girls predominated (63 percent in 1967, 64 percent in 1968). Gil's explanation was that girls, when young, conform to parental expectations to a greater degree than boys do. As they mature sexually, parental anxiety increases as does use of physical force in controlling their behavior.

Two of the programs visited maintain data on large numbers of children. The Hennepin County child protective services program has aggregated data relating to 630 children over a 10-year period from 1963 to 1973; 56.8 percent of these children are male and 43.2 percent are female. Reporting on 373 abused and neglected children during a 6-month period of 1974, the Montana Department of Social and Rehabilitation Services shows that 49.3 percent of the children were male and 50.7 percent were female. However, their breakdown by age and sex shows that the proportion of males and females varies according to age. There is a higher proportion of males than females in the 0-2, 6-7, and 8-10-year-old age groups and a higher proportion of females than of males in the 3-5 and 10-18-year-old groups, paralleling Gil's (1970) findings.

While there may be some slight tendency for boys to be abused more than girls at younger ages because of their greater degree of activity and because of the greater incidence of hyperactivity in boys, these tendencies seem slight. Similarly, the tendency to report more girls than boys in the older age groups may be a function of greater anxiety and tendency to punish adolescent girls on the part of the parents, as suggested by Gil, or it may be a function of more vigilant reporting by community resources which may be more likely to define girls as fragile and in greater need of protection. In other words, physical punishment of boys may be more acceptable than physical punishment of girls.

Birth Order

There seems to be no agreement as to the relationship between birth order and abuse. In two studies the majority of children were oldest or second-born children (Elmer et al. 1971; Glazier 1971). Sample sizes in these studies, in the order cited, are 34 abused and neglected children and 50 children with failure-to-thrive. Youngest children are more frequently abused in three studies (Bennie and Sclare 1969; Cameron, Johnson, and Camps 1966; Jackson 1972) based on sample sizes of 10, 29, and 18 abused children, respectively. Other authors who mention birth order simply state that the abused child is generally one child in the family selected as a target for abuse.[4] Cameron (1972) states that the target is most likely to be either the oldest or the youngest, representing an unwelcome and unwanted beginning or addition to the family. In her study of 33 children admitted to a hospital with abuse related injuries, Elmer (1967c) found that there was no statistically significant relationship between birth order and abuse, but rather, that a particular child might be targeted for abuse because his position in the family had special significance for the abusive parent.

Multiple v. Singular Abuse: Repeated Abuse of One Child Abuse of Siblings

Many abused children are not just victims of a single, isolated incident. In the studies reviewed, the proportion of children with a history of repeated abuse varies from 21 percent to 50 percent.[5] Duration of exposure to abuse is included in Nurse's (1964) discussion of 20 probation cases. In these families, abuse occurred over a period ranging from 6 months to over 5 years. The Georgia League for Nursing estimates the average duration of abuse to be from 1 to 3 years. These studies suggest that abuse is not an isolated, one-time event and that therefore, without some form of intervention, abuse will be repeated. Neglect is more likely to be ongoing and chronic and is far more likely to involve all of the children in a family.

Several studies provide evidence that abuse is not limited to one child in the family. Skinner and Castle (1969) found that in the 41 families with more than one child, 49 percent battered more than one of their children. These figures are based on case records of the British NSPCC of abused children under 4 years of age who were in need of medical attention. Simons et al.

(1966) reported a history of sibling abuse in 16 percent of the 313 cases reported to the New York City Bureau of Child Welfare. Glazier (1971), studying 251 reported abuse cases in the Buffalo area, found that 12.5 percent of the incidents concerned more than one child in a family. While these percentages are lower than the 49 percent reported by Skinner and Castle, it should be noted that there may have been unreported cases in which siblings were abused. In the absence of a specific study of each child in the family it cannot be assumed that only the reported child has been abused.

In all probability single v. multiple abuse depends on whether the abuse is primarily motivated by the dynamic relationship between a particular child and his parent(s) or by general stress factors within the family, on whether only one child has been removed so that another child becomes the target of abuse, and on the age of all of the children in the family.

In part I, cases are reported in which all of the children in a particular family have been abused and cases are reported in which only a single child has been abused. In those cases in which only a single child has been abused, it generally seems that the child has particular significance to the parent because the child represents the bad and unacceptable parts of the parent; because the child resembles a hated relative, boyfriend, or exhusband; or because the child is in someway different or special, e.g., hyperactive, colicky, irritable. In some reported cases the abuse, or even murder, of one or more children is seen by program staff as a displacement of the feelings of revulsion toward a particular child who is actually the least abused. Our impression, based on a review of cases presented by the programs visited, is that in at least half of the cases it is not one, but all, or at least several, children in a family who are abused. While only one child may be reported by a hospital or by another source, further investigation shows that several of the children have been abused. In general, when programs receive an abuse report on one child, all of the children should be checked for evidence of bruises and old fractures.

CHILD-SPECIFIC PRECURSORS TO ABUSE

In virtually all studies, some abused children had significant medical histories and disabilities prior to the abusive incident. Nearly one-half of the 20 abused children on which followup study was conducted by Elmer and Gregg (1967) had a history of medical problems. Several had low birth weights, were premature, were ill during the neonatal period, had convulsions or brain damage, or were seemingly predisposed to failure-to-thrive.

Low birth weight and prematurity are discussed by other authors as well. In Silver, Dublin, and Lourie's (1971) sample of 34 hospitalized abused children, the proportion of premature infants was over two times the national average. However, since prematurity is higher among low income groups, comparisons with the national average tend to be misleading. Skinner and Castle (1969) report that 13 percent of the children referred to the NSPCC in 1 year were premature; in all cases early mother-child separation occurred.

Prematurity and low birth weight contribute to the vulnerability of the child. Hospitalization after birth is prolonged, amounting to an enforced separation between the mother and child; a normal relationship or bonding may be difficult to establish. Klein and Stern (1971) studied 51 battered children hospitalized in Canada over a 9-year period. Twenty-four percent had low birth weight as contrasted with an expected United States and Canadian national rate of only 7 or 8 percent. The mean neonatal hospital stay for those infants was 41 days.

Elmer's (1971) accident study also included some abused children who were born prematurely. Approximately one-third of the 34 abused children weighed less than 5.5 pounds at birth. None of the nonabused children weighed below that level. Elmer explains that premature infants cry more, are more irritable, and thus place a greater strain on families with few resources.

In addition to prematurity or illness during the neonatal period, a number of authors have studied physical or developmental deviations which antedate abuse. Johnson and Morse's (1968) sample of 101 children included 70 percent who had physical or developmental deviations before the injury was reported (Costin 1972). However, in most cases it is difficult, if not impossible, to differentiate between those factors specific to a child which may predispose him to abuse and those factors which may as easily be the consequences of abuse. This chicken and egg problem makes it impossible in most cases to determine to what degree a particular child, by virtue of his special physical, developmental, or intellectual handicaps, was predisposed to abuse.

Gil (1970) found that 29 percent of his sample cohort were deviant in social and intellectual functioning during the year preceding the reported incident. Fourteen percent were physically deficient. Nearly 13 percent were below their age appropriate grade level. Prior to the reported incident, 17 percent had been hospitalized for physical illness, 9 percent were in foster care, 4 percent were known to juvenile courts, and nearly 4 percent had been in child care institutions. Gil states that this level is "... in excess of the level of any group of children selected at random from the population at large ..." (p. 108). However, Simons et al. (1966) report that the proportion (10 percent) of their sample (313 children reported abused in New York City) that had severe prior defects, e.g., brain damage, eye and orthopedic impairments, was not that different from the percentage of such disorders in the total New York City child population.

The literature on behavioral characteristics is of a descriptive rather than analytic nature. The problems of deciding whether these behavioral characteristics are the cause or the result of abuse is monumental.

Johnson and Morse (1968) differentiate between the behavior of children younger than, and older than, 5 years of age. Younger abused children are described as whiny, fussy, listless, chronically crying, restless, demanding, stubborn, resistive, negativistic, unresponsive, pallid, sickly, emaciated, fearful, panicky, and unsmiling. Older abused children are described as gloomy, unhappy, depressed, insincere, inconsiderate, deceitful, openly expressive of disrespect toward their fathers, and ingratiating toward their mothers. However, these two sets of characteristics do not appear to be that different from each other. The authors state that the children most likely to be abused are the ones who are overly active and most difficult to manage. Because of their failure to respond to care and to grow in a normal manner, they are seen as threatening or at least not gratifying to the parents' self-image.

Terr (1970) delineates three types of relationships of the abused child to his family. First, the presence of a physical abnormality such as failure-to-thrive may be an irritant and guilt

producer to the mother. The fact that the child does not develop properly is a reflection on the mother's child care skills. The second type of relationship concerns ego defects which are secondary to maternal deprivation. Thus, there exists a shallow relationship between parent and child. The child withdraws and becomes indifferent to the mother. The third relationship consists of retaliatory activities on the part of the child. Hostile behavior by the child worsens an already strained interaction.

Program staff was asked to consider all of the abused children they had known and to make an estimate of the proportion of these children who presented a problem which an independent observer agreed could make that child especially difficult, e.g., physical handicap, colicky baby, hyperactivity. Estimates within and across programs ranged considerably from 10 percent to 40 percent, but the majority of estimates were approximately 20 percent. Thus, about one-fifth of the children, according to program staff, could be considered as predisposed to abuse; the majority of children are described as attractive and appealing youngsters or infants.

DISABILITIES AND DEFICIENCIES RESULTING FROM ABUSE

As a result of abuse, children suffer, in varying degrees, from both physical and mental defects. When abuse is first diagnosed, prevalent physical characteristics include large heads, protruding bones, bruises, poor skin hygiene, multiple soft tissue injuries, malnutrition, and smallness for the child's age.[6]

Holter and Friedman (1968a) describe the nature of abuse injuries and compare them with neglect and accident injuries. The authors completed two surveys: in the first, 69 accident cases involving children under 6 years of age seen in a hospital emergency room were reviewed in terms of type of injury, explanation, and signs of abuse or neglect. In the second survey, 87 cases were similarly reviewed and home visits were made by a public health nurse. Eleven percent of the two survey samples were suspected to be incidents of abuse. Injuries displayed by suspected abused children (who were all considered high risk) consisted of head injuries, fractures, dislocations, limb injuries, burns, abrasions, contusions, and bruises. The accident (nonabuse) group exhibited lacerations and ingestions. An additional important difference between the groups can be seen in the delay between time of injury and emergency room visit. The timespan amounted to 4½ hours for neglect cases, 2 hours for abuse, 1 hour for accident, and three-quarters of an hour for repeated accident cases.

A followup study of these same children 5 years later (Friedman and Morse 1974) found that over 70 percent of the suspected abuse and neglect groups had injuries requiring medical attention in that interval. Only 50 percent of the accident group needed additional medical care.

Neurological damage is a common after-effect of abuse. Morse, Sahler, and Friedman (1970) report that 71 percent of the 25 children (all surviving children treated for abuse from 1963 to 1966) they studied 3 years after hospitalization for abuse or neglect were outside of the normal range of intellectual, emotional, social, and motor development. Forty-three percent were mentally retarded. Martin (1972) also reports that same proportion having permanent brain damage in his sample of 42 abused children followed by a child development center. Thirty-three percent of his sample was also diagnosed with failure-to-thrive. He found that syndrome occurred twice as frequently in children who were functionally retarded as in children who could subsequently function normally.

Elmer's (Elmer and Gregg 1967) studies also show a high proportion of retardation. Fifty percent of the 20 abused children restudied after a span of from 1½ to 10 years after hospitalization for multiple bone injuries were retarded; one-third had physical defects; and eight were emotionally disturbed. Her comparison of another group of 34 abused children with 67 accident victims produced the following results: The abused children had twice the incidence of neurological problems as the children with accidental injuries.

Johnson and Morse (1968) discuss the disabilities of 101 abused children known to the Denver Welfare department. The following problems were present: "uncontrollable" severe temper tantrums (19 percent), below normal speech development (18 percent), mental retardation (16 percent), toilet training problems (15 percent), feeding problems (13 percent), physical handicaps (7 percent), and brain damage (1 percent). Twenty-five percent of the 52 children under 5 years of age were below normal in language development; one-half suffered from malnutrition, dehydration, and failure-to-thrive.

Galdston (1971a) lists two types of behavior displayed by physically abused children. They may be listless, apathetic, and unresponsive to all but painful stimuli or they may be extremely fearful, recoiling from contact with anyone. While abused children may, in fact, recover from the harmful experience, Galdston states that once a child reaches the age of 3½ or 4 there is great difficulty in correcting the damage.

Lukianowicz (1971) characterizes the long- and short-term effects of battering. Short-term effects refer to changes in appearance and behavior (listlessness, withdrawal, apathy), changes in attitude toward parent (fear), and psychosomatic symptoms of emotional stress (refusal to eat, vomiting, bedwetting). Longer-term effects which can occur include, again, withdrawal, timidity and fear, rebelliousness, and becoming an abusing parent. Brain damage is also a possibility.

A number of other authors also describe the emotional and relationship problems of abused children. Costin (1972) states that abused children are shy and have low self-esteem; Zalba (1967) reports that they tend to be depressive, hyperactive, destructive, fearful, withdrawn, as well as bedwetters, truants, fire-setters, and overreactive to hostility. They are described as having a lack of trust in the parent and difficulty in mastering the stages of autonomy and initiative (Martin 1972). Bryant et al. (1963) states that the abused child has a seriously impaired relationship with the abusive parent. The child may also accept the parents' bad image of her/himself, as a form of loyalty (Kempe 1969). Acute anxiety is exhibited through such symptoms as speech problems, sleep difficulties, thumbsucking, and nail biting (Lewis et al. 1969). Leontine Young (1964) describes the children she studied as detached from feelings and from other people and lacking in energy and purpose. They take on the role of scapegoat of the family and feel unloved; their needs go disregarded (Steele and Pollack 1974). Curtis (1963) reports an unusual degree of hostility toward the parents and toward the world in general. Some of the above characteristics could lead to the child's inviting others to hurt him (Milowe and Lourie 1964).

Typical hospital behavior of abused children is described by Morris, Gould, and Matthews (1964). When brought in for treatment, these children: (1) cry hopelessly, (2) do not look to parent for assurance, (3) do not expect to be comforted, (4) are wary of physical contact, (5) are apprehensive when other children cry, (6) are apprehensive when adults approach other crying children, (7) are alert for danger, (8) continually ask what will happen next, (9) are in search of such things as food, favors, things, services, (10) show a "poker face" when discharge home is mentioned, and (11) do not suggest that they want to go home.

Violent behavior has been frequently mentioned as characteristic of abused children. Galdston (1975) describes its presence in children attending the Parents' Center Project, a therapeutic day care program. The author states that these children use violence as a major way of seeking attention. After several weeks in the program the children were able to express emotions in other, more acceptable, forms; however, none lost their violent behavior completely. Another specific behavior manifested by these children is the "grabbing reaction." The children, wanting a belonging relationship, will grab an object from someone else. Once taken, however, the object ceases to be an attraction.

Neglected children are discussed by several authors; however, their descriptions are no different from those dealing with physically abused children: withdrawn, hostile, depressed, antisocial, and passive.[7] There is difficulty in establishing a one-to-one attachment, a bonding, between child and mother. The same traits are used to describe children diagnosed as failure-to-thrive.[8]

Gardner (1975), in summarizing the work of the Gilday Center in Boston, a day care center for abused children, described the children as follows:

> We cannot offer any typical behavior or personality pattern which would fit every abused child, although we have certainly learned what kinds of behavior to expect. For example: these children are much more apt to comfort an upset adult than to expect comfort when they are upset. They may be wary of physical contact of any kind. Their capacity for being 'given to' is boundless. They show little or no distress at separation from parents. They can be very manipulative of adults from a very early age, and they are often accomplished actors. They sometimes respond negatively to praise as if it were safer to be 'bad.' They are generally reluctant to engage in any messy activities. Some seem highly skilled at provoking adults to anger, while others indiscriminately seek

affection from any adult. Their language development is generally slow, and many have speech impediments. They demand immediate gratification and find it almost impossible to wait or take turns. Some are extremely well coordinated and others have little sense of body awareness. Initially, they seem completely without the normal childlike sense of joy (pp. 149-150).

The Bowen Center, one of the programs described in part I, has had 9 years' experience in the treatment of abused and severely neglected children. Their description is as follows:

> The limited backgrounds of our children, their suspicion, their unfamiliarity with success, make them view each new experience as a potential threat, and we must literally decoy them into participation in any new activity. The sense of fun one normally sees in preschoolers is totally lacking.
>
> One is struck by the differences our children display as compared to less deprived youngsters. The expression on their faces is old and worried, they rarely smile. They relate to staff either by clinging to anyone available, or they attack. They are all frightened and share a general distrust of a new situation. Their behavior is provocative, literally inviting violent response.
>
> Their initial approach to materials is indiscriminate hoarding, trying to accumulate as many things as possible, but with no drive to use them, only to collect. They are unable to use free play periods constructively.
>
> Although we observe little overt difficulty with separation, the children appear to be undifferentiated from their mothers, i.e., if mother is sick, they experience themselves as being sick, if a parent is away from home they tell us 'Daddy dead' in a flat tone.

Children manifesting the failure-to-thrive syndrome exhibit different characteristics than do physically abused children, although both types of abuse may be present in one child. Gregg (1968) makes a distinction between the failure-to-thrive syndrome and physical abuse. Whereas physical abuse may represent a one-time occurrence, failure-to-thrive is generally of longer duration. Children with complaints suggesting systemic disease not related to trauma instead suffer from longstanding neglect which may be accented by abuse. Barbero and Shaheen (1967) divide the syndrome into four clinical forms. Failure-to-thrive may occur: (1) without systemic disease but with family disruption, (2) with clinical manifestations, e.g., vomiting, diarrhea, anemia, respiratory problems, neuromuscular disorders, (3) accompanied by trauma (physical abuse) and (4) as an accompaniment to primary systemic disease which precipitates family disruption and contributes indirectly to the syndrome.

2. PARENT

Bullard et al. (1967) studied hospital records of 151 children exhibiting the failure-to-thrive syndrome. Fifty of the children studied had no primary organic illness. In most cases, the syndrome began in early infancy, progressing until the child was 6-12 months old when hospitalization occurred. As in physical abuse cases, other disorders were present. More than one-half of the 41 children followed up from 8 months to 9 years after hospitalization showed continued growth failure, emotional disorders, mental retardation, or a combination of those problems.

Glaser et al. (1968) report that of the 50 children with failure-to-thrive in their study, 37 percent (N = 19) had failed or had difficulties completing the first year of school. Over 40 percent (N = 40) continued to show physical evidence of their earlier state between 6 months and 8 years after discharge. Of course, school failure and later physical problems cannot be attributed to failure-to-thrive alone as both of these can be consequences of poor parenting.

Exploited children, as described by Galdston (1971a), are children who do not act their age, whose attitudes, interests, and behavior are not appropriate to their age. The child functions to gratify the parent and fulfill the parents' image. Galdston gives several situations of exploitation. An obese child may be fulfilling the parent's desire to eat; a child with disordered behavior who is often involved in accidents may be gratifying the parent's desire for violence. Sexual abuse is another category of exploitation. The parent is fulfilling his needs through the child. Sexual abuse is also dealt with by Tormes, and Schultz (1973). Tormes characterizes the sexual abuse victims by their lack of socializing and exposure outside of the family. Schultz describes the deep relationship established between the abuser and the abused as one where the victim seeks out affectionate behavior from the parent.

There are two additional studies in the literature which offer insight into the behavioral effects of abuse. Babow and Babow (1974) have published a verbatim case study of a 21-year-old female with a long history of abuse by her mother. She had repeatedly tried to commit suicide and was diagnosed as schizophrenic. Her explanation for the suicide attempts and other self-destructive behavior was that they were a punishment for what she saw as the bad thing she had done: being born when not wanted. The second study (Green 1968) involved school-age schizophrenics with a history of abuse who were enrolled in a residential treatment center. The parent-child relationship in these cases alternated physical abuse with periods of withdrawal and threats of abandonment. The abused children attempted to inflict pain on themselves in order to recreate whatever parental contact existed.

The behavioral characteristics of children as reported in the literature are certainly supported by program experience. Multiple foster home placements are often precipitated by the behavioral problems manifested by the children whose behavior can be so difficult to tolerate that they lead to one rejection after another. Many of the children feel that the abuse is a punishment for their fundamental badness and they experience out of home placement as proof of their badness. Thus, in the new setting they continue to act out their negative self-image and to precipitate the punishment they know must be forthcoming. In addition, many of these children, having never experienced a firm and consistent limit-setting approach, are in fact very difficult to live with in a home which is not given to chaos.

****

The contrast between the vast amount of literature reviewed in the previous chapter and the relative paucity discussed in this chapter is no accident. It points up the fact that most authors, most researchers, and in fact most programs are addressed primarily to the needs of the parents. Much of the interest in parents is based on a desire to deal with root causes so that precipitating social problems can be eradicated and so that treatment can be focused. But beyond this interest in parents in the name of prevention and treatment is an interest in adults which supercedes interest in children. In general, in the field of abuse and neglect, children are second-class citizens.

Of all the programs visited, only one is seriously addressed to the needs of abused and neglected children. By and large, as will be discussed in the next chapter, treatment programs are designed to meet the long-range needs of parents rather than of children. Children suffer incredible pain and hurt, children are placed in long-term foster care storage with little opportunity to understand or to work through what has happened to them, and children continue to live in homes which are harsh and rejecting. In all too many cases, children are seen by a worker only in passing as she/he visits with the parents and in many cases are asked to leave so that parent(s) and worker can talk. No one works with the children or helps them to cope with the same life conditions which are felt to be too difficult for adults. The majority of social workers and protective services workers have no training in how to work with children or adolescents; many of them state openly that they are not comfortable dealing with children and adolescents.

Our review of the literature suggests that not only are children's needs underaddressed but that in addition there has been little attention devoted to a study of the interaction, under a variety of circumstances, between abused children and their parents. Efforts at developing typologies which can be useful for prevention and treatment are primarily centered on the dynamics of the parents rather than on the kinds of interaction which may be causing abuse. This lack of attention to parent-child interaction is also reflected in the kinds of treatment modalities that have been developed in abuse programs. As will be seen in the next chapter, family therapy which focuses on interactional variables is in a barely nascent state in this field.

NOTES

1. Corbett 1964; Costin 1972; Fontana 1971 and 1973c; Galdston 1965 and 1971a; Gelles 1973; Georgia League for Nursing; Skinner and Castle 1969; Solomon 1973.
2. Cameron, Johnson and Camps 1966; Ebbin et al. 1969; Elmer 1967c; Elmer et al. 1971; Evans, Reinhart and Succop 1972; Friedman and Morse 1974; Heins 1969; Holter and Friedman 1968a; Jackson 1972; Lauer 1974; Paulson and Blake 1969; Zuckerman 1972.
3. Bryant et al. 1963; Glazier 1971; Johnson and Morse 1968.
4. Boardman 1962; Brown and Daniels 1968; Caffey et al. 1972; Costin 1972; Joint Commission on Mental Health of Children 1973.
5. Bennie and Sclare 1969; Gil 1970; Joint Commission on Mental Health of Children 1973; Lauer et al. 1974; Morse, Sahler and Friedman 1970; Paulson et al. 1974; Simons et al. 1966; Skinner and Castle 1969.
6. Kempe et al. 1962; Leivesley 1972.
7. Galdston 1971a; Polansky et al. 1972; Polansky, Hally and Polansky 1974.
8. Bullard et al. 1967; Elmer et al. 1971; Evans, Reinhart and Succop 1972.

Psychiatric characteristics of abusing parents

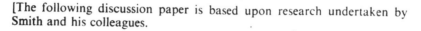

Selwyn M. Smith

[The following discussion paper is based upon research undertaken by Smith and his colleagues.

Index cases

Over a period of two years 134 battered infants and children under five and their parents were studied. All the parents had either confessed to battering or could give no adequate explanation of their child's injuries. Ninety-one (68 per cent) were referred from eight hospitals. Eighteen (13 per cent) were prison cases. Twenty-five (19 per cent) came from other sources.

Control Group

The controls comprised 53 children under five years. emergency admissions to hospital and where there was no question of battering, accident and trauma cases were excluded. Parents of these children were matched with the index group on the basis of the mother's age and the age of the infant. Other variables were held constant.]

Age

The young age of mothers closely compares with the age distribution described by other authors (Gil 1968b; Skinner and Castle 1969). On average index mothers were aged 19.7 years at the birth of their first child. This compares strikingly with the national average of 23.3 years (Registrar General 1972a). Even in the lowest social class the average was 22.6 years (Newson and Newson 1963). Index mothers were thus nearly 4 years younger than the national average when they gave birth to their first infant. Considering that most battered babies were first or second born and that more than half were under 18 months old when battered it may be concluded that battering is associated with youthful parenthood. This argument is further exemplified by the infrequent occurrence of battering in older parents with large families observed in this and other series

---

SMITH, S. M. (1975) *The Battered Child Syndrome*, London, Butterworth, pp. 197–202, 213–15.

(Bennie and Sclare 1969; Lukianowicz 1971) and suggests that the risk of battering diminishes with parental age.

Social class

The parents in this series were predominantly from the lower social classes. The association of low social class with battering parents has been commented on by several other workers (Young 1964; Skinner and Castle 1969). No support was found for the statement that all social classes are represented (Kempe 1969). Of the index group 76 per cent were from social classes IV and V compared with only 32 per cent in the Birmingham population (City of Birmingham 1972). It may be argued that such a large discrepancy is due to the youthfulness of the parents and type of admission (emergency) of the children. Nevertheless, despite allowing for these important factors it was found that the control group also contained 33 per cent of social class IV and V. This strongly suggests that battering is mainly a lower social class phenomenon. Furthermore, as the criteria for referral of cases were medical it may be reasonably assumed that if more children from high social class families had been admitted with unexplained injuries then consultant paediatricians would have referred them.

Abnormal personality

Abnormality of personality was a significant finding among the parents of battered children. The less severe types of personality disturbance were more commonly found among the mothers, who in general had features of emotional immaturity and dependence. Many of these mothers had in addition little concept of appropriate child-rearing practices. Battering may at best be regarded as an ineffectual method of controlling their child's behaviour. Techniques of teaching child-rearing skills based realistically on their low intelligence should perhaps be explored further as a possible means of correcting such ineffectual parent care.

Among the fathers studied 33.3 per cent were psychopaths. The association of battering with psychopathy has been commented on . . . (Birrell and Birrell 1968; Lukianowicz 1971: Scott 1973) but contrasts with Kempe's (1969) finding that psychopathy is a feature in only 2 or 3 per cent of battering parents. . . .

Criminal records

Twenty-nine per cent of the fathers had a criminal record. Though the follow-up period was brief, nevertheless 6.7 per cent went on to commit subsequent crimes. Furthermore though 19 per cent of the children's siblings had been previously battered only 1 per cent of the parents had been charged with cruelty or neglect, highlighting the capriciousness of the legal system towards parents who batter babies. Criminality and recidivism particularly if associated with a psychopathic personality should caution against an optimistic outcome, and invoking a care order is essential if further battering incidents are to be prevented. No association was found with alcoholism or drug addiction, which agrees with Steele and Pollock's (1968) findings but differs from those of Young (1964) and Gil (1968a) who maintained that battering is precipitated by alcoholism.

Neurosis

It was found that mothers were neurotic by three different measures. Fifty-eight per cent were non-psychotically disturbed on Goldberg's

General Health Questionnaire and 48 per cent were diagnosed as neurotic at interview—the usual symptomatology being depression, anxiety or a mixture of both. The diagnosis of neuroticism on the Eysenck Personality Inventory lends some support to the clinical finding of neurosis and the questionnaire results. Thirty-four per cent reported having an unhappy childhood. In general neurotic mothers—in contrast to psychopathic fathers—confessed to harming their children and expressed willingness to discuss their difficulties further. For this particular group of mothers the combination of symptomatic relief with a programme of social re-learning conducted by skilled therapists seems to the author to be far more beneficial than relying solely on programmes of 'mothering' and other methods (Kempe and Helfer, 1972) that tend to reinforce their dependent behaviour.

Neuroticism was also found to be an important characteristic of those mothers who confessed to battering their children. Among the fathers neuroticism was masked by the high proportion who denied battering the child. However, among the fathers who were identified as perpetrators the mean scores on both the Eysenck Personality Inventory and the General Health Questionnaire were abnormally high. The need for these parents to act out their hostility was not detected for the sample as a whole but emerged when only those who confessed to battering were singled out. This is not surprising considering that items on this scale would be particularly pointed for a battering sample—for example, 'When I'm angry I feel like smashing things'.

Hostility

Foulds has shown that as a general rule the hostility of neurotics is of the introverted kind (Caine, Foulds and Hope 1967). The results from this study, however, showed that baby batterers who were neurotic were not predominantly intropunitive, but were characterized equally by extrapunitiveness. The most clear-cut for both mothers and fathers were the bizarre forms of hostility, hitherto found only in psychiatric populations (Philip 1969) namely projected hostility and guilt. While guilt and remorse have often been dismissed as symptoms unrelated to actual circumstances in psychiatric populations and as glib sophistication among psychopaths (Hare 1972), there is no reason to suppose that the guilt experienced by the sample is not reality-orientated or genuine, considering recent events. Considering their impaired relationships their high level of paranoid hostility is perhaps also understandable. . . .

Self-criticism was also not detected for the sample as a whole, so that on first inspection of the results the pattern of significant types of hostility was most reminiscent of psychopaths who 'may regard themselves as hot-tempered, cynical, interestingly mad or diabolically wicked; but . . . draw the line at appearing faintly inferior or incompetent' (Philip 1969). However, those who confessed to battering did not draw the line in their self-descriptions. This group of baby batterers may possibly, as previously suggested (Smith, Hanson and Noble 1973, 1974), be more amenable to treatment.

Thus the results depict baby batterers as neurotic—chiefly depressed—and characterized by all kinds of hostility directed against both others and themselves. This description resembles that of the depressive psychopath (Sattes 1972). Indeed in the backgrounds of the sample there was considerable evidence of psychiatric disturbance; childhood neurotic symptoms, childhood unhappiness, a family history of psychiatric illness, physical handicaps, head injuries and lack of school success. Despite such adversities very few baby batterers had received any formal psychiatric treatment.

Psychomotor performance

The spiral maze

A test of risk-taking while under pressure has demonstrated that delinquents have relatively fast and careless performances, while behaviour disordered children are likely to be either fast and careless or slow and careless (Gibson 1964). West and Farrington (1973) have pointed out that clumsiness, although significantly predictive of both juvenile delinquency and recidivism, seems to be 'of importance only because of its association with low intelligence'. It was found that index and control mothers did not differ on the 'quick and careless (to slow and accurate)' dimension but that index mothers were more slow and clumsy. The prevalence of depression in this sample probably contributed something to the slow tempo (Mayo, 1966) but the clumsiness may be regarded as a reflection of low intelligence. The relative effects of personality and intelligence on the psychomotor behaviour of baby batterers deserves more attention. However, risk-taking when under pressure does not appear, from the results of the Spiral Maze Test, to be a characteristic of battering parents.

Psychosis

The findings confirm the view that only a minority of battering parents are psychotic (Steele and Pollock 1968). The bizarre nature of the injuries inflicted by psychotic parents suggests that they form a separate sub-group among baby batterers whose management must differ accordingly.

Abnormal EEGs

Because the numbers who underwent EEGs are on the small side, tentative conclusions only may be drawn from this aspect of the study. Nevertheless, the prevalence of abnormal EEG findings strongly suggests that some baby batterers at least are much more closely related to other groups committing acts of violence than they are to the general population. This is borne out also by the results of psychological testing, particularly of the group with abnormal EEGs, which also showed a consistent variation from the normal population. It would, therefore, seem clear that baby batterers are not a homogenous group about whom it is safe to generalize. Whereas in some instances battering may be a response to unusual and excessive stress situations—though this needs further investigation--the presence of a definitely abnormal EEG in almost 25 per cent of cases points to what may well be a separate sub-group to which special attention should be paid. This is further borne out by a demonstrable relationship between personality diagnosis and abnormal EEGs. Indeed five female batterers and one male batterer all with abnormal EEGs could undoubtedly be classed not only as having a personality disorder, but as aggressive psychopaths (Walton and Presly 1973). The male subject also had a criminal record. The two other female patients exhibited a personality disorder though this was not primarily of an aggressive type.

Violence breeds violence?

Steele and Pollock (1968) have suggested that baby batterers were deprived both of basic mothering and of the deep sense of being cared for from the beginning of their lives. Some of the findings from this study are at variance with this suggestion. Significant proportions of index mothers said they were physically maltreated in childhood and that their parents were unreasonable, rejecting and harsh. High proportions of index fathers also experienced punitiveness from their own parents, and significant proportions said their parents were unreasonable in their disciplinary methods, supporting those authors (Gibbens and Walker 1956; Tuteur and Glotzer 1966; Steele and Pollock 1968; Fontana 1968) who suggested that such child-rearing practices reflected childhood experiences. On the other hand the sample did not report lack of affection to any greater extent than others of low social class. Considering the parents were willing to report unreasonable discipline, there is no reason to assume that lack of affection was not reliably reported. Such inconsistencies may be realistic illustrations of the backgrounds of baby batterers. . . .

Management aspects

Recent comments (New Society 1973) have suggested that social workers have been 'too soft' and have often misjudged situations because of their enthusiasm for keeping the child and family together. Medical personnel are, however, also reluctant to notify authority particularly if they consider that this might result in parents being prosecuted. This reluctance may, of course, partly be due to the fact that medical and social welfare considerations on the one hand, and legal rights and safeguards on the other, are often hard to reconcile. However, by reserving to themselves this discretion of whether to pass on relevant information the doctor or social worker concerned may deprive the child of his legal rights of protection.

The results showed that there was a failure to ensure protection of the child. It was disconcerting to observe that the majority of cases were not brought to the attention of the juvenile court, reliance instead being placed on voluntary supervision. In view of the high mortality and morbidity reported in this and other series (Helfer 1968; Hall 1975; White Franklin 1975) and the high frequency of re-battering that occurs, it is alarming to observe that no arrangements for supervision took place in 21 instances. It is the author's opinion that local authorities are failing in their statutory role of protecting the child by being reluctant to institute care proceedings.

The quality and quantity of supervision available varies in different areas, and may, of course, influence a local authority's plan of management. Nevertheless, supervision whether it be voluntary or by court order does not overcome the inherent difficulty in managing these cases—namely, that no supervisor can be with the child or his family for more than a fraction of the time. Social workers in their desire to help parents and keep families together may embark upon a programme of casework. Considerable emphasis has been placed upon intensive casework with families since the passing of the Children and Young Persons Act 1963. The success of this has never been systematically evaluated. Furthermore management at present is hampered, in the author's opinion, by the local authorities' practice of imposing a dual role on the social worker. By appearing as the person who had made an application to deprive the parents of their parental rights the social worker's task of establishing and pursuing a therapeutic relationship is made even more difficult. In the light of the findings from this study it is already apparent that casework will not succeed in many instances and that trusting the parents unduly may have damaging consequences to the child.

Management of the problem has in the past too often been plagued by a tendency to rely on the case conference on the assumption that discussion alone is in the child's best interests. It has been the author's experience, however, that this method is often extremely inefficient. I would propose instead that a regional team, hospital based, consisting of a paediatrician, psychiatrist, social worker and psychologist should be established to tackle the overall problem.

An alternative but somewhat complementary scheme has been proposed by Bevan (1975) who suggests that a new office of 'Children's Guardian' should be created. The guardian would be a social worker with some legal training whose primary duty would be the protection of children's rights. Either of these appointments would perhaps improve the poor liaison that presently exists between the various agencies which concurrently and sequentially are involved in managing a case. It would also circumvent the unilateral action that often occurs through these agencies and go some way towards overcoming the present practice of returning the children home where re-battering takes place.

Other remedies rest with the courts. The case in the juvenile court is a civil and not a criminal one. It is not the court's duty to establish whether a particular individual has inflicted the injuries. It is only necessary to prove that a state of neglect or injury exists and that the parents are not preventing this. At present juvenile court magistrates have no powers to either request a psychiatric report or to recommend where appropriate that parents attend a treatment centre. It is the author's belief that improvements in child care would come about if magistrates were granted these powers.

In deciding upon an appropriate sentence, the court can follow the Criminal Justice Act 1972 (and its amendments) which gives it wide powers—particularly if the accused has not previously been in prison. In order to decide whether other measures are more appropriate in dealing with the offender—for example, probation with a condition of treatment—the court is empowered to obtain psychiatric and social reports. This procedure allows an opportunity for reaching a sentence determined in the best interests of all concerned.

The methods used by the courts in sentencing baby batterers in this study varied. Probation with a condition of psychiatric treatment was the most frequent method used in the case of the mothers, while for fathers, imprisonment was the more likely outcome. This difference in sentencing may be due to the higher incidence of previous criminality among the fathers. It could be argued that as adult courts already have these wide powers there is no need to provide juvenile court magistrates with similar ones. However, the hesitation of doctors and social workers to facilitate criminal investigation procedures, the legal rights of the parent to remain silent and to have certain prejudicial evidence excluded and the high burden of proof on the part of the prosecution to prove their case, may all go some way towards explaining why the majority of these parents did not appear in the adult courts. Observations during this study revealed that a surprising lack of liaison occurs between the juvenile and adult courts. Furthermore, a mistaken belief is often apparent that it would be improper to mention any other proceedings in connection with the same set of facts. It is the author's belief that if the juvenile court also had the power to request psychiatric reports on the parents it would overcome some of these difficulties.

Consumer's Viewpoint

Most people become users of social services through no fault of their own. They may be poor, sick, homeless, grief-stricken, frightened or even aggressive—but their pride is usually intact. However, I am a consumer because I am a battering parent, and my child is in care. So for me, guilt replaces pride as an additional factor. My guilt inevitably colours my attitude to social services.

Initially, I sought help myself, now I am writing this because I am concerned that people in a similar situation—my peers—also receive adequate help. I worry too about breakdowns in communication, because I know how easy it is for my mood to be misinterpreted, and how it is possible to manipulate someone in authority. These 'breakdowns' have occurred elsewhere, with sickening consequences, and will I am afraid, occur again. A layman can sometimes spot a potential batterer a mile off, yet a trained social worker may miss one at five paces. We all know at least one person without the necessary 'O' levels, who has the insight to see 'underneath' a problem. There is an enormous gulf between tea and sympathy and the social worker's case-notes. To err is human, social workers are human, and inevitably there will be tragic mistakes.

The hardest path I tread is the one between support from social services and an over-dependence on them. I find my confidence can easily be undermined, albeit by well-meaning people. Occasionally I wish they would foster my independence, and curb my leaning. On the whole however, I receive a balanced service. For example, the delay experienced in being allowed to care for my son by having him at home for reasonable periods of time, ideally coincided with my own feelings of ability to cope. There have been occasions where milestones have been reached too slowly, and conversely sometimes, too quickly, but my frustration has been shared with my social worker.

Social services take over where the family unit left off. Sometimes, as in a family, there is a conflict of personalities, between worker and client. Guilt makes me concede that my ensuing unhappiness is fair retribution, but at times I become rebellious. The family unit recognizes such conflict, but social services surrogate parents know no such bounds. So at one point I hated my child, my social worker and myself. Most of these feelings are now resolved, but it was a painful experience for us all. However, I do now have a viable relationship with my son.

In an 'ideal' society, I'd like to see a surfeit of social workers, so personalities could be matched more closely. In four years I have come across intelligent, intellectually inferior, patronizing, understanding, moralistic, punitive and even supercilious social workers. The same can be said for doctors, police, health visitors, and other officials. I feel ambivalent about all these agencies, because of the variation in my experiences. By reacting differently to all these approaches, I became more unsure of my *own* identity. Also, the workers' reactions differing so greatly made co-operation difficult to say the least. One social worker's undisguised abhorrence of what I had done to my son, initially made me feel like a monster. Then I rationalized that as she was a mother herself, but unable to identify with even a small part of my hate towards my son, then she was the freak not me. After all, isn't it a now widely accepted fact, that all parents hate their children at times?

Sometimes I overcame this 'holier-than-thou' attitude by showing my superiority in other ways. Intellectually I could run rings around some of

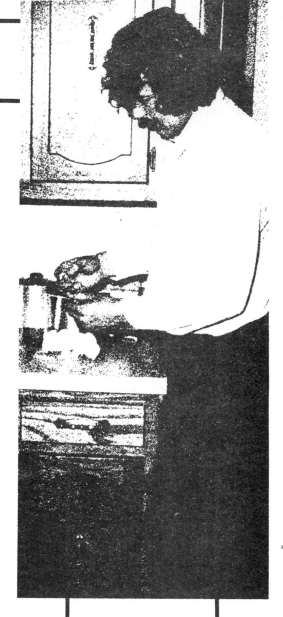

A battering parent

the social workers, and took delight in doing so. They would flounder in my sea of words, and I would go away triumphant. My only net gain though, was a bolstered ego, because the time wasted inevitably made slower my rehabilitation as a mother. The only recurring pattern to emerge from these varied confrontations, is my guilt.

I'd like a generic worker, who could deal with any aspect of her clients' problems, whether germane or not, without referring me to another agency. She would also deal with the problems of other members of the family herself—after all, these invariably interact with your own problems. For example my daughter was at a school for emotionally disturbed children, but my social worker was unwilling to discuss her case with me, although I needed to talk about the feelings aroused, by having her temporarily 'beyond my care'. A further example of a non-generic worker's drawbacks, is the NSPCC inspector (who dealt with my case previous to social services) who refused to discuss my ailing marriage but referred me to the Marriage Guidance Council.

In addition to possessing a compatible personality, I'd like one worker to see a case through from start to finish. As I am now working with my sixth social worker, I am well aware of the pitfalls in the lack of continuity. I realize that when people move this is not always feasible, but could the case-notes be forwarded quickly, too? Could the social worker make herself known to the family, soon after the move, in a supportive role and not as an obvious deterrent? Sometimes families are determined to disappear behind a mask of anonymity, despite all efforts to keep track of them. It is for this reason that I am all in favour of a central register of both confirmed and suspected batterers. The information would be computerized, and housed in one building. Ideally it would be continually updated with information from all branches of the medical profession, and associated services, and the police and other agencies, possibly even extending to teachers. Care would have to be taken that only authorized persons could have access to these records. Even over the telephone some way would have to be evolved to stop undesirables, i.e. the press, from obtaining this information. There would of course be 'teething problems' and there may also be administrative problems that I have not foreseen.

I would also like to see more group therapy (although I had a very satisfactory one-to-one therapy), more attention to those 'silent' cries for help and more 'safety nets'. By safety-nets I mean 24-hour relief centres where you can temporarily, and voluntarily relinquish responsibility during a traumatic period. These would be like a creche, but with trained social workers to initially advise the parent, as well as offering temporary relief. Also, more short term fostering or short stay accommodation in a place of care, i.e. hospital, or a children's home, to ease the burden, while the parents receive help. A general vigilance is needed by all concerned with child welfare, possibly aided by more films and lectures on the subject of child abuse.

Greater liaison and the following up of information may lead to a reduction, but I believe the nearest thing to a cure of society's ills, especially that of cruelty to children, is to be found in our own communities. If we ever revert to the time when generations of families lived in the same neighbourhood, then things may be different. If, once again the grandparents become the hub of the family, acting as midwives, health-visitors, baby-sitters and general advisers, baby battering may be reduced. Social services could well be replaced by the family incorporate.

You Can Change Behavior You Don't Like Without Using Punishment

DR. THOMAS GORDON

When children's behavior interferes with their parents' needs, as it inevitably will, parents naturally want to try to modify such behavior. After all, parents do have needs. They have their own lives to live and the right to derive satisfaction and enjoyment from their existence. But parents make two serious mistakes.

First, much to their regret, many parents ignore unacceptable behaviors and watch their children grow up to be terribly inconsiderate or even oblivious of their parents' needs. If parents permit this, they will develop strong feelings of resentment and even grow to dislike such *ungrateful* or *selfish* kids. Second, most parents choose punishment as their first approach in trying to modify unacceptable behavior. If parents permissively ignore behavior they don't like, they suffer; if they rely on punishment, their kids will suffer. And in both cases the relationship suffers. But what can parents do so that children will learn to respect their parents' needs and rights? There are effective methods for infants, toddlers, and for older children.

With Infants and Preverbal Children

Very young children present a special problem for parents because they may be unable to understand verbal messages. Nevertheless, it is actually quite easy to influence infants and preverbal children to modify behavior unacceptable to parents, provided the right approach is used. Parents can choose from four different approaches—all very effective.

Reprinted from the booklet *What Every Parent Should Know,* by Thomas Gordon, Ph.D., by permission of the publisher, the National Committee for Prevention of Child Abuse, Chicago, Illinois.

1. The Guessing Game

Effective parents must learn to be good guessers with infants and toddlers simply because these children can't tell parents much about what's going on inside them. Barbara, six-months-old, starts to cry loudly in the middle of the night. Her parents are awakened from the sleep they need and naturally find this behavior unacceptable. But how can they get Barbara to stop crying? Quite simply, they start guessing. Finding the cause of her crying so that they can remedy the problem is something like a puzzle:

Maybe she's wet and cold. We'll check first on that. No, she's still dry. Well, could it be we didn't burp her enough and she is feeling uncomfortable with gas? Let's pick her up and start the burping process. Bad guess again—Barbara won't burp. Wonder if she's hungry? There is still some milk in her bottle, but it got pushed down to the end of the crib. We'll act on that hypothesis next. Success! Barbara sucks for a few minutes and then gets sleepy. They put her back into her crib gently and she falls asleep. Her parents can go back to bed now and get their own needs met.

That is an example of the guessing game, an approach that parents have to use very frequently with infants when they whine incessantly, when they are restless and pestering, when they can't get to sleep, when they throw their food on the floor. The guessing game works effectively because when infants do things that are unacceptable to their parents, there's a reason for it—usually a very logical reason. When parents start using the guessing game, they stop resorting to punishment.

PRINCIPLE VI   WHEN INFANTS BEHAVE UNACCEPTABLY, THERE IS A GOOD REASON, BUT YOU HAVE TO TRY TO GUESS WHAT IT IS

Sometimes parents will find the guessing game easy, other times more difficult. The cliché, "If at first you don't succeed, try, try again," is the soundest advice I know for parents. Actually, parents can get quite good at the game, because they get to know their offspring better and better. Parents have told me that they eventually learned to tell the difference between a wet-cry, a hungry-cry and a gas-cry.

2. Let's Make a Trade

Another effective approach for changing unacceptable behaviors of infants and toddlers involves trading: substituting the unacceptable behavior for another behavior that would be acceptable to the parent.

Laura, your curious one-year-old, has found a pair of your new nylons, which she finds enjoyable to touch and tug on. You find this unacceptable because you're afraid she'll snag or destroy them. You go to your drawer and pull out an old pair that is already snagged and beyond being wearable. You place this pair in her hands and gently take away the new pair. Laura, not knowing the difference, finds the damaged pair equally as enjoyable to touch and tug. Her needs are met, but so are yours.

Dave is jumping up and down on the couch and mother fears he will knock the lamp off the end table. Mother gently but firmly removes Dave from the couch and proceeds to jump up and down with him on the pillows which she removed from the couch and put on the floor.

Shirley, age eighteen months, starts to get up on her dad's lap on the very night he is dressed in his freshly cleaned light-colored suit. Dad notices that Shirley's hands are covered with jam mixed with equal parts of peanut butter. Dad gently restrains Shirley, but then immediately goes to the bathroom, gets a wet washcloth and wipes her hands clean. Then dad picks Shirley up and puts her on his lap.

Again, when parents start thinking in terms of trading they stop using punishment.

PRINCIPLE VII WHEN YOU CAN'T ACCEPT ONE BE-HAVIOR, SUBSTITUTE ANOTHER YOU CAN

3. The Nonverbal I-message

Older children often modify their behavior after a parent sends them an honest message that conveys how the parent is affected by the child's behavior, as in:

"I can't hear on the phone when there's so much yelling."

"I'm afraid I'll be late if you take so long to dress."

"I love that little dish and I would be sad if it got broken."

But children too young to understand words won't be influenced by such messages (called "I-messages" because they convey to the child, "Let me tell you how *I* am feeling."). Consequently, the I-message has to be put into a nonverbal form, as in the following examples:

While dad is carrying little Tony in the supermarket, he starts to kick dad in the stomach, laughing with each kick. Dad immediately puts Tony down on his feet and continues walking. (Message: "It hurts me when I get kicked in the stomach; so I don't like to carry you.")

Judy stalls and pokes getting into the car when mother is in a terrible hurry. Mother puts her hand on Judy's rump and gently but firmly guides her onto the front seat. (Message: "I need you to get in right now because I'm in a hurry.")

PRINCIPLE VIII LET KIDS KNOW HOW YOU FEEL, EVEN IF YOU CAN'T USE WORDS

The key to employing this method of trying to modify unacceptable behavior is avoiding any kind of behavior that will be punishing or painful to the child. After all, you only want him to know how you are feeling. Slapping, hitting, thumping, pushing, jerking, yelling, pinching—all these methods inevitably communicate to the youngster that he's bad, he's wrong, his needs don't count, he's done something criminal, and he deserves to be punished.

4. Changing the Environment

Most parents intuitively know that one effective way of stopping many kinds of unacceptable behavior is to change the child's environment, as opposed to efforts to change the child directly. What parent has not watched a whiney, pestering, bored youngster get totally (and quietly) immersed when his parent provides him with some materials that capture his interest such as clay, finger paints, puzzles, picture books or old scraps of colored cloth. This is called "Enriching the Environment."

At other times kids need just the opposite. They're keyed up and hyperactive just before bedtime, for example; so the wise parent knows how to "Impoverish the Environment." Overstimulated children will often calm down if they are read a fairy tale, told a story (real or fiction), or perhaps, a quiet period of sharing their days' events. Much of the storm and stress of bedtime could be avoided if parents made an effort to reduce the stimulation of their children's environment.

Most unacceptable (and destructive) behavior of toddlers can be avoided by serious efforts on the part of parents to "Child-proof the Environment," as with:

Buying unbreakable cups and glasses

Putting matches, knives, razor blades out of reach

Locking up medicines and sharp tools

Keeping the basement door locked

Fastening down slippery throw rugs

PRINCIPLE IX IT'S OFTEN MORE EFFICIENT TO CHANGE THE CHILD'S ENVIRONMENT THAN TO CHANGE THE CHILD

With Children Old Enough to Talk

Modifying the unacceptable behaviors of children old

enough to speak and understand verbal language involves talking straight so that they will listen. Then they will take into consideration your needs and decide on their own to change their behavior.

By far the most effective method is to send a verbal **I-message**. As explained previously, an I-message is one that communicates to the youngster only what is happening to you as a consequence of his behavior, as in the following examples:

> "When the TV is on so loud, I can't talk with your mother."

> "I'm not going to enjoy the flowers I planted if they're trampled on."

While it appears to be straightforward, sending I-messages is not easy to learn, primarily because most parents are so locked into the habit of sending **You-messages** when they encounter unacceptable behavior. You-messages contain a heavy component of blame, judgment, evaluation, threat, power, or put-downs. Here are the most common types of You-messages:

> YOU clean up that mess. (ORDERING)

> If YOU don't stop that, you'll go to your room. (WARNING)

> YOU shouldn't come to the table without washing your hands. (PREACHING)

> YOU could go outside and play. (ADVISING)

> YOU ought to know better. (MORALIZING)

> YOU are acting like a baby. (EVALUATING)

> YOU are just showing off. (PSYCHOANALYZING)

> YOU need to learn about courtesy. (TEACHING)

> YOU are driving me to an early grave. (INDUCING GUILT)

> Look at these gray hairs YOU have caused me. (BLAMING)

Instead of influencing kids to change, You-messages make children defensive and resistive to change, and over time they seriously shatter children's self-esteem. What's more, they provoke youngsters to strike back with a You-message of their own, causing the situation to escalate into a verbal battle royal, often bringing tears, hurt feelings, slammed doors, threats of punishment, and a fractured relationship.

I-messages, on the other hand, are much less apt to provoke resistance to change. When kids hear that their parents are *hurting*, their natural desire to help out emerges. Furthermore, when kids are not put down or blamed for having *their* needs, they are much more willing to be considerate of their *parents'* needs.

**PRINCIPLE X   TO CHANGE UNACCEPTABLE BE-
HAVIOR OF YOUR CHILD, TALK
ABOUT YOURSELF NOT THE CHILD**

Probably the greatest reward for parents who learn to send I-messages is that their children eventually take after them. To tell your child honestly how you feel is revealing your own humanness—he learns you can be hurt, tired, disappointed, harried, worried, and fearful. Such honesty on your part will serve as a model, and you will see your children begin to be honest and real with you. Instead of strangers in the same household, as in so many families, parents and children develop an authentic and open relationship. Parents experience the job of having honest children, and the children are blessed by having real persons as parents.

Maternal Alcoholism and Fetal Alcohol Syndrome

BARBARA LUKE

BARBARA LUKE, R.N., R.D., is a clinical specialist in maternal nutrition at Sloane Hospital for Women, Columbia-Presbyterian Medical Center, New York, New York.

Patty is 18 months old, but her size and development are about those of an eight-month-old child. In utero, she had been small for gestational age, and she weighed only 2,300 grams at birth.

She was born with bilateral hip dislocations and limited motion of both elbows.

At two months, she was admitted to the hospital in congestive heart failure, secondary to an atrial septal defect. At 18 months, she was diagnosed as mentally retarded. Patty's mother is an alcoholic, and Patty has fetal alcohol syndrome.

About three years ago, alcoholism was clearly related to a "pattern of craniofacial, limb, and cardiovascular defects associated with prenatal onset growth deficiency and developmental delay"(1). This was the first reported association of maternal alcoholism with birth defects in the offspring. It became known as the fetal alcohol syndrome.

Some correlation has been made of maternal alcoholism and defective offspring since the time of the early Greeks. What, then, are the reasons for the seemingly recent development or the increased incidence of this syndrome? I propose that there are three principal reasons.

The most obvious answer could be an *improvement in antepartum care* over the past decade. There is more emphasis on screening and treating high-risk mothers, and alcoholism is a risk. Because of more intensive antepartum care, many alcoholic women who otherwise would have aborted carry their infants to term.

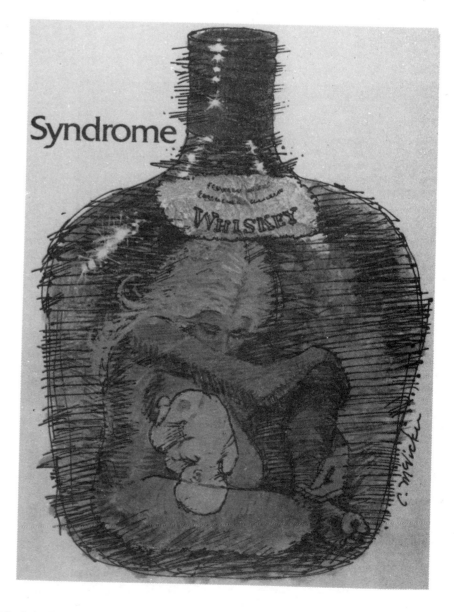

Syndrome

"Maternal Alcoholism and Fetal Alcohol Snydrome," Barbara Luke, *American Journal of Nursing*, Vol. 77, No. 12, December 1977. ⓒ1977 American Journal of Nursing.

Another reason is that over the past several decades, our *food supply has improved* greatly in quality, quantity, composition, and availability. In turn, this probably has reduced the nutritional deficiencies of alcoholics(2). Foods are processed so that they remain edible longer, and more foods are fortified, especially with B vitamins and iron.

Fortification of breads and cereals with thiamine has reduced the incidence of Wernicke's syndrome (a mental condition often seen in old age, consisting of defective memory, loss of sense of location, and confabulation), alcoholic beriberi, and the polyneuropathy often previously seen in the alcoholic because of the constant and accelerated metabolism of this vitamin by alcohol. Fortification of cereal products with niacin has reduced the incidence of alcoholic pellagra, with its accompanying classic symptoms of peripheral neuropathy (sensory disturbance with burning paresthesia of the feet). Recently, government assistance to the low-income population through food stamps and Women, Infants, Children (WIC) programs, have provided more food to pregnant and lactating women.

The third factor contributing to the fetal alcohol syndrome is the *increased incidence of alcoholism.* HEW has warned that an alcoholic intake above three ounces of absolute alcohol or six drinks a day can lead to birth defects(3).

The National Committee on Alcoholism has established criteria for the diagnosis of alcoholism, based on physiological, clinical (including major alcohol-associated illnesses), behavioral, psychological, and attitudinal manifestations(4).

Alcoholism is one of the more difficult diseases to recognize for several reasons. Drinking produces a socially accepted, legal "high." Neither the nutritional value nor the hazards of alcohol are stressed to the consumer. Because alcohol interferes with protein synthesis and with the absorption of many nutrients, and thus causes deficiencies, heavy drinking during pregnancy can affect the mother adversely and damage the fetus irreversibly.

Alcoholism often is not screened for by health professionals. Many patients will state the type, amount, and frequency of their alcohol intake if questioned honestly and nonjudgmentally.

Many alcoholics want to be helped, but need to have a door opened for them(5).

During routine antepartum evaluation, a history of any, or a combination of any, of the following alcohol-associated illnesses should alert the health professional to maternal alcoholism(6):

- fatty degeneration in the absence of other known causes
- hepatitis
- cirrhosis
- pancreatitis in the absence of cholelithiasis
- chronic gastritis
- hematological disorders—anemia—hypochromic, normocytic, macrocytic, hemolytic with stomatocytosis, low folic acid clotting disorders—prothrombin elevation or thrombocytopenia
- Wernicke-Korsakoff syndrome
- cerebellar degeneration
- cerebral degeneration in the absence of Alzheimer's disease or arteriosclerosis
- toxic amblyopia
- myopathy
- cardiomyopathy
- peripheral neuropathy/beriberi
- pellagra

Once the diagnosis of maternal alcoholism is suspected or a patient confides that she has drinking problems, a thorough nursing evaluation is important in planning care. A valuable nursing history tool to use with alcoholic patients can be found in a recent AJN article(7). The interview is divided into two sections: the first deals with the patient's drinking history and the second with symptoms related to the gastrointestinal system. Supportive services, such as social service, psychotherapy, and nutrition counseling, are often helpful during the antepartum and postpartum periods. A high degree of patient motivation is needed, which can be indicated by the regularity of antepartum clinic attendance.

Alcohol interferes with the absorption and the utilization of nutrients and with protein synthesis.

Heavy alcohol consumption is most likely to affect fetal structure during the first trimester, when organogenesis is taking place. Frequently, the alcoholic who does conceive will spontaneously abort, often during the first trimester. During the second trimester, when there is mainly an increase in cell

size rather than in cell number, poor diet, heavy alcohol consumption, or both are most apt to affect infant weight. Because a woman who chronically drinks may be malnourished, even a decrease in alcohol intake just before conception may leave her with depleted vitamin and protein reserves.

Daily food habits, allergies, and dislikes, as well as dietary supplements, should be considered in evaluating the adequacy of the maternal diet. The recommended daily food allowances during normal pregnancy appear in the box on the next page.

Because food prices vary so much across the country and from month to month, cost is difficult, if not impossible, to estimate. In general, a low-cost diet for gestation might include milk, eggs, cheese, grains and legumes, less expensive meats, and chicken. Higher-priced diets could include seafood, more fresh vegetables and fruits, more expensive meats. I recommend the same diet for both income groups (see sample menu).

Dietary supplements may be indicated, depending on the degree of alcoholism, secondary illnesses, presence of fetal growth retardation, maternal antepartum complications, such as anemia, weight loss, or poor gain, and the patient's customary diet intake.

If anemia is present, therapy depends on the specific type. Macrocytic anemia, common among chronic alcoholics, can be corrected by folic acid and concurrent vitamin C therapy. Green leafy vegetables, liver, and mushrooms are all plentiful sources of folic acid.

Anemia due to iron deficiency (hypochromic, microcytic) is common in pregnancy, but is aggravated by maternal alcoholism. Therapy for this anemia, as well as for fetal growth retardation, is a high-protein, high-iron diet. The best foods for this diet include animal proteins; elemental iron helps correct the anemia and meet the fetal demands for iron. Absorption of elemental iron and nonanimal sources of iron also is enhanced by vitamin C.

If an alcoholic mother has seizures, perhaps during withdrawal while she is hospitalized for the treatment of other complications, the daily administration of 100 mg. pyridoxine (vitamin B₆) may be beneficial. Delirium tremors have been associated with low serum magnesium levels and may respond to parenteral magnesium sulfate therapy.

2. PARENT

Health professionals should suspect fetal alcohol syndrome when prenatal growth deficiency, low birth weight

FETAL ALCOHOL SYNDROME

(2,500 grams or below), breech presentation, and poor Apgar scores occur in combination with an antepartum history of maternal alcoholism. A study of three infants of alcoholic mothers revealed these abnormal findings at birth and in early infancy(9): Craniofacies—microcephaly, short palpebral fissures, epicanthal folds, maxillary hypoplasia, cleft palate, and micrognathia; Limbs—joint anomalies, and altered palmar crease pattern; Performance: postnatal growth deficiency and developmental delay. Other defects included cardiac anomalies, anomalous external genitalia, capillary hemangiomas, and fine-motor dysfunction.

Fetal growth retardation, a discrepancy between the fetus's actual and expected size for its gestational age, can be detected as early as 16 weeks gestation. Serial ultrasonography, at two-week intervals (16, 18, 20 weeks, and so on) is the best way to monitor intrauterine growth. The ultrasonogram clearly indicates the biparietal diameter of the fetal head, and deviations from the norm after 16 weeks of gestation can be detected easily.

After birth, depending on the extent of fetal retardation and the time and amount of the mother's last alcohol intake, the infant is either drowsy or irritable. For example, when ethyl alcohol is given to suppress labor, the infant often arrives in the nursery in either state.

The signs of fetal alcohol syndrome can range from severe retardation with extensive brain stem involvement to such slight retardation that it is not detected at all until much later when developmental problems arise. If there is brain stem involvement, the sucking reflex may be poor, and tube feedings are given. If sucking and swallowing reflexes are affected, gastrostomy feedings may be done. No food intolerances have been demonstrated.

Even if the syndrome is not detected at birth, several factors may lead the nurse to suspect it when the mother returns for a check-up with her infant. These include apathy, eating problems,

SAMPLE MENU FOR A PREGNANT WOMAN			
Breakfast:	2 eggs 8 oz. milk (whole or fortified) 2 slices toast (whole wheat) 4 oz. juice	**Midafternoon:**	crackers cheese fruit
Midmorning:	ice cream fresh fruit	**Dinner:**	hamburger baked potato (with margarine or butter) salad 8 oz. milk
Lunch:	tuna fish sandwich lettuce & tomato 8 oz. milk oatmeal cookies	**Before bed:**	pound cake ice cream

RECOMMENDED DAILY FOODS DURING NORMAL PREGNANCY*		
Food	*1st half of pregnancy*	*2nd half of pregnancy*
Milk, cheese, ice cream	2-4 servings	4 servings
Meat, fish, beans, poultry	3-4 ounces	6-8 ounces
Eggs	1	1-2
Vegetables (dark green or deep yellow)	1 serving	1 serving
Citrus fruits or juices	1-2 servings	1-2 servings
Other fruits & vegetables	1 serving	2 servings
Breads & cereals (whole grain or enriched)	3 servings	4-5 servings

* An alcoholic, pregnant woman will need additional protein and vitamin supplements because of her decreased reserves in these two areas.

failure to thrive, poor development and growth in the infant, as well as maternal behavior and attitude toward the child and her seeking of health care for him.

If the nurse cares for a pregnant woman with a drinking problem, she encourages her to stop drinking or to reduce the amount. Explore with her the reasons for the heavy use of alcohol and refer her for counseling. Explain the infant care problems, such as difficulty in eating and sleeping, that she may expect after her baby is born. She may need assistance in the home, and referrals to the public health nurse and social service.

An infant with FAS may be kept in the hospital or even placed in a home temporarily if the mother is unable to cope with the newborn.

Success in working with these mothers depends largely on their reasons for becoming pregnant in the first place and their motivation for completing the

pregnancy. If she truly wants the baby, almost every woman will do everything in her power—including breaking such habits as smoking and drinking—to ensure a healthy pregnancy and baby.

References

1. JONES, K.L., AND OTHERS. Pattern of malformation in offspring of chronic alcoholic mothers. *Lancet* 1:1267-1271, June 9, 1973.
2. LUKE, B. The nutritional implications of alcohol abuse. *RN* 39:32-34, Apr. 1976.
3. ALARM sounded on alcohol, pregnancy. *ACOG Newsletter* 21:3, Aug. 1977.
4. NATIONAL COUNCIL ON ALCOHOLISM, CRITERIA COMMITTEE. Criteria for the diagnosis of alcoholism. *Ann.Intern.Med.* 77:249-258, Aug. 1972.
5. MUELLER, J.F. Treatment for the alcoholic: cursing or nursing? *Am.J.Nurs.* 74:245-247, Feb. 1974.
6. NATIONAL COUNCIL ON ALCOHOLISM, CRITERIA COMMITTEE. *op.cit.,* p. 252.
7. HEINEMANN, EDITH, AND ESTES, NADA. Assessing alcoholic patients. *Am.J.Nurs.* 76:785-789, May 1976.
8. LUKE, B. Guide to better evaluation of antepartum nutrition. *JOGN Nurs.* 5:37-43, July-Aug. 1976.
9. JONES, K.L., AND SMITH, D.W. Recognition of the fetal alcohol syndrome in early infancy. *Lancet* 2:999-1001, Nov. 3, 1973.

The Predicament of Abused Children

Carolyn Okell Jones

JONES, C. O. (1977) revised version of 'The predicament of abused children' in White Franklin, A. (ed.) *The Challenge of Child Abuse*, London, Academic Press (in preparation).

Even without damage from trauma, even without the associated effects of poverty, parental mental illness, neglect, under-nutrition or deprivation, the child cannot be expected to thrive in a home in which fear of bodily harm is an unrelenting spectre. It has long been recognised that imagined fear of physical harm affects the developing psyche. Abused children live with a continual fear of harm, that is not a fantasy but an ever present reality.

Martin et al., 1974

1 Introduction

1.1 When one surveys the rapidly increasing volume of world literature on child abuse, it is striking how relatively few publications have focused on the experiences and development of the surviving affected children and their psychotherapeutic needs. Yet, on reflection, it is very understandable. In the decade following the publication of Kempe's (1962) classic article on the battered child syndrome, which drew attention to its high mortality rate and the associated brain injury, the main concern was to protect the child from lethal physical harm and the main thrust of professional intervention was directed towards life-saving procedures. Emphasis was placed on clinical manifestations in order to improve diagnosis, on the complex legal issues, and on the psychodynamics of the abusive parents in relation to the type of psychiatric and social work treatment that they could use with benefit. It was soon recognized by practitioners that these parents could rarely tolerate the child becoming the focus of attention and were quick to sabotage any arrangements made on the child's behalf unless their own dependency needs were being met first.

1.2 Regarding the children, the tendency was to make theoretical generalizations about their development and to stereotype them in terms of their characteristics and behaviour on the basis of early anecdotal data. Although clinical observations suggested that many of the children were considerably damaged emotionally as well as physically by the time they came to professional attention, direct work with the children was, in the main, neglected. Also overlooked, when their physical safety was so much at stake, was the potentially damaging effect on the children's personality and emotional development of separating them from their parents, placing them in hospital often for extended periods, and moving them from one caretaker to another.

1.3 It is only now, in the second decade of child abuse research, that professionals have begun to ask, 'for what are we saving these children and what is the quality of their subsequent life?' Knowledge about abused children's long-term development is still limited but the depressing data from existing follow-up studies on their neurologic, cognitive, social and emotional development have prompted us to acknowledge that there is an urgent need to broaden our therapeutic goals.

2   Developmental problems of abused children

2.1   In order to appreciate some of the problems of abused children this paper will give an overview rather than detailed consideration of the follow-up studies. Apart from identifying common consequences of abuse some consideration will also be given to what extent these are consequences of:

1.   The physical injuries per se.
2.   Other malevolent environmental influences of the kind frequently associated with abuse, each of which is already known to have the potential to impair and disrupt the growing child's development. These include under-nutrition, emotional and physical neglect, social and/or economic disadvantage, emotional disturbance in the parents and family instability.
3.   Professional intervention and treatment planning.

2.2   The literature shows that common sampling problems have been met by most of the researchers conducting follow-up studies of children diagnosed as abused. Abusive families are difficult to trace because of their frequently high mobility rate; parents resist evaluation of their children; the children may have died or been placed far away from their family of origin in institutions or adoptive or foster homes. While the morbidity in children who are traced has been shown to be serious, one feels even more pessimistic about the fate of many of the other children, who were not available for study, as they are likely to be living in considerably worse environments with minimal or no professional intervention.

2.3   Other methodological problems associated with the follow-up studies include failure to employ matched comparison groups so that the findings may be skewed by uncontrollable variables such as social class, and failure to document the type of intervention the families have received. Methods of assessing the children vary from study to study, some researchers having used a range of formal and developmental tests whereas others have relied mainly on clinical impressionistic data.

2.4   In spite of the difficulties described above, the findings of a variety of follow-up studies in different countries, concur that abused children are clearly at high risk for damage to the central nervous system and maldevelopment of ego function. Mental retardation, learning disorders, perceptual-motor dysfunction, cerebral palsy, impaired speech and language, growth failure and emotional disturbance are documented with depressing frequency (Elmer, 1967; Elmer and Gregg, 1967; Birrell and Birrell, 1968; Johnson and Morse, 1968; Terr, 1970; Martin, 1972, 1974, 1976; Sandgrund et al., 1974; Morse et al., 1970; Smith and Hanson, 1974; Baldwin and Oliver, 1975; Straus and Girodet, 1976; Kline, 1976). However there are conflicting findings on the extent to which such physical or developmental deviations antedate abuse and are of a congenital nature or are the result of rearing in an abusive environment.

2.5   The hard data from follow-up studies relate chiefly to mortality and significant intellectual and neuromotor handicap. Considerable variation has been noted in the type and severity of neurologic damage sustained by abused children. Physical assault on the head may itself be the cause of the child's neurologic handicap but it is important to emphasize that a young child can suffer significant damage to the brain through violent shaking (Caffey, 1972, 1974) with no outward sign of damage to the head such as bruises or fractures of the skull. Martin (1974) reports that as expected neurologic dysfunction is highly related to IQ and a history of head trauma. However he emphasizes that some children with serious head injury were not retarded and that significant neurologic dysfunction occurred in 16 children with no obvious explanation of the cause and no documented history of head trauma. Hence Martin, Baron (1970) and others conclude that the nervous systems of abused children are also at risk from the psychological and environmental stresses to which they are exposed, and that neurologic dysfunction may be an adaptation to the abusive environment. Galdston (1975) on the basis of observations of abused children recently admitted to a day care centre, reports that some children were so retarded in their development and that their movements were so clumsy and uncoordinated that brain damage was suspected. However after a short period of daily attendance at the centre the same children demonstrated such rapid improvements in motor activity that the diagnosis of organic brain damage was precluded.

2.6   In a number of studies under-nutrition has been reported in approximately 30–35 per cent of abused children at the time abuse was recognized (Elmer, 1967; Birrell and Birrell, 1968; Martin, 1972). Martin (1974) refers to convincing evidence that under-nutrition during the first year of life can and does result in permanent effects on the nervous system, including motor dysfunction and mental impairment; and in older children may reduce the child's ability to focus on, orient to or systain interest in learning tasks. Martin's (1972) report of 42 abused children as well as Elmer's (1967) report indicate a significant difference in intellectual prognosis when under-nourished, abused children were compared with well-nourished abused children. It appears that children who are under-nourished as well as physically abused have a much poorer prognosis in terms of mental function and neurologic integrity.

2.7   The psychological damage sustained by abused children has been, in the main, the subject of speculation. For example, Green (1968) postulates that early physical abuse which occurs in a matrix of overall rejection and stimulus deprivation may enhance the development of pain dependent behaviour. The children may become accident prone, indulge in self-destructive behaviour or establish a pattern of inviting harm and playing the victim (Bender, 1976). The latter may be one reason why some children get rebattered in foster homes. Other writers have emphasized the tendency of the children to identify with aggressive parents and pattern themselves on the parents' behaviour. Clinical experience suggests that the young child physically abused at a pre-verbal stage of development is particularly prone to develop violent behaviour as a character trait (Galdston, 1975). The most detailed study of the emotional development of abused children to date has been completed by Martin and Beezley (1976). The nine characteristics and behaviour noted with impressive frequency and intensity in the 50 children studied included:

1.   Impaired capacity to enjoy life.
2.   Psychiatric symptoms (e.g. enuresis, tantrums, hyperactivity, bizarre behaviour).
3.   Low self-esteem.
4.   School learning problems.
5.   Withdrawal.
6.   Opposition.
7.   Hypervigilance.
8.   Compulsivity.
9.   Pseudo-mature behaviour.

Over 50 per cent of these abused children had poor self-concepts, were sorrowful children and exhibited a number of symptomatic behaviours which made peers, parents and teachers reject them. Martin and Beezley's data do not confirm any relationship between the type of injury nor the age at which it was inflicted with subsequent emotional development. Psychiatric symptoms were on the other hand significantly correlated 4.5 years after abuse with environmental factors such as the impermanence of the subsequent home, instability of the family with whom the child was

2. PARENT

living, punitiveness and rejection by caretakers and the emotional state of the parents or parent surrogates. Elsewhere Martin et al. (1974) noted that even the intelligence of abused children, when brain damage was controlled for, correlated quite highly with the subsequent stability and punitiveness of the home.

2.8 Scant attention has been paid to the siblings of abused children in the existing literature yet the psychological effects of witnessing or being aware of repeated ill-treatment are likely to be profound. A few studies that have involved siblings of the presenting children indicate that they are also at risk of physical abuse, be they older or younger, and that they often appear as deviant in their functioning as the child identified as abused (Johnson and Morse, 1968; Skinner and Castle, 1969; Baldwin and Oliver, 1975; Smith and Hanson, 1974; Baher et al., 1976; Straus and Girodet, 1976). It would seem that these children have few healthy ways of adapting to the abusive environment. However variations in the inherent equipment of the child, which determine his capacity to adapt to these stresses or to surmount the damaging influences of earlier developmental insults when placed in more favourable environments, warrant further exploration.

2.9 A major mechanism of survival for an endangered child is modification of his behaviour according to his surroundings. Malone (1966) has noted that pre-school children living in dangerous environments (including danger of abuse from their parents) have certain areas of overdeveloped ego functioning, areas of advanced ability. These include extreme sensitivity to parental moods and discomfort and role reversal with parents such as making decisions for them or taking care of younger siblings: such 'precocious' behaviour is constantly reinforced by the parents. While the child's ability to cope and his areas of overdeveloped ego-strength are highly adaptive and assets to survival, they are weaknesses insofar as they contribute to the child's literalness and inflexibility. Similarly Martin and Beezley (1976), out of their total sample of 50 abused children, identified a group of 10 pseudo-adult children who demonstrated precocious behaviour and a group of 11 children who demonstrated marked compulsivity. Both groups tended to have a high frustration tolerance and were extremely attentive and co-operative in the testing situation. Martin and Beezley stress that although these behaviours appeared to be more successful modes of adaptation they are not necessarily healthy ways of coping. 'The compulsive and pseudo-adult children were locked into styles which are not conducive to age appropriate enjoyment or flexibility. Compulsivity, by definition, connotes rigidity and inflexibility. The pseudo-adult child has forfeited his right to feel and act like a child, instead planning his life for the pleasure of adults rather than for himself.'

2.10 The above examples describe the behavioural characteristics of a small group of children who appear to have learnt certain adaptive coping mechanisms in order to survive in dangerous environments but at considerable cost to themselves. However we can no longer assume that the abusive environment results in either a specific personality or a neurologic profile. Some abused children have been observed to be passive, withdrawn, unresponsive and apathetic while others present as hyperactive, aggressive, attention seeking and extremely provocative (Baher et al., 1976; Martin and Beezley, 1976). Some with extremely high intelligence do well at school and keep pace with their parents' high expectations, but they more commonly present with school learning problems (Martin, 1974; Martin and Rodeheffer, 1976; Kline, 1976).

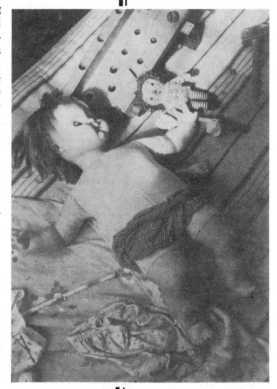

3 The effects of professional intervention and treatment planning

3.1 Another basis for the varying effects of abuse is related to what happens to the children after the diagnosis of physical abuse. Hospitalization, separation from parents, frequent home changes and poor quality foster homes or institutional placements may be more damaging to the child in the long term than the physical trauma itself. Martin and Beezley (1974a) discuss how professional intervention and treatment planning often contribute to the abused child's difficulty in developing a sense of object constancy or a concept of self. In Martin's own study (1976) seventeen children had from three to eight home changes from the time of identified abuse to follow up (mean of 4.5 years). The more seriously maladjusted the child, the more likely he was to have had three or more home changes. Similarly the more maladjusted a child was, the more likely he was to have perceived his present home as lacking permanence. Martin comments 'there is no data to show that any of these study children had been physically injured in foster homes but we know that in foster care they were frequently subjected to inappropriate discipline, indifference, rejection or seductiveness. Moreover efforts to reunite the family may prevent consideration of the optimal home placement for the child in foster care. Many children were placed back with their parents on a trial basis repeatedly.'

3.2   Baher et al. (1976) emphasize the urgent need for information on the relative merits of various type of protective placements for abused children in comparison with the home environment. They describe the difficulties that arise when choice of placement is governed not only by the extent to which it will meet the child's emotional needs but also by the extent to which it will encourage and enhance the parent–child relationship. They comment 'with hindsight, we now feel that in several cases, the child's interest might have been better served if the focus of our intervention had been on helping the parents to accept permanent separation rather than on working towards rehabilitation.' Baher et al. (1976) also note that disrupted caretaking featured prominently in the childhood of many of the abusive parents studied.

3.3   Besides considering the possible damaging effects on the child of professional intervention, what needs examining is the extent to which such intervention is capable of improving the abusive home environment. The intervention by many child protective agencies still seems concentrated on the prevention of recurrence of physical assault with little attention to improvement of the home environment. As soon as the home seems reasonably safe for the child from the standpoint of physical abuse, professionals tend to decrease their visits and support. However it is distressing to those who are concerned about the abused child that the few studies that have attempted to evaluate progress in families in relation to the type of therapeutic intervention experienced, suggest that even intensive long-term treatment programmes have had little ostensible impact so far on the parents' distorted views of the child or on the aberrant child-rearing practices.

3.4   In 1970, Morse et al., reported a follow-up study of 25 children who had been hospitalized three years previously for injuries or illnesses judged to be the result of abuse or gross neglect. During that three year period one-third of the children were again neglected or abused. The data from this study are discouraging. Only 29 per cent of the children were within normal limits intellectually and emotionally at the time of the follow up; 42 per cent were considered mentally retarded and 28 per cent were significantly emotionally disturbed. Ten out of 19 children were below the tenth percentile in height and weight. The study attempted to relate the degree of agency intervention to the status of the abused children at the time of the follow-up study. No pattern of relationships could be found. The authors comment, 'neither the amount of time nor skill expended by agency workers and nurses was predictive of how well the children progressed'. In fact the only characteristic common to the majority of children who appeared to be developing normally was a good mother–child relationship *as perceived and reported by the mothers*. Additional data from Morse's study suggest that the milieu of the abused child and more specifically the parents' perception of the child are critical influences on the child's development.

2. PARENT

3.5 Martin and Beezley (1976a) also report on the relationship between the therapy received by the abusing parents and the subsequent developmental status of 58 abused children at a mean of 4.5 years after abuse had first been documented. They comment 'It was disheartening to note the current behaviour of the parents towards the previously abused child'. Parents of 21 of the children had had psychotherapy as part of their treatment programme; 90 per cent of the children of these parents were still living in the biologic home. Even though the children were no longer being battered in the technical or legal sense, 68 per cent of them at follow-up were still experiencing hostile rejection and/or excessive physical punishment. However, these children were faring much better than those whose parents had received no formal treatment. Of those parents who had received only casework or services from a public health nurse, only 43 per cent of the children were living with them at follow-up. Thirty-six per cent were still in foster care and 21 per cent had been adopted. The families where no formal treatment had been instituted for the parents were even less satisfactory. In this group of children only 40 per cent were living with the parents, and of those, 83 per cent were the objects of rejection and excessive physical punishment. In all three groups of parents there remained considerable chaos in the family function. As already stated in this paper, the severity and frequency of psychiatric symptoms in the children correlated significantly with unstable family function and punitiveness and rejection by caretakers.

3.6 Baher et al. (1976) have evaluated the progress made in families referred to the Battered Child Research Department of the NSPCC, after a substantial period of intensive therapeutic intervention. This was of value to the abusive parents and improvements in several aspects of family functioning are reported. Also the supportive, intensive care provided, was, in the main, associated with an absence of rebattering or a reduction in its probable severity. The findings on the cognitive development of the children are encouraging. They show that the Department's system of care helped to restore the child's overall developmental status in most cases with those in the special therapeutic day nursery showing the greatest improvement of all. However, psychological assessment also indicated that these children's family relationships remained distorted, especially their relationship with their mothers, and differed from those of non-abused but deprived controls. This was substantiated by the fact that only slight positive changes were noted in most aspects of parent–child interaction, leaving many doubts about the effectiveness of the treatment service in improving the quality of parenting. The majority of the children were still living in homes where empathy and sensitivity to their needs were still lacking, where inconsistent and often harsh discipline remained the mode, where parental expectations remained inappropriately high and where little positive reinforcement took place.

3.7 In the author's estimation only eight out of twenty-three children seemed to be making reasonably satisfactory and *sustained* emotional development at the time of final evaluation. Of the remainder, a few had serious emotional problems which caused grave anxiety about their future development. A few were like weathervanes who reflected the moods of their parents by regressing or displaying disturbances when the home situation was particularly stressful. The authors comment '... we now feel that our dual and interlinked emphasis on treatment of the parents and protection of the children, neglected an important area, the psychotherapeutic treatment of the children, which could well be provided in a day care setting'.

4 Implications for future therapeutic intervention on behalf of abused children

4.1 It is apparent from the material presented in this paper that abused children (and frequently their siblings) undergo considerable physical and emotional suffering and that their proper development is impaired in a variety of ways for a variety of reasons. We still have a long way to go in devising methods of intervention that will improve the quality of life for these children. In future professionals must concern themselves with the needs and rights of the child in a broader context than that of physical safety. We must try to find ways of counteracting other malevolent aspects of home life which result in emotional disorder, inhibited intellectual capacity and a propensity to resort to violence in adult life (Curtis, 1963; Silver et al., 1969; Steele, 1970).

The need for child abuse treatment programmes to include comprehensive developmental assessment of all battered children at the time abuse is diagnosed cannot be over emphasized. Only then can their special needs be recognized and appropriate services such as speech therapy, occupational therapy, play therapy and psychotherapy be provided. Subsequently all abused children should be required to be kept under periodic review by medical, psychological and social work staff so that their development can be closely monitored. In accordance with the current interest in child advocacy it would be helpful if a key worker for the child could always be designated at the initial case conference. This person would then assume special responsibility for reporting on the child's development and representing his interests at subsequent reviews.

We can no longer cling to the assumption that treatment of the parents will automatically improve the quality of life and relationships for the child. Direct work with the children is essential since their whole personality organization is endangered. Some children may benefit greatly from short-term support from a sensitive, understanding adult such as their doctor, nurse, social worker, concerned teacher or friend, who can help them deal with the immediate stress of physical injury, hospitalization, court hearings, separation from parents and placement with substitute caretakers. Other abused children will undoubtedly require more intensive therapy to assist them with persistent and deep-seated problems. For example, they may need help in improving their self-concept; in dealing with their own anger; in loosening their inhibitions; in learning to enjoy age-appropriate pleasures, that adults can be trusted and that love is not always conditional on the gratification of adult needs.

4.4 Dr. Ruth Kempe (1975) has discussed the relative merits of individual and group psychotherapy for the pre-school abused child. She describes the difficulties of engaging pre-school children in individual therapy, not the least being parental resistance. She has found group therapy in a special nursery setting easier to arrange and more appropriate for this age range. Individual therapy is often more suitable for the school age child for two reasons. Firstly, the school age child is already used to coping with two environments and sets of relationships and making the shift from one to the other. Secondly school-age children are more able to verbalise, more aware of their difficulties and are perhaps better motivated towards treatment. Group therapy for latency age abused children and their siblings is currently being investigated as a mode of help at the National Center for the Prevention and Treatment of Child Abuse and Neglect in Denver.

4.5 Bearing in mind the acute shortage of child psychiatrists and psychotherapists, play therapists and social workers skilled in communicating with young children, we must enlist other personnel, such as experienced nursery nurses and carefully selected, sensitive foster parents to help meet these children's needs. At the same time the stress on those workers who become involved in the treatment of the children and are able to share in the horror and pain that many of these child clients have experienced, should not be overlooked. They, in turn, need regular support and consultation themselves.

4.6 Ideally the workers treating the parents and those involved in providing therapeutic day care for the children should be based under the same roof. Galdston (1975), Ten Broeck (1974), Ounsted et al. (1975), Bentovim (1976), Alexander et al. (1976) have discussed the great value of

2. PARENT

special day or residential family centres in which a multi-faceted treatment programme can be offered, including vital work on the abnormal and distorted parent–child interactions. For example, this may include individual and/or group therapy for the parents, parent self-help groups, specific therapeutic attention for individual children in a day-care setting and joint play therapy sessions for parents and children. This kind of setting also helps to facilitate close communication, mutual understanding and support between all staff involved in the treatment process.

4.7   The parents may also benefit from direct education in alternative methods of child rearing (Paulson and Chaleff, 1973; Savino and Saunders, 1973; Smith et al., 1973). However it is important for practitioners to recognize that many abusive parents suffer from an emotional rather than an intellectual block to understanding their children's needs and development and that their receptiveness to instruction on child management is highly contingent on the establishment of a relationship of trust with the workers involved. Jeffrey (1975) describes a very interesting programme based on education and behaviour modifications for changing parent–child interaction in families of children at risk. Practical techniques utilised in the homes of abusive parents include: interventions to change the negative quality of general interaction between children and care givers, interventions to change attitudes and interventions to change the children's responses.

4.8   Undoubtedly permanent separation of the child from his family is another therapeutic option which should be considered more frequently than it is at present in child abuse cases. Clarke and Clarke (1976) have collated evidence that against expectation even severe deprivation can be reversed. They include Koluchova's reports (1972, 1976)[1] on a pair of identical twins in Czechoslovakia who, after being isolated and cruelly treated from the age of 18 months to 7 years by their stepmother, have made surprisingly good progress since placement in a therapeutic foster home. Reference is also made to Kadushin's (1970) work on the successful placement of older children for adoption despite earlier neglect and ill-treatment. While it is impossible to lay down rigorous rules of thumb regarding decisions over permanent removal, the need in some cases remains not only to ensure the child's safety but also to facilitate his development in the broadest sense. In the recent move in child care thinking towards a greater emphasis on the rights of the child as an individual (Goldstein, Freud and Solnit, 1973) there has been a tendency to assume that it is relatively easy to decide that a child has no long-term future with his family. In the experience of practitioners, however, such a prognosis may be difficult to make until the family has been known for some time, and yet only if decisions about separation are made early in the casework process, can frequent disruptions of caretaking for the children be avoided. Of help here would be the setting up of more residential assessment centres similar to the one at the Park Hospital, Oxford, England or the Parental Stress Centre, Pittsburgh, USA, where the whole family could be intensively observed in a safe place over a period of weeks or months. The family's response to efforts to augment their caretaking capacities and capacity for change could then be evaluated as well as the quality of parent–child interaction. At the same time the child is protected and assured optimum growth and development by means of a stimulating environment. Another goal would be to establish more scientific and legally acceptable criteria for court determination and disposition than are available at this time. This seems vital in view of many of the provisions of the Children Act (1975), for example, the provision which brings in, as additional ground for dispensing with parental agreement to adoption that the parent or guardian has seriously ill-treated the child and, because of the ill-treatment, or for other reasons, the rehabilitation of the child within the household of the parent or guardian is unlikely.

4.9   In conclusion, it has to be acknowledged that detailed study of the

---

[1] [Papers 29 and 30 in this Reader.]

phenomenon of child abuse forces us to consider uncomfortable issues relating to the status and treatment of children in the population at large. Regardless of whether they have been physically abused, many children who may never come to professional attention are living in sub-optimal environments and experiencing the kind of inadequate parenting described in this paper which could permanently impair and disrupt their development. Abused children as a group are currently the focus of much public and professional concern in many different countries. It is to be hoped that by devoting considerable attention and resources to them and their families, we shall learn more about preventing the transmission of all kinds of damaging patterns of child rearing from one generation to the next.

References

ALEXANDER, H., et al. (1976) 'Residential Family Therapy', Ch. 19 in Martin, H. P. (ed.) *The Abused Child—A Multidisciplinary Approach to Developmental Issues and Treatment*, Cambridge, Mass., Ballinger.

BAHER, E., HYMAN, C., JONES, C., JONES, R., KERR, A., MITCHELL, R. (1976) *'At Risk' An Account of the work of the Battered Child Research Dept*, NSPCC, London, Routledge.

BALDWIN, J. A. and OLIVER, J. E. (1975) 'Epidemiology and Family Characteristics of Severely Abused Children', *Brit. J. Prev. Soc. Med.*, **29**, 205–221.

BARON, M. A., et al. (1970) 'Neurologic Manifestations of the Battered Child Syndrome', *Pediatrics*, **45**, 1003–1007.

BENDER, B. (1976) 'Self-Chosen Victims: Scapegoating Behaviour, Sequential to Battering', *Child Welfare*, **LV**, no. 6, 417–422.

BENTOVIM, A. (1976) 'A Psychiatric Family Day Centre Meeting the Needs of Abused or At Risk Pre-school Children and their Parents', *Paper presented at the first International Congress of child abuse and neglect, W.H.O., Geneva.*

BIRRELL, R. G. and BIRRELL, J. H. W. (1968) 'The Maltreatment Syndrome in Children: A Hospital Survey', *Med. J. Aust.*, **2**, 1023–1029.

I AM YOUR CHILD
AND I NEED YOU BADLY.

Please look at me carefully the next time you see me.

Please notice that I am small and weak.

Please listen to me carefully the next time you see me.

Please notice that I don't know much.

Like you, I was born helpless. And growing up so I can take care of myself will take me a long time, too.

I need food.

I need rest.

I need to be kept clean.

I need to be kept warm in winter and cool in summer.

I need to be taken in your arms or sat on your lap.

I need to feel your skin against my skin.

I need you to help heal my hurts.

I need you to play with just so you and I can have some good times together.

I need you to teach me everything you can so I'll have a chance in this world when I grow up.

I need your patience. I know I'm not very orderly. I cry out for things like food and attention the second I need them. I can't help it, and I know that bothers you sometimes. All I can hope is that you will be patient with me until I can learn to be patient, too.

Above all, I need to know you love me. Even if your parents gave you no love, try to give a little to me so I can give a little to my children and they can give a little to their children.

I need so much from you, yet I have only one thing I can give you in return.

That is my love.

Today and tomorrow and as long as I live.

The Phenomenon of the Abused Adolescent: A Clinical Study

IRA S. LOURIE

National Institute of Mental Health

The abuse of adolescents is a problem of epidemic proportions. Although this problem has many factors in common with the phenomena of child abuse, it has many unique factors. These factors relate to the developmental processes present in adolescence and to how youth and their families react to them. The total picture of this problem is not nearly complete, but this study indicates that (1) there is a great variability in the patterns demonstrated by families of abused and neglected adolescents; (2) the abused and neglected adolescents usually have developmental problems in the areas of separation and control; and (3) the parents are similarly in the midst of a crisis related to their own stage of development.

Every year millions of adolescents are involved in some form and degree of physical violence in their homes. This violence ranges from what most people would consider acceptable punishment to what all would consider abuse. For those young people who are abused or perceive themselves as abused there is little help available. Very often the recognition of abuse leads them to further victimization by their families and by agencies ill equipped to deal with them.

This phenomenon of the abused adolescent has received relatively little consideration in the field of child abuse and neglect. Although recent statistics demonstrate 25–30 percent of protective service caseloads across the country are adolescents, the literature is devoid of pertinent information as to specific factors in the identification, etiology and case management of adolescent cases. Gil (1970:105) found in his national study on the incidence of abuse that 16–17 percent of the children reported were over 12 years of age. These apparent underestimates are also reflected in the child abuse literature where such major works as *The Battered Child* by Kempe and Helfer, *The Battered Child in Canada* by Van Stolk, *Somewhere a Child is Crying* by Fontana, and *Children in Jeopardy* by Elmer mention hardly a word about the adolescent. Recently Straus, Gelles and Steinmetz (1976) have been exploring physical violence in American families. As part of this "Family Violence Research Program" it has been reported that 58 percent of 285 college freshmen interviewed had been struck by their parents the year preceding college and that six percent had received significant physical injury (Mulligan, 1976). Rigg and Tripp in a personal communication report 10 cases of adolescents hospitalized in a six-month period as the result of abuse and 31 adolescent cases referred as outpatients to a child abuse team in the following eleven months. Steele and Hopkins report that among 100 first pickup juvenile offenders, 92 had been abused in the year and a half prior to pickup. In her national sample of 1000 girls, Konopka (1976) mentions the surprising amount of abuse prevalent as well as the serious psychological repercussions of this abuse. In recent experience with runaway houses, this author has been impressed with the high percentage of unreported abused adolescents in their caseloads. This incidence is presently under formal investigation.

Table 1. Reported Incidence of Abuse of Children 12 Years Old or Older

Jurisdiction	Time Period	Percent of Abuse Reports on Children 12 Years Old or Older
Connecticut	1/74–12/75	24.0
Montana	1/74–12/74	29.7
Arizona	1970–1974	25–28*
Montgomery County, Md.	1/75–9/76	49.0

* Includes neglect.

Lourie and Cohan (1976) describe the failure of professionals working with child abuse to extend their thinking beyond the "battered baby" of the early 1960's to this large abused population over 12 years old. They question the advisability of accepting the present working assumption that what is known about child abuse and neglect is generalizable to the adolescent. An exploration must be made of the differences between the two age groups so that adolescents can be adequately served and protected.

As stated before, the basic fund of knowledge concerning abused and neglected children was developed from the frame of reference of the battered infant. The generally accepted model for this, as described by Kempe and Helfer (1972), consists of three major factors: (1) the parent with the potential to abuse; (2) the special child; and (3) the crisis situation. Steele and Pollack (1974) show that parents with psychological problems may distort the normal needs of their children and abuse them and that hyperactive children, unwanted and premature children ("Special Children") are thought more likely to provoke abuse. Environmental and social stresses whether related to society or directly to the individual are felt to be a factor in abuse.

While there are many children who have been abused and neglected from their childhood into adolescence, for many the abuse and neglect start in adolescence. For these cases we must search for the factors which allowed the family to avoid abuse during the child's early years and which precipitated the abuse during adolescence. Similarly, in those cases where abuse continues from childhood into adolescence, we must look for ways to explain why abuse can exist unnoticed in these families for so long only to become manifest in adolescence.

A CLINICAL STUDY

The Protective Service Unit of the Montgomery County Department of Social Services, Rockville, Maryland, is the recipient of all reports of abused and neglected children up to 18 years of age in a suburban Washington, D.C. county with a population of 550,000. This study was initiated in September 1975 reviewing cases back to January 1975 and seeing new cases through October 1976, and continuing to the present time. During the 12 months from September 1975 to August 1976, the agency received reports on 258 adolescents out of a total caseload of 751 abused and neglected children. One hundred fifty-seven of these adolescents were reported as physically abused, 89 as neglected (which includes emotional abuse) and 12 as sexually abused. All of these cases were reviewed and 25 cases were studied in greater depth using an individual psychiatric interview with the child and an interview with the family. Included in this sample were 10 physical abuse cases, nine neglect or emotional abuse cases, and 6 sexual abuse cases. They ranged from 12–17 years of age; 18 were females and 7 were males. The interviews focused on patterns of family interaction and the psychosocial developmental status of the youth and the parents.

Family Patterns

The patterns of family interaction demonstrated by the families seen in this study were extremely variable. As a result it was not possible to develop any concise typology. The following two cases demonstrate the wide extremes in these patterns and address several pertinent issues.

Linda E. is a 14-year-old white female who was referred by her mother, who was provoked by Linda's "talking back." Linda is an obese, depressed, and oppositional girl whose provocations are the result in part from feelings of loneliness and emptiness. Linda also has a history of grand mal seizures since an early age. Her mother is an angry woman who was deserted by her husband shortly after Linda's birth. She has always been resentful of Linda who "restricted her life," and has found caring for her a terrible burden. Four years before the abusive incident, Mrs. E's mother on whom she had been quite dependent died, heralding a rapid decline in the relationship with her own needy child. This decline ultimately led to the abuse incident.

Becky B. is a 14-year-old white female who was referred after a rather severe beating at the hands of her father following her "talking with a boy I told her not to talk with." Becky is a pleasant, rather seductive girl who presents herself in a way more reminiscent of an 18 or 20-year-old. She has had numerous struggles with her parents over limits. These conflicts in the past have precipitated a runaway episode. She sees herself as having been a shy dependent girl until reaching seventh grade, when she "grew up real fast." Becky's parents appear as a rather close couple who are interested in the welfare of their daughter. However, both parents are extremely rigid. This is especially true for the father, who has many preconceived generalizations about what girls should be and which young people, "hippies," are bad. This rigidity led to the assessment of unrealistic limits which Becky continually tested. The conflict between parent and child led to the abusive incident.

In the first case, Linda and her mother represent the typical abusive pattern with an extremely demanding and injured child living with a dependent mother who is lacking a vehicle for her own needed emotional support (in this case following the loss of her mother). Contrariwise, in the second case, Becky's father presents a picture of a man with many interpersonal strengths and a strong relationship with his wife and children. Becky, unlike Linda, has shown strength in her psychosocial development. The conflicts between Becky and her parents appear to be related to conflicts based on their strengths, while those between Linda and her mother appear to represent their mutual frustration at not having their exaggerated needs satisfied by each other.

Another issue which these cases demonstrate is that of impulse control. Linda's mother, in contradistinction to her interpersonal needs, shows strength in the area of impulse control. It was this strength that kept her from physically acting out her frustrations earlier in Linda's life, and more importantly prevented her from severely beating Linda during the present episode when her frustrations finally overwhelmed her. Becky's father, again, represents the other end of the spectrum. He has trouble controlling his impulses. This is represented first by his rigidity and secondly by his need to control Becky to the extent that he does. When he became overwhelmed, his angry impulses were easily unleashed in a vicious attack on his daughter.

Although no specific family or individual patterns were established for abused and neglected adolescents in this study, invariably we found either the adolescent or his parent dealing poorly with an expected developmental task. In the sample, the youths were usually struggling with developmental problems of separation and/or control. The parents were dealing with a broader range of issues which were less amenable to classification. The following discussion will focus on both these adolescent and parent issues.

THE ADOLESCENT

The developmental tasks and stresses of adolescence have been demonstrated to be monumental for many. Most often the reactions to this process by youth and their families disrupt long-standing family adjustments. As families readjust, abuse and/or neglectful episodes may occur as a reaction to this process. In other cases, abuse and neglect, ongoing since childhood, become manifest as a reaction to the developmental process. Relating back to the concept of the "special child" as a major etiological factor, *every adolescent is a special child*. However, even though every youth is a special child, each youth's specialness is different: what makes for these differences and increased vulnerability must be looked at in terms of the expected developmental struggles of adolescence.

Adolescence is a stage in life where the school-age child must relinquish a comfortable position as a controlled and dependent family member. He must then move toward a position separated from his family, taking the responsibility for his or her well-being and social behavior. Simultaneously the adolescent must adjust to marked changes in his or her body, both in the areas of physical and sexual development. To arrive at a productive and comfortable adult stage each child must integrate his new body, new sexuality, new individuality, new responsibility, and control. All this must be done in the context of an ever-changing society, one which usually assigns to youths a role which is much different-looking from that assumed for them by their parents. The fact that so many young people make the bridge to adult life successfully is a testimonial to the resilience of the human organism and its basic wish to be normal.

The application of these developmental principles to the area of abuse requires looking at those developmental lines that are most often a problem in these youth and/or their families to see what makes this one "special." As stated earlier, case studies indicate that the two most common developmental problems which lead to family violence are separation and behavioral control.

Separation

William L. is a 16-year-old Oriental male who has become a social isolate at school due to his own perceptions of Orientals as being "half men" and fostered by his parents' desire for isolation from peers in general and the non-Oriental population specifically. This was accompanied by exceptional school performance and appropriate behavior. William's failure to separate kept him at home where he struggled with his father about home responsibilities. These struggles led to a violent act by the father in which the boy's arm was lacerated by a thrown ashtray.

The case of William is one in which separation is a prominent issue ultimately leading to abuse. This issue is manifested by a youth's failure to move smoothly from his family to a peer group. This separation task is one in which both parents and children play a role. For the separation to take place, the binding forces which hold a child in his family must be overcome by the forces toward separation and individuation. This is similar to the concepts of Steirlin (1974) who has reviewed the work in this area and describes centripetal and centrifugal forces ("binding and expelling") in families.

As a youth separates he is then able to develop an individual identity. Erikson (1968) describes this as the move from a position in which the usefulness of childhood identification ends and identity formation begins. For this to happen, not only must the family dynamics of binding and separation forces be favorable, but the individual must be ready to accept an individual identity. To do this there must be adequate ego strength and a solid base of early identification.

Failure to move smoothly in this separation task has many possible manifestations. Most of these, when viewed from the proper perspective, are seen as attempts by a youth to respond to a developmental lag in the task of separation and are, therefore, reactions toward or against binding forces. These behavioral manifestations tend to: (1) represent the presence of forces binding them to past ties and needs; (2) create the need for increased binding; or (3), represent a flight toward separation in order to escape unwanted binding needs. Most adolescent behaviors, whether seen as problems or not, have components which rely on this drama.

In turn, these adolescent behaviors disrupt family systems, causing stress. These behaviors are often provocative to others, including parents. The dynamics of such provocations are usually in the service of forces toward separation but can be used as a binding vehicle as well. The case of William demonstrates the interweaving of these dynamics. His failures to separate were due to his lack of readiness and were enhanced by binding forces of his family. This led to provocations between himself and his father, which served the dual purpose of creating a system in which he was more closely bound to his father (through struggle), while at the same time asserting his independent strivings, immature as they may be. In families such as his, where violence is a form of expression, this drama can be expressed in violent ways which in turn can become abusive. The adolescent can also tap in on the hidden violence in even the most outwardly gentle parent.

When abuse occurs, it in turn becomes another factor in determination of separation dynamics. Sometimes the reaction to abuse is to run away, a case in which separation forces supercede. On the other end of the spectrum is the teenager who accepts all the abuse given, even though he is perfectly able to fight back or run. This is not an unusual outcome where dependent needs, as a result of binding forces, are dominant.

Control

Kim G. is a 16-year-old female with a three-year history of struggles with her parents about her indiscreet sexuality, drug usage and for being involved in minor delinquent acts. The parents reacted to her behavior by setting limits in order to help control her behavior. These limits invariably tried to keep her closer to home. She objected vehemently to this and reacted by breaking each new limit. During these struggles she was beaten by her frustrated mother.

Control is a second major issue in which developmental lag can easily lead to abuse. The case of Kim is such an example. Although many of the behaviors which led to abuse in her case may be explained on the basis of the separation issues described above, there are issues concerning the ability to control which are prime. Beginning at birth the amount of behavioral control exercised by individuals and their parents is in an ever-changing balance. By the time adolescence has been reached every youth must have incorporated a certain level of self-control. If not, there arises a situation which creates a need for closer binding in order to solicit control from the outside, which then replaces ineffective internal controls. The need for control is accentuated in adolescence as drives, physical strength, and freedom increase.

As adolescents strive for competence in these areas of control, they must set limits for themselves and test those limits. This is followed by modification of the limits and exertion of self-control as needed. As with all developmental tasks, this is a variable one in which various levels of control are needed at different times. This requires a variable degree of parental control, based on the youth's rapidly fluctuating capacity to control himself.

Often a struggle arises in families over this issue of control. These struggles are based on a misalignment between a youth's ability to control and a parent's (1) need to control, (2) need to avoid control, or (3) inability to offer realistic controls. In the case of Kim, she demonstrated a poor ability to set her own limits. Her parents reacted to this by setting limits for her. Not only were these limits unrealistic, they were unenforceable. The struggle created led to violence, based on the fact that violence was a major form of expression in that particular family.

Typically, the issues of separation and control are intertwined. Most cases tend to have problems in both areas. A determination as to which is primary is often difficult, but is extremely important to the construction of a treatment plan. There are two major patterns between which to differentiate. In the first, there is a youth who has strong binding needs. Because the direct expression of these needs is developmentally unacceptable, they remain hidden behind a false sense of independence. In order to get closer binding the child loses control and performs an act which causes the parent to exert external control, thereby pulling the youth closer.

In the second pattern, there is a youth who does not have the capacity to control. This forces the parents to exert external control. No matter how much independence the youth can tolerate he is still bound closely in order to make up for this deficit in control. Although the two patterns have similar behavioral manifestations, in the first we must treat the need for binding and in the second we must treat the need for control.

THE PARENTS

Mid-Life Development

Having addressed the issues in youth development which lead to stresses implicated in abusive situations, the parental side must be addressed also. Little is written about the development of the midlife adult. Steirlin (1974) describes this process, as it pertains to separation, as "running counter to what we find in adolescence. . ." Although admittedly abridged, he points to several important factors: the "declining of libidinal drives," "the relative blunting of alertness and inquisitiveness" and the "need to assess and confirm existing loyalties." These and many other unexplored factors make the adolescence of their children a difficult period in parents' lives. This area needs more exploration and will be the subject of future publications.

We have already seen in the discussion of the child how the adolescent's reaction to development is affected by the needs and capacities of the parents. When parents face a turbulent period in their development they are less able to tolerate changes in their lives. In an attempt to adjust to developmental changes the parents rely on prior support pathways that have developed in their families. When this attempt is met with an adolescent whose dynamics, either appropriate or exaggerated, represent a stress to the support pathways system, the adults are left without a mechanism to rely on as they attempt to consolidate their own developmental changes. This leaves both the parents and the youth vulnerable to these stresses. Abuse is then one of the possible reactions to stress.

CONCLUSION

The abuse of adolescents is a problem of epidemic proportions. Although this problem has many factors in common with the phenomena of child abuse, it has many unique factors. These factors relate to the developmental processes present in adolescence and to how youth and their families react to them. The total picture of this problem is not nearly complete, but this study indicates that (1) there is a great variability in the patterns demonstrated by families of abused and neglected adolescents; (2) the abused and neglected adolescents usually have developmental problems in the areas of separation and control; and (3) the parents usually are similarly in the midst of a crisis related to their own stage of development. These phenomena must be studied further before this population of young people receive the care and protection needed for normal growth and development.

REFERENCES

Elmer, E.
1967   Children in Jeopardy: A Study of Abused Minors and Their Families. Pittsburgh: University of Pittsburgh Press.
Erikson, E. H.
1968   Identity: Youth and Crisis. New York: Norton.
Fontana, V.
1973   Somewhere a Child is Crying. New York: MacMillan.
Gil, D.
1970   Violence Against Children. Cambridge MA: Harvard University Press.
1975   Unraveling Child Abuse. Am. Journal of Orthopsychiatry 45, No. 3, April.
Helfer, R. E. and C. H. Kempe (eds.)
1974   The Battered Child. Chicago: University of Chicago Press.
Kempe, C. H. and R. E. Helfer
1972   Helping the Battered Child and His Family. Philadelphia: J. B. Lippincott.
Konopka, G.
1976   Young Girls. Englewood Cliffs NJ: Prentice Hall.
Lourie, I. S. and A. M. Cohan
1976   Abuse and Neglect of Adolescents. Child Abuse Reports 1:6
Miller, D.
1974   Adolescence. New York: Aronson.
Mulligan, M.
1976   An Investigation of Factors Associated with Violent Modes of Conflict in the Family. Unpublished Master Thesis.
Steele, B. and C. Pollock
1974   A Psychiatric Study of Parents who Abuse Infants and Small Children. Pp. 103–145 in R. E. Helfer and C. H. Kempe (eds.), The Battered Child. Chicago: University of Chicago Press.
Steirlin, H.
1974   Separating Parents and Adolescents. New York: Quadrangle.
Straus, M. A., R. J. Gelles, and S. K. Steinmetz
1976   Violence in the Family: An Assessment of Knowledge and Research Needs. Unpublished paper.
Van Stolk, M.
1973   The Battered Child in Canada. Toronto: McCelland and Stewart.

The views expressed in this paper are not necessarily official positions of the National Institute of Mental Health.

Speaking Out For Their Rights

The Illinois Foster Children's Association

William T. Perozzi

William T. Perozzi, A.C.S.W., is Assistant Guardianship Administrator, Illinois Department of Children and Family Services—East St. Louis Area Office, East St. Louis, Illinois.

"Why was I sent away from home? My father abused me—*he* should have been the one to go!"

"Just because you're a foster child, the teachers and the police automatically assume you're emotionally disturbed, or a juvenile delinquent."

"I'm a Catholic, but my foster parents made me go to a Baptist church. They said if I didn't co-operate I'd be sent to an institution."

"I really didn't want to leave my last foster home. Sure I complained, but it didn't do any good."

At the residential emergency shelter where he worked part time as a child care aide, 17-year-old Mike Mulligan heard many comments like these from the foster children there. Many of the "veterans"—those who had been in one or more foster homes and were awaiting placement in another—were angry and bitter. The "new kids"—those just entering the foster care system—were confused and concerned about their future.

Like the children at the shelter, Mike was a foster child, a ward of the state. He understood their feelings, for he had experienced the same frustrations in trying to gain some control of his life. He knew what they meant when they complained of being treated as second-class citizens—of being "looked down on" just because they were foster children, of being used or inferior clothing while their foster families' natural children were more stylishly dressed. Like many foster children they felt worthless, and powerless to change their situations.

Mike, however, was luckier than most foster children. When he was 15 and living in an institution, he had been befriended by an agency case-worker who became his foster father. Through their relationship, Mike began to learn about the state bureaucracy that had controlled over a third of his life—the way the foster care system is supposed to operate, its problems of communication, its financial problems and the large caseloads carried by its workers. He realized for the first time, for example, that the agency had earmarked a certain amount of his foster care money for his clothing and personal needs, and that he could legally appeal any major decision affecting his case.

As Mike learned to communicate and deal effectively with the agency, he was soon successful in getting many of his needs met through the system. He talked with foster children at the shelter, explaining the system to them, and he encouraged them to speak out for their rights. The problems and frustrations they shared could be alleviated, he believed, if foster children united. He envisioned an organization of and for foster children: an organization that would make foster children feel that they were being listened to, one that would teach them how to deal effectively with the system and how to help make agency workers more sensitive to their rights and needs.

Although Mike left for college and was not able to take an active part in the formation of the organization he had envisioned, the need for such a group was evident and others did carry the project to fulfillment.

Getting It Off The Ground

As the Assistant Guardianship Administrator for the East St. Louis area of the Illinois Department of Children and Family Services, I am responsible for protecting the rights and welfare of foster children. An association of foster children could, I thought, give me a better opportunity to deal directly with the children I was supposed to be protecting. A social work graduate student from Washington University, who was then doing field work at the agency, was also interested in seeing an organization formed and, together, we decided to take on the project.

We agreed that the organization had to be separate from both the agency and the Foster Parents Association because of possible conflicts of interest. The first step, however, was to obtain agency approval.

The original proposal presented to the agency emphasized an organization for support, recreation and education rather than advocacy, since there were many in the agency who were hesitant to organize foster children. After obtaining agency approval, we decided to start a group in Alton, Ill., where a large number of teenage foster children were living and where the idea of an association of foster children had been well received by the local field office.

A meeting with the Foster Parents Association was next. We had anticipated that its members might feel threatened by the existence of a foster children's organization. However, after discussing the proposal with the group, the foster parents gave the children's association their full support. They were concerned about problems with the agency and felt that a foster children's association could work with them in bringing about desired changes.

The student then wrote to all foster children living in the target area, inviting them to a meeting to discuss plans for an organization. Twenty foster children, ranging in age from 12 to 18, attended the first meeting in March 1976. After discussing mutual problems with the agency and foster parents and ventilating their anger and frustrations, the foster children were ready to begin thinking about how they could organize to deal constructively with their concerns. Before the meeting was over, the Foster Children's Association had been formed and temporary officers elected and given power to further develop it.

Once the foster children had selected their own leaders, we worked with them, helping them learn how to organize an association, conduct meetings, prepare by-laws and be effective leaders. All of the decisions regarding issues and strategies were formulated by the foster children, and we acted only as advisors, coordinators or liaison persons.

Goals and Philosophy

A philosophical approach to the Foster Children's Association was established through general agreement on the following points:

☐ Foster children have individual needs and concerns, and they are in the best position to know what their needs and desires are.

☐ Because of their early life experiences, many foster children do not trust adults or adult institutions.

☐ Foster children are discriminated against in the community because the label "foster child" has a negative connotation.

☐ As individuals, foster children are economically and politically powerless; they are dependent on the agency and courts for their welfare.

☐ Foster children are additionally disadvantaged because they usually do not know all the agency rules and regulations which govern workers' actions and which were planned as safeguards for them. Foster children generally know only what they are told by their caseworkers and foster parents—information that is usually incomplete and which may, at times, consist of lies devised to threaten them into cooperating.

☐ The agency and courts are too impersonal, overburdened, political and underfinanced to meet the individual needs of foster children and to provide adequate resources to meet those needs.

☐ Foster children need to organize in order to have a greater influence within the community and with the people who control the agency. Through such an organization, foster children would have a better chance of having their needs met through the system, thus reducing the need to rebel against the agency.

Although there will be some who may not agree with all of these points, the foster children gave many vivid examples—which we found to be true—to support each point. Most of the foster children related stories of being moved abruptly, without explanation, from one foster home to another. None of them understood the court process. They did not realize, for instance, that the guardian ad litem was their lawyer and that they could have testified as to how they would have liked to have seen their problems solved. Nor did they know that they had a right to appeal decisions. Most reported feeling like culprits rather than victims of situations over which they had no control.

The foster children told of encountering resentment against them among teachers, the police and others in the community who believed that foster children would be a bad influence on other sudents. All also cited examples of what they considered to be unfair treatment by foster parents and caseworkers.

The older foster children had a special complaint. The state, which had been giving them up to $290 a month for support while they were attending school or job training programs, suddenly cut that amount to $200. No provisions were made for those who had signed leases or entered into other financial contracts.

Article II g of the association's by-laws spells out its purpose: to work together to improve the image of foster children in the eyes of the community; to improve the quality and quantity of foster homes; to enhance communication among foster children and to advocate for their legal and natural rights; and to promote the development of programs, resources and recreational activities for foster children.

Securing Funds

The association's first headquarters was in a foster home. However, members realized after the first two meetings that they needed operating capital for an office, telephone, secretarial help and basic supplies.

To raise money the association held a bake sale and a car wash. A second graduate social work student who had become involved with the association happened to be on the board of the local Economic Opportunity Commission and he managed to convince the Commission that the group's project deserved its support. The Commission secured a $5,000 grant for the purpose of starting a Foster Children's Association. Although the association did not have any control over this money, arrangements were made to allow the group autonomy while the E.O.C. supplied an office, equipment, phone and transportation.

The next problem was staffing the office. An agreement was reached with the local C.E.T.A. program (a program funded by the Labor Department's Comprehensive Employment and Training Act) to pay the expenses for two part-time, year-round positions and two part-time summer positions. The association selected four foster children who had the interest and ability to fill these positions and, by July 1976, the Foster Children's Association had an office (located at Lewis and Clark Community College in Godfrey), staff, supplies, transportation and operating capital.

Improving Their Image

As one foster child put it, "Maybe we can change the community's opinion about foster kids so that when something goes wrong they won't always think we did it!"

The group was aware that any time a foster child received press coverage, it was usually for something he or she had done wrong—and the fact that the child was a foster child was always mentioned. The members felt that foster children's achievements deserved attention and that the only way to counter negative press coverage was to make reporters aware of their accomplishments and encourage them to write positive stories about foster children. By the time of the third meeting, several of the members had become acquainted with a local newspaper reporter, whom they invited to their meetings. She talked with the group about how reporters operated and the importance of good public relations, and agreed to write some articles about the association. As a result, reporters were regularly invited to cover stories on the association's projects and, in the past year, several positive stories about foster children and the association have appeared in local papers.

Members of the group have participated in radio talk shows, and the association was the subject of an article in a statewide agency newsletter and in a foster parent publication.

Since all of the publicity that the foster children have received thus far has been positive, they are certain that their image in the local community is improving.

"The cops used to come to my house when anything happened," a 17-year-old foster child told an interviewer recently. "They figured if I hadn't done it, then I knew who had. Now the police don't come any more."

Improving Foster Home Care

On radio shows, the foster children always point out the need for more and better foster homes. They have also distributed leaflets about foster care throughout the community in an attempt to recruit new foster homes.

Members of the association have become involved in the series of training workshops which the agency holds for all new foster parents. One session has been turned over to the foster children, who lead discussions and present skits showing how foster parents might handle such problems as drug use, runaways, initial placements and communication.

The foster children have also testified at public hearings on licensing standards. One of their goals is to raise such standards by making foster parent training mandatory.

Enhancing Communication

Before each monthly meeting, the association sends letters to every foster child in the area, giving the meeting agenda and any additional information that may be helpful to them. The letters are followed up by phone calls and transportation, if necessary, is arranged.

Guest speakers from the community and the agency participate regularly in the meetings, presenting information on such subjects as foster home recruitment and training and agency rules and regulations. The association also held a series of meetings as part of the League of Women Voters' project, Community Education on Law and Justice, in which a judge, a lawyer and a police officer helped inform community groups about the operation of the criminal justice system.

Advocacy

The group soon learned that it needed a power base from which to operate. Although the fact that they were organized did provide them with more power than they would have had as individuals, members realized that

they needed the support of other influential groups and individuals in the community to be truly effective.

The association made itself known to such national groups as the Children's Defense Fund, the Child Welfare League of America, National Action for Foster Children and, on a state level, the Illinois Commission on Youth, the League of Women Voters and the Illinois Foster Parents Association. The foster children were pleasantly surprised to find that all of these groups were interested in the formation of a Foster Children's Association and in offering it help. The press and radio coverage served to legitimize the group in the eyes of the community. Soon the association had representatives on a local youth advisory council and on the Illinois Youth Council.

Issues of Concern

In initiating their advocacy role, the foster children developed a number of position statements on subjects important to them. The first concerned a proposed change in the agency's rules concerning corporal punishment. The agency did not allow foster parents to use corporal punishment on foster children, but it was reconsidering this position. The children's association wrote letters to the agency and spoke at public hearings in a successful effort to prevent any change in policy.

Another issue concerned a foster child's right to be involved in agency staff meetings when major decisions affecting the child are being made. The agency had been holding internal staff meetings to discuss and formulate case plans. Although at times the foster child had been involved in these meetings, this was not a routine occurrence. The association wanted to make it mandatory that foster children over the age of 12 be invited to the meetings to present their own cases. After the association had presented its position to the administrative staff, the local agency agreed to do so.

Other issues which the association wants to address concern foster care payments and the foster children's right to privacy in regard to phone calls, correspondence and personal belongings. The association has also been effective in bringing individual case problems to the attention of the agency and in supporting foster children whom they felt were being treated unfairly.

Members of the association have also discussed the need for a hotline and a runaway center with other community groups and are looking into possible funding for such services.

Providing Recreational Activities

Realizing that there was no need to supplement community recreational programs with separate programs for foster children, the association decided to use recreation as a means of bringing foster children together and enhancing the group's progress. Parties have been held for older children who were leaving the group, and the association has sponsored hay-rides, cook-outs and trips to an amusement park.

Problem Areas

It is always difficult to sustain young people's interest in projects which yield few immediate results—and maintaining the foster children's continued interest is, of course, a problem in the organization. There are very few opportunities for immediate gratification, since resolution of many of the problems the group is now working on will require much time and effort. Thus, the group chose to develop a highly motivated and trained executive committee which conducts most of the organization's work. A majority of the members of the core group maintain their involvement because they like the status and the attention that membership gives them within the agency.

Short-term goals and objectives of the association have also been established so that members can see immediate progress.

Meetings are planned on school nights early in the week so that they won't compete with other community activities. However, since the members are scattered throughout the county, getting the children together for a meeting has been a major problem. The association does occasionally have use of a van, and some members who have cars transport others. At times, foster parents have been enlisted to bring some foster children to meetings. However, it is important that the association not become a burden on foster parents and one of the group's objectives is to purchase its own van.

Since foster children are extremely mobile, moving from foster home to foster home and from community to community, it is difficult to maintain a well-trained core group. In one year, for example, the group has had a complete turnover of six group leaders. However, so long as there is an existing structure and organization, it is possible to bring in new people and still carry on business as usual.

The turnover problem occurs not only with the foster children, but also with the student advisors. In one year we have had four student advisors, each involved for a few months at a time with the organization.

Current Projects

Members of the association are writing a handbook for foster children—a "survival manual" spelling out their rights in the foster home, the agency and the community and offering suggestions for getting one's needs met through the system. It is hoped that the handbook, which will be distributed to all foster children in the state, will contribute to ensuring the rights of foster children and upgrading services to them, as more children demand the services to which they are entitled. The handbook should also serve to promote a more open and honest relationship between foster children and their foster parents and caseworkers.

Both the children's association and the Foster Parents' Association are supporting a bill submitted to the state legislature which would increase payments for foster care.

The association has received inquiries from others interested in forming a similar organization and the first goal for the coming year is to expand statewide and, possibly, nationally.* The association has also applied for incorporation as a nonprofit organization.

Benefits to Children and Agency

The Foster Children's Association has grown to 60 active members. We have noticed that foster children seem to have a greater tendency to cooperate with the agency once they are involved with the association—and we have observed marked changes in the behavior and attitudes of some of the members.

Agency staff members have not only overcome their initial concerns about the organization but have also shown a willingness to work with it and to use the organization to improve child welfare services. Although it is too early to adequately assess any long-range benefits to the foster children or agency, the association has demonstrated that it is needed and that it has the potential to effect changes both within the agency and the community in their approaches to and attitudes towards foster children. We are confident that an attitude of working together will emerge. For now, we are gratified that an organization planned by and for foster children is alive and well in Madison County, Illinois.

Photo: Office of Human Development Services

SEXUAL CHILD ABUSE

The statistics may vary, but all of the literature on sexual child abuse report that in at least 65 percent of the cases the victim knows the assailant. Reports show incest to be one of the most common yet least reported crimes. Generally authorities are not contacted until the victim is incapable of dealing with the stress or is pregnant. Sex crimes are usually committed by younger people and girls are victims more often than boys.

Education and increased public awareness are the most effective weapons against this form of child abuse. In the case of molestation, it is the children themselves who need to be taught protective measures. Children are not consenting adults but victims who's bodies and minds are being violated.

The helping professional, volunteer worker and parent must take an active, direct approach. An understanding of child development, child behavior and crisis intervention are important in the ability to help the child and parent in alleviating guilt. Consistent and open follow-up discussions with the child will help ease developmental problems that may possibly occur during adolescence.

All of the articles included in Section III emphasize the importance of increased public awareness. A section from the National Committee for the Prevention of Child Abuse pamphlet "Sexual Child Abuse" provides a concise overview of the problem. "The Terror of Child Molestation" is directed toward parents and explains ways to help children protect themselves from and cope with molestation. Judianne Densen-Gerber, a lawyer and founder of Odyssey Institute (a metropolitan program designed to help runaways, and now assists in the cause of sexually exploited children) calls attention to the increased number of exploitative films and magazines involving young children. Society is so terrified of the problem that it makes reporting difficult. In "Sexual Abuse Begins At Home," the author writes how serious this problem is. "The Sexually Abused Child" explains techniques for a nurse to use in assisting with the child after sexual abuse occurs. It is a valuable guide for helping professionals, volunteers and parents. Brian G. Fraser, a lawyer and director of the National Committee for the Prevention of Child Abuse is interviewed regarding the legal rights of the parents and the sexually abused child. He concurs with others in the field, that legislation can do little for the already abused child.

The public needs to make a commitment to sexually abused children and provide proper treatment facilities, education and a prevention network.

Sexual Disturbance in Young Children

That adults abuse children sexually is a cruel reality, but one which nurses must face, for they are responsible for helping the child. In intervening the nurse needs to keep the child's total emotional environment uppermost in her mind.

ROBERT L. GEISER/SISTER M. NORBERTA

DR. GEISER, PH.D., *is chief psychologist at Nazareth Child Care Center in Jamaica Plain, Massachusetts, where* SISTER M. NORBERTA, C.S.S.F., R.N., *also serves as a pediatric nurse practitioner. Formerly a psychologist with the Psychiatric Services for Children at Tufts–New England Medical Center, Boston, Dr. Geiser is the author of several articles and a book on foster care and child psychology.*

Because sexual abuse of children is an occurrence that horrifies laymen and professionals alike, when health care providers intervene their attention is likely to be focused on the behavior itself. They make every effort to separate the child from the adult abuser, and there may even be some concern with punishing the adult or with psychiatrically alleviating the child's supposed trauma. But the problem is rarely conceptualized in broader terms. Often the assumption is made that, once the child has been separated from the adult, the problem is solved. Failure to recognize the broader implications of sexual abuse means that these children do not receive the help they desperately need.

Sexual abuse is usually only one sign that a child is in psychological trouble. While it *may* indicate a disturbance in the child's sexual development, often it does not. Such abuse does, however, always indicate a primary disturbance in the child's emotional relationships with adults. Most people, because of the child's dependence and vulnerability, think of adult sexual behavior with children as specific, forcible acts of rape. Actually, less than five percent of all offenses against children involve the use of physical force. This is true because the adult offender is usually someone with whom the child has had a long-standing, emotionally meaningful relationship(1).

As a result, what a health professional may label as sexually abusive behavior may not be considered abusive by the child. Frequently children who are sexually abused are willingly engaging in affection-seeking behavior and do not perceive the sexual behavior as abnormal, abusive, or traumatic. In such cases, it is unlikely that the sexual behavior by itself upsets the child's personality development.

On the other hand, sexual abuse usually occurs in the broader context of a disturbed psychosocial environment. Adults who have failed to protect the child from sexual abuse may also have failed to protect the child in other areas. It is common, for example, to find that a sexually abused child lives in a deprived environment. There is always emotional deprivation and sometimes physical deprivation and neglect as well. Thus the child may learn to use sexual behavior to satisfy nonsexual needs—especially needs for affection.

In the case of the foster children we see who have been sexually abused, besides deprivation there is often a high incidence of violence within their natural families. Often the sexually abused children or their siblings have been battered or have witnessed much violence between their parents. This overexposure to violence in addition to emotional and physical deprivation is far more harmful to the child's personality development than actual sexual abuse.

The sexual abuse itself is harmful in that it may stir up feelings in the child such as guilt, fear, and anxiety. These feelings may be expressed in ways ranging from sexual acting out to disturbed behavior in areas quite unrelated to sex. In the latter case, the process of diagnosing a disturbed sexual environment becomes complicated.

Since the child victim is unlikely to show signs of physical injury, most times a disturbed environment must be diagnosed from direct observations of the child's behavior and/or parent-child interaction, supported by inferences made from case history material. At times either the child or his caretaker may tell the nurse about the sexual abuse, but this is unusual in initial contacts. Such information is usually shared with a nurse only after the patient or his guardian has established a relationship of trust with the professional. Even then a direct revelation must be carefully assessed, for it may be nothing more than the child's fantasy.

Once a diagnosis has been made, if intervention is to help the child, it must explore the child's total environmental adjustment. Special attention must be paid to what factors allowed the sexual abuse to happen, what nonsexual needs the behavior met in the child, and in what ways the child's emotional relationships with adults are disturbed. The following cases demonstrate how incidents of sexual abuse fit into a child's total environment and create difficulties for the child in other areas. Two of the cases involve the sexual abuse of a male child, an instance which has received little attention in the literature but which is nonetheless a problem. Through discussion of these cases we will explore some of the behavioral indications of abuse from both parents' and child's view, the reasons for the behavior, and methods and approaches to dealing with it.

CASE I—MARK

Mark was eight and a half when he was admitted to a child-care center from the foster home where he had been living for over a year. His foster mother had become increasingly incapable of dealing with Mark's aggressive behavior toward other children and his nightly bed-wetting.

The staff at the institution observed that Mark showed many signs of disturbed behavior. Besides wetting his bed every night, he sucked this thumb constantly and was preoccupied with sexual activity and stimulation. He masturbated frequently and crawled into bed at night with the younger boys and tried to initiate sex play. When the staff began to supervise his nighttime behavior more closely, they reported with considerable agitation that Mark turned his sexual attention to the cottage pet, a dog.

Mark's case record revealed that he and his four siblings were originally placed in foster care because of severe emotional and physical neglect. They were the natural children of two immature and inadequate parents, who had themselves been deprived and neglected as children. Mr. S was a sporadic

While sexual abuse may indicate a disturbance in the child's sexual development, often it does not. Such abuse, however, always indicates a primary disturbance in the child's emotional relationships with adults.

drinker and Mrs. S had been in a mental hospital. She still had many physical complaints and used these as an excuse to stay in bed much of the time.

The home environment was chaotic. The children slept on urine-soaked mattresses, lived in incredible filth, and often went without food and adequate clothing. They also witnessed frequent verbal and

The adult offender is usually someone with whom the child has a long-standing, emotionally meaningful relationship.

physical fights between their parents and were left on their own for days at a time while the parents were out drinking.

In the course of investigating the home situation prior to putting the children in foster care, it was discovered that a frequent visitor to the home was a young, retarded uncle in his twenties, who was well known to the local police for sexually molesting children and dogs. The uncle often slept at Mark's house, and when he did, he shared a bed with one or more of the children. The parents allowed this in spite of the fact that they were well aware of the young man's deviant sexual behavior.

When a social worker asked if the uncle might have molested Mark, the boy's father just shrugged his shoulders and said, "Kids have to learn about that stuff sooner or later." Mrs. S, on the other hand, vehemently denied that Mark had been singled out, protesting, "He (the uncle) has sex with all the kids!" She herself frequently took all the children to bed with her, not for sexual reasons but to ward off her sense of loneliness and isolation.

Commentary

The first obvious deviation in Mark's psychosocial environment is his parents' failure to protect him from his uncle's sexual abuse. (Incidentally, failure of the mother to protect a female child from the father's advances is known to be a contributing factor in some cases of father-daughter incest.) The lesson that Mark and other children learn from this parental failure is that you can't trust adults to protect you. Mark's basic lack of trust in adults, greatly augmented by the parents' failure to physically care for and nurture him, will be an obstacle to other adults in helping him in the future.

A second point which Mark's case dramatically makes is that child victims are often susceptible to adult seduction because of severe emotional deprivation in the home environment. Rarely, if ever, does sexual behavior in a young child have sexual motivation. To understand the sexual behavior of a child, one must look more closely at the child's nonsexual needs. It is often found that at the time the sexual abuse occurred, the child was engaged in affection-seeking behavior in his or her relationship with the involved adult. In foster children with severe emotional deprivation, their need for affection may be an even stronger motivational force than usual. Satisfaction of this need through sexual encounter reinforces a deviant childhood pattern of obtaining affection through sexual behavior.

Another pattern which is encouraged in the absence of parental protection is that often the child defends himself against being victimized by identifying with the aggressor. In Mark's current behavior in foster care, he repeats the trauma that he experienced at his uncle's hands—with one difference. Instead of being the victim, Mark has now become the aggressor. Like his uncle, he seeks out defenseless others to molest.

Mark's Development

Separating Mark from his uncle, while desirable, has not solved the boy's problems. After nearly four years of foster care, his difficulties in relating to others have become fairly clear. He shows a continuing pattern of preoccupation with sex play with other children. Since he has developed into a fairly large 13-year-old, he is physically able to dominate and intimidate other children.

Mark has also demonstrated a chronic failure to learn in school, a consequence of many factors. One is his fixation with sexual matters, which disrupts his ability to concentrate in school. Failure to learn is a common difficulty in children who have been sexually abused. Some of these children show an intellectual bewilderment. Having been overwhelmed by their emotions at a vulnerable time, they seem to be unable now to understand the world around them. Also, because these children cannot trust

The child learns to use sexual behavior to satisfy nonsexual needs—especially needs for affection.

adults, they cannot accept help and knowledge from their teachers.

Mark's relationships with all adults, especially child-care staff, are highly ambivalent. With men Mark is submissive, docile, and often fearful. He is afraid that a relationship with a man will expose him to sexual attack. At the same time, he admires men who are strong and wants to build up his body and muscles, enabling him to defend himself.

With female staff Mark still alternates between being loud, defiant, and hostile and being affectionate, coy, and babyish. This alternation is typical of many sexually abused and emotionally deprived children. On one hand, Mark wants to be the child who is loved, cared for, and protected, and he inap-propriately expresses this (for a 13-year-old boy) by hanging onto and caressing female staff.

On the other hand, Mark is angry at women, for he sees them as depriving, as his mother was. At times he acts out that anger by being quarrelsome, verbally abusive, or even striking out. Thus, he also repeats the pattern of conflict between the sexes that he was exposed to in his home environment.

Because of Mark's mother's rejection, deprivation, and neglect of him and both his parents' failure to protect him from environmental dangers, Mark's anger at his mother is very intense. In fantasy children who have been either sexually or physically abused often direct considerable aggression toward the parent(s), at times even imagining their parents' destruction. (In reality the children may show a paradoxically strong desire to be reunited with their parents and direct their aggression against their substitute caretakers.)

Mark's fantasies, as revealed in psychological testing, are filled with violence and sadistic injury. The stories he makes up to correspond with pictures in-

Emotional and physical deprivation, as well as overexposure to violence and sexuality, are far more harmful to the child's personality development than is actual sexual abuse.

volve women, often identified as mothers, who are repeatedly stabbed, shot, or strangled. Strong sexual overtones run through most of the stories, and they clearly show the fusion between sex and aggression which is a legacy of Mark's environment.

Needless to say, Mark is extremely confused in his sexual identity. He has been the sexual object of another male, and on the verge of adolescence, he finds that his normal sexual object, the female, is someone with whom he is intensely angry. Mark's models for masculinity and femininity have been poor ones, and his picture of the interaction between the sexes is even worse. Men dominate, fight with, and hurt women. Women deprive, reject, and are victims of men's brutality. Is it any wonder that Mark still has frequent nightmares of monsters and violence? Or that he did not respond to medication and continues to wet his bed three times a week?

Mark has avoided any efforts to help him talk about his relationship with his uncle. Though he has received some psychiatric help, he needs much more—especially in relation to sexual matters. When he was a small child, it is unlikely that his sexual encounters aroused feelings which bore much resemblance to adult sexual feelings (though adults often assume they do). Now that Mark is entering adolescence, however, the entire area of sexuality will become a major battleground.

CASE II—SALLY

Sally was admitted to a pediatric hospital after her mother told the emergency room staff, "I have just beaten her, and I'm afraid I'll kill her." On subsequent work-up no bruises or evidence of trauma were noted, and a skeletal survey for fractures was negative. Yet Mrs. J insisted that she had beaten the child a number of times in the past to the point of unconsciousness. She claimed the child never did anything right and that she had to beat her to get her to do anything. "That kid is driving me crazy!" the child's mother told a nurse. "I don't want to kill her and have to go to jail."

In the next few days Sally's mother's concern abruptly shifted from physical abuse to focus instead

---

A child's direct revelation of sexual

abuse must be carefully assessed,

for it may be nothing more than fantasy.

---

on Sally's sexual behavior. "She's a fast woman," Mrs. J told the staff. "She kisses like she means business." Sally's mother told of finding the child naked in a closet with a boy on one occasion and of catching her masturbating with her doll on another.

Sally was *not* a teenager. At the time of her admission the child was four and a half years old. Her mother had long seen Sally as acting like a grown woman, especially in sexual areas. Mrs. J confided that as a baby Sally had always "stared at you like an adult." What's more, as a newborn Sally had had breast and vaginal discharges, which her mother saw as signs of mature sexual functioning. This did not seem strange to Mrs. J, who reported that she herself had menstruated at five years of age and was fully developed at nine.

Staff observation of the interaction between Sally and her mother showed Mrs. J to be extremely rejecting of Sally, calling her "worthless and horrible." Once she pushed Sally away forcibly, hard enough to send the child crashing into a wall. The possibility that Sally has been and will continue to be physically abused by her mother must be taken seriously.

Sally herself was insecure and frightened in the hospital. She reacted negatively when she did not receive total attention. The slightest frustration would trigger a barrage of vulgar language from her. The child spoke explicitly of sexual matters to the staff and acted out sexually with other children. During bath times she would compulsively wash her genitals and once she asked a nurse to touch her genitals. "I like you," she explained. "My mommy does it to me, because she likes me." This incident led members of the hospital staff to suspect that Sally had been

directly stimulated sexually by her mother at times.

To a nurse not secure in her own sexuality, Sally's request might be a threatening invitation. As a result she might be punitive and rejecting of Sally. The inclination is for the nurse to place an adult interpretation on Sally's behavior, to see this as a sexual invitation and to react accordingly. One needs to look at this interaction through the child's eyes.

Sally's request is a way of seeking affection. She sees the nurse as an extension of her mother and expects her to react to her in the only way Sally knows adults can act, as her mother does. Since Mrs. J shows her love for Sally by directly stimulating her sexually, Sally sees such behavior as a natural way of communicating affection between adult and child.

For Sally to unlearn the patterns of relating to adults that her mother taught her, she must first come to realize that there are alternate ways of relating that are also satisfying. The nurse must model for Sally these methods of relating. She does this not by taking on an artificial role but simply by being herself with the child.

The nurse's most valuable treatment instrument is her own personality. "I don't have to touch you there to show I like you" can be a therapeutic response. To touch Sally's genitals would be to act as her mother does. Giving her a hug and a kiss or pointing out the other things one does that show affection—feeding her, talking with her—is showing Sally another pattern of demonstrating affection.

Often adults are hesitant to make a response until they are sure how much the child understands about sex. The important issue is not what the child understands, but rather what the adult understands about the child's needs. A child from a disturbed sexual environment needs to be shown loving acceptance in a way that doesn't overstimulate him.

A child can be traumatized by the arousal of strong feelings—whether they are of anxiety, grief, abandonment, excitement, panic, or anger—when he is too emotionally immature to deal with them. And so the child uses all his energy to ward off the stimu-

---

Another pattern which is encouraged in the

absence of parental protection is that often

the child defends himself against being victimized

by identifying with the aggressor.

---

lation which produces these feelings. In this way he tries to avoid being overwhelmed and to prevent the threatened destruction of his personality. He has no resources left to learn how to master the feelings—or, in many cases, to carry on successfully any other activity in his daily life.

Sally was seen by a child psychiatrist, who observed that her doll play was reflective of exposure to overt sexuality. She placed two dolls in a bed together and banged them violently against each other while talking explicitly about sexual behavior. Mrs. J denied that the child had witnessed her in sexual intercourse but thought that Sally might have watched a baby-sitter during such an encounter.

Commentary

There are many factors in this case typical of physical abuse cases. Mrs. J is a lonely woman, without a husband, and living in near poverty. Secondly, Sally was the product of an unwanted pregnancy, which made her a prime target for rejection. And to make matters worse, Mrs. J was herself a battered child. According to the record, she was battered more than any of her siblings, but the more her parents battered her, the more she defied them.

Mrs. J's sexual complaints against her child were a mixture of the commonplace—masturbation—and the bizarre, as in the meaning she gave to Sally's breast and vaginal discharges as an infant. As such they point out one of the difficulties in working with young children, especially in the area of emotional and behavioral problems. Often what is reported as the child's problem is really a matter of the adult's perception. Much of the time parents are fairly accurate observers and reporters, but sometimes their interpretations are markedly at odds with reality. Such is the case with Sally's mother, who sees the child as functioning sexually as an adult.

One might suspect that Sally's mother is seriously disturbed. A social worker saw her as a disorganized

---

Often what is reported as the child's problem is really a matter of the adult's perception.

---

woman who at times appeared psychotic. Mrs. J was evaluated by a psychiatrist, who said that she was extremely "needy and primitive, but not psychotic." Her need for love was so great that she used Sally to meet it. Thus the mother-child relationship satisfied Mrs. J's own momentary needs, and she did not even see Sally's needs.

The primitiveness of which the psychiatrist speaks is reflected in the fact that Mrs. J does not see Sally as a separate individual, but rather as an extension of herself: she named the child after herself. Other indications of her primitiveness are her impulsiveness and immature thinking patterns, characterized by projecting her perception of herself as bad onto her daughter.

Direct observations of Sally's behavior showed a preoccupation with sexual matters and suggested an overstimulating home environment. While children do engage in direct sexual talk and open sexual behavior, such activity in front of adults is rare and in-

dicates that the child has troubling sexual concerns.

Children who are overstimulated by strong feelings usually translate them into some form of motor activity. And so sexually abused children may exhibit overt sexual behavior or a variety of nonsexual behaviors such as fire-setting and hyperactivity. Through such behavior some children hope to alert an adult to their troubled emotions and to secure help. Often the child is looking for information, reassurance that the behavior is acceptable, or relief from feelings of guilt and anxiety.

Because of the premature and excessive stimulation of both sexual and aggressive feelings provided in

---

A child's basic lack of trust in adults, greatly augmented by the parents' failure to physically care for and nurture him, will be an obstacle to other adults in helping him in the future.

---

her environment, Sally has been overwhelmed by these feelings and has not learned healthy means of control over them. Many children from similar situations perceive sexual behavior in violent terms and may become adults for whom fighting is a way of making love or for whom violence brings sexual pleasure. Sally alternates between sexual and aggressive ways of relating to other people.

From the case record it is possible to pick up early clues that the mother-child relationship in Sally's case was to be a troubled one. First of all, it wasn't until the beginning of the fifth month of pregnancy that Sally's mother sought out prenatal care. The history taken at the time revealed there had been two prior miscarriages. Furthermore, Mrs. J informed the nurse that this was an unwanted pregnancy and that her husband had deserted her when he had found out about it. Though vitamins and iron were prescribed by a physician, she did not take them.

As the pregnancy drew to a close, Mrs. J had to give up a job that she enjoyed in order to have Sally and voiced her resentment about this to a nurse. While none of these clues are decisive by themselves, they do add up to a picture of a mother who is experiencing considerable conflict over her pregnancy. Such conflict can be the foundation of rejection, neglect, or physical abuse. The prenatal nurse was in an excellent position to have seen these difficulties.

The nurse who cared for the mother and infant as the child grew also should have noted signs of trouble in the mother-child interaction. Mrs. J's description of Sally "staring at me like an adult" is one. When a mother complains of unusual hostility toward her on the child's part, this is usually an indication that mother herself has strong negative feelings toward the child. Another clue is the meaning Mrs. J attributed to Sally's breast and vaginal discharges, which is indicative of Mrs. J's disturbed sexuality and can only bode ill for the relationship between mother and child.

There was further evidence that the relationship was not going well. At six weeks Sally was hospitalized with diaper rash and diarrhea. The admission was noteworthy in that Sally had become ill while being cared for by another woman. Mrs. J had abruptly turned Sally's care over to a friend for an indefinite period of time because she was "tired of caring for her."

When an infant is abandoned for indefinite periods for ill-defined reasons, the mother is expressing negative feelings about her role as a mother and her relationship to the child. During Sally's brief hospitalization the staff indeed noted poor mother-child interaction. Upon Sally's later hospitalization as a potentially battered child, all of this past evidence came to light.

The presence of either blatant or subtle clues might suggest to the nurse that she look further into the child's background for signs of a deviant sexual environment. In Sally's case the overstimulation of sexual feelings can probably be traced directly to her mother's manipulation of Sally's genitals during bath times. Of course, it is not just the simple presence of any of these clues that is crucial, but rather how they fit into the child's total environment.

Sally's Development

Because Sally was deemed a child in crisis (her hospital diagnosis was severe psychological disorder of early childhood), she was placed in foster care through court action. The major reasons for placement were the poor mother-child relationship and concerns about Mrs. J's physical and sexual abuse of her daughter.

Sally's foster parents made no mention of any sexual difficulties or acting out by the child. Instead, removed from the overstimulating home environment, Sally became quite aggressive and rough with other children. Thus, when Sally's need for love was met in other ways, she no longer had to initiate sexual behavior to get affection. She is now able to concentrate solely on expressing the other strong feeling that overwhelms her—anger at being rejected and abused. Sally was seen in individual therapy twice a week for many months. The focus of the psychotherapeutic work was this anger.

CASE III—HARRY

While most people would not question that direct exposure to sexual activity with an adult affects a child, they overlook the impact of other forms of environmental sexual stimulation on the child. For example, a child may be overstimulated by sharing a bed with a sibling or parent of the opposite sex; lack of privacy and modesty in the family; having a pregnant mother; or even inappropriate sex education information. In the following case a male child witnessed the unreported sexual abuse of a sibling, and the event caused disturbances in his behavior over the next few years.

Harry was admitted into foster care when he was five years old. He and his siblings had all been battered by their mother. The child initially caused no particular trouble, but there were indications from

While most people would not question that direct exposure to sexual activity with an adult affects a child, they overlook the impact of other forms of environmental sexual stimulation.

the child-care workers that Harry was engaging in frequent masturbation and some sex play with other children on the unit.

A month or so later Harry had a routine psychiatric evaluation. He undressed a number of dolls, noting their underpants carefully, removed these, and inspected the doll's body. He commented that boys are different from girls but did not display any anxiety. The psychiatrist felt Harry showed a normal anatomical curiosity for his age.

A few months later a report by his kindergarten teacher included the cryptic remark that "Harry has a rather sophisticated concept of sexual relationships." She offered no explanation. Almost a year passed and staff on Harry's living unit began to report more frequent escapades of sexual involvement with other children, regular bed-wetting, and occasional episodes of fire-setting. Harry was then scheduled for individual therapy.

Inadvertently, the child was assigned a young, inexperienced social worker as a therapist. During the second session he grabbed at the therapist's groin and asked if that was where babies came from. She asked him not to grab her like that, answered his question, and was met by a demand to see her genitals. When she turned down this request, Harry made an obscene gesture and rebuked the therapist in explicit sexual language. The session ended on this note, leaving the young therapist shaken.

The next six months of therapy passed with no recurrence of sexual incidents. Harry, however, was acting out sexually more and more in his living unit. Then, shortly after the therapist announced she was leaving the child care facility, Harry—not quite seven and a half years old—pulled a toy gun on the therapist and ordered her to lie down on the floor.

Had she been a more experienced therapist she might have been more wary. As it was, she complied with the request. Harry promptly dropped the gun and jumped on top of the therapist. When the surprised therapist pushed him off and jumped to her feet, Harry exposed himself, asking her if she would let him have sexual intercourse with her. "I won't tell anyone. It'll be our secret," he coaxed. When the therapist told him he couldn't, Harry threw a temper tantrum, smashing toys and throwing the pieces at her. The therapist was unable to calm Harry down. Harry left the session extremely angry at her.

During the next session Harry spent all his time playing with cars and trucks, smashing them into each other in collisions. Harry filled the air with sounds of sirens, as police, fire trucks, and ambulances rushed to the scene of his accidents. He even had the therapist make a sign saying: "Stop! Emergency! Do Not Get Close," which he posted.

The next and final session between the therapist and Harry was marked by Harry's showing considerable anger. The therapist made a standard interpretation, that Harry was angry because she was leaving. Harry immediately screamed back at her that she was wrong, that he was angry because she had refused his sexual advances.

Over the summer Harry's sexual behavior continued; meanwhile he was no longer in therapy. After a few months he was referred for a psychiatric reevaluation. That session was quite revealing. Harry picked up the receiver of a toy phone and called the police, reporting that there was an emergency and asking that they hurry right over. The new therapist, pretending he was a policeman on the other end of the telephone line, showed concern and asked: "What's wrong? What's happening?"

Harry's reply was, "A big man hurt a little girl by jumping on her. The girl is crying because the man

---

Frequently children who are sexually abused are willingly engaging in affection-seeking behavior and do not perceive the sexual abuse as abnormal, abusive, or traumatic.

---

is hurting her. You have to come and arrest the man and put him in jail and get an ambulance to bring the girl to the hospital." Becoming very agitated, Harry picked up a toy hammer and began to hit himself on the head.

The therapist immediately stopped him. "Why are you doing that? You're not a bad boy," he said.

"I am a bad boy!" Harry protested and tried to resume hitting himself.

The therapist again stopped him and repeated, "Don't hurt yourself. You are a good boy." Having read the summary of the previous therapist's contacts with Harry, he continued, "You saw a man jump on a girl and hurt her. You jumped on your therapist like he did to the girl. Now you're worried that maybe you hurt her and you'll be sent away like the

---

The mother-child relationship satisfied the mother's own momentary needs, and she did not even see her child's needs.

---

man was. You didn't hurt her and you're not bad. Nobody will send you away. Why don't you tell me about the man and the girl?"

Harry poured forth a story of seeing a man sexually abuse one of his older sisters in his house. It was not clear who the man was or which sister was involved, but Harry exhibited considerable anxiety and fear about the attack. Harry and his therapist discussed the matter in considerable detail, and Harry was relieved and reassured by the discussion.

Commentary

Harry, traumatized by witnessing a sexual assault on his sister, tried to deal with the anxiety and fear this aroused in him by recreating the upsetting scene. In reproducing with his first therapist the incident he had watched, however, Harry no longer remained the helpless, frightened observer. Instead he identified with the aggressor.

Harry probably repeated during his reenactment the same words he had heard the assailant say to his sister. The statement "It'll be our secret" was an important clue. A more experienced therapist might have picked up on the language and helped Harry to talk about what was bothering him.

Unfortunately, the inexperienced therapist reacted to the event as if it were a sexual act—that is, as if it reflected sexual motives and needs on the part of the child. Many adults make this simple mistake. It was only when the second therapist acknowledged Harry's nonsexual feelings, paid attention to his anxiety and guilt, that the boy shared with the therapist the traumatic sexual event he had witnessed.

It is important to note that Harry's story came out only after many months of disturbed behavior. When a mental health professional helped him to express what was troubling him, Harry readily revealed his trauma and was able to begin resolving his problem.

Harry's Development

Remarkable changes in Harry's behavior followed the single session with the second therapist. His sexual acting out in the living unit stopped. Even more gratifying, Harry suddenly began learning in school. It was as if energy he had spent in trying to understand the sexual trauma he had experienced was now being diverted into constructive school activity.

Some months later Harry dictated a story into a tape recorder in school for his teacher. In it he told about an 8-year-old boy who falls in love with his attractive teacher. The boy decides he is going to marry the teacher, but he waits until he is grown up to approach her and they have a beautiful wedding. Afterward the boy takes his bride to their new house, and they immediately go upstairs to the bedroom.

The story indicates that at least Harry is now

The important issue is not what the child understands about sex but rather what the adult understands about the child's needs.

---

placing things into some perspective. In it Harry sets aside sexual behavior for when he is grown up. For the time being, he is willing to return to the world of childhood and more appropriate concerns.

Implications for Nursing Staff

Because sexual abuse of children is so horrifying, it's often difficult for adults to accept that it really happens. Nurses are no different than anyone else in this respect. Nevertheless, they must accept sexual abuse as a fact and become alert to the indications of it. They are in the frontlines of the health care delivery system—in schools, in homes, in emergency rooms, in hospitals, and in clinics—and often would be the first to detect behavior problems in children which need further investigation.

When sexual disturbance is found and appropriate care instituted, then the role of the nurse is to help sexually abused children to make a transition in their relationships with adults. In a sense, the children are testing the adults around them to see if they are like their parents. The children's behavior can arouse complex feelings in those who are trying to care for these children, combinations of anger, disgust, anxiety, and shock. Acting on any of these feelings would not be helpful to the children. The two most important qualities for the nurse to possess in this regard are patience and consistency.

The Problem's Panorama

Dealing with child victims of sexual abuse or overstimulation is far from simple. One must look at the sexual abuse not as an isolated episode, but rather in the context of the child's total emotional functioning. Separating the child from the adult aggressor is a necessary but only a first step. Even if such a move eliminates the disturbed sexual behavior that the child may show, it is not enough. For sexual behavior is only the tip of the iceberg. Beneath those superficial manifestations lie many related difficulties.

There will certainly be difficulties in emotional relationships with others and frequently there will be learning difficulties in school and other disturbed behaviors such as bed-wetting, fire-setting, aggressive behavior, age-inappropriate behavior, and nightmares. Feelings of fear and guilt concerning their sexual behavior are also a factor. And since the child victim is likely to have lived in an emotionally depriving environment, the sexual relationship with the involved adult often has satisfied the child's need for affection and closeness.

When separated from the adult, the child will therefore often experience a sense of loss. He has been deprived of what to him has been an emotionally meaningful relationship, probably the only one he has known in his life. The child needs help in handling his feelings of guilt and depression and needs to come to understand that the adult has problems and is unable to care for him in an appropriate manner.

The cases presented in this paper point out how sexual difficulties are a part of a larger, disturbed environment in which the child lives. If intervention is to help the child, it must address itself to this larger environment. It is this environment that allows sexual abuse to occur. The sexual behavior is used to meet other nonsexual needs that the child has, and is

---

Sexual behavior on the part of the sexually abused child is only the tip of the iceberg. Many related difficulties lie beneath.

---

reinforced as a disturbed pattern of relating to others, when these needs are filled by it.

Nurses and other health professionals should not try to deal with the many problems involved in sexual abuse by themselves. Psychiatric consultation should be sought, and in some cases psychiatric treatment for the child may be necessary. The health professional's role is to provide these children with emotionally healthy relationships with adults. The most healing experience for sexually abused children is to learn that there are adults who will care for them, protect, and love them without overstimulating them or overwhelming them with feelings such as those of guilt and fear.

REFERENCE

1. TORMES, Y. M. *Child Victims of Incest.* Denver, Colo., American Humane Association, 1968, p. 10.

BIBLIOGRAPHY

AMERICAN HUMANE ASSOCIATION. *Protecting the Child Victim of Sex Crimes.* Denver, Colo., The Association, 1965.
————. *Sexual Abuse of Children.* Denver, Colo., The Association, 1967.
EATON, A. P., AND VASTBINDER, E. The sexually-molested child. A plan of management. *Clin.Pediatr.* 8:438-441, Aug. 1969.
LEWIS, M., AND SARREL, P. M. Some psychological aspects of seduction, incest, and rape in childhood. *J.Am.Acad.Child Psychiatry* 8:606-619, Oct. 1969.
SCHULTZ, L. G. Child sex victim: social, psychological and legal perspectives. *Child Welfare* 52:148, Mar. 1973.
SWANSON, D. W. Adult sexual abuse of children (the man and circumstances). *Dis.Nerv.Syst.* 29:677-683, Oct. 1969.
WEISS, J., AND OTHERS. Study of girl sex victims. *Psychiatr.Q.* 29:1-27, Jan. 1955.

WHAT PARENTS SHOULD KNOW AND DO ABOUT «KIDDIE PORN»

The production and sale of sex magazines and films— a million dollar business — still threaten thousands of runaways and other vulnerable children.

by Peter Bridge

Child pornography or "kiddieporn" is a hideous aspect of modern life which has spread across the nation. It is really child abuse for profit—big profit. This commercial enterprise involves children as young as three years of age to about seventeen or eighteen, when they usually look too old to be convincing as child performers or models, at which time, almost inevitably, many turn to prostitution as a continuing way of life.

"What Parents Should Know and Do About Kiddie Porn," Peter Bridge, *Parents Magazine,* Vol. LIII, No. 1 January 1978. ©1978 Parents Magazine.

More boys than girls are involved, but both sexes have been used. All told, it's estimated that some 300,000 children are being victimized at any given moment; their numbers are augmented each year by about 60,000 or 70,000 children, recruited mostly from the ranks of the runaways. (These numbers include not only teenagers, but also frequently children under ten who often have no idea of what they're getting involved in.)

Currently there are some 260 magazines featuring juvenile sex themes, illustrated by photographs of young boys and girls involved in a variety of provocative poses and sexual activities; they are shown by themselves, in pairs and groups, or in acts involving both children and adults.

In addition, there are thousands of film "loops" (short films which keep repeating as long as the film

PHOTOGRAPH BY J. B. CUNY-PANICKER/PHOTOREPORTERS

is run) and reels, as well as posters, books and other materials still being sold throughout the country. These materials cost only pennies to produce, for the most part, but up to hundreds of dollars to buy. Thousands of film reels, for example, are made from a single negative so that the cost of making these films vanishes by the time they reach the marketplace, where they bring anywhere from $25 to several hundred dollars each. Magazines produced for 25 cents or less a copy, market for up to ten dollars each.

"Moppets," a magazine which depicts children of both sexes, three to eight years old, sells for between five and seven dollars; "Lillitots," featuring children eleven to fourteen, sells for about the same price. Other titles include: "Incest, the Game the Whole Family Can Play," "Torrid Tots," "Suckulant Youth" and "Chicken Brats." The term "chicken" refers to the child prostitutes who become the victims of "hawks," or adults. Police know the whole activity as "chicken-hawking."

The manufacture of child pornography is a repulsive activity condemned even by those who advocate the rights of adults to view, or participate in, pornographic activities. Stanley Fleishman, a West Coast attorney who represents the Adult Film Association of America, and David Friedman, the Board Chairman of this association are both on record supporting measures to control the production of "toilet material," as they describe pornographic materials involving children.

The existence of kiddieporn as business—big business —first came to public attention less than a year ago through the efforts of Professor Frank Osanka of Lewis University in Glen Ellyn, Illinois, and Dr. Judianne Densen-Gerber, founder of Odyssey International, an organization devoted to the rehabilitation of drug-abusers.

Dr. Osanka discovered that child pornography had become a widespread commercial enterprise at about the same time that Dr. Densen-Gerber made a similar discovery. Dr. Osanka was teaching his class on child abuse—the only accredited college-level course on the subject—when a student showed him a magazine and asked how he related it to child abuse. Dr. Densen-Gerber said she received a copy of a kiddieporn magazine in the mail with an unsigned note asking for her reaction.

Their response was immediate and energetic. Together and separately they held a series of press conferences in cities throughout the country call-

ing attention to these activities and demanding action. Dr. Osanka observes that when "the heat was on," while they were loudly and vigorously protesting the availability of such material, it did become scarce in the cities in which they were speaking. But after they left, it went right back on the shelves.

Professor Osanka regards all kiddieporn as a special form of child abuse and, indeed, some pornographic materials are specifically geared to child-abusers whose fantasies link violence against children with having sexual relationships with them. "Child Discipline" is a primer on how to derive sexual satisfaction from beating children. "Lust for Children"—complete with instructions on how to avoid successful prosecution— claims that a little girl's

screams when she is being sexually attacked are actually cries of pleasure.

But all of the children involved in kiddieporn are abused. As Dr. Osanka emphasizes, taking part in such activities deadens and corrupts children's feelings; it leaves them empty of natural emotion. "They reach a point where they cannot relate to anybody except on a sexual plane," he observes. "They are shells."

Dr. Osanka argues that the members of the middle class are deceived if they suppose that the victimized children come entirely or mainly from poverty or crime-ridden areas. The children involved are mainly runaways from all classes, backgrounds and parts of the country. "Most of them wind up in the cities—New York, Chicago or Los Angeles," he points out. "It's no accident, then, that these cities are also the centers for the production of kiddieporn." Recruiting runaway youngsters is heartbreakingly easy. Often little more than a kind word will do it. Knowing this, manufacturers and purveyors of child pornography have scouts out at bus stations, train terminals and airports where they expertly and easily spot the runaways.

Who are the consumers of kiddieporn? According to undercover police in New York City who operated a porn shop in Times Square last year, "The customers are usually white, middle-class men. They're dressed in suits and ties, and carry attaché cases. They pay whatever the price is and walk out with magazines, playing cards, films or what have you. Their favorite subjects are young boys and very young girls. A week or so later, if it's a film they've purchased, they'll bring it back and trade it in for a part of its purchase price on another. They usually come in during lunch or just after work. Women rarely, if ever, buy child pornography."

This description of the typical customer is particularly shocking because it describes seemingly well-adjusted people. One tends, in thinking of such tastes, to suppose that they're held by real "freaks," easily recognizable as deranged.

Why our society harbors so many people driven by inner weaknesses, fear or anger, which surface as compulsions to view or engage in this kind of debased behavior is a question too complicated to take up here. Whatever the causes, and whatever help might be forthcoming for the

consumers of kiddieporn, some people believe that their actions—as buyers of this material—should also be punishable by law. This might be difficult to accomplish, since a purchaser of a magazine could claim he had no idea of the contents—though the titles alone make that clear—but just bought it without really looking inside. The sellers, too, as well as the producers of these materials, might be subject to criminal proceedings. An analogy can be made to the inappropriateness of punishing prostitutes by law, while their clients, the "johns," are deemed legally innocent.

If sellers and purchasers of this material were subject to arrest, crackdowns would be more effective. As it is, when "the heat is off," as Professor Osanka's past experience shows, the pornographic retailers are back in business.

That's why he and Dr. Densen-Gerber have continued to urge for legislation prohibiting the use of children in pornography. To date they have been partially successful. Both the Senate and the House have adopted bills applying criminal penalties for using children for such purposes and for transporting children—including males—across state lines for pornographic purposes.

However, such federal legislation will solve only part of the problem. Strong state laws are also needed. Dr. Osanka points out that today only twenty-two of the 50 states have laws relating to the subject, and approval is expected in six other states. As the 1978 congressional sessions begin, eleven other states are expected to consider child pornography bills. Most of them are open to constitutional questions.

Still, the crusade against child pornography has caused widespread awareness of the problem, and this, in the long run will be a powerful deterrent to the continuation of this "industry." As pornographic material disappeared from the shops when it came under attack, so does it disappear when groups picket stores marketing such items.

Redoubling efforts in the home to communicate sympathetically but firmly with children will also be an important help, says Dr. Osanka, because it can substantially reduce the number of runaways and therefore the "raw material" for the kiddieporn producers.

The common trait of runaways, as Dr. Osanka points out, is alienation. "They come from homes in which

constructive communication with their parents has altogether broken down." Include here parents who want to be "involved" but have somehow lost touch with their children. Re-establishing communication when there is distrust between the generations is admittedly terribly hard. But it is essential. If a child is already hostile and rebellious, the parent's role is very difficult. Any parent who has been there, has learned—the hard way—that two things count the most. The first is to be unequivocally clear about your own views of right and wrong. Don't be swayed or put down by a child who says you're square. Don't be afraid to be unpopular with your child, or think you'll lose his or her love.

The second course to follow if a child is close to an open break is *not* to present the child with a final either-or choice. Do what you can to stop him from acts you consider wrong, but always leave the door open for him or her to retreat from his stance without losing face.

Actually, some runaways are running to save their lives. Dr. Osanka points out that thousands of children —again not just from deprived backgrounds—are in more jeopardy in their homes than they would be alone in some faraway city.

In any case, runaways are not the only source of "actors" for pornographers. There are some adults who are quite willing to "sell" or "rent" their children or wards to pornographers. A social worker in Rockford, Illinois, was arrested and jailed for "renting" his three foster sons to pornography producers for $150 each an "appearance." Some drug-addicted adults, stooping to anything, have "leased" their children to pornographers, for the price of a fix.

Even now, books, magazines, films and playing cards are for sale throughout the nation. Dr. Osanka, who travels the country appearing on television and radio programs, campaigning against child pornography says, "I grew up an orphan and, as far as I'm concerned, a molested child." Had child pornography been as widespread and active an enterprise when he was growing up as it is now, he believes he might have ended up one of its victims. That strong sense of "there but for the grace of God, go I," is a part of the reason behind Dr. Osanka's intense efforts to protect children from this most corrupt and abusive of activities.

THE TERROR OF CHILD MOLESTATION

Whether or not a child is ever assaulted is not simply a matter of chance; there is a great deal parents can do to help their youngsters protect themselves against dangerous strangers.

The Terror of Child Molestation

There is no more hideous crime than the sexual molestation of a child. Even in the criminal world—among those convicted of assault and murder—the child molester is viewed with scorn and disgust. Yet, it happens. And though reliable statistics don't exist, it's evident from the cases that are reported that child molestation is not uncommon, and may be increasing.

Although there are no national figures on forced sexual activity with prepubertal youngsters, isolated studies suggest that of every 50 victims of rape, at least three, and perhaps as many as six, are children. Jack L. Paradise, M.D., Associate Professor of Pediatrics and Community Medicine at the University of Pittsburgh School of Medicine and Medical Director of the Ambulatory Care Center at Children's Hospital of Pittsburgh, estimates that his hospital's emergency room sees one such victim each month.

These cases represent only those that are reported and recorded. They don't include the unreported incidents and cases seen by private physicians, which don't become part of the public record. Nor do they include those emotional and physical assaults on children which fall short of rape—that of the exhibitionist, the seducer, the pawer. These are as real, and maybe as damaging, as rape, itself.

All parents hope their children will never have such a terrible experience. And though parents cannot wholly control the environment in which their children live, there are steps to take to help protect a daughter—or a son, for boys, too, are sometimes the victims of sexual molesters—from the threat of such assault.

"The basics that have been taught by our parents and grandparents are a good place to start," says Dr. Virginia E. Pomeranz, Associate Clinical Professor of Pediatrics at Cornell University Medical College. "Both boys and girls, should be

---

SAFETY QUIZ FOR YOUNG SCHOOLCHILDREN

prepared with the cooperation of Detective Jack Meeks, Crime Prevention Section, New York City Police Department

Q. You are walking home from school with your friend Tony, when a car comes along and a nice-looking man leans out and calls, "Hey, Tony! Your mother had to go to the store and she says I should drive you there to meet her. Come on, climb in!" Tony says, "I don't know you!" but the man says "That's okay, I'm a friend of your mother's. Come on!" What should you and Tony do?

A. Neither you nor your friend should go with anybody you don't know, no matter what he says. If something like this happens, walk as fast as you can in the direction opposite to the way the car is traveling, even if that means going back the way you came. Tell the first policeman you see, or a teacher, or grownup you know, about the man.

Q. The telephone in your house rings, and you answer it. A man's voice you don't know says, "Hi! Are your Mommy and Daddy home?" What should you say?

A. If a strange person calls, always ask, "Who is this, and who do you want?" If the person doesn't then say who he is and ask for somebody by name, hang up. Never tell anybody you don't know whether or not your mother or father is home, or who else is or isn't there home, or who else is or isn't there.

Q. Your doorbell rings. There is just one thing you should do. Do you know what it is?

A. Tell your mother, father, babysitter, or another older person that the bell rang. Don't answer the door yourself until you are older. Note to parents: Young school-age children shouldn't be left alone in a house or apartment; there is always the possibility of forced or deceptive entry, as well as the risk of fire or other mishap.

Q. You and your friends are playing in the schoolyard at lunchtime, and you notice a man standing on the other side of the fence watching the kids. After a few minutes he takes some candy bars or cookies or a toy out of his pocket, and motions for you and your friends to come over. Is it okay to go?

A. No. Don't approach, and never accept anything from a stranger. If something like this happens, tell a teacher right away.

PHOTOGRAPH BY ED LETTAU

taught to play in well-lighted areas within sight of adults and to stay away from dark, deserted areas such as alleys, lonely roads, abandoned buildings or the basements of apartment houses—as much to avoid muggers as sexual deviates.

"Young children should be warned to clear out without delay when approached by strangers—whether such persons are offering candy, suggesting car rides or asking the time or directions; it doesn't make sense for an adult to ask the time or directions of a young child, and an adult who does has something less than good intentions. The key word is: run—preferably home, or to the nearest home or neighborhood business where there are adults known to the child."

Dr. Paradise adds, "Most children have enough sense to avoid seedy-looking characters; but they should also be wary of strangers who may look perfectly presentable but whose behavior—say, in trying to start a conversation in an isolated situation—is questionable."

Nor should a child tolerate aberrant behavior on the part of someone she knows. Susan Brownmiller, author of *Against Our Will* (a history of rape), reports that three-quarters of the molesters in one study were previously known to the child. "Children should be told," says Dr. Pomeranz, "to avoid anyone acting 'funny'—in a manner that doesn't seem normal to the child—and to report such behavior to the parents, whether or not any sexual advance or assault has occurred." If it is the custom of your neighborhood candy-store proprietor to dispense free lollipops to the children on the block, that's one thing; but if, say, an elevator operator in an apartment building suddenly singles out one child, riding alone, for special gifts or attention, that may be something quite different.

It is important, too, to always know where your children are, and with whom. If your child walks to and from school, or goes part of the way on foot, and the route is not well lighted and well traveled, make sure that the child does not walk alone. You should know your child's schedule and be sure that there is no dawdling on the way to and from school. If a child must come home after dark, see that the child is escorted by an adult or a responsible teenager. Know your children's exact whereabouts when they are playing outside your home.

Most parents are concerned about how to forewarn a child without unduly frightening the youngster. Should you go into such detail that the child is likely to develop an inordinate fear of strangers?

Child-care authorities agree that you should not. Most youngsters, exposed to daily reports of violent behavior on the news media, are well aware that there are dangerous and disturbed people in the community. Children should not be led to feel that they are likely to be singled out as victims, but that you are acquainting them with the kind of precautions taken by all prudent people—precautions especially applicable to relatively small and weak people, children.

David A. Kahn, M.D., Assistant Professor of Child Psychiatry at Hahnemann Medical College in Philadelphia, says, "It's best not to lay down a set of 'don't' rules, but rather to discuss protective measures which should be observed by all members of the family, parents and teenagers as well as younger children. It is important for the child to understand that these are not merely directives pertaining to polite and impolite behavior; they are important matters of family concern. A news item reporting a violent incident, whatever the age of the victim, can be conveniently used to initiate such a discussion."

Steven Levenkron, a psychotherapist associated with the Department of Psychiatry at Montefiore Hospital and Medical Center, agrees. "Parents should not carry their warnings to an excessive point. Children should not receive the impression that all grown men are bad or suspect. It is best to characterize people who interfere with the persons and liberties of others as exceptions. The point to be emphasized is that it is not

by DODI SCHULTZ
Co-author (with Virginia E. Pomeranz, M.D.), "The Mothers' and Fathers' Medical Encyclopedia"

always possible to distinguish one from the other on first appearance—and it is particularly difficult for a young child, who has had little experience in judging human nature and behavior."

A related question is: How should a parent explain a news item referring expressly to "sexual molestation" and perhaps involving a child?

It should certainly be stressed that sex is not evil, Steven Levenkron points out, "A youngster growing up with that idea will have great difficulty later on in a marital relationship. Sexual relations properly take place between consenting adults, in private. Those few individuals who do not respect this basic principle, who try to force their attentions upon others and who sometimes are attracted to children rather than to adults are, I think, best characterized as 'strange' and 'not quite right'—men who are ill and need help but, who meanwhile represent a danger to others."

An incident involving exposure can be used, Dr. Kahn notes, as an opportunity to further enlighten a child. "This can be done without moralizing. A parent can describe such behavior as sick, pointing out that those of us who care about our bodies show them only to those we know and love. A child thus learns that sexual activity is right and acceptable under special conditions, but not under others."

Despite all precautions, there remains the possibility that an assault might be attempted upon your child. Physical assault on a child, with sexual intent, can range from kissing to attempts to fondle the child's genitals to actual penetration. Whatever the nature and degree of the assault, it can prove extremely shocking to the child. Physicians and psychologists report many tragic instances of the effects of such experiences haunting the youngsters for years. But they also emphasize that lasting trauma can be prevented—with appropriate management by the child and the parents.

Appropriate behavior on the child's part is simply reporting the incident fully—but it is the parents' task to see that the child will be able to do so. Steven Levenkron points out, "No one, child or adult, can be truly prepared for the violation of mind and body that takes place in a sexual assault. But children can be given the language which will enable them to relate the experience and to express their feelings about it. The inability to do so has led to a great deal of persistent misery—lasting in cases I have seen, into the person's teens, twenties and thirties.

"A child should be able to report to you with no hesitancy, that, 'The man was walking around with his penis hanging out,' or that 'He wanted to touch my vagina.' If the child does not know the proper words, or you

have made the youngster feel that certain parts of the body are unmentionable, then she cannot communicate either the details of the event or her distress. If a child has an accurate vocabulary which she feels comfortable using, such an incident is more likely to be reported to you as readily as any other unsettling experience.

"Another point is that the child must feel free to complain about adult behavior which she senses to be strange or repulsive. Most children, for example, are used to being kissed by their parents and relatives; many are also greeted in this manner by close friends of their parents—and while they do not all like it, they accept it. It should be made clear to a child that not all adults have that privilege, and that a person's body is one's own. Kisses are normally perceived by a child as simple gestures of affection, but the youngster need not and should not be afraid to object fiercely if a stranger tries the same, no matter how innocent his appearance and bearing.

"This concept should be communicated to children in simple language, with no sexual overtones. People simply should not embrace or caress others who do not wish to be so touched, and the child who objects is wholly in the right, despite the fact that the aggressor is a grownup and hence part of a group the child has normally been encouraged to obey.

"Simple verbal objections raised by a child can, in fact, be a significant defense against intended or attempted assault. Experts point out that a man who makes advances to a small child may actually be aroused by his victim's fearful compliance, but may be effectively put off by the child who is able to say boldly, 'Don't do that! I don't like it!' "

A young child who has been sexually molested, whether or not actual rape or other physical harm has occurred, has been through a terrifying and, perhaps, incomprehensible experience. It is difficult for any parent to remain calm under such circumstances—but it is vital to the child's future well-being.

Any parent would react, initially, with anger. "It is probably foolish," Dr. Paradise concedes, "for parents to try and hide their outrage. On the other hand, it is a mistake to treat the situation differently than if the child had been molested in any way other than sexually. The issue should be dealt with as one of injury or attempted injury by someone who is disturbed, without emphasizing the sexual aspects."

It is also important that there be no mistake, in the child's mind, as to the target of the parents' anger. The child has been embarrassed, humiliated and, very likely, physically overpowered. She may wonder if some

weakness on her part played a role in what happened. Further, the child may feel truly guilty—not only because of actual disobedience (she may, in fact, have ignored parental directives to avoid a particular area), but in another, more subtle sense.

Dr. Kahn explains: "Many adults don't realize that small children have not yet learned that events take place independently of them. They connect pleasant experiences with adults to their own good behavior. Conversely, unpleasant ones are associated in their mind with misbehavior on their part, with some violation of the mysterious and complex rules of the grown-up world. It's very common, for example, for children of divorcing or separating parents to feel that they must be responsible, and to view the event as a punishment for their faults or misdeeds. So, a child who has been assaulted may feel that she has somehow caused or contributed to the event, that she has been bad."

If there has been a rape or other injury, that should be the first concern, and the necessity for a doctor to see the youngster should be explained to her, but with no sexual overtones, whether or not the injury involves the genitals. It is best, Dr. Pomeranz believes, for the child to be seen by a physician they know. "Probably the best person to examine a girl is the mother's gynecologist. A boy—or a girl, if the mother has no regular gynecologist—can be taken to a pediatrician or family physician. If your doctor is not available, the child should be taken to a hospital emergency room. In any case, a parent—preferably the parent of the same sex—should stay with the child throughout the examination and any treatment that may be necessary."

Psychotherapist Levenkron adds: "Be sure the child understands what's happening during the examination of the genital or rectal area—the doctor is 'checking to make sure that everything is okay.' The parent should give the child a reassuring but honest and realistic explanation should there be physical damage to be repaired. Pain that may occur is best described by

saying something like, 'This may hurt and you may be somewhat uncomfortable for a while, but it will be better very soon.' "

Next, whether or not the child has been physically injured, the incident should be reported to the police. Some parents are reluctant to do this, perhaps because they feel it will subject the child to a further reliving of the event, and that it is best dismissed from the child's mind as quickly as possible. But such things cannot really be forgotten that quickly or easily. Further, it is a disservice to all children not to try to help apprehend a child molester.

Before the youngster faces the police, parents should try gently to elicit a full report of the incident and description of the attacker. Then, when the child does speak to the police, be sure you're also present, and try to keep the interview as brief as possible.

In talking to the police, as well as in private discussions, it's important not to grill the child. Dr. Kahn suggests that parents listen quietly and show serious concern. Prompt the child to recall details without demanding instant answers. Be patient. The child may not understand that an adult is anxious to get the facts quickly so the offender may be apprehended quickly. Bear in mind that in most instances, the child has not been suddenly and violently accosted. Most often, there has been a friendly approach or prelude, the child's confidence has been gained, and then what may have begun as a casual "touching game" turned without warning to serious, purposeful aggression or violence. The child is understandably confused. It is probably best to point out that the individual must be quite sick, and that you would like to find him because he needs help.

How can parents help children who have been assaulted, avoid lasting emotional trauma? Is professional counseling necessarily needed? Should the child be seen right away by a psychiatrist or psychologist?

Dr. Kahn doesn't think therapy is necessarily indicated for the child. It is rather the parents, he thinks, who may benefit most by discussing their initial feelings and reactions with a trusted counselor. "That person might be a psychiatrist, a psychologist or any other qualified individual—anyone the parents trust, whether physician, psychologist, social worker or other counselor who understands interpersonal relations. Only if there are hints, after a couple of months, that the child remains disturbed is therapy advised."

Certain kinds of temporary distress are to be expected and are not causes for additional concern. The child may, for instance, have recurrent nightmares, dreams in which the event is relived. "That," says Dr. Kahn, "is a common and normal reaction to a frightening event in which the pervasive emotion was helplessness. The bad dreams will lessen over a period of time. Meanwhile, the parents should assure the child that they understand, that one can have things on one's mind which are very scary and that these sometimes come out at night instead of in the daytime. Of course, the child should be reminded and reassured that the frightening experience is over. It won't recur, and she is safe."

Nor should parents be unduly concerned if, for a time, there is a certain sensitivity associated with the part of the child's body, that has been treated roughly. "This, too," Dr. Kahn observes, "is a normal reaction. Even in the absence of actual physical injury, the child may deliberately refrain from touching the area or having it touched by anyone else. The parents should express sympathy—'I understand, you feel kind of uncomfortable'—and reassure the child that there will be no lasting injury and the feeling will in time go away."

If these effects persist after two or three months, the child should receive therapy in order to prevent the possibility of more serious problems occurring in the future.

Parents should be alert, too, to the possibility of persistent guilt feelings on the child's part, which—if allowed to continue—may cause difficulties in subsequent teenage boy-girl relationships and later on in marriage. "A sign which may indicate a persistent feeling of guilt in the child," says Dr. Kahn, "is continued deliberate misbehavior. The child feels bad or evil and may start to behave badly at home, at school or both. It is important for parents to recognize such changes in the child's behavior and to seek help promptly."

Finally, Levenkron suggests that even if all seems well, it is advisable for a girl who was raped in childhood to have the benefit of preventive therapy when she becomes an adolescent. This is essentially an emotional checkup to make sure that the tumultuous teen years will not be further complicated by a girl's distorted attitude resulting from the earlier frightening experience. "Counseling at this crucial time can resolve conflicts and help to assure that her future emotional and sexual relationships will be healthy and happy."

WHAT PORNOGRAPHERS ARE DOING TO CHILDREN: A SHOCKING REPORT

A new pornography—magazines and films showing very young children in explicit sexual acts—is growing rapidly. The time has come to stop this moral outrage before it goes any further. Here is a frank discussion of the challenge we face

by Judianne Densen-Gerber

On January 12, 1977, at the Crossroads, an adult bookstore in New York City, I purchased Lollitots, a magazine showing pornographic pictures of girls aged eight to 14, and Moppets, a magazine illustrated with pornographic photographs of children three to 12. I bought a deck of playing cards that pictured naked, spread-eagled children. I looked at a film showing children violently deflowered on their First Communion day at the feet of a "crucified" priest replacing Jesus on the Cross. I saw a film showing an alleged father engaged in bizarre sexual practices with his four-year-old daughter. Of 64 films presented for viewing, 35 showed children; 16 of these involved incest.

In the months since January, I have personally purchased magazines carrying the titles Nudist Moppets, Chicken Delight, Lust for Children, Schoolgirls, Naughty Horny Imps, Chicken Love and Child Discipline, and seen films such as Children Love and Lollipops #10. I found them in New York, Philadelphia, Boston, Washington, New Orleans, Detroit, Flint, Chicago, San Francisco, San Jose and Los Angeles— and even in Sydney, Melbourne and Canberra, Australia. And I have become angered beyond description.

I first became aware of the million-dollar sex-for-sale industry that is exploiting America's children through my work with Odyssey Institute's Concerns of Children Division.

Since then I have traveled all over the country amassing evidence, holding news conferences, determined to bring this disgrace to the attention of the public—and to put a stop to it.

According to the book *For Money or Love: Boy Prostitution in America*, by Robin Lloyd, an investigative reporter for NBC News in Los Angeles, there are at least 264 different boy and girl porn magazines being sold in adult bookstores nationwide. These magazines— slickly produced—sell for prices averaging more than $7 each. Most of the children exploited are runaways from extremely abusive and neglectful homes—most of the children, that is, who are eight years old or older. But younger children used in the production of pornography—some as young as three—must be provided by their parents or guardians, who themselves often are drug addicts, porn performers, prostitutes or, more frequently, parents having incestuous relationships with their children that they wish to memorialize in photographs or movies to exchange with others who belong to clubs or groups advocating this type of activity. There is one group in southern California—it claims 2,500 members!—whose slogan is "Sex by eight or it's too late." Too late for what? To grow up loved and protected and unscarred?

Robin Lloyd's book documented the involvement of 300,000 boys, aged eight to 16, in activities revolving around sex for sale, including both pornography and prostitution. A common-sense "guesstimate" on my part leads me to believe that if there are 300,-000 boys, there must be a like number of girls, but no one has bothered to count the females involved. (Lloyd postulated but cannot substantiate that only half the true number of these children is known. That would put the figure closer to 1.2 million nationwide—a figure that is not improbable to me, considering the nation's 1 million runaways. How many ways are there for a 12-year-old to support himself or herself?)

In an April Ms. magazine article titled "Incest: Sexual Abuse Begins at Home," the following startling fact was noted: "One girl out of every four in the United States will be sexually abused in some way before she reaches the age of 18." Researchers working with deviant women report that 50 to 70 per cent were sexually traumatized as children. This is truly an illustration of the sins of the parents' being visited upon the children.

We hide from the knowledge of incest; we have been even more ostrichlike in the area of the commercial sexual abuse of children. Only six states specifically prohibit the participation of minors in an obscene performance that could be harmful to them (Connecticut, North Carolina, North Dakota, South Carolina, Tennessee and Texas), although other states are considering such legislation. There is no Federal statute that specifically regulates or restricts the production, distribution or marketing of pornographic material involving children. Neither is there a Federal statute prohibiting the distribution of pornographic material to children.

Forty-seven states and the District of Columbia have laws in some way pertaining to the dissemination of obscene materials to minors. But state criminal statutes that deal with sex crimes often are not helpful, either because the physical activity does not meet the criteria of the statute—for example, rape, sodomy, sexual abuse—or because they are so broadly worded as to discourage courts from applying them in terms of significant penalties.

Many states have child-welfare provisions within their education laws that regulate the employment of children in commercial activities. Unfortunately, either these same laws abdicate control when the child is working for a parent or the sanctions are so limited—a $10 fine or ten days in jail—as to pose no deterrent.

Given the paucity of legislation that relates specifically to child pornography,

there can be little wonder at the relatively few attempts at law enforcement. The problems of case-finding and evidence are compounded by a confusion between sexploitation as a form of child abuse and adult-obscenity matters. These problems and the attitudes of many judges discourage and actually thwart the few criminal investigations attempted.

This year, for instance, when one of America's leading pornographers, Edward Mishkin, was arrested in New York, one third of the enormous quantity of material confiscated involved children. Mr. Mishkin pleaded guilty, and in spite of the fact that he had had many previous convictions, acting Justice Irving Lang, of the New York State Supreme Court, sentenced him to 27 consecutive weekends in jail—I assume so that his workweek destroying children would not be interrupted. We as citizens must ask why Judge Lang did not give Mishkin the seven-year maximum sentence. Mishkin went right back to work, and was rearrested on like charges within one week.

If you want to do your part in putting an end to this vicious abuse of children, I urge you to write to your Federal and state legislators, asking that they support the three-pronged approach suggested by Odyssey's Law and Medicine Institute. First, to make changes in your state education law to require licensing of all media involving children and to prohibit children from participating in any sexually explicit acts, any material produced in violation to be confiscated. Second, to strengthen the child-abuse and neglect statutes to include commercial sexual exploitation of children and to make the findings of venereal disease in children under 12 an automatic presumption of child abuse and neglect. (In 1976 Connecticut passes such a law on venereal disease because there has been two cases of gonorrhea of the throat in children under 18 months of age and one in a child nine months old with that state.) And third, to create greater penalties under the obscenity laws if the offending material involves persons under 16.

There comes a point at which we no longer can defend atrocities by intellectualization of forensic debate. We must simply say: "I know the difference between right and wrong and I am not afraid to say

no or to demand that limits be imposed."

Common sense and maternal instinct tell me that these abuses are not a question of freedom of speech and press. Children are not consenting adults; they are victims whose spirits are mutilated as their bodies are violated. This is a matter of child abuse and should be dealt with through child-abuse laws.

It is outrageous for someone to publish a primer instructing a sex molester on how to pick up a child in the park and subsequently assault her sexually ("Lust for Children") or for someone else to issue a booklet advocating that a father have incestuous relations with his daughter and illustrating positions to be used if she, at nine, is too small for normal penetration ("Schoolgirls" and "Preteen Sexually").

We are not going to produce mentally healthy and happy children by issuing an executive order that all children must be loved. But we can author legislation to protect them and give them a fighting chance in this world. To paraphrase the French writer Camus, speaking for all of us who in some way work with children or care about them:

"Perhaps we cannot prevent this America from being an America in which children are tortured...but we can reduce the number of tortured children. And if you don't help us ... who else in this world can...?"

You and I can make a difference. Since my initial news conference in January, 1977, in front of the Crossroads store, much of "kid porn" has disappeared from New York's adult bookstores--and the Crossroads itself has been closed. It was so simple; the answer was so clear: If we can still be outraged, if we can still care, we can begin to nurture a soil for all children to grow straight and strong.

As psychoanalyst Erik Erikson wrote: "Someday, maybe, there will exist a well-informed, well-considered and yet fervent public conviction that the most deadly of all possible sins is the mutilation of a child's spirit; for such mutilation undercuts the life principle of trust, without which every human act, may it feel ever so good, and seem ever so right is prone to perversion by destructive forms of consciousness."

NO FAMILY IS SAFE FROM CHILD ABUSE. NOT EVEN YOURS.

Let's say you're lucky. Your family isn't one in which child abuse occurs.

But, because it is estimated that there are more than one million cases of child abuse in America each year, the chances are someone you know, or someone your child knows, is a victim of child abuse.

Child abusers are as much the victims of a vicious cycle as the children they abuse — whether the abuse is physical, sexual, emotional, or neglect. Abused children learn abuse as a way of life. When they become parents, they pass that learning on to their own children. If your child were to marry an abused child, you probably wouldn't know about it until your first grandchild was born. And then it might be too late, unless those parents receive help. Get more information, now, on how you can help break the cycle of child abuse.

HELP DESTROY A FAMILY TRADITION. WRITE:
National Committee for Prevention of Child Abuse, Box 2866, Chicago, Ill. 60690.

106

SEXUAL
INCEST
ABUSE
BEGINS
AT HOME

BY ELLEN WEBER

One girl out of every four in the United States will be sexually abused in some way before she reaches the age of 18. Although it is widely assumed that her assailant will be a mysterious pervert, according to a 1967 survey conducted in New York City by the American Humane Association, only one quarter of all sexual molestations are committed by strangers. Only 2 percent take place in cars; only 5 percent in abandoned buildings. In a full 75 percent of the cases, the victim knows her assailant. In 34 percent, the molestation takes place in her own home.

Molestations by a stranger are generally one-time occurrences, but in the case of incest or sexual abuse by a known assailant, the victim may be trapped in a relationship for years. And while the guilt and shock of a sexual encounter with a stranger are often defused by supportive parental reaction, the family of a sexual abuse victim often fails to intervene on her behalf.

Sexual abuse occurs in families of every social, economic, and ethnic background and runs the gamut from "fondling" to fellatio, cunnilingus, sodomy, and, ultimately, full intercourse. Little girls as young as four or five may be shown dirty pictures in magazines, or forced to pose nude in seductive poses. The average age of sexual abuse victims is 11 years, and victims have been as young as eight months.

Since sexual abuse often begins before a child understands its significance, force is rarely involved; the perpetrator uses his position of authority or trust to convince the naïve child that their relationship is "for her own good," or a normal part of growing up. According to several psychiatrists, when the victim learns the truth, she may feel both betrayed by the offender, and guilty and ashamed about her own cooperation. At this point, the victim will usually resist the relationship, only to be frightened with stronger and stronger threats; but her own sense of complicity may prevent her from asking anyone else for help.

Even when help is sought, the family may close its eyes to the charge out of a sense of loyalty to the offender, the fear of public embarrassment, or perhaps the loss of a father's income. The mother may not want to believe her husband capable of such atrocious behavior, or she may simply feel powerless to do anything about it. Dorothy Ross, coordinator of a sexual abuse treatment center in California, explains "Sometimes mothers are afraid of being beaten or of their family's being broken up or of the loss of financial support. Often it's a vague fear of not knowing what to do, where to go, what's going to happen." Sometimes the girl is actually blamed.

Some experts have found a correlation between sexual abuse and later antisocial behavior. Dr. Richard Burnstine, a Chicago pediatrician, has found that nearly all the girls at Chapin Hall, a home for disturbed and homeless children, had been sexually abused. A large portion of adolescent runaways are children trying to escape from a sexually abusive relationship. When physical escape proves impossible, they may embark on long careers of drug use. John Siverson, a family therapist in Minneapolis who has treated more than 500 cases of adolescent drug addiction, reports that some 70 percent of his clients were caught in some form of family sexual abuse. The same is true of 44 percent of the female population at Odyssey House—a residential drug treatment program with centers in seven states—and out of the 52 cases only two had ever been reported to the authorities.

Women who have been sexually abused as children [the ratio of girls to boys in reported cases is 10 to 1] report adult sexual problems, ranging from an inability to achieve orgasm to a total revulsion for heterosexual relations. Many of the victims interviewed for this article strongly believe that the only thing any man is after is sex, and that all they (the victims) are good for is sex. Not surprisingly then, many sexual abuse victims turn to promiscuity or prostitution at some time in their lives. In a recent study of adolescent prostitutes in the Minneapolis area, it was found that 75 percent of them were victims of incest. It is also suspected by several clinical psychologists that the victim's feelings of low self-worth, and distaste for sex, make victims prone to marrying men who will sexually abuse their daughters.

The National Center on Child

ent," says Dorothy Ross, a California probation officer and the coordinator of the Child Sexual Abuse Treatment Program in San Jose, California. "But the idea of a father having sex with his own daughter is so horrible, so abhorrent, we don't want to believe it goes on."

In a study of 20 families involved in incest, the American Humane Association noted that 10 of these families had had contact with several public agencies "without revealing that the violation of society's most fundamental taboo was a feature of their home life."

As Dr. Jacob Lebsack, associate director of the National Study on Child Neglect and Abuse Reporting in Denver, explains, "Many social workers will report and talk

attorney, and, if she qualifies as a witness, to the defense attorney under cross-examination in open court.

Usually, however, the abuser is never brought to court because there is not enough evidence to prosecute. The Los Angeles Police Department, for example, receives about 100 reports of sexual abuse by a parent or guardian each year, but no more than 30 percent of these ever reach the stage of a formal complaint; and only a very small percent ever get to court. Corroborating evidence is difficult to obtain in any sex crime, but in a case reported weeks, months, or years after the offense, it is practically impossible. Other members of the family may refuse to testify,

ASK ANY GROUP OF A DOZEN OR SO WOMEN IF ANY OF THEM WERE SEXUALLY ABUSED IN CHILDHOOD. STATISTICS SHOW THAT AT LEAST ONE WILL ANSWER YES... IF SHE DARES.

Abuse and Neglect estimates that there are at least 100,000 cases of sexual abuse each year, though it is the most unreported category of criminal activity. Other professionals, such as Hank Giarretto, director of the Santa Clara Child Abuse Treatment Program in San Jose, consider a quarter of a million cases a conservative estimate.

Vincent De Francis, director of the Children's Division of the American Humane Association in Denver, Colorado, says that the incidence of sexual abuse is "many times greater" than that of physical abuse. Yet in comparison with society's efforts for the battered child, the sexual abuse victim has been virtually ignored. For instance, while every state specifically requires the reporting of physical abuse, nearly half of the states do not specifically mention sexual abuse in their mandatory reporting laws.

"People can more easily identify with the physically abusive par-

about bruises but are unwilling to press further to determine if this is a case of sexual abuse in which the bruise is only a secondary characteristic."

"I think you're sort of embarrassed to ask the question," says Dr. David Friedman, a pediatrician at USC Medical Center where child abuse has become a central concern. He admits having missed a good deal of sexual abuse when he was in private practice. "You're afraid you will lose the patient by implying that it's possible."

On the average, sexual abuse reports are not made until the victim can't stand it any more and tells someone, or becomes pregnant. Even then, the victim herself is usually removed from her home and placed in protective custody or a foster home, a procedure which unfortunately reinforces her conviction that she is the offending party. She is then asked to repeat the embarrassing details of the abuse to police, investigators, protective service workers, the district

even after they have brought charges, and the victim herself may not make a credible witness if she's fallen into the predictable pattern of promiscuity or drug use. The result is often a one-on-one situation which most D.A. offices— interested in a good conviction rate—are reluctant to take to court. The offender is released, but for her own protection, the victim resumes her "sentence" in the foster home.

Many professionals find it hard to say whether the abuse, or its aftermath, is more traumatic for the victim. Often the victim's mother is forced to go on welfare, her sisters and brothers are also placed in foster homes; her parents—usually at the court's urging—are permanently separated or divorced.

Certainly, says Dorothy Ross, "If the abuse hadn't made an impact, then by the time the system gets through with her it has become the most important thing that ever happened in her life." While law enforcement officials would like to see more cases prosecuted, so that the offender—and not the victim—is punished, others feel that the child's welfare is often sacrificed in the massive onslaught against the perpetrator. De Francis of the Humane Association feels that if a child is involved in legal proceedings, she should be surrounded by social services that will cushion the impact. As a preventive measure, he also stresses the need for schools to give children some understanding of parenting roles, responsibility, and behavior so that they will recognize when they are being mistreated by adults.

At present the only comprehensive program designed to meet the needs of both victims and offenders is the Santa Clara Child Sexual Abuse Treatment Program in San Jose, California (CSATP). Started five years ago CSATP provides therapy and counseling for daughters, fathers, and mothers, as well as practical assistance and emotional support through the maze of courtroom procedures. Therapy for the victim is aimed at relieving her own feelings of guilt over the abuse and family breakup, and helping her deal with her anger and resentment toward both parents. For the offender, the program emphasizes "taking respon-

sibility for what [he has] done," says Director Giarretto. Offenders and their wives are helped to recognize the marital (not just sexual) problems which, according to Giarretto, are often a primary cause of sexual abuse.

Some of the families in the program are referred by the courts—as an alternative to the father's imprisonment or as a condition for probation. Many of the cases police formerly had to drop for lack of evidence are now referred to CSATP. The program lasts for an average of six months to a year, although many of the graduates continue to attend Daughters United or Parents United—the two self-help groups generated by CSATP. About 400 families have completed treatment in the past five years, and only two repeat cases of sexual abuse have been reported.

CSATP is being looked to as a model for other state programs in California. Last year Governor Jerry Brown signed into law a measure that would create statewide treatment centers for abused children and their families. Elsewhere in the country, police departments and district attorneys' offices now have special units trained to handle sexual abuse problems with greater sensitivity. In some places, child-abuse hot-

lines, rape crisis centers, and hospital sexual assault services are expanding their facilities to recognize and treat sexual abuse. In California the National Organization for Women has set up a Task Force on Sexual Abuse; it hopes to establish a national task force during the April NOW convention to coordinate local efforts to help victims.

The magnitude of the problem of incest is perhaps only matched by the degree of secrecy which surrounds it. As more assistance becomes available, more of the hidden victims are reaching out for help. For example, in 1974, the number of cases referred to CSATP increased from 31 to 145. In 1975, there were 169 referrals, and in 1976, 269 cases were referred—all from the vicinity of Santa Clara County. (In Los Angeles, there were only 107 cases reported last year.)

The taboo against family sex, far from preventing it, only keeps us from recognizing and treating those who violate it. If society is going to help the victim of sexual abuse, it is going to have to become less terrified of it. And then we will see just how big the problem really is.

Ellen Weber, a free-lance writer living in Berkeley, California, has researched and written for films on child abuse.

THE SEXUALLY ABUSED CHILD

BY KAREN LEAMAN, RN, MSN
PHOTOGRAPHS BY DAVID FREESE

THE LITTLE GIRL and her mother are in tears. The mother believes her 8-year-old daughter, Janie, has been sexually abused by a neighbor's 17-year-old son. The mother's tears stop, and her expression becomes grimly determined when she requests a physical examination of her daughter. She wants evidence to prove the boy's guilt. She wants him put behind bars.

Nurses are often the first people outside of the victim's family to learn that a child has been sexually abused. You may see such cases in the E.R., in a clinic, in a psychiatric unit, in a doctor's or school nurse's office, or in the home, if you're a public health nurse.

You may see it almost any time — maybe tomorrow. Sexual abuse is thought to be one of the most common but least reported crimes committed against children. Some experts estimate that as many as 500,000 cases occur in the U.S. annually.

Almost a hundred cases of suspected sexual abuse are seen yearly at the Child Protection Center of the Children's Hospital at the National Medical Center in Washington, D.C., where I am a psychiatric nurse clinician. Nearly all of these children are preadolescent girls. How do we deal with the challenging needs of these children and their families? Let me tell you — and thus give you some pointers that might be useful in your own practice.

Janie — the 8-year-old — is typical.

Today she told her mother that the neighbor boy had been "touching me under my panties." The attending physician does a complete exam. It reveals that the vulva is reddened and the hymen is intact. It proves nothing. The girl might have been sexually abused — or she might not have.

The police are notified, but they need physical evidence to support a complaint of child abuse. Janie only sobs and clutches at her mother more tightly when the police ask her questions. Later the same day, the police question the boy. He denies any sexual contact with the child. The case is dropped for lack of evidence.

Is it or isn't it?

Was Janie actually sexually abused? To proceed with intervention in such cases, you have to make up your own mind from the evidence as you see it. Sexual intercourse occurs in relatively few cases (and usually with post-puberty minors), so often a medical exam cannot prove or disprove sexual abuse.

Sexual abuse of children is also hard to define. It includes the entire range of sexual activity a child might be willingly or unwillingly subjected to by adults. (The act does not necessarily have to be against the child's will to constitute abuse.) The sex acts vary from mere exhibitionism in front of the child, or fondling of the child, to rape.

What things point to sexual abuse?

Gonorrhea or other inflammatory diseases of the pelvic region; suspicious physical findings, such as blood in the child's undergarments; itching or scratching of the genitals; or evidence of physical abuse, such as bruises.

The indications may be more subtle. Sexual abuse is sometimes discovered during inpatient services when a child does not want to be discharged because the abuse occurred at home. Occasionally sexual abuse is indicated by subsequent sex play between peers or when the child acts out the sexual incident with dolls.

Usually, however, most cases of sexual abuse of children are brought to professional attention by parents or other caretakers who have witnessed the incident, heard about it from other witnesses, heard about it from a friend or teacher the child has confided in, or heard it directly from the child herself.

The nurse's role

Sexual abuse creates a situational crisis for the child and family. Nursing intervention can be based on the crisis model for treatment where you, the nurse, take an active and direct approach with the family. This approach is particularly effective with families where the child is sexually abused by a stranger or someone known to the family but with whom the family has no personal commitment. The intervention goal: resolution of the feelings about the abusive event so that family functioning is returned to normal as soon as possible.

Not all nurses feel comfortable working with sexually abused children and their families. Indeed, any nurse who tries to help in this kind of crisis should have a good understanding of child development, child behavior, and crisis intervention techniques. And she should also be free of any serious sexual hangups of her own.

I've found that best results can be achieved by focusing intervention on the parents. The way they respond to the child and manage her at home is probably what determines how the child will resolve her own feelings. You can, in fact, help the child through the parents.

Ideally, intervention should start as soon as possible. At the moment when the parents reveal their knowledge (or suspicions) of the abusive event, they need help the most. Now is when they will be most receptive to your efforts. Early management of the family can be divided into a series of steps.

"The Sexually Abused Child," Karen Leaman, *Nursing 77*, Vol. 7, No. 5, May 1977. ©1977 Intermed Communications, Inc.

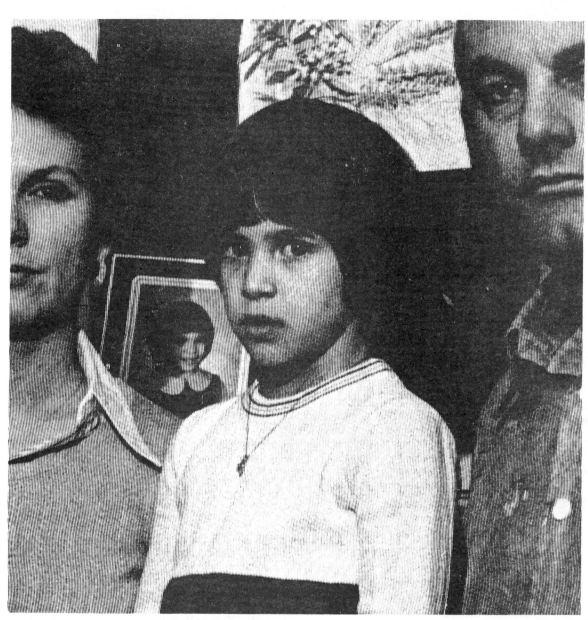

photos: David Freese

1. Interview the parents and the child separately to find out as much as you can about the sexual abuse.

2. Explain in detail to both parents and child all the medical procedures that will be necessary. These usually include a complete medical exam with special attention given to the body orifices. (A complete pelvic exam will usually not be necessary in the case of preadolescent girls.) In some cases, such as those where rape is suspected, swabs may need to be taken for medical and legal purposes. The child and her family should understand what all of these procedures involve before they are performed. Some of the children I have seen were more frightened by the medical exam than they were by the sexual abuse. In cases where the child is out of control or extremely frightened, better postpone the exam until the child will tolerate it without being frightened.

3. Prepare the parents for the fact that the medical findings may not prove nor disprove sexual abuse.

4. Explain to the parents any results of the exam that are significant, such as finding of traumatized tissue.

5. Assure both parents and the child that the abusive event almost certainly will not leave the child marked for life, either emotionally or physically if the event is dealt with reasonably and calmly.

6. Make sure the parents understand that their reaction to the assault will, to a large degree, determine the reaction of the child.

7. Encourage the parents to prevent

3. SEXUAL

The abusive event almost certainly will not leave the child marked for life, either emotionally or physically if the event is dealt with reasonably and calmly.

further trauma to the child by returning the home life to normal as soon as possible.

8. Explain to the parents that the child will probably react to the family's reaction more than to the abuse itself.

9. Inform the parents of the authorities' role. In some states, reporting the incident may be required by law. (The nurse herself needs to be familiar with the child-abuse laws in the local community.)

10. Encourage the parents to ventilate their feelings of anger, frustration, or remorse over the incident.

11. Help the parents mobilize support from their relatives, friends, physician, or other professionals, such as the local public health services personnel.

12. Document the results of your interview and the medical exam. Remember that these records may be used in court, so stick to the observable and avoid inferences.

Anticipating reactions

Now let's look at some of these guidelines more closely. In focusing on the parents, you must be able to anticipate their reactions to head off conflicts. Generally, parents feel anger at the offender and want him prosecuted to the limits of the law. They are apt to be angry with hospital personnel when the medical findings neither confirm nor disprove sexual abuse. They may direct this anger toward you in no uncertain terms. Remember that their hostility is not directed toward you personally, but toward an institution they feel has let them down. If you can sympathize with them, without being patronizing, you may be able to help them deal with their crisis.

Reporting the abusive event to the authorities and to other agencies and services, such as the local Suspected Child Abuse and Neglect (SCAN) center, may not only be legally mandatory, but also will be therapeutic for the parents as well. This is, in effect, a safety valve for their anger.

Parents may also feel depressed and worthless after their child is sexually abused. They may feel guilty, particularly if they feel responsible for the event because they didn't adequately protect the child. Their anger and guilt can be greatly reduced if you persuade them that their child will, in all probability, go on to lead a normal and happy life, in spite of the abusive event.

The anger and guilt that parents normally feel is one good reason they and the child should be interviewed separately. Typically, the child will pick up her parents' anxiety and will feel responsible for upsetting the household.

Incest
Parental feelings are hardest to resolve when a member of the child's family, or someone the family likes, is the offender. An example is when the mother's boyfriend is the offender. Yet these are the families that need help the most. Not surprisingly, studies have shown that the closer the offender is to the family, the more disturbed the family's inter-relationships are.

In situations where a stranger is the offender, the parents can easily support the child and direct their anger at the offender. But when the offender is a close friend or relative, the parents' loyalties are divided. They may deny that sexual abuse has occurred and instruct the child not to "tell" on the offender, to preserve their relationship with the offender. These children are often ones brought to the hospital with gonorrhea or those children who disclosed the incident to someone other than their parents.

Incest, of course, complicates intervention, but does not prevent it. You can let the parents know that you discern the incestuous nature of the abuse, without accusing anyone. This attitude will usually show the parents that they have nothing to gain by denying the abuse — to themselves or to outsiders. You can, perhaps, get them to face the problem squarely and start to deal with it. If at all possible, you should persuade the parents (or the mother and her boyfriend) to seek psychiatric help. Make sure they follow through and keep the initial appointment. If you suspect incest, you must notify the appropriate child-abuse authorities in your area.

If you have any reason to believe that sexual abuse of the child may recur, you have a professional duty to contact the appropriate protection agency in your community. (Some of the agencies to call on for help are: the juvenile court, the police, the local social-welfare agency, or a child-abuse center.) The decision to report a family is a difficult one and should be made jointly by you and your supervisor, possibly with a psychiatric consultant.

Through a child's eyes
The child's reaction to sexual abuse is often the hardest thing for the parent

Point out to the parents that the child has an immediate and overwhelming need to feel loved and secure after the abusive event.

(and the nurse) to understand. But doing so is obviously imperative if the family's to return to normal. Otherwise, the traumas of the child and of the parents may continue to feed each other indefinitely.

Most people don't realize that a child views sexual abuse completely differently than an adult. The reactions vary greatly with the child's age, emotional maturity, relationship with the offender, and the family's reaction to the abusive event. One researcher has found that in cases of forcible assault of young children, when the event is dealt with calmly, the memory will dim and can disappear from the consciousness of the victim within 18 months and will leave no detectable trace.

The young child (about 4 to 8 years) responds more to the behavior of the offender than to the abusive event itself. If the offender was gentle and caring, the child may not even be disturbed by the event until it is disclosed to the family or a friend. If the offender was threatening, or if the child experienced considerable pain, she may be more upset by the experience.

If you treat the event calmly and help the parents to calm down, trauma to the child will be greatly reduced. You should point out to the parents that the child has an immediate and overwhelming need to feel loved and secure after the abusive event.

Follow-up
Follow-up is needed in most cases of sexual abuse. Who performs this service depends largely on the organization of your local social agencies. The family may be followed by a social worker, officers from the youth division or the police sex squad, in addition to a public health nurse, or some other professional. At our hospital, the Child Protection Center continues to serve those families with sexually abused children whose needs warrant further attention and help. If your hospital or agency doesn't provide follow-up services, you should refer the family to an agency that does. I believe that *some* sort of follow-up is always necessary for 3 to 6 weeks after an abusive event.

Follow-up serves three important purposes:
1. You (or whoever handles follow-up) can continue to reinforce the initial efforts at intervention — help the parents find friends or social workers who can help them through the crisis, determine if

3. SEXUAL

the parents can return the child's home life to normal, and explain to them any questions they may have about their child's reaction.

2. You can assess the child's continuing reaction to the abusive event. Young children often resolve their feelings through play, because they lack the cognitive and verbal development necessary to talk about the incident or verbalize it in their own minds. This can often be seen when the child engages in some sexual or aggressive play with dolls or invents doctor-nurse games that re-create her experience in the hospital. The child should be encouraged to channel sexual feelings through toys, rather than sex play with peers. Older children may need to talk to you about the abusive event to reassure themselves by your response.

Follow-up assessment gives the opportunity to discover phobias that the child may have developed as a result of sexual abuse. She may be afraid to go to school, if the abuse occurred there. If the child remains confused and anxious about the event, she may have trouble sleeping. The parents may continue to exhibit anxiety about the event. If this continues a week or two after the event, the family probably should be evaluated by a psychiatrist or mental-health professional. If psychotherapy is needed, you should continue to provide follow-up services until it begins. Don't cut the family adrift on their own.

3. You can assess what measures, if any, have been taken to assure sexual abuse won't be repeated. If abuse occurred because of parental neglect, as when a child is left unattended, try to determine if the practice has continued. If it has, you should, of course, encourage the parents to be more responsible. If the child continues to be in danger, the family must be reported. Your first priority is always the well-being of the child. That, after all, was why the child was brought to you in the first place.

Sexual Child Abuse and the Law

Brian G. Fraser, J.D.

Mr. Fraser, is incest against the law?

Yes.

Whose law?

Society's, as a matter of fact. In almost every civilization it is considered a taboo, but it is specifically a crime in all 50 states and the District of Columbia.

Do you think incest is the most frequent sexually abusive act against children?

I don't know. One of the problems when you are talking about sexual abuse or molestation is that no one has accurate figures.

What sort of procedure would help to acquire accurate figures?

Well, child abuse is a generic term that has four components. There is nonaccidental physical abuse. The second is neglect, the third is sexual molestation or abuse—which could cover many activities including incest—and the fourth is mental injury or emotional abuse. For all practical purposes a good mandatory reporting statute includes sexual abuse in its definition. Unfortunately, abuse cases in some states are lumped together to include all four of those elements. To get a count on the number of sexual abuse cases depends entirely on how a state's central registry is set up and if the department is capable of breaking down those figures. Some states just can't.

How do most state laws define incest?

Sexual intercourse between family members.

Would it only include blood relatives of the child?

It varies from state to state, but in most states it would be blood relatives.

Discussions and articles about the sexual abuse of children frequently refer to the First Amendment. What is the significance of the reference?

First of all, you have to distinguish the First Amendment from criminal laws. The First Amendment issue usually comes up when legislators are drafting legislation that deals with pornography, including child pornography.

The federal government cannot pass any laws that would infringe upon basic states' rights. It is the right and responsibility of each state to protect the safety, health, welfare, and morals of its citizens. That means that any legislation concerning sexual abuse is a primary responsibility of the individual state and not the federal government.

Reprinted from the booklet *Dealing with Sexual Child Abuse*, Vol. 2, by permission of the publisher, the National Committee for Prevention of Child Abuse, Chicago, Illinois.

115

3. SEXUAL

when legislators are drafting legislation that deals with pornography, including child pornography.

The federal government cannot pass any laws that would infringe upon basic states' rights. It is the right and responsibility of each state to protect the safety, health, welfare, and morals of its citizens. That means that any legislation concerning sexual abuse is a primary responsibility of the individual state and not the federal government.

How do state governments do that?

The states have passed two different types of laws. These laws allow sexual abuse cases to be filed in the criminal court or in the juvenile court.

If the district attorney decides to pursue the sexual abuse case, he may file charges in the criminal court. The purpose of the criminal court is to punish the perpetrator. The criminal court does not address the needs of the child.

Secondly, every state has enacted statutes that allow the department of social services to file a case of sexual abuse in the juvenile court. The purpose of the juvenile court is to protect and pursue the child's safety and interests. The juvenile court does not punish.

Hypothetically, a case of sexual abuse involving a child could be filed in both the criminal court and the juvenile court.

Are city governments involved in sexual abuse legislation?

No. The only time a city would become involved would be when it is debating ordinances for zoning x-rated theaters or massage parlors or something like that. A city doesn't have the right to pass laws about child abuse; that is the state's responsibility.

If the sex offender is outside of the family situation, would the case be more apt to go into the criminal court?

Yes. The fact is that juvenile court does not have jurisdiction over the perpetrator. It has jurisdiction over the child. If a parent is suspected of incest, for example, what the juvenile court usually does is to say: "We think the child is in danger. We would like to return the child to you, but we feel unsafe about doing that. We would like to see you involved in a treatment program. We will reconvene in six months or a year, and if there has been some progress, we will return the child to you." This is like dangling a carrot in front of a horse. That doesn't work particularly well if the perpetrator is not a member of the family because he has no real interest in having the child returned to the parent.

The criminal court is the court that has jurisdiction over the perpetrator of a crime. The first issue to be resolved in criminal court is whether or not a crime has been committed, and the second is the penalty.

Hypothetically, the criminal court can act as a therapeutic tool *if* the perpetrator is found guilty of sexual abuse. Then, rather than sentencing him to jail, the court can offer probation on the condition that he become involved in some treatment program.

Does the sex offender receive any therapy or counseling while in prison?

It varies from state to state and county to county, but probably the answer is no in most places.

When released from prison for incest, does the offender usually

return to his own home?

Yes.

If he doesn't receive any counseling or therapy and he returns to his own home, what happens to the child that was molested?

It depends. Although criminal prosecution in these cases satisfies a need for retribution, it usually doesn't address the issue of what is wrong with the father, or what is wrong with the stepfather, or how behavior can be corrected.

There is no measurement of the offender's rehabilitation before he goes back into the home?

Not in the criminal court.

In the juvenile court?

The juvenile court is not concerned about criminal prosecution or jail sentences, but it is concerned about whether or not the child will be safe and whether or not treatment for the parents is adequate. As far as the juvenile court is concerned, the father is always free to go back into the family. The question for the juvenile court is whether or not the child should be there when the father returns. While the juvenile court cannot stop the father from returning home, it can make sure that the child is not there when the father does return; that, however, is not a solution.

Of all the sexual abuse cases the juvenile court hears, how many families are strengthened?

Nobody knows that.

How do most states define sexual abuse for purposes of the criminal code and the juvenile code?

It varies from state to state.

Are there any acts that are crimes in every state?

Incest is one. Forcible rape is another. Other than that, it varies from state to state.

Is the variety of state laws helpful or confusing to the issue?

If you are considering a particular state, it is not especially confusing because the state's law is the one that governs behavior within that state. Looking at it from a national perspective is somewhat confusing.

Would agreement on the definition of sexual abuse be helpful?

For purposes of evaluation, yes.

Every state has a mandatory child abuse reporting statute. In addition to that statute, does each state also have other laws that deal with sexual abuse of children?

Yes.

What should a person do if he suspects a child is a victim of sexual child abuse?

Every state has at least one statewide agency to receive and investigate suspected child abuse. By all means, report your suspicions to that agency. Frequently it is only by calling the situation to the attention of the authorities that the family receives help.

What is the name of the agency?

It depends upon the state in which you live. It is usually called the Department of Social Services, Department of Protective Services, Social and Rehabilitation Services, or the Department of Children and Family Services.

Is child abuse and neglect totally regulated by specific child abuse and neglect statutes?

Not necessarily. Anytime a child is badly physically abused,

3. SEXUAL

for example, it could fall under the common-law definition of assault, assault and battery, or assault with a deadly weapon.

Other laws may also come into play?

Sure. I'd say that about half of the states have specific crimes of child abuse. To a certain extent, the crime of child abuse is redundant. An assault and battery statute, for example, could be used to prosecute the perpetrator of physical abuse. However, to establish a crime in the criminal court, the district attorney has to show a criminal act and intent to commit that act. In some cases a statute that deals specifically with the crime of child abuse makes it easier to establish the element of intent. In other words, a specific criminal statute for child abuse can sometimes make it easier for the district attorney to prove his case.

Wouldn't there be some advantage in unifying these laws and defining abuse under one law?

There is some value in uniformity, but the value usually comes in dealing with transient families who move from one state to another. Since the definition of child abuse varies from state to state, what may be classified as child abuse in one state and one court might not be child abuse in another state and another court.

Every state has a mandatory child abuse reporting statute. Does every state include sexual abuse as part of the child abuse that must be reported?

Only 42 states specifically require that sexual abuse be reported as part of child abuse.

Do the existing state laws require the testimony of the child victim?

No, I don't believe that any law in any state requires the testimony of the victim. The more important question is whether or not the child victim can testify. That varies from judge to judge. In most states children can testify at the discretion of the judge if they meet two criteria: one, they are old enough to articulate; and two, they are old enough to know the difference between right and wrong. These are basically the criteria that are used to determine if a child can testify, but there is no requirement for the child to testify.

Do most laws tend to place the burden on the victim for proving her (his) own innocence?

No. In order to successfully establish a case of sexual abuse in the criminal court the district attorney must show a criminal act and must show intent to commit that act.

In some cases the defendant's attorney may attempt to smear the reputation of the victim, implying that she slept with a number of men. The implication, if that type of evidence is allowed to be presented, is that the victim egged the perpetrator on, and the requisite intent is not established. In some situations, therefore, the victim *is* forced into a position of defending her reputation.

Today fewer and fewer courts are allowing this type of evidence to be presented. In any event, in cases of sexual abuse involving a child, this should not be an issue. Incest is incest. Rape is rape. In most states children are not considered able to give consent to sexual activities. The only issue is whether or not incest has taken place or whether the child has been raped.

Why do so many articles cite the fact that most children are not believed and that most of the trauma is placed on the victim, while the suspected offender walks out free and clear?

Well, for one, sexual abuse is a difficult case to prove, especially in the criminal court. Two, I think, is the very simple reason that we just don't believe, or we have a difficult time believing, that a parent or other adult would sexually abuse a child.

Do you think we need any more laws governing the sexual molestation of children?

I think we need *good* laws. That doesn't necessarily mean that we need more laws. We could probably do with fewer laws. We need good laws that specifically delineate what sexual molestation is, make it easy to establish the case legally, and provide a therapeutic thrust.

What is the first and foremost legal objective in handling a case of the sexual abuse of a child in the juvenile court?

The protection and safety of the child. The second is the reconciliation of the family, if possible.

Can the law prevent the sexual abuse of children in any way, or does the law always respond to misdeeds?

The law primarily reacts to problems. In very few cases does it anticipate solutions. That is not to say that it is impossible to draft legislation that deals with sexual abuse from a preventive point of view. But, currently, I would have to say that the preventive approach is very unusual in America.

What do you think are the most important actions legislators should take now in the area of sexual abuse?

I think that legislators need to be somewhat more realistic in their approach. It is very easy to pass legislation that requires the reporting of child abuse. It is quite easy to pass legislation that allows this kind of case to proceed quickly to the court. It is somewhat naive to believe, however, that this will cure the problem. Once you identify the problem, you have to be able to provide treatment. Legislation that details a specific problem should also make an appropriate allocation for establishing treatment programs.

Is there anything else you would like to recommend?

Yes. The sexual abuse of children is something that the general public doesn't talk about much. It is something that people have a difficult time conceptualizing. It seems to me that one of our priorities should be public awareness and education about sexual abuse. People don't do anything about a problem until they know that the problem exists.

What we have been talking about is really legislation and the courts. Legislation is simply a vehicle for identifying these cases *and* a framework that allows us to deal with the various aspects of the problem. The courts deal with the problem once it has occurred. A more prudent approach, I believe, would be to concentrate on the preventive aspects of the problem.

Finally, until we develop good treatment programs and until we can develop the capability to make that treatment available to large groups of people, it is rather naive to believe that we can have much of an impact. As a society we have to admit to ourselves that sexual molestation happens, and we have to make a commitment to provide enough resources to develop a good treatment and prevention network.

SCHOOLS, INSTITUTIONS AND THE COMMUNITY

Section IV deals with three issues: the involvement of the educator in identification and as perpetrator of child abuse and neglect, or the status of the child in our correctional facilities, and the ignored needs of the abused rural child; and community (lay) efforts to work with parents in providing support to interrupt abusive patterns.

Teachers are mandated by law to report suspected cases of child abuse and neglect. Diane Divoky is opposed to the extent of the legal involvement of educators. She feels that few teachers have the expertise to do little more than guess, let alone determine whether a truant or a shabbily dressed child, a rebellious or withdrawn child, is an abused child. Legislation should concentrate on the problems of the most severely and obviously threatened.

Each state has an agency (usually the Department of Social Services) required to investigate reported cases. The teacher's legal involvement is generally limited to identification and the adjucatory hearing. Immunity is provided when a report is made in "good faith." Teachers are civally liable. "What Can Be Done About Child Abuse?" provides general guidelines for the roles teachers play in suspected cases of abuse. This is followed by the Education Commission of the States' "Model School Policy."

Another issue facing the teaching profession is the use of corporal punishment. A recent Gallup pole cites discipline as the single largest problem in the schools. In 1977 the Supreme Court upheld the use of corporal punishment as a disciplinary measure in certain cases. "Paddling, Punishing, and Force: Where Do We Go From Here?" defines the current status of the law and responsibilities of the teacher to the student.

The New York State College of Human Ecology at Cornell University held the first National Workshop on Institutional Child Abuse in June, 1977. Three articles are taken from the University's magazine "Human Ecology Forum," which devoted two issues to the subject. Poetry appearing on these pages was written by residents of the South Lansing Center operated by the New York Division for Youth in Lansing, New York. The movement to replace large, isolated rural facilities with small foster care centers and community based institutions is caught in the many demands on tax dollars. Recommendations from the workshop are included.

Cities have a number of facilities available for helping the troubled family. The rural child and his/her family are virtually on their own. "Advocacy for the Abused Child" encourages communities to assume the responsibility to develop and increase the delivery of support services to their areas.

One of the most successful of the self-help programs (over 800 chapters) is Parents Anonymous. At weekly meetings, battering parents are helped to channel anger and frustration, and learn to feel good about themselves. Two articles are included that offer suggestions for starting a community (volunteer) program and pitfalls to avoid. Dr. Vincent J. Fontana feels that in combatting child abuse and neglect it is important to have a "human network of support," involving a multidisciplinary team of professionals, paraprofessionals, a 24 hour hot line, a hospital residential setting, individual and group therapy, and parenting and consumer education. In all approaches, the involvement of unskilled workers, or volunteers, is integral to the interruption of the repetitive cycle of abuse.

CHILD ABUSE

MANDATE FOR TEACHER INTERVENTION?

BY DIANE DIVOKY

Ready or not, teachers are being assigned a major role in the national crusade against child abuse now moving at fever pitch. In most states new or updated laws require teachers and other school personnel to report suspected cases of abuse and, often, neglect. In Montgomery County, Maryland, all school employees are required to report physical abuse, sexual abuse and neglect—with the neglected child being one who is ill-clad and dirty, unattended, emotionally disturbed due to friction in the home, emotionally neglected by being denied "normal experiences that produce feelings of being loved," or exposed to unwholesome and demoralizing circumstances. The policy emphasizes that any doubt about reporting should be resolved in favor of the child.

In Adams County, Colorado, elementary grade teachers are told to be on the lookout for children who exhibit reticence in class, aggressive acting-out behavior, poor peer relationships, poor hygienic habits, or a fear of adults. In junior high school, the signs of neglect or abuse include sexual promiscuity and an inability "to conform with school regulations and policies." New Jersey warns its teachers that classroom "signposts" of abuse are "disruptive or aggressive" behavior, "withdrawn or quiet" behavior, "poor attendance or chronic lateness," and dirty and torn clothing. Abusive or neglectful parents, the teachers are told, display a "lack of maturity," "low frustration level" and "impulsive traits."

In the state of New York, teachers are required to report any student whom they have "reasonable cause to suspect" is "maltreated" by a parent; i.e., the child's "emotional health" has been impaired so that a "substantially diminished psychological or intellectual functioning" can be noted in, for example, the "control of aggressive or self-destructive impulses." *Guidelines for Schools*, the widely distributed child abuse advisory pamphlet of the American Humane Association, says an alert teacher looks for symptoms in the parents as well as in the child: "Are they apathetic or unresponsive?" "Do they fail to participate in school activities or to permit the child to participate?"

At last fall's Child Abuse Training Seminar in Houston—part of the federally funded model program for the identification and referral of abused children by school personnel—the approach was simple: show the gruesome color slides; use dramatic language ("If you were a nine-year-old and your parents were torturing you every night of your life, wouldn't you be grateful to the person who reported you?"); talk about signs like nail biting, thumb sucking, masturbation and uncontrolled urinating; and insist there's no relationship between "abuse" and other kinds of physical force used against children ("Corporal punishment is reasonable and it is meant to teach; abuse is the venting of anger and frustration").

Guidelines Are a "Judgment Thing"

In California, where 120,736 children were reported as abused or neglected in 1974, a school system like the Hayward Unified School District already feels confident about "accepting the moral responsibility to monitor," according to Joan Chambers, administrative director of pupil services. If a teacher sees bruises or some other physical sign of abuse, or hears a child talking about a disruptive incident at home, she arranges for the nurse or other designated staff member to talk to the child to get some indication of what happened and, if warranted, to call a report in directly to the police. Chambers said all reports are supposed to be made directly to one of two police officers with special in-service training in child-abuse cases, but in practice these people are often not around, and any available beat

There are no guidelines as to what signs justify transferring a child from school to the police station—without parental permission.

man comes to the school to interrogate the child, remove the clothing, examine the body, and then, perhaps, take the child into protective custody. "Once we've called the police, it's out of our hands," Chambers said.

There are no guidelines as to what signs justify transferring a child from school to the police station—without parental permission. Marks on the buttocks, what one police officer called "overcorrection," is considered "borderline" by that officer. Some school officials admitted they were a bit squeamish about sending a child off in the police car, but one officer disagreed: "Often it's a thrill for the kids to drive off in a police car," she said. "Sometimes I say I'll buy them candy." Margaret Outman, a nurse for the children's centers in the neighboring Oakland schools, concurred: "The

children are better through all this than we are."

At the station, the child is booked, Polaroid shots are taken of the bare body, and the parents are called. Social agencies are checked by phone to see if the family has a history of problems, because at some point the children's division of the county probation department must decide whether the child will be returned home immediately or put at least temporarily into a children's shelter or foster home. Again, guidelines are fuzzy, a "judgment thing," but the attitude of the parents when they get to the station or shelter—how contrite they seem —is a major factor, two officers said.

Within 36 hours of phoning the police, the school employee must make a written report, including information about the nature of the injuries

and the student's statement. Copies of this report go to the police, the probation department, the school district office, the school principal's "confidential" file and, when appropriate, the welfare department. One copy gets sent on to a state register of suspected child abusers, maintained by the Department of Justice.

Even when they are found to be unsubstantiated, these written reports are never removed or expunged from the various agency files. The Hayward school district personnel do not know which of the reports in their own files represent actual abuse and which are false alarms. What services the family receives as a result of reporting and what impact there is on the child aren't known by the school staff, either. "Hopefully, good things come out of reporting," said Chambers, "but

One expert has suggested a national policy of health visitors who would regularly visit every home to check on the well-being of young children.

there's a possibility that ultimately you may have done more damage, because even the abused child is afraid to lose its family. But our job is to report, to shore up teachers and convince them it's helping and not finking."

The Child Protective Services Act

The message is to look for signs and symptoms and, when in doubt, report. The state laws themselves use both a carrot and a stick to make mandated reporting more palatable: they all grant anonymity as well as immunity against criminal and civil prosecution to those who report suspected cases, and most attach a criminal penalty, usually a misdemeanor, to the failure to report.

And if the Model Child Protective Services Act currently proposed by HEW's Office of Child Development is approved and promulgated by the Secretary of Health, Education and Welfare—and OCD officials are assured it will be—the reporting network will get broader and more active still. The mere existence of the model act, which "seeks to encourage fuller reporting," will move many states still tinkering with their own legislation to adopt it wholesale. Frank Ferro, associate chief of OCD's Children's Bureau, said there will be pressure on states to comply if they want their federal grants.

The model act would require teachers—as well as social workers, day-care workers, podiatrists, religious healers and a raft of other public and private employees who have some contact with children—to report immediately to a single statewide toll-free telephone number "their reasonable suspicions" of parents or other caretakers who abuse or maltreat children. To be reported are those child custodians who create or allow "to be created a substantial risk of physical or mental injury to the child, including excessive corporal punishment" or who fail "to supply the child with adequate food, clothing, shelter, education (as defined by state law), or medical care." The "mental injury" to be reported involves "failure to thrive; ability to think and reason; control of aggressive or self-destructive impulses; acting out or misbehavior, including incorrigibility, ungovernability, or habitual truancy."

Under the model act, the teacher would first call in a report and then immediately notify the principal or his agent, who would take color photos and, if medically indicated, have a radiological examination of the child be performed. Once the report was made to the hotline, it would be transmitted—ideally by facsimile telecopier—to the local social service agency. (Local school officials could also use the statewide number—and a remote-access computer terminal—to check out a parent's record of prior reports in order to decide whether to report "suspicious circumstances" or

not.) After the report, the action begins. The child protective service worker or police officer can take the child into protective custody without the consent of the parents if there's an imminent danger to the child's health. A thorough investigation ensues. If the parents refuse to give the protective service access to the child or the home or to allow the child to be removed from the home or to accept the "service plan" of the agency, court proceedings or other legal action can be taken against them.

A New Institution Is Born

The model law, and the growing campaign against child abuse it will cap, possibly represents the most extensive system of intervention into the lives of families that this nation has yet conceived. What began as an intensive but very limited movement in the early '60s to save physically battered and ravaged children—usually preschoolers—from death or permanent physical damage is suddenly a national social welfare system, complete with data banks, a whole new army of social workers, and enormous legal authority, capable of subtly and not so subtly directing parents and guardians as to how they will raise and treat their children. Teachers and other mandated reporters are installed as snoops; everyone else is permitted to play the game, with their reports given equal status. Local social workers, bestowed the new title

124

of "child protective service team," become instant experts on family dynamics, with the capability of working up "appropriate service plans" that will heal wounded families and relieve the strains of poverty. If the family declines the plan, it can be referred to the police or criminal court.

And the model act is not a lonely example of overkill. Brian G. Fraser, attorney for the federally funded National Center for the Prevention and Treatment of Child Abuse and Neglect in Denver, has suggested a national computer to hook up all the state data banks "so that abusive and potentially abusive parents may be tracked as they move across the country." Dr. C. Henry Kempe of the University of Colorado School of Medicine, the father of the "battered child syndrome," has suggested a national policy of health visitors who would regularly visit every home to check on the well-being of young children.

The overreaching thrust of the model act—and similarly ambitious plans—has not met with universal approval. Senator Walter F. Mondale of Minnesota, the author of the 1974 Child Abuse Prevention and Treatment Act, which set the stage for the current crusade, has expressed his "deep concern" about the model, noting that resources are not available for the problem of "child neglect," and that the act may be unevenly applied to poor families and minorities. Mondale stated that the intention of his legislation was "to address the problems of the most severely threatened and abused children in this country," quite a different goal from that now being pursued. "I feel so strongly about this that, if HEW should decide to promulgate the law in its present form, I would personally write to all of our state legislatures and recommend that it not be adopted."

Judge James Lincoln, chairman of the Neglected Children's Committee of the National Council of Juvenile Court Judges, is equally critical of the model's inclusion of "mental injury" and "neglect" and of its information-maintenance procedures. Lincoln has recommended its postponement and has backed instead a much more limited model system for the handling of physical child-abuse cases to be published by the Justice Department. And 12 members of the model act's own advisory committee have damned the model as being "the Trojan Horse of child protective services," so zealously broad "as to preclude effective delivery of services to those acutely in need or prevention of serious injury to children. Coercive intervention into family life in vaguely defined

situations of suspected neglect and maltreatment is inappropriate to a social service agency and violates due process of law. . . . The provisions governing access to information in the central register are inadequate to protect the privacy of families and children."

But while the model act gets battered about, the child-abuse industry grows and grows. HEW's National Center on Child Abuse and Neglect spent some $19 million in 1975, and a raft of other agencies, from the Health Resources Administration to the Law Enforcement Assistance Administration, have money in child abuse. Because the field has become a pork barrel for researchers and clinicians in an otherwise hungry era, any number of social scientists and private consultants are busy designing scales and tests to uncover potentially abusive or neglectful parents, indexes and schemes to note the early warning signs, and blueprints for prevention.

What has allowed the best-intentioned of social programs—salvaging the battered child from the truly psychopathic or incompetent parent and reclaiming the most dysfunctional of families—to turn so rapidly into both a glamor industry and an ominous threat to our civil liberties and family autonomy is a number of myths that have caught on in the highly charged environment that surrounds the child-abuse issue. The myths—interfering with any true understanding of who the child abusers are, what abuse is, the extent of the problem and the possibilities for curbing it—don't necessarily support one another; in fact, at times they seem in total conflict. But each has contributed, in its time, to a precipitate growth in the campaign against child abuse.

Who Is the Child Abuser?

The first-born of the myths, the one that initially fixed public attention and wrath on child abusers, depicted child abuse as an aberration in a culture that generally treats children very well, and child abusers as deviants—usually pathological misfits—in an otherwise healthy population of parents. The "battered child syndrome" —first explored in the early '60s— certainly suggested extremes of behavior and personality, and early conclusions about abuse were drawn from a small sample of those families involved in severe attacks on their children. Presentations of the child-abuse phenomenon, whether before a Senate subcommittee or in the popular press, were hallmarked by full-color photos of the ravaged bodies of babies and toddlers and sensational

stories of sadists and torturers who happened to be parents. Indeed, emotion-packed voices, like that of Dr. Vincent Fontana, director of the Mayor's Task Force on Child Abuse and Neglect in New York City, still insist that "the important battle continues between the child murderer and the child saver."

But as early as the late '60s, the results of the first and still only reliable nationwide survey of child abuse (conducted at Brandeis University with U.S. Children's Bureau funds) were indicating, according to its chief researcher, professor of social policy David G. Gil, that "violence against children is not a rare occurrence, but may be endemic in our society because of a child-rearing philosophy which sanctions, and even encourages, the use of physical force in disciplining children. Furthermore, . . . abuse of children committed or tolerated by society as a whole, by permitting millions of children to grow up under conditions of severe deprivation, [is] a much more serious social problem than abusive acts toward children committed by individual caretakers." Gil also found that "children living in deprived circumstances were, for a variety of reasons, more likely than other children to be subjected to abusive acts by their caretakers," and that such acts are triggered by the strains and frustrations of poverty.

"Finally," Gil noted, "the study revealed that children are being abused both physically and emotionally not only in their own homes, but also in the public domain, in schools, and in other child-care settings, especially those schools and institutions that serve children from economically depressed neighborhoods." He concluded that "the dynamics of child abuse were thus found to be deeply rooted in the fabric of our culture. Consequently, the widespread notion that this destructive phenomenon was primarily a symptom of individual psychopathology appeared to be too narrow an interpretation of the wide spectrum of child abuse." Gil's recommendations were to attack all violence at its source by changing the prevailing practices of disciplining children and to work to eliminate poverty.

A brand-new study by Elizabeth Elmer of the University of Pittsburgh takes the relationship between abuse and poverty one step further. In comparing three groups of lower-class children—one of abused children, one of youngsters who'd suffered accidents, and one with no history of abuse or accidents—she found a large percentage of the entire sample had serious problems in speech, emotional development and school achievement. These problems "were distributed quite evenly among abuse, accident and comparison children. The entire sample . . . appeared sad and fearful. . . . Mothers' reports indicated that the families, whether abuse, accident or comparison, experienced constant violence, both environmental and personal. It must be concluded that the effects of abuse on child development are insignificant compared to membership in the lower classes."

James Kent, a pediatric psychologist who heads the research and demonstration child-abuse team at Los Angeles' Children's Hospital, admits that the child-abuse issue is "a red herring." "Getting beaten is the least of these kids' problems," he said. "The bones will mend and the bruises will heal. It's everything else that goes on in their lives and in their families that's overwhelming." Sit in on a disposition of abuse cases at the hospital, and the talk is of parents without education, jobs, a telephone to break their isolation, or bus fare to get a child to a clinic for orthopedic shoes; of mothers of five who already are old in their early 20s; of people who spend their days being tossed from one social agency to another, who finally turn on each other in their frustration and anger.

But the abuse issue is popular in this time when our social policy is such that benign neglect is the answer to poverty and when our former good intentions about coming to terms with hunger and ghetto schools and hopelessness in our society seem all but forgotten. As Gil said, looking at the relationship between poverty and child abuse: "Public and professional concern with child abuse in individual homes tends to exceed by far the concern with this massive, collective abuse of children by society as a whole. Could it be that the oversensationalized interest in the former serves as a smoke screen to cover up society's destructive inaction with respect to the latter? Are abusive parents perhaps seized upon as convenient scapegoats to expiate society's collective guilt for abusing countless numbers of its young?"

If few wanted to hear Gil's argument that poverty breeds abuse, fewer still wanted to heed his words about attacking the sanctioning of violence —especially violence against children —at its roots. There is a long tradition to overcome: infanticide, abandonment, exploitation, maimings, child labor and brutal beatings are all part of our cultural legacy. Bizarre punishments seen as "for the good of the child" are woven into our history. Even today, children are the only persons in society who legally do not have the right to what Gil calls "the dignity of their bodies."

In 1970, Dr. Brandt F. Steele, professor of psychiatry at the University of Colorado Medical Center and a leader in the child-abuse movement, wrote that violence is endemic to our society, that "individuals as well as various cultural and social groups tend to use aggression and violence that they consider good or right to enforce their good and right standards." Among these are sane parents who really believe—as their parents did— that they are teaching their child right from wrong and respect for authority with beatings and physical punishment. "If we are really to understand the mechanisms of violence and how to control it in our culture, we must pay attention much more than we have in the past to those moral forces within us that tell us to direct violence in certain ways, and that enable us all to do evil under the guise of doing good."

In 1973, Dr. E. F. Lenoski, director of the Pediatric Emergency Center at the University of Southern California Medical Center in Los Angeles, told a Senate subcommittee: "The flood of venom that has spewed forth from many authors has painted the perpetrators of abuse to children as only fit for the gallows or some other similar fate. . . . I would agree with those who have written and spoken out that between 5 and 10 percent of the people who are involved in child abuse are mentally ill. . . . The remainder of child abusers appear to be essentially normal, intact human beings."

Is There a Child Abuse Epidemic?
The myth of the child abuser as deranged sadist has lost some credibility, but only to be replaced by an opposite notion: that we are all potential abusers and that child abuse is a raging and terrifying epidemic in the land. Gil had said early on that the "quantity and quality of abuse as a serious social problem has been exaggerated"; that more than half of abused children received only cuts and bruises; that abuse does not "constitute a major social problem"; and that "even if allowance is made for the gross under-reporting of fatalities, physical abuse cannot be considered a major killer and maimer of children."

Yet the myth of an epidemic of abuse, with all its attendant hysteria, keeps growing. Often the hysteria is engendered by those who have the responsibility of knowing better. A case in point: on November 30, 1975, the Sunday New York Times ran a story headed "Child Abuse Rate Called 'Epidemic.'" The subhead: "U.S. Says Fifth of the Million Annual Victims Die." The lead sentence: "More than a million American children suffer physical abuse or neglect each year, and at least one in five of the young victims die from their mistreatment, the government announced today." Many other papers across the nation ran similar stories, all taken from a United Press International release. The "government" speaking here was Douglas Besharov, director of HEW's National Center on Child Abuse and Neglect and author of the Model Protective Services Act. Besides announcing that at least 200,000 children die each year from child abuse, Besharov was quoted as saying that statistics indicate that 1.6 million cases of abuse and neglect are reported each year, that more than a million of these are substantiated, and that about three fourths of the neglect reports come from people in the same cultural life as those accused, eliminating any cultural bias in reporting.

The statement that 200,000 children a year die from child abuse should have been taken for what it was—a ludicrous charge (620 deaths were verified in 1974). The other assertions, all inaccurate and unfounded, could have been, and in fact were, taken at face value by the unsuspecting. Besharov had told the reporter that all his statistics came from the American Humane Association, which has a contract with the National Center to compile reporting statistics. The people at AHA, who had been working as rapidly as possible to put together a responsible statistical estimate for release in 1975, described Besharov's statements as "groundless" and "excessive." "We have no idea what Doug is talking about," one staff member said succinctly.

In spite of assurances from Besharov's staff that at least the 200,000 deaths figure would be corrected in the Times, no correction ever came. Instead, Walter Cronkite picked up the startling statistics as the basis for a feature on the CBS nightly news the following day, and practitioners in the field began to use them as reliable data, thus further alarming the public groundlessly.

When Is a Child Abused or Neglected?
One of the major problems in gathering real statistics is, of course, the absence of a meaningful definition of abuse or neglect. In spite of the myth that all of us can recognize abuse or

neglect on its face, that there are universally understood standards of acceptable treatment of children, neglect and maltreatment—and even abuse—are almost impossible to define. Are the four children of the welfare mother who all sleep in a single bunk bed under lead-based peeling paint neglected? Or is the middle-class child in the tense home so perfectly appointed with fragile art objects and white carpets that he can't function as a child the victim of maltreatment? Or are both, and a lot of children in between, whose parenting doesn't live up to some utopian ideal? Are children in understaffed day-care centers or authoritarian boarding schools neglected? Is corporal punishment in the schools abusive? (Authorities such as Gertrude Williams, editor of the *Journal of Clinical Child Psychology*, think so.) Is the abusive parent the one who doesn't let his child participate in neighborhood activities, or the one who forces his boy to make it in Little League?

Is the child of an alcoholic parent automatically an abused child? One child may fall apart in such a stressful environment; his sibling may cope quite nicely. As Norman Polansky, professor of social work and sociology at the University of Georgia and perhaps the most respected authority on neglect, notes: "The environment's impact, after all, is experienced as 'stressful' only as it impinges on individual feelings." Psychologist Sheldon White, an authority on child development at Harvard University, adds: "Neither theory nor research has specified the exact mechanisms by which a child's development and his family functioning are linked." Polansky describes attempts to define neglect as "premature and scientifically presumptuous," pointing out what other researchers have also observed: that neglect is "inevitably relative," depending on the knowledge and state of child development and care as well as the wherewithal of any community; and that "children of disorganized, multiproblem American families are nearly all better off than those now starving in Africa's drought countries."

Besides, as Michael Wald, professor of the Stanford Law School and an authority on juvenile law, explains, "We cannot predict the consequences for a child of growing up in a home environment that lacks affection or stimulation, or with a parent who suffers from alcoholism, drug addiction, mental illness, or retardation. . . . In fact, by focusing solely on parental behavior, child-care workers often ignore the many strengths a given

child may be deriving from his environment. . . . The complexity of the process by which a child relates to any environment defies any attempt to draft laws solely in terms of environmental influences."

Even serious physical abuse, apparently the most specific and incontrovertible form of maltreatment, is not always easy for doctors to identify, much less nonmedical persons. In what was to be "a simple, straightforward study of clearly abused children and clearly abusive families" funded by the National Institute of Mental Health, researcher Elizabeth Elmer of the Pittsburgh Parental Stress Center found the "totally unexpected": that of 33 children who met the "powerful criteria for admission to the study"—multiple bone injuries acquired at early ages when the children couldn't "propel themselves into positions of danger" and "a history of neglect or abuse"—four had not, in fact, been abused, and for seven others, the evidence was inconclusive. Elmer calls for the "painstaking" evaluation of suspected abuse cases and describes the psychological damage suffered by parents and children as the result of erroneous accusations by the hospital staff: "It cannot be emphasized too strongly that false accusations of the parents can be harmful in the extreme."

Richard J. Gelles, professor of sociology and anthropology at the University of Rhode Island, agrees with Elmer, and suggests that what has been taken as the personality characteristics of child abusers—anxiety and depression—may actually be the results of being publicly labeled as abusers: "At least it ought to be recognized that the effects of being labeled an abuser may be more damaging to the individual caretaker and his or her child than is the actual instance of abuse."

Can We, Should We, Intervene?

The extensive reporting networks now in the planning are based on the most preposterous myth of all: that beneficial and significant social intervention will automatically follow identification. Again and again, child-abuse authorities stress that a reporting system is only justified by the benefits and services to families which are triggered by reporting. Yet there is simply no evidence to suggest that intervention is both possible and good, that enormously expensive public services can save families.

One hears much from the media about a few high-powered, well-funded demonstration projects that seem to be having some success in

treating a carefully selected group of abusive parents. For example, the Children's Trauma Center, part of the Oakland (Calif.) Children's Hospital, has a $387,000 annual budget, a highly trained, full-time staff of 15, plus two consultants and a large volunteer corps, to service some 175 cases a year. Their reabuse rate is under 10 percent.

But no comparable funding or expertise is—or can be expected to be —available in most other communities. And the Trauma Center deals exclusively with the abusing parent. For the much larger group of neglectful parents, the outlook is more bleak. According to the newsletter *Child Protection Report*, "Parents Anonymous [the self-help group for abusive parents] and other organizations which have attempted to involve neglectful parents in their group experiences report little or no success." Leonard Lieber, the founder of Parents Anonymous and a former social worker, stated that neglecting parents need more individual attention over much longer periods of time than abusive parents: "Neglecting families characteristically express infantile behavior problems, and it becomes a problem of raising the parents all over again from infancy. We're talking in terms of a time period that can extend from five to ten years, and even then, when the support system is withdrawn, the family often regresses to where it was before."

Professor Polansky—in addition to painting in elegant detail the totally ineffective "rituals in which welfare workers participate with their clients," the neglecting parents—makes a powerful case that "half measures may be worse than nothing," dismisses most conventional forms of intervention as useless, and suggests some radical steps which would be loathsome to those who take the Constitution seriously. He endorses the early and permanent removal of children from homes where there is "even persuasive evidence" of abuse, substantial prison terms for abusive parents, the promotion of sterilizations subsidized by the government, and institutional placement of many neglecting mothers.

Short of this side of 1984, the outlook for stepped-up intervention is dim for a number of reasons: it assumes proven methods that we haven't begun to find; it would cost staggering amounts; and it just might do more to undermine our social fabric than the problem of abuse itself.

Arguing for parental autonomy and against coercive intervention except in cases where a child evidences serious physical or emotional damage,

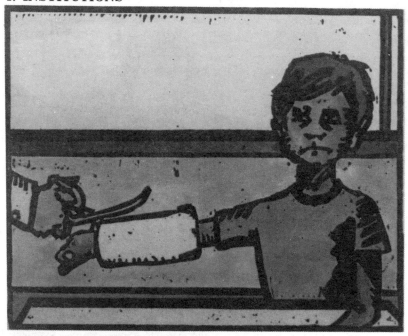

Says one psychologist: "Getting beaten is the least of these kids' problems. The bones will mend and the bruises will heal. It's everything else that goes on in their lives that's overwhelming."

Professor Wald states that "there is substantial evidence that, except in cases involving very seriously harmed children, we are unable to improve a child's situation through coercive state intervention. In fact, under current practice, coercive intervention frequently results in placing a child in a more detrimental situation than he would be in without intervention. This is true whether intervention results in removal of the child from his home or 'only' in mandating that his parents accept services as a condition of continued custody."

Carefully documenting the detrimental effects of institutional or foster home placement, the at best ineffective and often harmful attempts of social workers to provide services, and the vagaries of the system by which the government makes decisions about intervention, Wald concludes that "we lack sufficient knowledge and agreement about child development and 'proper' parenting to justify either the state's undertaking the functions now assumed by parents or assuming a more extensive role in monitoring parental decision-making. . . . If the law required all parents to provide a home environment that maximized the opportunity for their children to realize their inherent potentials, intervention might be necessary in most American homes."

Wald continues: "Such a system is

possible. According to one observer, in the Soviet Union, 'when mothers take their babies to the clinics, they are given quizzes to see if they are doing the "right thing." Workers are frequently sent into the home to observe the parents' relationship with each other—and with their children.' Given the plight of many children, it is tempting to adopt policies along these lines. However, the history of failure of previous state efforts to improve children's lives through substitute parenting demands rejection of this notion."

"Finally," Wald suggests, "adopting a policy of minimal coercive intervention may encourage the creation of more extensive services available on a voluntary basis to all families. Hopefully, this will improve the well-being of many more children than now are aided through the almost haphazard application of neglect laws. . . . It should be remembered that our societal commitment to child welfare has not extended to guaranteeing all families adequate income to assure that all children can receive basic nutritional and medical care, adequate housing, or any of the other advantages we would like parents to provide. Nor have governmental bodies been willing to make day care, homemakers, or other services available to all who would use them voluntarily. Yet every study shows a strong corre-

lation between neglect and poverty. In a society that is committed to protecting individual freedom and privacy, it is preferable to attempt to solve problems by noncoercive means before relying on coercive methods."

What Role Should the Teacher Play?
No one, of course, would advocate leaving children who are suffering severe physical or emotional damage to the mercy of their abusive caretakers. Clearly, there is a group of children whose very existence depends on the state's ability to intervene rapidly and skillfully. But these children are almost always the very young, who will not come to the attention of those mandated to report under the new schemes, and they are just the children who may very well be lost in the rush to identify and service hundreds of thousands of families who are—in one way or another—delinquent or deviant in their child-rearing practices. Services, expertise and funds are limited; the existing social agencies can do only so much repair work. Better to husband the available resources for those in the most urgent need than to diffuse it in creating a vast new bureaucracy with slim prospects of helping anybody.

Teachers, like all those who work intimately with children, can see flaws and deficiencies in the nurturing and home environments of many of their students. There is a tendency to want to move in and save the child, to reconstruct the family. The instinct is natural; but the doing is something else entirely. Few teachers have the expertise to do little more than guess, let alone determine, whether a truant or a shabbily dressed child, a rebellious or withdrawn child, is an abused child. And few social workers assigned to intervene in such cases can do more than perform holding operations.

If teachers really care about the quality of life of their youngsters, there are, however, a number of steps they might take. They can call for a rejection of the overly broad reporting laws and demand narrowly focused laws that, as Senator Mondale recommends, "address the problems of the most severely threatened and abused children in this country." At the same time, they can fight for the voluntary child welfare services—day care, homemakers, parent-support services—that are now available to few families. They can lead the way in promoting the social policies that would guarantee that no child would go hungry, ill-clothed or poorly housed, and that no parent would live day in and day out under stresses that finally turn them against their children.

What Can Schools Do About Child Abuse?

- A kindergartener is found to have multiple bruises and lacerations, new and old scars over most of his body. He has been beaten with an extension cord, the latest in a series of abuses that has included previous beatings, burnings, and an attempted drowning.
- A high school girl sustains a black eye and extensive facial bruising during an argument with her parents over which college she should attend.
- A first grade boy is beaten and punched in the face by his father when the boy fails to recite his alphabet perfectly.

Isolated incidents? Unfortunately not. It is currently estimated that the majority of the abused and neglected children in America are of school age. Yet very little has been written about this forgotton population; even less has been done. Most of the literature about child abuse and neglect concerns the young child: the child under three whose youth and small stature make him more vulnerable to life-threatening injuries. But the older child—the child over five—is at risk, too. While his injuries are less often life-threating, they are frequently serious and may have long term physical and psychological effects.

The number of abused and neglected children of school age is enormous. According to preliminary data from the American Humane Association National Clearinghouse on Child Neglect and Abuse, *two-thirds* of the cases reported to the Clearinghouse in 1975 involved children between the ages of 5 and 17. Despite the fact that these children are in school day after day; despite reporting laws in every state which mandate reporting of suspected child abuse and neglect, only a few forward-looking school systems are involved in detecting and preventing child abuse and neglect among the school-age population.

Diane D. Broadhurst

What can the schools do about child abuse? A great deal. There are at least four important roles schools can play in the fight against child abuse and neglect:

- Reporter of suspected incidents
- Partner in decision-making and treatment programs
- Agent for primary prevention
- Child advocate.

Reprinted by permission from *Victimology: An International Journal,* Vol. 2, No.2, 1977, pp. 268-276. ©1977 Visage Press Inc. All rights reserved.

4. INSTITUTIONS

Reporting

Where school systems have been involved in child abuse and neglect management, it has usually been as reporter of suspected incidents, and the value of this traditional role cannot be over-emphasized. Schools are where children are—six hours a day for nine months of the year and twelve years of their lives. These children are seen daily by professionals trained to observe children, people skilled in the recognition of normal, or usual childhood behavior. Nowhere else in the community does this observation occur regularly. When school staff know the signs and symptoms of child abuse and neglect; realize they are required to report suspected incidents, and are aware of the legal immunities provided them, then they can become active participants in child protection. There is a growing trend across the country for school systems and local Board of Education (and some State Departments and Boards of Education) to enact policy requiring staff to report incidents of suspected child abuse and neglect. Such policies reflect state law regarding form and content of reports and usually include procedures for how, when, and to whom to report in the local community. Reporting policies have been adopted by school systems in California, Colorado, Hawaii, Maryland, North Carolina, Wisconsin, and other states, but *every* school system should have such a policy. It should be the first step in any system's involvement in the direction and prevention of child maltreatment.

Those school systems which adopt reporting policies and procedures usually find that staff are more comfortable about reporting and that the reporting process moves more smoothly. They usually find a significant increase in the number of cases reported as well. The Montgomery County, Maryland Public School, one of the nation's largest school systems, has been a pioneer in the development of school-based child protection programs. Data from that system amply demonstrate that the schools are an important means of case-finding. In the 1972–73 school year, the Montgomery County Schools reported fewer than 20 cases of suspected child abuse. During the 1973–74 school year, the Board of Education of Montgomery County adopted a policy requiring the reporting of suspected child abuse and neglect by all school staff. In addition, each school administrator was required to attend one of a series of programs on child abuse and neglect, held during the annual summer administrative workshop. In the 1973–74 school year, 63 cases of suspected child abuse were reported—a threefold increase (Project Protection, 1976).

Early in the 1974–75 school year, Montgomery County instituted Project Protection, a child abuse and neglect detection and prevention program funded by the US Office of Education as a model for school systems. Following an intensive three level staff development program designed to reach every school staff member from superintendent to classroom teacher—more than 7,000 persons in all—139 cases of suspected child abuse were reported, more than twice the total for the previous school year. Reporting for the 1975–76 school year continued at the same high level. Significantly, very, very few reports concerned families reported the previous year.

Though nationally only about half the reported cases of suspected abuse are valid, better than 70 percent of those reported by Montgomery County schools staff during 1974–76 were valid. But reports from county schools were not confined to suspected abuse alone. During the three year period 1973–76, 285 cases of suspected neglect were reported, in a community with one of the highest median incomes in the nation. Child neglect and poverty are not synonymous, and it is well to keep that in mind.

Clearly, staff who can recognize a child at risk and who know what to do about it can be a significant element in finding and bringing help to abused and neglected children, as the following case illustrates:

> Kenny T., an 11-year old, was new to his school, though his younger brother and sister had been students there the previous year. Kenny's teacher had taken particular notice of him because for all of the first week of school he wore the same tattered shirt and pants, though his brother and sister wore new and different clothes each day.
>
> During the second week of school Kenny appeared in class one morning with a bruised cheek and a large and ugly wound on his head. He was obviously in pain, and his teacher took him to the nurse at once. Asked about the injuries, Kenny stated that his mother had struck him with a bed slat. He was afraid of her, he said, and he begged not to be sent home. The nurse and the teacher told the principal of the incident, and Protective Services was called immediately. The social worker who responded to the report of suspected child abuse took Kenny to the hospital, where his head wound was sutured and bandaged. A routine physical examination disclosed multiple new and old bruises and lacerations on the boy's buttocks, thighs, and lower back. There was little doubt Kenny has been subjected to repeated abuse. The Protective Service investigation revealed that Kenny had only recently come to live with his mother and stepfather. Born when his mother was 16 and unmarried, Kenny had been raised by his grandmother who lived in a distant state. When she died in early summer, he was sent to live with his mother and her husband, neither of whom wanted the boy. Though they related fairly well to their own children, they had no use for Kenny and resented "wasting money on him."
>
> Kenny is currently in foster placement, where he is well and happy. He continues to express fear of his mother who has refused all contact with him and all offers of counseling and assistance. It is likely that Kenny will remain with his foster family, something he has indicated he would like very much.

Decision-Making and Treatment

Although the role of reporter is vitally important, it is not the only role for schools in the fight against child abuse and neglect. In some communities the schools are coming to be regarded as partners in case planning, decision-making, and treatment. The partnership is a logical one. For the abused or neglected school-age child, his school may be his one stable reference point. He needs that stability to continue; he needs the support and caring of people he knows and trusts—the people in the community he sees most often and with the greatest regularity. It makes perfect sense, then, for the schools to work in concert with other community agencies to plan what will best serve the child's interests, and some communities have begun to do it. In the San Francisco Unified School District, for example, school staff work closely with Children's Emergency Services (CES), the agency which investigates reports of suspected child abuse and neglect. San Francisco has a school board policy which not only mandates reporting of suspected child abuse and neglect to CES, but also encourages local schools to participate in the assessment of the child's needs performed by the CES team (San Francisco, 1976).

In other communities such as Albemarle County, North Carolina and Anne Arundel County, Maryland, the partnership takes the form of school participation in a Child Protection Team. At team meetings cases are discussed, treatment plans made, and services committed. Frequently the schools are called on to provide tutoring, special classes, free or low-cost meals and activities, psychological, auditory or visual testing. School staff may also work with child and family in other ways, as the following case illustrates:

> Jeff, a seventh grader, was often absent from school. When he came, he was apathetic and inattentive. One morning he appeared in his counselor's office with a black eye and split lip which he said had been caused by his mother. After explaining that the law required him to report the incident, the counselor called

the local department of welfare. Subsequent investigation revealed that Jeff's parents were recently divorced. Beset with problems, angry and frustrated, the mother blamed her husband for the break-up of the marriage. She felt that Jeff, who closely resembled his father physically, was "just like his father—no good" and unappreciative of her "sacrifices." This case was staffed by the local child protection team whose membership included a representative of the school system. After extensive discussion it was determined that Jeff could remain at home if Mrs. G., his mother, could be given strong support and Jeff helped too. Mrs. G. agreed to attend a therapy program at a local mental health clinic, and Jeff's counselor and teacher agreed that they would work with him. The school staff gave Jeff special attention, tutoring and counseling him and encouraging him to participate in school activities. They scheduled frequent conferences with Mrs. G. to inform her of Jeff's progress and to underline their interest in his welfare.

Mrs. G. has responded well to group therapy, and she is learning to handle her anger and frustration. Jeff, with a calmer home life and extra attention in school, has shown marked improvement. He attends school regularly now and is beginning to take an interest in his work. The home situation is not yet considered completely stable, however, and the school continues to work closely with Jeff and his mother.

Undoubtedly many school systems would prefer to avoid working with abused and neglected children. They may no longer have that option. In fact, they may already be providing services to these children, whether they realize it or not. Martin (1976) reported both neurologic deficits and significant delays in the acquisition of gross motor skills among the abused children he tested. Blager and Martin (1976) reported on several studies which found significant language delay among abused children. Kline and Christiansen (1975) in a study of 138 abused children of school age in Utah, reported that 26.8 percent were placed in special education classes, as compared to 8 percent of the school population not classified as abused. The largest number of these children were in classes for the emotionally disturbed. Academically the majority of the study group were below grade level in reading, spelling, and math. In addition, a statistically significant number of children were resident in psychiatric care facilities.

Child abuse appears to be on the increase. If more children are injured, undoubtedly more will require special educational service. The implications for schools are clear, particularly in light of recent federal legislation which mandates the provision of public education to *all* children.

Preventing Child Abuse and Neglect

Perhaps no single agency is better suited to engage in primary prevention of child abuse and neglect than the schools. The inability to handle stress and the tendency to have unrealistic expectations and demands of children are common among maltreating parents. Schools should provide information on parenting to *all* students, not just the few girls who are traditionally found in child development classes. In addition, *every* student should learn means of coping with stress, and finally, each student should be familiar with community resources that exist to help people in need. Similar information should be made available to the community at large through adult education classes. Two excellent courses of study are available to school systems which want to begin such programs. *Exploring Childhood,* a parenting curriculum, is designed to prepare students to be better parents. It includes a unit on stress which deals with child abuse and neglect. The course was developed by the Education Development Center under grants from the Office of Child Development and the National institute of Mental Health. *Understanding Child Maltreatment: Help and Hope,* developed by Project Protection, is a course of study about child abuse and neglect. Currently in use in selected Montgomery County, Md. schools, it has also been referenced in the new

Maryland Home Economics curriculum and has been taught as an inservice course for teachers. The curriculum guide, which is available through the Educational Resources Information Center (ERIC), is also being used by school systems in other states, either as a course of study or as a resource document to help those systems develop curricula of their own. Negotiations are now under way with the National Center on Child Abuse and Neglect to reprint *Understanding Child Maltreatment* and make it more widely available. The abuse and neglect of children is a community problem requiring community solutions. If abuse and neglect are to be prevented, it will take the entire community, working as a whole, to accomplish it. The schools must be willing to do their part.

Speaking Out for Children

As Donald Kline has pointed out (Council, 1976), when children need special programs, special consideration, it is usually parents who press for them. In the case of the abused or neglected child, this is unlikely to happen. Someone else must speak out to protect the child from those responsible for his care. Someone else must begin the process by which a troubled parent may be helped to protect his own child. The responsibility for speaking out must be shared by each member of the community. Schools already stand *in loco parentis* to those in their care. They must be prepared to exercise that duty to protect children from abuse and neglect, children who cannot protect themselves, children like those in the following case:

> Janet B., a six year old, was thin, frail, and unkempt. She was a shy, retiring, and always silent little girl. Janet often came early to school, but one morning she arrived even earlier than usual, sought out her teacher, began to cry, and complained that her back hurt. Janet's teacher took her to the nurse where examination revealed her back to be a mass of cuts and bruises. Asked about the injury, Janet, clearly frightened, said that her father had hit her with a board that morning when she had been unable to find something he wanted. She added that her father and mother were often "sick" and that she had a younger brother and sister at home. A report of suspected child abuse and neglect was made immediately by the school, and authorities went to Janet's home. They found the family living in a filthy, vermin-infected shack, without food, beds, or running water. Mr. and Mrs. B. were drunk, and the children unsupervised. Susequent investigation disclosed that both parents were alcoholic. Mr. B. had a small income from a military disability pension, but most of the money went to buy beer and wine. The children's needs were ignored. Janet and the other children were removed from the care of their parents and placed with relatives in another city. They have been there for almost a year now, and they are thriving. Mr. and Mrs. B.'s living conditions remain unchanged, despite repeated offers of assistance. The children's placement is considered permanent.

What the schools can do about child abuse and neglect is limited only by the imagination of those responsible for them. Schools can begin to address the problem by:

- Learning about the phenomenon
- Adopting policy requiring staff to report suspected incidents
- Reporting incidents of suspected child abuse and neglect
- Joining other community agencies in case management and treatment
- Offering courses on parenting and related topics to students and others as a means of primary prevention
- Speaking out for the child who has no advocate
- Reaching out to parents in need of assistance.

If just one child is helped, just one family made whole again, it will have been worthwhile.

Considerations for Policy Development from a report by the Education Commission of the States

A policy regarding child abuse and neglect is a commitment by the school (or other education group or institution) to cooperate with other agencies and professions in identification, treatment and prevention programs. The ultimate purpose of a child abuse and neglect policy is to protect children whose health or welfare is threatened through nonaccidental injury or neglect by parents, guardians or caretakers.

The guidelines that follow are practical suggestions to help education policy makers develop and implement effective child abuse and neglect policies. These are not intended to be cookbook instructions that spell out what to do and how to do it. Rather, the guidelines are offered as points to consider when developing policy. They are designed to assist in the development of policies suitable to the needs of institutions and groups. Because of variations among state laws and among school district policies and regulations, it is impossible to develop uniform "model" policies and procedures applicable to all the American school systems.

The first and strongest suggestion is that every school system adopt and issue a child abuse and neglect policy, particularly a policy on reporting. Almost every state reporting requires or encourages school personnel to report suspected child abuse and neglect. An effective child abuse policy should inform school personnel of their legal obligations and immunities in regard to reporting, as well as inform the local community that school personnel are legally obligated or encouraged to report suspected child abuse and neglect.

Any policy regarding child abuse and neglect must be in compliance with state law. To ensure that a proposed policy complies with current statutes, consult an attorney or the state's attorney general.

"Education Policies and Practices Regarding Child Abuse and Recommendations for Policy Development," the Education Commission of the States, Report Number 85.

should cite the elements listed below. Sample wording for such citations is listed to the right.

Elements to be Cited	Sample Wording
1. *A brief rationale for involving school personnel in reporting.*	Because of their sustained contact with school-age children, school employees are in an excellent position to identify abused or neglected children and to refer them for treatment and protection.
2. *The name and appropriate section numbers of the state reporting statute.*	To comply with the Mandatory Reporting of Child Abuse Act (Section 350-1 through 350-5), Hawaii Revised Statutes (1968), as amended (Supp. 1975),...
3. *Who specifically is mandated to report and (if applicable) who may report.*	...it is the policy of the _____ School District that any teacher or other school employee...
4. *Reportable conditions as defined by state law.*	...who suspects that a child's physical or mental health or welfare may be adversely affected by abuse or neglect...
5. *The person or agency to receive reports.*	...shall report to the department of social services... *or* ...shall report to the principal, who shall then call the department of social services...
6. *The information required of the reporter.*	...and give the following information: name, address and age of student; name and address of parent or caretaker; nature and extent of injuries or description of neglect; any other information that might help establish the cause of the injuries or condition.

School employees shall not contact the child's family or any other persons to determine the cause of the suspected abuse or neglect.

It is not the responsibility of the school employee to prove that the child has been abused or neglected, or to determine whether the child is in need of protection.

7. *Expected professional conduct by school employees.*

Any personal interview or physical inspection of the child should be conducted in a professional manner...

8. *The exact language of the law to define "abuse" and "neglect"; if necessary, explain, clarify or expand.*

"'Abuse' means the infliction, by other than accidental means, of physical harm upon the body of a child." "'Neglect' means the failure to provide necessary food, care, clothing, shelter or medical attention for a child."

9. *The method by which school personnel are to report (if appropriate, list telephone number for reporting) and the time in which to report.*

An oral report must be made as soon as possible by telephone or otherwise and may be followed by a written report.

10. *Whether or not there is immunity from civil liability and criminal penalty for those who report or participate in an investigation or judicial proceeding; and whether immunity is for "good faith" reporting. ***

In Illinois, anyone making a report in accordance with state law or participating in a resulting judicial proceeding is presumed to be acting in good faith and, in doing so, is immune from any civil or criminal liability that might otherwise be imposed.

or

In Maryland, there is no immunity from civil suits for untrue statements made by one citizen against another.

11. *Penalty for failure to report, if established by state law.*

Failure to report may result in a misdemeanor charge: punishment by a fine of up to $500, imprisonment up to one year or both.

12. *Action taken by school board for failure to report.*

Failure to report may result in disciplinary action against the employee.

13. *Any provisions of the law regarding the confidentiality of records pertaining to reports of suspected abuse or neglect.*

All records concerning reports of suspected abuse or neglect are confidential. Anyone who permits, assists or encourages the release of information from records to a person or agency not legally permitted to have access may be guilty of a misdemeanor.

In its child abuse and neglect policy, a school system can specify its role in multidisciplinary cooperation, professional training, public awareness and programs of primary prevention. Although such statements are not necessary, they can help clarify previously ambiguous or ill-conceived positions.

The simple process of articulating a clear position can help refocus current programs and even allow new program development.

Policy makers may also find it helpful to articulate a clear policy on evaluation of the school system's child abuse and neglect programs. What are the school system's goals regarding its child abuse and neglect programs? What are the expectations? Are they realistic, measurable? By spelling out realistic expectations and some means to evaluate goals regularly, policy makers can help ensure more effective programs.

A final suggestion: to be useful, the adopted policy must be widely disseminated. Distribute copies to all school employees and parents and throughout the community every year. Well-conceived, clearly written and fully circulated policy is an essential first step toward meeting education's potential role in child abuse and neglect programs.

*While every state provides immunity for those reporting child abuse, many do not provide immunity for reporters of child neglect. School systems in these states may be able to extend immunity to school personnel via the state public school laws. Many of these laws grant immunity to educators who act under a requirement of school law, rule or regulation. By enacting a regulation requiring school personnel to report suspected abuse *and* neglect, school systems can ensure full immunity to their employees who report.

Paddling, Punishing and Force:
Where Do We Go From Here?

by Irwin A. Hyman, Anthony Bongiovanni,
Robert H. Friedman and Eileen McDowell

On April 19, 1977 the United States Supreme Court, in a five to four decision, decided that the bodies of schoolchildren are not protected under the Eighth Amendment to the Constitution, which forbids the use of cruel and unusual punishment (*Ingraham v. Wright*, 1977). In the case in question, two teenagers were severely beaten with wooden instruments jokingly referred to by many as "boards of education." The medical treatment required for the students would have resulted in reports of suspected child abuse had parents wielded the paddles. The Court did not approve of the use of such force by school authorities, noting that "Public school teachers and administrators are privileged at common law to inflict only such corporal punishment as is reasonably necessary for the proper education and discipline of the child; any punishment going beyond the privilege may result in both civil and criminal liability." Nevertheless, it refused to grant schoolchildren the same protection afforded adult criminals.

Both educators and parents immediately expressed concern about the ruling, which has different meaning for different factions among educators.

Proponents of paddling view the ruling as a clear mandate to "toughen up" on kids. Many educators among them feel that their role *in loco parentis* has been strengthened and that they may now freely swat their charges without fear of reprisal. Although they understand that severe abuse could lead to law suits brought by parents on

Irwin Hyman, Ed.D., is associate professor of school psychology and Director, Center for the Study of Corporal Punishment and Alternatives in the Schools, Temple University, Philadelphia. Anthony Bongiovanni and Eileen McDowell are doctoral students in school psychology at Temple University, and Robert H. Friedman is a school psychologist with the Bridgewater-Raritan, New Jersey, School District.

"Paddling, Punishing and Force: Where Do We Go From Here?" Irwin A. Hyman, Anthony Bongiovanni, Robert H. Friedman and Eileen McDowell, *Children Today*, Vol. 6, No. 5, September/October 1977. ©1977 Children's Bureau, Office of Child Development, Washington, D.C.

behalf of their children, they also realize that few parents will devote the time, money and energy needed to buck the school system.

Those who oppose paddling regard this decision as the "Nixon Court's" way of halting the movement of the preceding decade toward the recognition that children, as citizens, are entitled to protection under the Constitution. They agree with the minority opinion which indicated that by holding the Eighth Amendment as protection only for criminals, children in school would have to commit criminal acts in order to be protected from harsh physical punishment by school authorities. The minority opinion also pointed out that the ruling, by denying schoolchildren due process in cases of physical punishment, has deprived them of even rudimentary assurance "against unfair or mistaken findings of misconduct."

The forthcoming battle between the two camps will probably take place in state legislatures and local school board meetings. In preparation for the debates on these issues which are sure to follow, the National Center for the Study of Corporal Punishment and Alternatives in the Schools has prepared a number of papers on the subject.[1] Following is a summary of some of the issues involved.

Defining Corporal Punishment

The generally accepted definition of corporal punishment stems from a legal perspective and involves the infliction of pain, loss or confinement of the human body as penalty for an offense. Black's *Law Dictionary* (1968) defines it as "physical punishment as distinguished from pecuniary punishment or a fine; any kind of punishment of or inflicted on the body, such as whipping or the pillory. The term may or may not include imprisonment according to the individual case." As applied in the schools, corporal punishment has generally been defined as the infliction of pain by a teacher or other school official upon the body of a student as penalty for doing something which has been disapproved of by the punisher.

Corporal punishment in the schools is not implied when a teacher or school official uses force to 1) protect himself or herself, the pupil or others from physical injury; 2) obtain possession of a weapon or other dangerous object; or 3) protect property from damage.[2]

Extent of the Practice

Corporal punishment is a widely accepted method of disciplining children in school. A recent survey revealed that only two states, Massachusetts and New Jersey, have statutes which completely prohibit the use of corporal punishment in public schools.[3] Three other states—Hawaii, Maine and Maryland—have imposed severe limitations on its use. In Hawaii, permission to use corporal punishment had been temporarily suspended (at the time of the writing of this article) in response to the ambiguity of a recent statute. Maryland's statute prohibits its use unless a county decides otherwise, and in Maine corporal punishment cannot be used except to bring a disturbance under control or to remove a student who is causing a disturbance. What constitutes a disturbance must be dealt with on an individual basis.

Twelve states have remained silent on the issue of corporal punishment and this lack of action may be regarded as an implicit sanction of the practice. For example, a recent survey by the New Jersey Department of Education reveals that of these 12 states, the only one in which corporal punishment is not practiced is West Virginia.

The remaining 33 states allow or specifically endorse the use of corporal punishment as a means of disciplining children in public schools. However, many municipalities—among them New York City, Chicago and the District of Columbia—have banned its use in their schools.

The survey also found that in 28 of these 33 states, the power to physically punish disruptive students is given to the classroom teacher. Often administrators are also entitled to use physical punishment, and two states even grant the privilege to noncertified employees.

In analyzing the restrictions imposed on the use of corporal punishment, the survey revealed that the most frequently mentioned limitation, one practiced by 10 states, is that the punishment must be administered in a reasonable manner. Two states require that each incident be approved by the principal before the child is punished. Other limitations include the requirement that either the principal or another teacher be present as a witness and that the punishment cannot be inflicted in the presence of other students. One state requires that the parents be notified afterwards; two others require that the teacher "not use deadly force" and that the punishment be inflicted "without undue anger"; and one state does not allow a child to be hit on the head or face.

The rationale most frequently offered regarding the use of corporal punishment, the survey found, is to maintain discipline in the classroom. Other justifications mentioned in the legislation of various states include: for purposes of restraint, to promote the welfare of the child, to quell misbehavior and to increase obedience.

To what extent—and how—is corporal punishment used in the schools? Consider the following examples:

4. INSTITUTIONS

• In Vermont, a young sixth-grader was beaten by the principal for striking another student. The principal first struck the child repeatedly, knocking him from his seat onto the floor. He then kicked the child in the abdomen, back and legs and pulled his hair, causing him to suffer severe bodily bruises. (*Roberts v. Way,* 1975.)

• After being caught with cigarettes, three schoolboys in Missouri were given the choice of receiving a "paddling" or eating the cigarettes, according to the October 20, 1976 edition of the Kearney, Nebraska newspaper, *Hub.* Two of the boys chose to eat 18 cigarettes and the ingestion of tobacco resulted in their both being hospitalized, one for a kidney infection and the other for aggravation of an existing ulcer condition.

• During the 1971-72 school year, according to an article, "It's Time to Hang Up the Hickory Stick" (*Nation's Schools,* November 1972), the public schools in Dallas reported an average of 2,000 incidents of physical punishment a month. Nearly double that number of paddlings were reported for students in the Houston Public Schools in 1972, according to a school administrator who said that a total of 8,279 paddlings were administered there during a 2-month period.[4]

• A study of the practice of corporal punishment in California schools, commissioned by the California State Assembly in 1973, showed that—among the 974 school districts responding to a questionnaire—603 reported that they used a paddle, 336 used the hand and the remaining schools used belts, light straps, yardsticks and other implements. The reported number of incidents of physical punishment in elementary through high school grades in these districts for the 1972-73 school year was 46,022. Only five percent of the cases involved female students.

How does the practice of corporal punishment in the United States compare with that of other nations? A list of those countries which have abolished corporal punishment would include the following: Belgium, Luxembourg, Holland, Austria, France, Italy, Portugal, Finland, Norway, Sweden, Denmark and all the Communist bloc countries in Europe, and Cyprus, Japan, Ecuador, Iceland, Jordan, Qatar, Maurituis, Israel and the Philippines.

Research on Corporal Punishment

In defense of corporal punishment, J. F. Killory cites four criteria of punishment to be considered: it should result in the greatest behavior change; it should demand the least effort on the part of the user; it should result in behavior that is relatively permanent; it should produce minimal side-effects.[5] None of these criteria are met when one considers the research evidence available on the use of corporal punishment in the schools.

The results of research studies on punishment, for example, cast serious doubt on the efficacy of corporal punishment as a method of inducing behavior change in schoolchildren. The maximum effectiveness of punishment has been demonstrated to depend upon adherence to certain basic principles and to the control of several closely related factors.[6] To the extent that such control is not achieved, the ultimate effectiveness of punishment decreases while the risk of actually strengthening the undesirable behavior increases. For just as the behavior of

a gambler is reinforced when he wins—even though he may lose more often—a child who is punished only intermittently, as are most children in school, has his undesirable behavior reinforced when it goes unpunished.

In addition to the problems associated with effective and controlled application, the use of corporal punishment presents several potential negative side effects, beyond the obvious danger of inflicting physical injury to the child. When corporal punishment is practiced in a school, disciplinarians provide students with a model of aggressive behavior that young children are known to imitate.[7] Not only do they imitate such aggressive behavior in situations similar to those observed in the classroom, but they also tend to become aggressive when faced with frustration in their own lives. In essence, children who observe the practice of corporal punishment are being taught that aggression is a proper method to use in solving problems. Children also tend to become anxious and fearful when they observe another individual receiving such punishment.[8]

Although there has been no research, using experimental and control groups, on the direct effects of corporal punishment on achievement, there have been studies of

Photo: "An Old Fashioned Boy's School, 1905"

Photos: *Library of Congress.*

the effects of extreme punitiveness by teachers. A review by B. Rosenshine and N. Furst suggests that the achievement of students is negatively correlated with the amount of criticism used by the teacher.[9] Corporal punishment, of course, may be viewed as an extreme form of criticism.

> **After being caught with cigarettes, three schoolboys in Missouri were given the choice of receiving a "paddling" or eating the cigarettes.**

The potential for social disruption constitutes a primary disadvantage of the use of punishment. When physical punishment is used there is a strong tendency for the recipient to actively avoid the punishing individual or environment. Such a tendency, when related to school or school personnel, has the potential effect of destroying the student-teacher relationship. This would not only have a negative effect upon the child's education but, among older children, could ultimately lead to withdrawal from school. In addition, research suggests that physical punishment increases the possibility of physical retaliation, not only toward the source of punishment, but toward other individuals—and objects—within the school environment.[10] Therefore, the use of corporal punishment within the school represents a potential danger to students, educators and school property.

Those who defend the use of corporal punishment as a practical method which requires little effort tend to view its practicality from the perspective of school personnel alone: it can be applied by anyone in any setting, there is no need for specialized training or special equipment other than a paddle, and there is no dollar cost. The fact that most school personnel are physically stronger than children also makes corporal punishment especially attractive.

Beliefs About Corporal Punishment

Four of the most common myths pertaining to the use of corporal punishment have been explored by H. Clarizio:

1) that physical punishment helps to develop in the child a sense of personal responsibility, thrift, learning, self-discipline and character; 2) that "occasional paddling contributes substantially to the child's socialization"; 3) that "corporal punishment is the only resource in maintaining order"; and 4) that "those individuals involved with the schools favor its use." [11]

In his recent, extensive review of the literature on punishment, A. Bongiovanni found enough material to cast doubt on the efficacy of punishment under the conditions it is used in the public schools. While it is true that punishment results in the temporary reduction of targeted behaviors, in order for punishment to be effective over a long term it must be extremely harsh and repeated. Even then there are enough variables to contraindicate complete success. In order for corporal punishment to be effective in stopping children's misbehavior the

results would often be hospitalization. The major paradigm for the successful use of punishment is traumatic avoidance learning. This teaches avoidance of a behavior, but it also has negative implications for the setting in which it occurs and toward the source of the punishment.[12]

We know that the degree of physical punishment used by parents has been positively correlated with various forms of psychopathology among children, particularly with delinquency and acting out behavior. Some studies have derived a near perfect correlation between the amount and the severity of physical punishment suffered by a child during the ages of two and 12 and the amount and severity of adolescent anti-social aggressiveness displayed by the same child.[13]

Previously mentioned research studies suggest that children learn aggressive behavior by modeling the aggressive strategies of adults. Other researchers claim that the authoritarian personality may be a result of discipline that is harsh and threateningly applied. If one considers teachers who use corporal punishment as aggressive adults, one could conclude that this practice heightens, or at least contributes to, the increasingly aggressive interpersonal strategies displayed between students and teachers. The result is aggressive children reared into aggressive adults who create a violent society—not a nation of self-disciplined individuals.

Regarding the second belief, the crux of the issue lies in refuting the fact that infrequent or "judicious" use of corporal punishment is beneficial to the child. To be effective, punishment, unless traumatic, must be applied immediately and consistently. Yet in the school setting, behavior that one wishes to eliminate can hardly be monitored closely enough to be punished each time it occurs. Thus the "occasional" use of corporal punishment results in a situation in which the undesired behavior is only intermittently attended to. Instead of weakening the undesirable response, occasional paddling may actually strengthen behavior that is intermittently reinforced.

The third belief, based on the assumption that corporal punishment is the only thing some students understand, simply indicates that attempts have not been made to expose children to other, more constructive forms of discipline. Physical punishment may be the only thing some *teachers* understand.

Concerning the last myth, that those individuals involved with schools favor its use, Clarizio does assert that students in general, but only one-third of parents, tend to view physical punishment as an effective way to make students behave in schools.[14]

In a 1972 Task Force report, the National Education Association (NEA) indicates several reasons why students prefer corporal punishment to other alternatives.[15] For some students it is an easy way out: it does not require much time or any real change in behavior. For others it presents an opportunity to demonstrate toughness and endurance. Still others who feel guilty about offenses find relief in punishment. None of these reasons is educationally defensible.

A good explanation for why some students say they are in favor of corporal punishment was offered in a study by E. Elardo, who interviewed a group of elementary

During the 1971-72 school year . . . the public schools in Dallas reported an average of 2,000 incidents of physical punishment a month. Nearly double that number of paddlings were reported for students in the Houston Public Schools in 1972 . . .

schoolchildren.[10] Most of them, he reports, said that some children would prefer paddling to other forms of punishment in order to "get it over with." But they also felt that the paddling did no good in changing behavior. One child added: "Sometimes you get falsely accused of doing something. If you get paddled and later prove you did not do it, you can't get unpaddled. But if you lose an activity, maybe by the time the activity should occur you can prove your innocence and still get your activity."

The NEA Task Force report also points out that support of corporal punishment by schools encourages people outside the school system to feel that they are justified in physical assault on children. Conversely, by abolishing corporal punishment in schools we might reduce the incidence of child-beating elsewhere.

In addition to Clarizio's four myths, three others deserve mention. One is the prevailing notion that corporal punishment is necessary because teachers have to be protected and the threat of punishment offers them a means of self-protection. However, there is absolutely no evidence that corporal punishment is effective as protection. In fact, it is more likely to increase counter-violence by students.

Ernest Norms, in the NEA Task Force Report, suggests that the adolescent against whom protection is sought will respond not with unruliness in the classroom—but with a zipgun in a dark hallway. Certainly this protection argument loses its validity in the light of figures presented in a survey on the use of corporal punishment in public schools in Pittsburgh.[17] There, the highest incidence of corporal punishment occurred in grades 1 through 4. Could even the most mature fourth-grader represent a real threat to the most diminutive teacher? If protection were a real issue we would certainly expect a higher incidence of physical punishment in the high schools.

Another myth asserts that corporal punishment is only used as a last resort. Adah Maurer, a leader in the fight against corporal punishment, feels that referrals to the school psychologist and mental health agencies are often scheduled *after* this so-called "last resort" of physical punishment. Although school regulations often require educators to make such referrals, they are commonly ignored as being "too much trouble."

Finally, there is a fallacious rationale that corporal punishment is justified within the concept of *in loco parentis.* However, the courts have increasingly limited school authorities' denial of children's rights under the rubric of *in loco parentis.*

Two other issues should be considered in regard to teacher sanction of corporal punishment. One is the possibility that many teachers use it simply because this was the disciplinary practice followed when *they* went to school. (Interestingly enough, many teachers we have spoken with explain that they avoid the use of corporal punishment *because* of their unhappy childhood experiences.)

A second issue pertains to consideration of the mental health of teachers and students. In an address before the Toronto Board of Education in October 1970, David Bakan, a social scientist, said: "Nor can we be assured of the wisdom in connection with the *use* of corporal punishment, even if one were to accept the *principle* of corporal punishment. I have no data on the mental health of teachers. It may be that . . . [it] . . . is higher than that of the general population at large. Yet the statistics on the mental health of the general population are such to give us pause in allowing a system-wide use of corporal punishment on children . . . If we add to this the observation of the Celdic Report [18] that approximately one in every 10 children is in need of special psychological . . . services, *the probability that either an ill teacher or an ill child or both will be involved in an incident involving corporal punishment is simply too high to allow it to go on at all.*"

Alternatives to Corporal Punishment

The need for discipline and adherence to rules is a necessary part of education. However, in school systems that prohibit the use of corporal punishment, both teachers and students survive nicely without it. Consider, for example, the States of New Jersey and Massachusetts, which have banned corporal punishment for many years. Effective alternatives do exist and are already in use in those states and in districts throughout the nation.

In its task force report, the National Education Association prepared a list of techniques for maintaining discipline without inflicting physical pain on a student. The NEA believes that one must consider short-range solutions while longer-range programs are being put into effect. Short-range solutions might include class discussion of the consequences of good and bad behavior, and reaching an agreement between students and teachers on immediate alternatives to physical punishment. As an intermediate-range solution, the NEA suggests revision of curriculum content by the staff and students, in order to help it better meet student interest, and expansion of work-study and other programs. Finally, as long-range solutions, NEA indicates that provision for support services to work with individual problem students and intensive in-service programs for teachers would be helpful.

Many people feel that a large portion of student conduct problems are rooted in students' academic failure and dissatisfaction with instructional or administrative demands. Following are two of the many suggestions that the South Carolina Department of Education's Task Force on Alternatives to School Disciplinary and Suspension Problems has underscored as most important for

Upon Fone a School-mafter

Fone fayes thofe mighty whiſkers he do's weare,
   Are twigs of birch, and willow, growing there:
Is fo, we'll think too, when he do's condemne
Boyes to the lafh,. that he do's. whip with them.

Illustration by Edwin Austin Abbey from the November 21, 1882 issue of "Harper's Young People."

reducing discipline problems: [19]

• *School Orientation*—According to the Task Force, frequent misunderstanding or lack of understanding of regulations causes students to become disciplinary problems. Students and parents cannot be expected to support and comply with regulations that they do not understand. Thus, in addition to being given information about a school's classroom schedules, curriculum, grading system and extracurricular activities, students and parents should also be told about school codes of conduct, administrative procedures for handling discipline problems, procedures for requesting parent-teacher conferences and special services for students.

• *Regular Attendance*—Students who attend school regularly create fewer disciplinary problems than students who are habitually absent. The report suggests that an accurate system of student accounting be followed and that parents should be advised of their children's absences. Students who attend regularly should receive appropriate recognition.

According to a survey of South Carolina educators, good teachers also tend to be the most successful "creative" disciplinarians.[20] The educators surveyed identified the following techniques as the most successful in preventing disciplinary problems: consistent application of rules (85 percent); strong administrative leadership (84 percent); small number of students per teacher (76 percent); teacher skill in diagnosing academic weakness and prescribing instruction (63 percent); and respect for stu-

dents (57 percent).

Programs have been developed to involve students and teachers in practical experiences that help them become more aware of their own and others' feelings and lead to better communication between teachers and students. Some of these include teacher effectiveness training, values clarification and approaches for motivating children.

Often the alternatives to corporal punishment are suggested by the very nature of the offense. For instance, in the incident described, when students were physically punished for carrying tobacco, a reasonable alternative might have been to assign the boys a project in which they would read literature and view films pointing out the dangers of smoking and then write a report suitable to their needs, interests and abilities.

Much of what has been outlined on alternatives to corporal punishment is based on the experience of educators. However, there is a growing body of literature on educational research that offers alternatives based on empirical findings. Jacob Kounin has discovered common mistakes made by poor classroom managers [21] and Hyman has developed Kounin's work into a system for training teachers to be better managers in order to avoid the need for paddling.[22]

In conclusion, it is apparent that our society has allowed the single largest institution dealing with children to continue barbaric procedures in order to establish a so-called "learning atmosphere." Over the last several years the Gallup polls have indicated that discipline is

4. INSTITUTIONS

considered the single most pressing problem in the schools. For many, discipline means physically punishing children in response to their misbehavior. However, such a response creates a syndrome of violence and counter-violence that can only lead to a self-destructive climate in the schools.

---

[1] The Center was established with grants from the Randen Foundation and the National Committee to Abolish Corporal Punishment in the Schools in September 1976. Housed and administered within the Department of School Psychology, Temple University, the Center cooperates with the American Psychological Association's Task Force on the Rights of Children and Youth and its Division of School Psychology; the American Civil Liberties Union and the California Committee to End Violence Against the Next Generation.
Since January the Center, which has assembled a reference library of over 500 documents related to the problems of corporal punishment, classroom discipline and violence in the schools, has published many papers and been involved in the development of legal briefs. Another major concern has been the development of educational strategies to serve as alternatives to corporal punishment. Staff members have designed clinics and in-service workshops to instruct teachers in classroom management techniques, and videotapes, bibliographies and a procedural manual have been produced to supplement this training. For further information write to: Dr. Irwin Hyman, Director, Center for the Study of Corporal Punishment and Alternatives in the Schools, 823 Ritter Hall Annex, Temple University, Philadelphia, Pa. 19122.

[2] National Education Association, *Report of the Task Force on Corporal Punishment*, 1972 (Library of Congress #22-85743).

[3] R. Friedman and I. Hyman, "An Analysis of State Legislation Regarding Corporal Punishment," a paper presented at the Conference on Child Abuse, Children's Hospital National Medical Center, Washington, D.C., February 1977.

[4] E. Elardo, "Implementing Behavior Modification Procedures in an Elementary School," a paper presented at the annual meeting of the American Educational Research Association, New York City, 1977.

[5] J. F. Killory, "In Defense of Corporal Punishment," *Psychological Reports*, No. 35, 1974.

[6] N. J. Azrin and W. C. Holz, "Punishment," in *Operant Behavior* (edited by W. K. Honig), New York, Appleton-Century-Crofts, 1966.

[7] A. Bandura, "Social Learning Through Imitation," in *Nebraska Symposium on Maturation* (edited by M. R. Jones), Lincoln, University of Nebraska Press, 1962.

[8] S. M. Berger, "Conditioning Through Vicarious Insignation," *Psychological Review*, Vol. 69, 1962.

[9] B. Rosenshine and N. Furst, "Research in Teacher Performance Criteria," in *Research in Teacher Education* (edited by B. O. Smith), Englewood Cliffs, Prentice-Hall Inc., 1971.

[10] N. J. Azrin, D. F. Hake and R. Hutchinson, "Elicitation of Aggression by a Physical Blow," *Journal of Experimental Analysis of Behavior*, Vol. 8, 1965 and A. Bandura, D. Ross and S. A. Ross, "Transmission of Aggression Through Imitation of Aggressive Models," *Journal of Abnormal Social Psychology*, Vol. 63, 1961.

[11] H. Clarizio, "Some Myths Regarding the Use of Corporal Punishment in the Schools," a paper presented at the annual meeting of the American Educational Research Association, 1975.

[12] A. Bongiovanni, "A Review of Research of the Effects of Punishment," a paper presented at the Conference on Child Abuse, Children's Hospital National Medical Center, Washington, D.C., February 1977.

[13] A. Buttons, "Some Antecedents of Felonies and Delinquent Behavior," *Journal of Clinical Child Psychology*, Vol. 2, 1973 and P. Welsh, "Severe Parental Punishment and Delinquency," *Journal of Clinical Child Psychology*, Vol. 3, 1974.

[14] Clarizio, op. cit.

[15] National Education Association, op. cit.

[16] Elardo, op. cit.

[17] S. M. Shafer, *Corporal Punishment Survey*, Pittsburgh, Pa., Board of Education, Office of Research, June 1968.

[18] *One Million Children: The Celdic Report, A National Study of Canadian Children with Emotional and Learning Disorders*, Leonard Crainford for the Commission on Emotional and Learning Disorders in Children, Toronto, Canada, 1970.

[19] South Carolina State Department of Education, *Report of Task Force on Alternatives to School Disciplinary and Suspension Problems*, Columbia, South Carolina, 1976.

[20] Survey: "Good Teachers Are Also Creative Disciplinarians," *South Carolina Education Association Emphasis*, August 20, 1976.

[21] J. S. Kounin, *Discipline and Group Management in the Classroom*, New York, Holt, Rinehart and Winston, Inc., 1970.

[22] I. Hyman, "Consultation in Classroom Management Based on Empirical Research," a paper presented at the annual meeting of the American Psychological Association, Honolulu, 1972 and "A Bicentennial Consideration of the Advent of Child Advocacy," *Journal of Clinical Child Psychology*, Winter 1976.

YOU ARE LOOKING AT AN ABUSED CHILD.

Most of the convicts in prison today were abused as children. Their parents committed crimes on them long before they entered lives of crime themselves.

Another sad fact: People who are abused as children tend to abuse their own children. It's the only kind of parenting they know.

Child abuse is a monumental problem in America, and it continues from generation to generation. It is estimated that there are at least one million cases of child abuse in America each year, and over 2,000 of those children die. And many more are scarred for life physically or mentally.

The one happy note in this message is this: **You** can help change things for the better. And we'll be glad to tell you how.

 **HELP DESTROY A FAMILY TRADITION. WRITE:**
National Committee for Prevention of Child Abuse, Box 2866, Chicago, Ill. 60690.

145

Our Children's Keepers: Institutions in an Abusive Society

"Our Children's Keepers: Institutions in an Abusive Society," from *Human Ecology Forum*, Vol. 8, No. 1, Summer 1977. ©1977 Cornell University.

Each community has its own human ecology, the system through which its members relate. A community's health can be gauged by how well it responds to members needs, how thoroughly it accommodates diversity, how easily it integrates the excluded, and how devotedly it encourages a common sense of caring for the problems of individuals.

As a nation of communities, the United States has developed through time a pattern of entrusting the care of troubled individuals to others. The pattern is based on the development of institutions — a new institution, it seems, for each newly defined problem. Until very recently, the pattern has resulted in a countryside dotted with large buildings: brick and mortar to house an expanding number of needful individuals: sizable places with hundreds or even thousands of beds whose occupants, once they get there, tend to remain there for many years.

Rurally located residential facilities have been idealized on and off throughout our history. The most idealized have been those created for the protection of children. From the earliest orphanages and hospitals to the most recent developmental centers and detention camps, such facilities have been described as places where the abandoned, abused, handicapped and deprived could get a new start and a protective environment far from the depraved conditions they might have faced back in their home communities. For the severely handicapped, the ideal reflects a social admission that the chore of caring is too great for even the most loving and giving of families. For the delinquent, the ideal reflects a social awareness that the road out of trouble probably didn't exist in the child's home or neighborhood.

The ideal was based in fact. From the earliest days of the republic to the turn of the present century, a "village idiot" syndrome persisted and was fairly widespread. The "abnormal" child and the downtrodden child of the street were subject to everything from public abuse to mob murder when temper or caprice moved the community's less humane members. The rural residential facility was designed to eliminate such incidents and to protect the most unfortunate children.

An increasing corps of critics has begun to repudiate the notion that such children benefit from care in large institutions. They argue that institutions are impersonal, disconnected from the rest of society, unresponsive to the needs of the children in their care, incapable of providing a healthy developmental environment, and that they sometimes abuse and brutalize children.

The major drive among today's reformers is to empty the large rural facilities and replace them with small residences, family (foster) care and day centers and programs in the child's hometown.

Massachusetts was a leader among the states in replacing its large juvenile correction centers with small community based facilities. Other states are following and certain federal regulations tie tax dollars to the concept. The courts have begun to take some strong steps. In Texas for example, juridical findings of inhumane conditions in the large congregate care institutions have led to a court order to the state's Youth Council to develop community based facilities.

Surfacing evidence of widespread physical, psychological and sexual abuse of children in large institutions has been one of the strong impetuses to the new trend of "deinstitutionalization." Such evidence includes child abuse by staff (directly), by administration and officialdom (indirectly) and by the children themselves (with the tacit permission of those responsible for the children's well-being).

The problems in some institutions have been well publicized. Even if the definition of institutional child abuse were limited to the most obvious categories — the physical, sexual, nutritional, drug and therapy-related mistreatment of children in other-than-home settings — there is compelling evidence that something is wrong.

In *Weeping in the Playtime of Others: America's Incarcerated Children*, author Kenneth Wooden has detailed the physical and psychological brutality perpetrated on children in the name of treatment in institutions around the country.

In the case of Texas, a year-long investigation by the FBI of the juvenile corrections system established that the facilities were operated with officially sanctioned brutality. Inmates were beaten, tear gassed in solitary confinement cells, put to hard labor and placed — as punishment — in dormitories with older inmates where they were sexually abused. In addition, there was racial segregation, a prohibition against speaking Spanish among a population one-third Chicano and a lack of effective treatment and schooling.

Jerome Miller, who dismantled the large juvenile correction institutions in Massachusetts earlier in the decade and who is now Commissioner of Youth in Pennsylvania, told *Corrections* magazine, "I think that most places that house juveniles are underneath [it all] brutal, I think that large institutions with coerced populations are based in violence.

BLAME THE SYSTEM

"There is a difference between a system that brings out the worst impulses in people and people who are bad. At Roslindale [an institution in Massachusetts], for instance, we hired young, radical students out of Harvard to work, and within six months, they were fascists. . . . I don't go around saying we had an evil staff; I said that we had a system that mistreated people and brought out people's worst impulses."

Social historian David Rothman (in "Decarcerating Prisoners and Patients" in *Civil Liberties Review*, Fall 1973) has written in a similar vein: "Earlier reformers always placed the blame for institutional failures on a poorly trained service staff, or insufficient funding, or faulty administrators. We, for our part, are blaming the system. The very idea of incarceration is now suspect. It is not the wardens or the guards or the attendants that are to blame for the inadequacies: it is the very notion of correcting or curing people by locking them up behind walls."

Although physical brutality is the most obvious and dramatic abuse, many authorities talk of more subtle and pervasive forms of institutional abuse.

Dr. Jeanne Deschner of the Center for Applied Research and Evaluation in Houston says instances of physical abuse are "fairly rare." But she points to "abuse in the sense that kids are not getting the treatment they need." She told us that "They're just being warehoused, tucked away somewhere.

Trapped inside an institution.
So scary at first — dull, dingy
rooms all around.
usually loud
or complete silence —
no in-betweens.
Chip stairs up.
People playing cards,
watching t.v.
wasting time.
Having a feeling of escaping,
running, but yet
staying because people
are friendly
plastic — but friendly
Staying or stuck?

That type of abuse is very, very common. In large institutions, you end up moving groups rather than dealing with people.

"When children are institutionalized, they are taken away from their communities and families," Deschner says. "They don't learn the skills that they will need as adults. They need treatment rather than being told what to do all the time. They should be learning to develop responsibility for their finances, food, entertainment and social life. Up to this point in our history, we have used the nuclear family to teach these skills. In institutions, we have not."

Additionally, the very structure of the institution isolates youngsters by age. They find themselves in the bizarre situation of spending their most formative years with only their peers and their keepers as models.

The result is that children are psychologically and socially crippled by their dependence on the custodial care of institutions. They develop a self-concept of being "different." Many cannot cope when they re-enter society and end up returning to institutional settings — jails or mental hospitals — as adults.

Like Deschner, George Thomas, president of the Regional Institute of Social Welfare in Georgia, states that in terms of the thousands of institutions in this country, the physical abuse of children "is not that widespread." He, however, argues that institutional child abuse occurs "in an administrative sense" because of "unjust practices leading to a child's inappropriate confinement."

"The primary abuse," he said in our telephone interview, "is in depriving children of the right to a decent home by placing them directly in institutions and keeping them there in prolonged care — deprived of a placement that at least approximates a natural home."

Thomas warns that the deinstitutionalization of children will not automatically end the problems of abuse normally identified with larger institutions. "Part of the answer to getting rid of that kind of abuse," he says, "is to acknowledge that there is no magical environment. There is nothing necessarily less abusive about a more individualized setting. The quality of care depends on how the people running the institution treat the children."

Similarly, Rothman warns, "The benevolent aims of the founders of prisons and asylums did not prevent the subsequent degeneration of those institutions, and the nobility of our ambitions is no guarantee that alternatives to incarceration will not be as awful as the buildings they replace.

LEGACY OF FAILURE

"It is one thing to give lip service to the concept," Rothman points out in his article "and quite another thing to implement it successfully." Rothman, a professor at Columbia University, wrote that our attempts to improve the institutional system reflect "a history of changes without reform." He says that "each generation discovers anew the scandals of incarceration, each sets out to correct them and each passes on a legacy of failure."

Implementing deinstitutionalization, some proponents predict, will mean difficult political struggles with a variety of factions.

At the pioneer National Workshop on Institutional Child Abuse held at Cornell in June 1977, Pennsylvania's Jerome Miller said, "Deinstitutionalization is not a technical issue, not a matter of knowing what to do. It is a matter of the will to do it.

"When talking about deinstitutionalization, we are not simply talking about making a decision to close big buildings; we are talking about vested interests, contracts, architectural fees [and state officials'] cozy relationships with contractors."

When these large public facilities were created, they engendered thousands of jobs and frequently became the most important economic force in the small communities where they were located. The swing to deinstitutionalization has thrown both those jobs and the economic stability of those communities into uncertainty, but even AFSCME (the American Federation of State, County and Municipal Employees) is on record as supporting the trend. The conditions they place on such support will surprise no one: they call for the guarantee for the well-being of institutionalized clients and for the guarantee of new jobs for workers displaced by the process of deinstitutionalization.

Miller pointed to a recent episode in Pennsylvania where he had announced plans to transfer juvenile offenders from an adult prison to smaller care settings. Miller said that AFSCME exerted strong political pressures against the move. AFSCME has, in fact, opposed Miller's attempts in the three states where he has worked — Massachusetts, Illinois and Pennsylvania.

At Cornell, Miller said that to break the political bottlenecks that stymie reform, deinstitutionalization proponents must address the problem of "the captive-keeper relationship" in state-run institutions that, in many cases, allows clients' interests to be ignored.

"I think we have to ask ourselves why, at a time when Dorothea Dix was campaigning against the use of leg irons and manacles in state institutions in the 19th century, McLean Hospital in Boston, (which served children of the wealthy) had a petting zoo and open-ended visiting hours. I think the reason was one of consumerism: wealthy people could come and go freely at McLean and they could take their money with them if they were unhappy with what it bought in the way of care for their children."

Based on the belief that the same type of consumer choice should exist among the residents of state-run institutions, some reformers are pushing for a voucher system that would allow greater consumer power over the services received. Under the plan, the institutionalized person or the person's family would receive an allotment of money to spend for institutional services and, if dissatisfied with the quality of care in one setting, could transfer to another. The voucher system is based on the rationale that if consumers are given the power of the purse, institutions would be more responsive to their needs. They believe this would lead to a wider variety and availability of services.

"A voucher system introduces some type of consumerism into the system, a greater questioning and more accountability than we have now," stated Berkeley's Martin Wollins in discussions at the Cornell conference.

Ronald Feldman, Director of the Boys Town Center for the Study of Youth Development, added, "A voucher system would create a free market economy where one does

not exist."

It is important to listen to Rothman and consider the possibility that a voucher system is yet another reform without change. What exactly does vouchering do for the welfare of the child and the child's family? Will vouchering end abuse? Would shifting children into smaller, more personalized settings in a location selected and approved by the family, break the child out of isolation from the normal rhythms of the community or would it merely be a new kind of isolation? What is the social outcome — does vouchering make for a better, less abusive society? Is it a clear step in that direction, with easily understood steps that follow?

UNHEALTHY URGE

Many observers have commented on the irony that Americans seem intolerant of differences between people even though "individualism" is one of the society's highest values.

Historically we have labeled hundreds of thousands as misfits to be put out of sight behind the walls and gates of institutions with names like Mountain Stream or Willowbrook. We seem ever ready to apply what Philip Slater refers to in the *Pursuit of Loneliness* as "the toilet assumption." We assume that "unwanted matter, unwanted difficulties, unwanted complexities and obstacles will disappear if they are removed from our immediate field of vision."

Neither a pocketful of vouchers nor a cadre of advocates can eliminate the unhealthy urge to flush away members of the society who do not meet an arbitrary definition of normality.

Cornell's family ecologist Urie Bronfenbrenner talked about community functioning and social isolation during an interview with *Human Ecology Forum*. "It used to be that children were isolated in institutions. Now they're becoming isolated outside of institutions. So very often deinstitutionalization means placing the child back into a world as alienated as the institution itself," he said.

The development of a healthy human ecology where the whole community accepts responsibility for the needs of each of its members is a critical priority in Bronfenbren-

---

Nine Ways of Looking at Death

1
Death is alright if it happens
at night / creeps up like dark
dies away like a spark.

2
Death isn't me
I don't like death.
Dead people or animals
make me cold
feels like ice.

3
Death is strange
Death means
Reincarnation to
some people. Death
is weird. People die
and people live / then
what's the use of living
if people die

4
It must be an experience
but I can't really say.
It's nothing anyone
has ever come back
to tell.
It must be an experience.

5
Death is dark
the unknown
it's scary and frightening.
Why must it
seem so bad

6
do it if you want
but don't not do it
for me.

7
I love life
but I dislike mystery
but I hate death — but
I shall not want to see
death.

8
I was born I know I'll die
but when it will come
it will be
short silent and peaceful
and beautiful because
the wind will be blowing
while I'll be
still and peaceful and my
spirit will rest.

9
death make me feel
like death.

Yesterday you loved me.
You said that you cared.
I'll never forget
The times that we shared
Today I turn
And find you're not there.
It's hard to believe
That you really did care.
I think of you often
With tears in my eyes.
I turn and I say
"I love you, good-bye!"

ner's analysis. "One of the fundamental problems with American society," said Bronfenbrenner, "is that we fragment everything. The essence of a social system is networks. You don't sever. You keep connections."

"I've argued that it is very important for all neighborhoods in every community to keep track of what's happening to their children and the people who are or would be available to become involved in the lives of those children. I think that applies immediately to the case where you have deinstitutionalized children in the community. Who's available for them? What type of place do they have? What is the community willing to do in order to give them a meaningful role?

"The Chinese have given that a tremendous amount of careful thought, so that what we call 'misfits' in our society are 'fits' in theirs."

In the context of Bronfenbrenner's analysis, it is conceivable that a voucher system could isolate the child and the child's family from the fuller community and separate the community from the realities of the needful child's life just as effectively as the present system does.

Larry King, who works as an advocate for institutionalized children in North Carolina, has expressed concerns about deinstitutionalization as a cure-all. In a telephone interview, King said, while he is opposed to big institutions because they are "innately evil in their concept and philosophy," deinstitutionalization is often undertaken "to comply with trends, not people's needs. Where do people go when they leave large institutions? The emphasis has been on discharge, not relocation." As a result, according to King, a population once invis-

ible to us in resident facilities is made even more invisible by being dispersed from those facilities.

Many people we interviewed pointed to problems that plague institutions: underbudgeting, overcrowding, unqualified staff and lack of proper training for personnel. Some also claimed that media reports had exaggerated and distorted the problem of institutional child abuse.

Douglas Besharov, executive director of the National Center on Child Abuse and Neglect in HEW (the sponsors of the Cornell workshops) said in a radio interview that "institutions are a necessary and very constructive mode of helping and caring for young children." Avowing that abuse of children in institutions is widespread, he pointed to the high cost of proper care and noted that the "great pressure" on tax dollars is a contributing factor.

He said that there is also a tendency in our society to use institutions as places where we can shuttle people off into the background — people whom we think are unattractive or ugly or uncared for. It's not just lack of money, but also a lack of humanity," he said. (See the complete interview on page 9.)

John Doris, a researcher in atypical development at the College of Human Ecology, argued another side of the question. Not only is institutional care expensive, but also it is necessary in the most severe and complex cases. Communities are simply incapable of providing services that the most needful require. Severe mental and physical disabilities cannot be properly attended to in small towns with anything like the effectiveness that they can in appropriate congregate care settings.

CARING COMMUNITIES

A final set of questions emerged for us. Can institutions exist without abusing children? Will communities take responsibility for children who need special help? Is there a plan to deinstitutionalize that promises anything but a new set of institutions at the local level — more humane, perhaps, but still institutions? Is deinstitutionalization, in fact, re-institutionalization?

In the end we concluded that if institutional child abuse is to disappear, communities must take back

responsibility for all but the most terribly handicapped of their children. Connections must be made, caring communities created.

Our informants led us to understand that institutions can play a primary role in making the necessary connections.

Those connections can be facilitated by people who provide a human service function: local government officials, governing boards of service, agency administrators and workers, and the media.

Three kinds of connections were suggested to us:

1. That the treatment of the most needful children — those who require care in a resident institution permanently or for an extended period of time and at a distance from home — be extended to the family so that the family can share in community life despite the special responsibility for their special child.

2. That institutions that do not require permanent residency break down the barriers between the institutions and the community.

3. That whenever possible children be released from institutions, and that the institutions assist those children, as well as their families, in becoming integrated into their neighborhoods and surrounding community.

The impulse must develop both from the community and from the institutions engendered by the community. Human service workers of all sorts — nutritionists, youth leaders, representatives of the mass media, governmental and institutional board members, volunteers, professionals, community service workers and organizers, Cooperative Extension agents, teachers, scholars and technicians — have roles to play that are definable at the local level.

One very discouraging aspect of our interviews was the almost unanimous admission that the institutions that are harboring abuse are functionally outside the boundaries of full accountability and monitoring. Self-correcting mechanisms are not even marginally effective. Administrative redress is generally unwieldy at best.

It gets down to this: institutions need to be well integrated into communities, and communities need to take direct responsibility for their children — even in a society that Bronfenbrenner points out gives no rewards for such caring.

Douglas Besharov, director of the National Center on Child Abuse and Neglect, was interviewed by Media Services radio specialist Michael Veley during the National Workshop on Institutional Child Abuse held recently at the N.Y. State College of Human Ecology, Cornell University.

Q First of all, what is your definition of institutional child abuse?

A There is no single definition. Institutional child abuse ranges from acts of beastiality and brutality, unreasonable and terrible corporal punishment, murder and sexual abuse, all the way to what may be the most pervasive form of abuse: the failure to adequately plan for and treat the long-term needs of children living in residential institutions.

Q How serious a problem is institutional child abuse in the United States today?

A We have no numbers as yet because institutional child abuse, like child abuse performed by parents, occurs behind closed doors. But we do know from the glimpses we've seen that it is a widespread problem involving many young children.

Q Some people say that the most serious form of abuse is institutionalization itself. Do you agree with that?

A Sometimes it can be, but I also think that the institutions are a necessary and very constructive mode of helping and caring for young people.

Q Are some types of institutions more likely to provide an environment for child abuse than others?

A Yes. I think the wisdom, which is both scientific and common-sense, is that the larger an institution is the harder time it has having heart and compassion. Federal standards recommend, and I personally feel, that institutions really should not be large congregate centers because such places breed inhumanity.

Q Why is child abuse, both in institutions and the home, so widespread today? What are some of the causes?

Q: Isn't money a small part of the problem of institutional child abuse? A: No.

A Probably the most significant cause of institutional child abuse and neglect is the fact that it costs a great deal of money to care for children properly. If institutional care for one child for one year costs $50,000, clearly it is difficult to deliver quality care in a time when there is great pressure on state and local tax dollars. And so I think money is a major problem. But I would be remiss if I didn't say there is also a tendency to shuttle people off into the background — people who are ugly or uncared for or unattractive. Many of the abused and neglected children, many mentally retarded children or handicapped children can be pushed aside. It's not just lack of money, but also a lack of humanity.

Q Do abused children tend to be abusive parents when they grow up?

A Although the scientific information is not yet in, it's clear that many, many parents who abuse their children were themselves abused as children. There are other social costs. Many violent criminals, many murderers, many muggers were abused and neglected as children. The evidence isn't in, but it appears there is a relationship between a positive, nurturant upbringing, a safe environment, and absence of later violent activity.

Q What are some of the goals of the National Center on Child Abuse and Neglect concerning institutional child abuse?

A The National Center's role is one of assisting others. We don't provide direct services. We help state and local agencies provide them. We are attempting with this [The College of Human Ecology's National Workshop], the first of our major activities related to institutional child abuse and neglect, to draw attention to the problem, to engage the interests of professionals, and from there to build our knowledge and then to help others use that knowledge to improve preventive and corrective programs.

Q Would a law similar to New York's law on reporting child abuse in the home be beneficial if adapted to institutional child abuse?

A It's sure to be a complicated process, and the law will have to change somewhat in relation to institutional abuse. But yes, I think that ultimately we will have to have a law that says that certain types of professionals must report the brutality they see in institutions. Lord knows there should be no objection to that.

Q Who actually is responsible for an abused child in an institution? Is it the institution or the staff member who might abuse the child?

A Aren't we all responsible?

Q You mentioned that money was a problem, but isn't money really a small part of the overall problem?

A No.

Q Will you explain?

A It costs money to have high quality institutions. If we want them, we'll have to pay for them.

Q Are institutions basically understaffed today with unqualified people?

A I can't generalize, but I can say this: if you have a person who is paid $4,800 a year to serve as a caretaker to children in an institution, yet a welfare client can receive $5,600 a year just by having children at home, I think you have a serious discrepancy. That says something about the quality of care that will go on in institutions.

"Q: Isn't money a small part of the problem of institutional child abuse? A: No." Michael Veley, *Human Ecology Forum*, Vol. 8, No. 1, Summer 1977 Cornell Universtiy.

151

Topical Storms
Recommendations To End Institutional Child Abuse

Large institutions are not good for children. That was the consensus among the 80 professionals who attended the National Workshop on Institutional Child Abuse at Cornell in June. They made 16 major recommendations aimed at eliminating the physical, emotional and intellectual abuse of children in institutions.

The recommendations are:

● Halt the construction of all large institutions for children.

● Replace existing large institutions with smaller institutions located near large cities.

● Treat children in their own homes whenever possible.

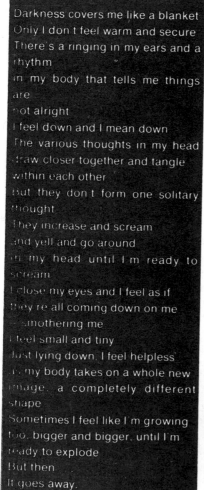

Darkness covers me like a blanket
Only I don't feel warm and secure
There's a ringing in my ears and a rhythm
in my body that tells me things are
not alright
I feel down and I mean down
The various thoughts in my head
draw closer together and tangle
within each other
But they don't form one solitary thought
They increase and scream
and yell and go around
in my head until I'm ready to scream
I close my eyes and I feel as if
they're all coming down on me
smothering me
I feel small and tiny
Just lying down. I feel helpless
As my body takes on a whole new
image, a completely different shape
Sometimes I feel like I'm growing
too, bigger and bigger, until I'm
ready to explode
But then
It goes away.

● Place children in a homelike setting — such as a foster or group home in their community — when they must be removed from home for their own safety.

● Keep mentally retarded children out of institutions.

● Jail only those juveniles who have committed violent crimes; never incarcerate 'status offenders' who are 'guilty' of acts such as truancy that would not be punished if committed by adults.

● Encourage private, competing agencies — not the government — to develop community child services; insure that those agencies are answerable to the communities in which they are located.

● Develop voucher systems — money that moves with each child — rather than financing institutions directly.

● Educate parents, neighbors and volunteers about the need for day care, group homes and halfway houses in their communities.

● Limit the size of institutions to 20 beds or less; provide one staff member for every three children.

● Establish standard rights and advocacy programs for all institutionalized children.

● Train institutional staff on their responsibilities in insuring children's rights.

● Allow the children the right to refuse treatment without being punished; require institutionalized children to do only what all children must do, such as attend school.

● Abolish the use of corporal punishment, drugs and isolation as restraints in institutions; use crisis intervention teams instead.

● Establish independent agencies in each institution that would have the power to investigate complaints about abuse and hold public hearings; report complaints about abuse to parents and police.

● Require all people dealing with child care services (including judges) to visit institutions for children; educate all child care personnel in children's rights.

The National Workshop on Institutional Child Abuse was conducted by the Family Life Development Center, a resource demonstration project on child abuse prevention located at the N.Y. State College of Human Ecology, Cornell and was funded by the National Center on Child Abuse and Neglect, U.S. Department of Health, Education and Welfare.

Participants represented child advocates, former inmates, social service agencies, labor unions, the White House, state and federal regulators, community groups, universities as well as institutions.

They placed the blame for current institutional problems on communities that want mentally retarded and delinquent children out of sight, and on a system of financing and staffing institutions that encourages the institutions to hold on to children rather than treating them for release.

Both the child and the community suffer, said Frank Schneiger, director of the Protective Services Resource Institute in New Jersey. "The child loses identity, the ability to make friends, family and cultural ties, family values, and suffers a great deal of unhappiness," Schneiger said. "Communities lose the capacity to deal with differences and diversity."

Louis M. Thrasher, director of the office of special litigation in the U.S. Justice Department's Civil Rights Division said that "Children should never be institutionalized for care and treatment unless every other alternative has been exhausted."

Unfortunately, he said, the current system not only puts children in institutions but guarantees that many will stay there for years. "All the economic incentives go to holding on to the body of the child," Thrasher explained. "The longer they have it, the more money they get. There ought to be guarantees that unless a child care agency meets specific goals by specific dates, it must give up the child to a more normal setting."

Jim Titus

Poems were written by residents of South Lansing Center, operated by the New York State Division for Youth in Lansing, New York.

Advocacy for the Abused Rural Child

Joseph A. Leistyna

Joseph A. Leistyna, M.D. director of Pediatric Ambulatory Services at the Univsity of Connecticut School of Medicine, Farmington, is chairman of the medical school's Child Protection Team and the project pediatrician for the Connecticut Child Abuse and Neglect Demonstration Center.

Much of what we have learned about child abuse and neglect in the United States stems from studies of lower-class, urban families. Little information has been available on the needs of many of our rural children, especially those from impoverished and developmentally crippling environments. However, several newly established child abuse programs are focusing on the needs of rural communities (see box insert) and more information on these activities should become available in the near future.

Joann Davies recently described some of the specialized skills that rural child protection professionals need in order to provide an effective program.[1] She also described such difficulties as the loneliness of decision making, the geographic distances involved, the isolation of the rural child protection worker and the lack of specialized resources, all handicaps which must be overcome in order to assure a successful program.

As the only practicing pediatrician in a rural county in Virginia during the years 1972 to 1975, I had an opportunity to work with a group of local professionals who served as volunteers in establishing, with the guidance of Anthony Shaw, professor of pediatrics and surgery, and his co-workers at the University of Virginia, one of the original community-based child protection teams in the state. This project later resulted in revision of Virginia's child abuse and neglect laws to include provision for the establishment of a network of hospital and community-based child protection teams throughout the state.[2]

Our multidisciplinary team consisted of two nurses, two social workers, three physicians (a surgeon, an obstetrician and a pediatrician), a mental health worker, a schoolteacher and a local attorney. Between 1974 and 1975, during the first full year of operation, the team investigated 47 cases of child abuse and neglect in a county of 18,000 people. These 47 cases, along with several others that the child protection team was not able to fully investigate by the end of the year, gave the county an overall incidence rate of 300 cases per 100,000 population. This rate exceeded C. Henry Kempe's original estimates of 25 to 30 cases per 100,000 population by tenfold[3] and closely approximated the current estimate of the National Center on Child Abuse and Neglect, Children's Bureau, ACYF, that a million children in the United States may fall victim to abuse and neglect each year.

Of the 47 cases evaluated by our child protection team, 29 involved physical abuse, including two deaths from severe trauma. The remainder included 10 cases of neglect, two cases of emotional abuse and six cases of sexual molestation. Forty-two of the children came from low-income families that were stressed by a number of environmental and social factors: poverty, deprivation, ignorance, apathy, social isolation (many of the families were without telephones or reliable automobiles) and inaccessibility to supportive health care systems. Home visits by the team's social workers often revealed the same desolate, non-nurturing, often violent lifestyle that Elizabeth Elmer found so lethal to normal psycho-social development in children of poor, inner-city families.[4]

A notable weakness in our child abuse program was the routine follow-up of active cases. In the entire county, there were only three social workers, four public health nurses and four mental health workers, three of whom worked part time. There were no parent aides, day care centers, crisis nurseries, hotlines or Parents Anonymous groups. Any therapeutic approach to working with abusive families was difficult—the county was large, entirely rural and without public transportation, and salaried personnel were too few to accomplish the tasks necessary to maintain an effective child abuse program. It was obvious that a cadre of child protective workers would have to be recruited and trained to supplement our inadequate staff. Since local funds were not available, the child protection team members evolved a comprehensive grant proposal which was submitted to HEW, without success. Urban study groups continued to attract most of the nation's research and demonstration funds.

It is of vital importance that attention be directed to increase the delivery of supportive services to rural children and their distressed families. Personnel capable of functioning in remote areas, far from the variety of resources found in the city, must be recruited and trained; the delivery of appropriate services demands a keen awareness of social and environmental factors unique to small towns and isolated farming communities. Supportive services require funding. Funding in turn requires an interested sponsor—a political figure seeking a large return at the polls, for example, or a demanding child advocacy group, neither of which abounds in rural areas.

Who, then, is to assume responsibility for advocacy for abused and neglected rural children? Local and regional governments bemoan their financial incapabilities and react slowly to public pressure and opinion. Rural politicians often fail to identify community needs; they may be suspicious of "big government" intervention through funded programs and fear a loss of local autonomy. Rural physicians are too few in number and fully occupied in providing care for those families who are motivated to seek help, capable of transporting themselves to the provider and able and willing to pay for necessary services.

Effective advocacy for abused and neglected children requires professional education and training so that symptoms of abuse, neglect and deprivation are identified and reported. It also requires professional ability to evaluate the special needs and problems of abused children and the effect of treatment programs for them, including any harmful effects. It is also necessary to make sure that children will receive continuing treatment until their homes are safe, the parents' problems are under control and the child's physical, psychological and developmental disorders are successfully treated.[5]

Who is to provide the special education and training to achieve these goals, especially in rural communities? Can medical centers provide such a resource? If so, medical institutions must first become more deeply involved in the broad concepts of child and family health, including the evolvement of interdisciplinary, community-oriented patient care models. The components of such outreach programs would address the social, educational, psychological, economic and ecologic exigencies that impact on healthy family function; the effect on the prevention, early identification and treatment of child abuse and neglect is obvious.

In order to generate institutional commitment to such programs, child service providers at every level (physicians, nurses, teachers, nursery and day care workers, advocacy groups, private and public agencies) must agitate and advocate that medical centers across the nation be induced to regionalize and organize their catchment areas. Effective agitation and advocacy demands concerted provider and interagency cooperation and a unified, interdisciplinary "assault" on the nearest medical institution.

Coordinated, direct contact by advocacy groups should be made with the following:

• Regional and state public health officials who can be useful allies when presenting statistics and community needs assessments to a medical center faculty.

• State legislators who have special interest in health issues and input into the policies of state medical schools.

• Representatives of private industry in the community (especially newly relocated complexes that have moved from urban areas) who recognize the need for outreach services for their employees.

• Department chairmen of medical schools, who are often very receptive to community needs once they have been systematically informed of the needs and community interest in meeting them has been demonstrated.

• Any local citizens who are associated with the nearest medical center, especially physicians and other professionals who are alumni of that institution.

A willingness to cooperate with any outreach programs that the medical schools may attempt is of utmost importance. This includes cooperation in providing a usable facility within the community; one successful program often leads to another. Advocates should also be willing to attend meetings and functions of local organizations and to speak about the needs of the community. Public awareness and an aroused community interest facilitate initiation and implementation of program proposals among legislators, health department personnel and medical school administrators. Medical institutions can thus be motivated to seek adequate funding to develop outreach units, mini-clinics and a corps of resource personnel to serve those rural areas which lack essential facilities.

Such program commitment would facilitate the establishment of workable child abuse programs, ongoing health and special therapeutic services for distressed rural families, expansion of rural school curricula to include family life and child development courses and the promotion of adult education programs to include courses in parenting and childrearing. It would also encourage the design and implementation of efficient patient transport systems.

It is crucial to the future well-being of many of America's rural children and their multi-problem families that all disciplines in the allied child health services advocate for the development, implementation and coordination of comprehensive and accessible supportive services, services presently non-existent in large areas of our nation.

[1] J. Davies, "The Specialized Skills of Rural Child Protection Professionals," National Child Protection *Newsletter*, V, (No. 1), 1977.

[2] Virginia Child Protection *Newsletter*, IV, (No. 2), 1977.

[3] C.H. Kempe and R.E. Helfer, *Helping the Battered Child and his Family*, Philadelphia and Toronto, J.B. Lippincott, 1972.

[4] E. Elmer, "A Follow-Up Study of Traumatized Children," *Pediatrics*, 59:273, 1977.

[5] B. Fraser and H.P. Martin, "An Advocate For The Abused Child," H.P. Martin (ed.), *The Abused Child*, Cambridge, Ballinger Publishing Co., 1976.

They Dare to Care
CHILD ABUSE VOLUNTEERS

*A report on a new and spreading approach to the problem of child abuse,
developed with the loving help of "ordinary" women*

By MARCIA KAMIEN Four years ago Sally Thompson, twenty-five-year-old wife and mother, drove down a deserted and unfamiliar country road outside of Schenectady, New York, feeling very nervous. Usually relaxed and cheerful, she was gripping the steering wheel so hard her knuckles were white; and she asked herself, "What am I doing here?"

It wasn't really a question. She knew what she was doing. She was on her way to visit a family she'd never seen before—a family recently reported to the county's Child Protection Unit for suspected child abuse and neglect. What bothered her was that she didn't know what might happen once she got there.

Although Sally Thompson was probably Schenectady County's first child-abuse volunteer lay therapist, she wasn't aware of it. All she knew that spring day was that she wanted to help and that perhaps this was the way to do it. But what

if it wasn't, she wondered? What if the parents became violent and abusive with her?

The lonely road seemed to go on forever. And then, at last, there was a farmhouse followed by three plain frame buildings, all exactly the same, all badly in need of paint. Six rural mailboxes in a row all said JENSEN. She was at her destination.

At the last house the door was opened by a very young woman—a girl, really—underweight and unkempt, her long red hair dirty and tangled. She eyed her visitor with suspicion and finally said: "Yeah?"

Sally, suddenly conscious of her neat blazer, her diamond engagement ring, swallowed and smiled. "Linda Jensen? I'm Sally Thompson," she said. "I understand you're having some trouble with your children and I'm here to help." (The names of Mrs. Thompson and Mrs. Jensen have been changed in order to protect Mrs. Jensen's privacy.)

Lay therapist Pamela Mason (right) visits with Sandy Pandori and twin daughters, Candice and Linda.

"They Dare to Care, Child Abuse Volunteers," Marcia Kamien, *Women's Day*, November 20, 1978. © 1978 Women's Day Magazine.

"Another social worker!"

"No, no. I'm a volunteer. I *asked* to come."

"Well . . . I don't know what you can do. But come on in."

The house was a shambles—dirty, cluttered, filled with broken furniture. A dark-haired sturdy little girl of about five sat on the floor eating potato chips out of a bag and watching television cartoons. Sally greeted the child, looking at her carefully for signs of abuse. The complaint, made by Grandmother Jensen, had said that "something funny" was going on. But nothing seemed strange about this little girl, Ingrid.

"Is there another child?" Sally asked. She noticed that Ingrid and her mother exchanged quick glances. It was finally Ingrid who pointed silently to a closed door at the far end of the room.

When Sally opened the door, she nearly gasped aloud. Lying in a metal crib among grayed, filthy sheets, was a skeletal child, perhaps three years old, with the distended belly and pipestem legs of a starveling. Her blond hair had been hacked unevenly all over her head and she wore only a torn shirt. She was attached to the crib bars by a leather harness and lay, apathetic and silent, turning listless blue eyes blankly to Sally.

The comparison between this pathetic creature and the healthy little girl in the living room was shocking. Sally had to swallow again. But when she turned to the mother, she did not demand to know why this child was tied up and being starved. She did not head for the phone to call the police. She did not take the child and leave.

She did none of the things she probably would have done six weeks earlier —before she had signed up for a special workshop on child abuse and neglect. Sally had learned her lesson well. She only said gently: "I can see you have a problem. What can I do to help you?"

She still remembers the look of utter disbelief in Linda Jensen's eyes, followed by the very small spark of an almost-smile. That half-smile was the beginning of a close relationship between Linda Jensen and her voluntary friend/big sister/mother/adviser/advocate. Their friendship—a genuine, two-way bond unlike the more formal client-caseworker relationship—continues to this day. And today's Linda Jensen is a very different young woman, thanks to Sally's time, patience, understanding and caring. As Linda herself puts it: "She saved my life."

Sally denies that kind of credit. Her training—in a workshop run by Ginny Davidson, supervisor of Schenectady County's Child Protection Unit—taught her that "rescue fantasies" are *out*. "We're there to help, not judge," she explains. "We're not missionaries; we're friends. We begin by accepting, not by tearing down." What Linda really means, Sally believes, is that she now likes herself . . ."and that's partly because she knew right from the beginning that I was prepared to like her, no matter what."

Not judging is a prime requisite of child-abuse and neglect volunteers, along with patience, the ability to empathize with someone else's problems, and a quality that can only be described as "unflappable."

Sally, who was the only such volunteer in Schenectady County four years ago, is today one of twenty workers in what has developed into the Schenectady County Lay Therapy Program. Other similar projects can be found dotted across the country: in Little Rock, Arkansas (one of the first, since 1972); in Philadelphia, Pennsylvania; Oakland, California; St. Louis, Missouri; Westminster, Colorado; Brooklyn, New York, to name a few; plus two very recent additions in New York City and Saratoga Springs, New York.

All of these groups have been formed in response to a new understanding of what causes child abuse. After years of considering abusive parents monsters, undeserving of their children, research with actual families has uncovered a different story.

Abusing parents are under stress (which could be from poverty, crowded conditions, loneliness, extreme youth, alcoholism etc.) and are unable to cope.

Abusing parents were never properly parented and so never learned parenting. Most of them were abused as children, too.

Abusing parents are suspicious and distrustful of others, which leaves them friendless and isolated.

Abusing parents are depressed, dependent and deprived and need care as much as their children do.

In short, there are always two victims in child abuse: the child *and* the parent.

When Sally Thompson first met Linda Jensen, for example, she found all these factors in operation. Linda married while still in high school in order to get away from home, where her foster mother (she had been abandoned as an infant) entertained men at night. Even though Nils Jensen, a classmate, couldn't hold a job, got into fights and drank heavily, Linda thought their marriage not all bad: "Oh, he hit me a lot, but never hard enough to send me to the hospital"—until the birth of their second daughter, Susan.

Nils was the youngest, smallest and only dark-haired son in a family of blond giants. He was considered the black sheep and did his best to live up to that reputation. The first child, Ingrid, was the image of her father, small and dark. Susan, however, was big and blond—not a surprise, considering her redheaded mother and her father's fair family. Nils then "got it into his head that Susan wasn't his . . . that I had been having an affair with one of his brothers, and nothing would change his mind," Linda told Sally. "He said to keep that bastard child out of his sight or he'd kill her." Nils did abuse the baby on several occasions, so her mother kept her harnessed to the crib to prevent her from wandering into the rest of the house, and fed her small amounts under the misconception that it would slow her growth and make her look more like her sister.

Says Sally: "Linda couldn't go to her in-laws; they already considered Nils a disgrace, and Linda was included. She had no neighbors closer than five or six miles, no means of transportation and nobody to talk to. It was actually a lucky day for Linda when she was reported because then she had someone to talk to and someone to help—me."

Sally began by telling Nils (who was, and remains, scared of her) that there are laws against beating small children and that he would have to stop. Nils complied—this is generally what happens—and Susan was freed from her prison and allowed to thrive at last. Then Linda needed tending. "Her teeth needed fixing," said Sally. "She needed to learn how to cook, how to shop for food. She had to learn her way around agencies so she could get assistance, food stamps, medical care—things like that. She's very bright, but when I met her she was totally disorganized and felt unable to deal with *anything*."

4. INSTITUTIONS

Now, four years later, the children are both well-nourished. Linda is neat, clean and attractive. She has separated from Nils until he gets help for his alcoholism. Life is far from middle-class perfection for

namics—which is a great deal, according to Dr. Arthur Green, a psychiatrist and director of the Brooklyn Family Center for the treatment of abused children and their families.

"Keeping the family intact is critical," he says. "Early separation from parents can harm a child more in the long run than the

anger, frustration and distrust."

A combination of anger, frustration, distrust, guilt and shame are not likely to create cooperation. Far from it. Over the years therapists, physicans and social workers have all found that these parents trust almost nobody. But people of the Establishment—those in authority who seem to be labeling them unfit and bad—such parents find positively threatening.

Patient, nonjudgmental, empathetic volunteers, though, are viewed quite differently. They don't come because they have to; they come because they want to. They aren't overloaded with work; they have plenty of time. They don't cry "shame"; they accept and soothe. They don't give orders; they suggest. They don't threaten; they help. And they don't move in for a short time and then disappear: volunteer workers in any program agree to stay with the assigned family for a full year, to visit at least once a week and to be available by telephone virtually all the time.

Every case history is crammed with phone calls. Sally says that the first year she worked with Linda Jensen, she was on the telephone every single day and often at night, sometimes talking Linda out of suicide. For the isolated family, telephone lines can be literally lifelines.

Even though, as Dr. Green says, "the first thing that happens when a family goes into treatment is that the abuse stops," this is only the first step. These parents need tender loving extended care to change their patterns of behavior. Often they are woefully ignorant of the most basic facts of child development, nutrition, health or budgeting. Most of them are doing the best they can. Given their backgrounds and the conditions of their lives, their best is just not good enough. They have to be taught higher standards.

This is not an easy task, and volunteers are warned that changes will be slow, small, sometimes almost invisible. Nancy Trimpoli, the originator and former director of Schenectady's Lay Therapists, says, "Sometimes the gains seem so pitifully small to the outsider. For instance, if a woman who has felt completely helpless and powerless—and as a result, furious—can pick up the phone and call for help, or maybe throw a few pots and pans around instead of hitting her child—this, in our work, is cause for celebration!"

Nancy Trimpoli studied fine arts in college; yet today she is an expert in child-abuse volunteer training programs. Ten years ago nobody had even heard of such a thing. Where did this growing idea come from?

The pioneer volunteer lay group was formed as a kind of experiment at the National Center for the Prevention of Child Abuse and Neglect in Denver less than ten years ago—in 1969. There for the first time it was clearly seen that caring voluntary workers were far more effective with abusing families than the best-trained (but overworked) professional.

Then in 1974 Congress passed the Federal Child Abuse Prevention and Treatment Act, encouraging states that had not

---

HOW TO START A VOLUNTEER PROGRAM IN YOUR COMMUNITY

1. Go first to your local child protective unit, explaining that you want to help. Go with a plan. Know what you want to do and have it in writing. You will get your cases from them.

2. Send a copy of your plan to a group that might fund you: this is called a support agency. It might be the church, a university group, the Junior League, a state or federal agency. Try more than one group. (Your support agency will also turn out to be a pool of help, equipment, supplies, space, etc.)

3. Develop a training course for volunteers. If you have no idea where to start, write or call those who have already done it. (A free booklet on the role of volunteers in child abuse and neglect treatment has been prepared by the federal government. Its appendix lists almost one hundred programs across the country that use volunteers. It can be obtained from the National Center on Child Abuse and Neglect, P.O. Box 1182, Washington, D.C. 20013.) Read books on child abuse and neglect treatment. Once you've examined other community programs, be creative. You know the people in your own community best.

4. Get experts in various fields involved. The best way is to ask them to be guest speakers at training sessions. One or two, at least, will become deeply interested in what you are doing. You will want a judge, a pediatrician, a nurse, a psychiatrist, someone in the police, a lawyer, public health people.

5. Get free space for talks, training sessions and an office, if possible. Try churches, schools, Masonic temples etc.

6. Get all the publicity you can. Send stories to the local papers about what you are doing. Tell all your friends, relatives and neighbors. Talk to any group interested in listening.

7. Find a coordinator for volunteers. She has to be familiar with local resources, so it can't be the new girl in town. She should be calm, well-organized, unbothered by crises, willing to work hard and have a high degree of common sense. These qualities are more important than specialized training.

8. Whenever and wherever you talk, always be sure to ask for help. You may not get volunteers or money, but you may get help, transportation, space, equipment, supplies.

9. Carefully prepare application forms for volunteers before training sessions begin. The form should show attitudes. (Sample question: "Any mother who hits her child is _____." Any applicant who fills in the blank with "evil" or "a bad mother" is probably unlikely to make a good nonjudgmental worker.) You'll also have to make up a final exam to be used at the end of training.

10. When volunteers are trained and ready, tell the child protective unit you are ready to go to work. It is the coordinator's job to "match" clients with workers, so that the worker becomes friend *and* role model.

Linda Jensen: She is on public assistance; Susan must attend a special school for the emotionally disturbed; the family can afford only a substandard neighborhood. To most of us, the changes in Linda Jensen's life may seem minuscule. But, says Child Protection Unit supervisor Ginny Davidson, "Nobody can expect to change a family completely, overnight. *Survival* is what we're talking about." Linda Jensen and her children are now among the survivors. And they have survived together.

Keeping the family together, even the family that abuses its children, is another new philosophy. Until very recently, it was considered of prime importance to get the child *away* instantly. As a matter of fact, in many places this is still the first thought. But while it solves the immediate problem of the particular child and the particular abuse, it overlooks what the act of separation does to the family dy-

physical abuse. The removed child is miserable and the parents are miserable—and you haven't done a thing to change the pathological climate that caused the abuse in the first place.

"When you place the child in foster care," says the doctor, "the parents almost always gets a replacement, by becoming pregnant or by choosing another child in the family for abuse. So rather than stop ping abuse, you're escalating it."

(Incidentally, keeping families intact saves taxpayers a lot of money. In New York State it costs about six thousand dollars per child per year for foster care, not including court and other agency expenses. Home-intervening volunteers cost the state exactly nothing.)

Furthermore, asserts Dr. Green, "most abusing parents already have a background of parental deprivation and disapproval to contend with. Removal of the child piles guilt with shame on top of their feelings of already done so to set up their own units for the protection of battered and neglected children. What had formerly been considered a family affair was now a matter of public concern.

Child-beating was out of the closet; and in New York State (to give just one example) the number of reported cases leaped from a bit over 3,000 in 1972, to almost 37,000 three years later! The work load was impossible for existing agencies to handle; there were simply not enough professionals to go around.

Ginny Davidson, supervisor of one such unit, recalls, "Every time I was handed another case by the Family Court, I'd have to say, 'We can't handle this. We don't have the money or the people.'" The judge's response: "*Get a volunteer!*"

Mrs. Davidson thought that was a very good idea. But where were the volunteers willing and able to spend the hours necessary to deal with these disrupted, guilt-ridden families and their multiple problems? Her answer was to go out and *find* them. She called every women's group in the Schenectady area, offering to speak at their next meeting. She's still doing it and believes this is the best way to spread the word and find the right kind of people. "*Talk,*" she advises. "Make yourself available to radio and television. To the local papers. To clubs and associations. Just keep talking."

Sally Thompson was in the audience when Mrs. Davidson addressed the Junior League in Schenectady. So was Nancy Trimpoli, with her natural administrative skills. Sandy Selby Spaulding was also recruited by Mrs. Davidson's talk; busy as she was with three young sons of her own, Sandy was eager to get involved, and is today director and trainer of volunteers in the Lay Therapy Program.

Nancy Trimpoli, Ginny Davidson and Sandy Selby Spaulding actually gave birth to the Lay Therapy Program all by themselves. They got in touch with Little Rock, where a program was in operation. They wrote a proposal and the publicity and the applications. They planned and gave talks, put up posters they had designed, set up and ran the workshops—everything.

They are especially proud of their program, not only because it has been so successful that they are now asked to help form new ones, but because they put it together with very little money, using whatever resources were available within their own community. "If you're willing to give the time to work hard," they say, "you don't need a lot of money." (See their step-by-step suggestions on starting a volunteer program in the box on page 188.)

Most volunteer projects begin this way: with the need and just a few dedicated people—sometimes with just *one*. In 1972, two years before Sally Thompson drove down that lonely country road near Schenectady, Sharon Pallone of Little Rock, Arkansas, spotted a malnourished young child and her very young dazed-looking mother in a store. Ms. Pallone thought they looked badly in need of help and discovered that they

had hitchhiked from Missouri, the mother running from a child abuse charge. They had no place to go and no one to turn to. Sharon Pallone took charge of the situation and thus became Arkansas' first volunteer lay therapist.

Eighteen months later Ms. Pallone, with the aid of a physician and the Department of Social Services, was busy training six new volunteers, the core of what would become SCAN (Suspected Child Abuse and Neglect) Services, Inc. In 1978 Little Rock's SCAN program has a staff of fifty and uses three hundred volunteers.

At virtually the same time that Sally Thompson was taking her fateful drive, a group of student nurses at Kings County Hospital in Brooklyn, New York, an affiliate of the Downstate Medical Center, were seeing severely abused children for the first time, in the pediatrics ward. They were shocked and appalled, and a small group of them begged Arlene Hurwitz, an assistant professor of nursing at Downstate, to think of a way they could help with the problem.

Professor Hurwitz was already concerned with the apparently rapid increase in child abuse. She designed for her students an elective course that was also a volunteer program, working in conjunction with Dr. Arthur Green of the Family Center.

"Volunteers," Professor Hurwitz explains, "serve as models of good parenting—something most abusing parents never had. Virtually all of the parents have suffered from early parental loss—through neglect, separation or death. That's another reason they should keep the children. Taking them away just repeats the trauma and keeps the vicious cycle in motion."

One student, Gail Maduri, wife and mother of three, was instrumental in putting a stop to such a cycle. Neighbors had reported the Faulkners to the police, saying, "They keep their kids tied up in the kitchen like dogs, and there's a lot of screaming all the time."

When Gail first visited the Faulkners, all six children—dirty, thin and ill-groomed according to the report—had been taken away and put into foster care. The parents sat at home, anxious, guilty, missing their children and drinking all day long.

It took several weeks to convince the Faulkners that Gail wanted to help and not blame them; but once they trusted her, they were glad to confide in her. Yes, they'd kept George (six years old) tied up, but they had to; he often acted crazy and went after the others with a kitchen knife. They didn't know what else to do. The couple, Gail discovered, had only the sketchiest notion of child care and didn't know how to handle stress except by screaming and hitting.

Gail Maduri's next few months were spent as the family spokesperson in Family Court. It was on her recommendation and her assurance that she would be in regular touch with the family that the judge allowed the five normal children to be returned to their parents. George was placed in an institution. With that problem gone, the abuse stopped. More important, it es-

tablished Gail's credibility. "After the children were returned," she reports, "they considered me their guardian angel." That meant they were now able to listen to her.

Gail has been teaching this family, by suggestion and example (she has, on occasion, cooked a meal or applied makeup), how to eat right, how to groom oneself, how to keep a home neat, as well as giving them a short course on child care and development. (They now know, for instance, that it is not appropriate to send seven-year-old Laura across a busy street to do the family marketing.) Gail's intervention has kept a family together, learning together and growing together.

The Downstate student nurses may very well be the only volunteer group composed of health professionals. It's not at all typical. The new Saratoga County Skilled Friends Program is. This began with the Daytime Circle, a women's group of the Presbyterian New England Congregational Church in Saratoga Springs, New York. These churchwomen were concerned with the growth of child abuse, and wanted to learn more about it.

At the same time, a woman named Beverly Lazar was taking a course called Child Abuse and Neglect Education for Administrators and Educators, even though there was no program yet in which to use those skills. Ms. Lazar and the Daytime Circle women met at a Saratoga Springs forum on child abuse sponsored by the National Humanistic Education Center and a local primary school; from this fortuitous meeting came a committee of eight that formed itself into a Task Force. Their goal: to deal with child abuse and neglect in Saratoga County. A year later, the goal is all but a reality. Thirty-four "Skilled Friends" are still in training, but they will soon be involved with their assigned families.

It isn't necessary to be a professional or a trained expert to help with child abuse problems. Most of the important intervention work being done right now is rising from the grass roots of America—from extraordinary "ordinary" people putting themselves on the line.

In Brooklyn they're student nurses. In Schenectady and Little Rock they're lay therapists. In New York City they're parent-aides (*consejera de padres* in Spanish). In Saratoga, they're skilled friends. Not everyone is suited to this kind of demanding work, of course. The best volunteers are people with high motivation, time, patience and empathy with others. Ideally, they are reliable, even-tempered, nonjudgmental and enjoy being with children.

With these qualities and some training (three full, intensive days in New York City; one hour a week for five months in Schenectady, for instance) anyone who wants to help alleviate the tragic consequences of child abuse can readily do so. One expert has remarked that the abuse is really a call for help.

Over and over again, volunteers recall how quickly abuse stops, once that cry has been answered. And much of the abuse, they say, is rooted in ignorance—not hatred.

They tell of the sixteen-year-old mother who marched into a busy department store one Saturday and thrust her wailing infant into the arms of a woman out shopping with her children. "Please!" shouted the girl. "Take him! I don't know what to do with him." Under the care of a motherly volunteer, this child-mother is learning how to be a parent—and is learning to enjoy it.

Sandy Pandori of Schenectady was another young woman who "didn't know how to cope" with the problems of caring for her twin babies single-handed. "We were together twenty-four hours a day," she recalled. "Just the three of us, trapped. I was getting to the point where I didn't care what happened to them. It was awful."

Into Sandy Pandori's life came lay therapist Pamela Mason, who visited two or three times a week, took mother and children out, together and separately, and was always available to talk things over in person and on the phone. "She suggested different ways I could handle things—that was a big help,"

says Mrs. Pandori. "A volunteer," she adds, "really gets involved. And it's not as if when things get all straightened out, it's over. I'm doing just fine now on my own, but Pam and I are still very good friends."

Parents will often accept from a friendly volunteer advice they would resent from professionals or from their own families.

"And when they know you're not being paid for helping," says Sandy Selby Spaulding, "but are doing it because you *want* to, it makes an enormous difference in attitude."

"These people need *more* than a friend," states Arlene Hurwitz. "With a friend, you have to give as well as take; and they're simply not capable of giving anything—at least not in the beginning. A friend might get disgusted, but the volunteer doesn't. She's there, no matter how bad things get."

If all this sounds like the role of a mother, it should. "Most of the time, we find a family consisting entirely of children," says Ginny Davidson. "Oh, there are people with adult bodies, but they've never really matured."

Jetta, a SCAN volunteer in Little Rock, recalls an incident which underlines this feeling. Her client was hiding in the woods, in the rain, in the dark. "Try to picture a woman who is five feet ten and who weighs maybe three hundred pounds, is strong as an ox and is crying to us in a little childlike voice, 'Go away, leave me alone. Just leave me alone.' That's what really gets to you, that's who you are working with, that little child inside."

Who is better at reaching "that little child inside" than women—normal, everyday, typical, usual, average women. When Nancy Fisher, founder and director of the year-old SCAN–New York and a one-time volunteer herself, gets on the subject of women volunteers her eyes flash. "Women

are especially suited to this work," she insists, "because they can use all the skills and talents in parenting and household management they already have—the kind of things women are noted for, yet never get a degree in and are rarely paid for doing." It is this expertise these families need so badly. A woman might well find special joy in using "what comes naturally" to help others in a very real way.

But the possibility of joy is overshadowed for many women by fear. What can I really do? Can I really help? Will it be too much for me? This fear runs both ways. Nancy Fisher and her first client (now her friend) remember together the first time they walked to meet each other, down a long corridor. Both were having the identical thought: "How will I find anything to say to her?" And their friendship has lasted two and a half years, even though they are no longer volunteer and client.

A one-time client of SCAN–Little Rock recalls: "I was scared when I picked up the telephone and called SCAN. I didn't know but what they'd come and get the children . . . (but) I've never been judged to this day. No one has ever judged me. I've judged myself harshly, or more harshly than anyone else possibly could have. Not a one has ever tried to change me, and through that, I've learned how to grow."

In her words of advice to volunteer workers, this woman speaks to us all:

"Bear the risk. Dare to care."

Community Task Forces: Getting It All Together

Frank Barry

Too often the public response to a serious social problem like child abuse and neglect is to demand legislation, to place responsibility for the solution on a public agency and then to drop back into complacency, content that the problem has been solved. Such a response to child maltreatment would be simplistic and inadequate. In New York, for example, state law designates the Department of Social Services (DSS) as the agency responsible in the area of child abuse and neglect, but few if any local DSS are able to provide all the services required by abusing or neglectful families.

This has not been the fault of the local social services department. With the passage of New York's Child Protection Act in 1973, local agencies focused on investigating calls and, when necessary, taking emergency action. The development of long-term services for families did not command the same urgency as emergency situations, if only because the state's fiscal crisis struck at the same time model child abuse legislation was passed.

Today, all counties have developed procedures for investigating hotline reports of child abuse and neglect, but there is growing realization that it does little good to report and investigate cases — even to remove a child temporarily from the family — unless the community

also has ways to help the families involved. The challenge communities face is to provide need services in a time of tight budgets.

In New York, more and more communities are demonstrating that solutions can be found when people at the local level get together to focus energy and attention on the problem. While one agency may be limited in funds and staff, task forces involving many local agencies and organizations can pool and coordinate community resources. The task force approach has resulted in new or improved services as well as better utilization of existing services in many New York communities.

HISTORY

Mayor John Lindsay appointed what was to be the state's first task force on child abuse in New York City in December 1968. Dr. Vincent Fontana, who published one of the earliest texts on child abuse in 1964, was largely responsible for bringing the problem to Lindsay's attention. The task force recommended a computerized city-wide central register for reporting suspected cases of child abuse.

In 1970, groups formed to deal with child abuse in three upstate cities. The Syracuse Citizens Committee on Child Abuse (formed in response to the death

of a young child) grew into the Alliance, a coordinating and support program for abusing families that has become a model for the rest of the state.

In Utica the Child Abuse and Neglect Committee, with a grant from a local foundation, initiated a demonstration coordinating project that was successful enough to be funded and continued by the DSS. Three programs are now being developed: Visiting Friends, a project to provide "modeling homes" of foster families for single teen-age mothers, and a project dealing with sexual abuse.

A third upstate group, the Binghamton Citizens Committee on Child Abuse, took an adversary role with respect to the local department of social services after the death of a child who had been hospitalized several times. The group developed three Parents Anonymous chapters and provided a parent aide program and a hotline.

In 1973, Ruth Humphrey, a volunteer, helped start a task force in Dutchess County. The Suffolk County legislature also started a task force that year.

By mid-1973, there were only eight task forces in the state. Then with the help of Cornell's Family Life Development Center, they began to appear more often; task forces now exist in 33 of the state's 57 counties.

Some task forces are composed mainly of agency professionals, some of

4. INSTITUTIONS

volunteers or interested citizens. Some are officially designated by local governments, others are formed by the local department of social services and some started when people came together on their own.

ACCOMPLISHMENTS

During the past year over 800 people representing at least 300 agencies have been meeting regularly in groups around the state to improve their community's response to child abuse and neglect. Their efforts have produced Parents Anonymous chapters, interdisciplinary consulting teams, Visiting Friend programs, training programs for Child Protective Service workers, speakers' bureaus and public awareness conferences.

These groups consist of people representing local agencies and organizations concerned about children. They consider themselves action groups, and their goals include generating change in their communities — usually by developing new services.

Generally, task forces do not operate new services; their committees work to find existing groups or agencies willing to offer them. Knowledge about funding sources and program development is pooled. New services start faster when one agency does not try to develop them alone. Some task forces have stimulated private funds that were virtually inaccessible to public agencies. Most have avoided expensive new services; they frequently use volunteers or nonprofessionals. Often the service is an adaptation or upgrading of an existing service.

ROLE OF THE FAMILY LIFE DEVELOPMENT CENTER

Working under a grant from the National Center on Child Abuse and Neglect, the Family Life Development Center (FLDC) at Cornell began to work in New York State in 1975 to assist communities in developing a response to abuse and neglect. In its first year, FLDC assisted three community groups in assessing the needs in their counties and identifying a course of action. The beginning was not easy, and there were no clear models. The idea of interagency coordination threatened traditions of agency jurisdiction. In some communities "the doctrine of confidentiality" was used to protect bureaucratic terrain and to prevent agencies from working together.

Much was learned by trial and error, but two years later the ideas developed in the early meetings had become reality in all three counties.

Encouraging the development of task forces became a major FLDC objctive in 1976. Through its newsletter and letters to local commissioners of social services, the center offered to provide technical assistance to emerging task forces in twelve counties. From interested counties, the center asked for a written request by the county commissioner of social services and assurance of support from several other commuty organizations.

The letters of request were a key part of organizational strategy because they required agency heads and community leaders to begin to commit themselves to the idea of a local task force. This meant that basic organizational steps were already taken by the time FLDC staff arrived.

We attended task force meetings, sometimes acting as facilitators until local groups could designate their own leadership. We shared our knowledge and materials about approaches that seemed to work with abusing and neglectful families. We helped groups define their goals and then put them in touch with people in successful programs around the state. We suggested procedures for the task forces to follow. We sometimes guided and encouraged professionals who were very competent in their own agencies but lacked confidence in relating to community groups.

Assisting in the formation of task forces became the center's chief goal during its final year of federal funding. FLDC staff trained 200 people to organize task forces by offering two-day "how-to" workshops around the state. Three months after the last workshop, ten new task forces were organized, mostly by people who had attended the workshops or read about task forces in the FLDC newsletter.

FLDC provided follow-up assistance to those organizing new task forces when requested. The center recently offered a series of workshops on projects task forces might develop, including education for parenthood, working with neglectful families, friendly visitors (parent aides), Parents Anonymous, interdisciplinary teams and special approaches to meeting the needs of children. These will be followed by workshops on obtaining funding for new and needed programs.

ISSUES IN FORMING A TASK FORCE

Those wishing to form a task force must deal with several crucial issues. A task force on child abuse and neglect will have little impact on the local system if it lacks support of top social services

officials. Yet, if this support turns out to involve "control," energy and creativity may be stifled. The organizing must inspire enthusiasm among task force members but should not threaten local officials as Welfare Rights organizing did in the 1960s.

For local officials the first questions are often, "Will it work? Will it be worth the time?" Newsletter articles, training sessions and technical assistance have helped answer these questions. So has success, especially when described by a social services official from a neighboring county.

An agency that permits its staff to work closely with outsiders in a setting beyond agency control knows its internal problems could become a matter of public debate. Many local agencies have decided that the potential benefits to their program outweigh the risk. Task forces have often boosted the morale of regular agency staff, improved their communication with counterparts in other agencies and improved their effectiveness by developing new services for their clients.

Once organized, the new task force faces several issues. Will it be primarily a professional or lay group? How will the differences in knowledge, orientation and vocabulary be overcome? How will the group set its goals? Can its members agree on specific projects and assign responsibility for accomplishing them? Who will lead it? Should the group raise money or rely on an agency for duplication and mailing? If it decides to raise money, how will this be done?

To be successful the group must learn to handle differences of opinion. This is an art that takes time to develop.

CONCLUSION

Task forces are a logical, perhaps inevitable, response to the shrinking tax dollar. Many public agencies find themselves forced to look for community help because they do not have the funds to do everything themselves.

Task forces generate a *community-wide* response to a social problem. They view community needs as a whole rather than focusing on a particular need through the perspective of a single agency. Relevant services are frequently created to meet the newly perceived needs.

The task forces operating today may dissolve after they have accomplished their goals, they may set new goals or they may move into entirely new areas. In any case they will serve as a precedent for problem solving in every community where they have been effective in reducing child abuse and neglect.

GUIDELINES FOR FORMING A CHILD ABUSE AND NEGLECT TASK FORCE

1. **Identify organizations, agencies and groups to be represented.**
Task force members should represent the Department of Social Service's Child Protective Unit as well as other agencies with mandated reporters (teachers, doctors, etc.) and those providing treatment and support services. They should also include representatives from civic or church groups with an interest in children and families.

2. **Get a commitment, preferably written, from the heads of organizations and agencies.**
The task force should not be organized "underground." A favorable endorsement from heads of existing organizations will encourage agency representatives to participate freely. First-hand reports as well as newsletter or newspaper articles about task forces elsewhere can help sell the idea.

3. **The first meeting should:**
• *Provide information* about child abuse and neglect, about the community's response to it and about the task-force approach.
• *Build enthusiasm* by describing other successful task forces and by demonstrating community concern and willingness to act.
• *Build individual* commitment by getting people personally involved and assuring that their opinions count.

4. **Plan the meeting to include the following:**
• Reason the meeting was called.
• What task forces are, what they have done elsewhere.
• Participation in small-group discussions. Ask groups to discuss: Why did you come to this meeting? How do you perceive the problem of child abuse and neglect in this community? What does this community need to develop a better rsponse? (Sheets of newsprint and magic markers can be used to record ideas for later discussion and reference.)
• Feedback: smaller groups should report back to the whole meeting.

5. **Define objectives and set priorities.**
In the second or third meeting focus on "what specific changes or improvements would you like to see in this community during the coming year?"; this will help the group set its goals. From the general idea, a list of specific projects can be developed and ranked by identifying not only those most important but also those most achievable.

6. **Form committees** to carry out specific projects.

7. **Develop leadership in the group.**
Selecting a leader is difficult. Experienced leaders may be reluctant to step forward to head an unproved group; on the other hand, the wrong person may volunteer to lead the group. Open nominations or nominating committees may help, but a good first step is for the group to discuss the kind of leadership it wants. Some task forces have temporary chairpersons, rotating chairpersons, or co-chairpersons.

8. **Develop an organizational structure.**
Initially by-laws and an organization chart are not important, but they often become so as the group develops. Some task forces in New York State have working committees with a steering committee of people selected from the working committees. A temporary committee may be set up to develop the structure and by-laws.

9. **Develop legitimacy and a working relationship with the community power structure.**
Collaboration and support from the community power structure is crucial. Including local political figures or United Way representatives on the task force is one way to get it. Newspaper and radio publicity can help.

10. **Develop public visibility.**
To present a solid image to the public, a public relations committee can be developed to speak for the task force. In this way the group will gain needed public support — new members, volunteers and financial contributions.

11. **Keep costs at a minimum.**
Often the county Department of Social Services will absorb the cost of meeting notices and mailings. However, some task forces have raised money for films, training materials, speakers and a full-time staff working to promote group goals.

Developing new programs should be the main objective of the task force. For instance, fund raising should not divert energies that could go into developing new programs. Once started, the programs and their operation should be assumed by existing groups or agencies.

12. **Provide information for members.**
Speakers and films can be used to educate members about child abuse and neglect. Although this is very important, it should not postpone action or hard decisions for long. A task force that becomes a study group will lose its most dynamic members and its sense of purpose.

13. **Understand the role of the organizer.**
An organizer builds a strong group by asking questions rather than making statements, by suggesting several solutions rather than one, by suggesting procedures rather than outcomes. Once a group has developed its own leadership, the organizer's role often becomes less critical.

Some Pitfalls
• Neglecting to involve or at least advise key people in the community about the task force.
• Spending months trying to define a purpose.
• Starting a study that takes a year and precludes decisions or actions until its completion.
• Becoming preoccupied with organizational structure.
• Developing beautiful plans but neglecting to assign responsibilities for carrying them out.
• Neglecting to assign deadlines.
• Failing to deal with issues such as group leadership, agency domain, or extent of Department of Social Services involvement.
• Turning into a discussion group rather than an action group.
• Failure to define a process of self-evaluation.
• Losing sight of abused and neglected children the group set out to help.

Photo: Office of Human Development Services

Help for Troubled Families

Abusing parents are often not capable of identifying their own needs. They cannot be expected to recognize the needs of their children. As indicated in previous sections, they generally have a low self-opinion and are isolated from their feelings. They are afraid of being singled out and many times react to intervention with hostility, or will adapt a conforming attitude. The parent will do or say anything to be rid of the worker as quickly as possible. The best chance for success in identifying and promoting permanent change is a multidisciplinary approach.

Professionals and volunteers must be aware of the "world of abnormal rearing cycle" (WAR). This describes the generational cycle of development of abused and neglectful parents. Instead of condemnation and punishment, the parent needs to feel supported. Workers must be non-judgemental and concerned with the family unit as a whole. Finding transportation, access to emer-gency loans, day care centers and ways to alleviate environ-mental stress are important in creating an atmosphere conducive to change.

Articles included in this section promote a multi-disciplinary approach that offers the parent and workers various sources of expertise to rely upon. Interagency communication is paramount. People cannot be expected to report suspected cases of abuse and neglect if they feel that the parents and child will become lost in a social services maze.

·It is impossible to include examples' of all the effective programs working in hospitals and communities. Dr. Vincent J. Fontana, director of the Center for Parent and Child Development, New York Foundling Hospital, describes the facilities for care provided for by the hospital. This article is followed by a discussion of the health visitor concept from a pediatric· seminar by Dr. C. Henry Kempe. Each author encourages communication, cooperation and coordination of activities among social services, educators, and the medical and legal systems.

Legislation is important for protection of the child and parent's rights. Programs like the Defender Child Advocacy Unit in Philadelphia (Room 234, 1801 Vine Street, Philadelphia, Pennsylvania) coordinates the skills of legal, psychological, social, investigative and administrative professionals to insure legal representation for the child's rights and best interests, and preserve the family unit. "The Medicalization and Legalization of Child Abuse" and "Model Child Abuse and Neglect Legislation" list the issues and concerns of the professional and legislator.

Readings in Child Abuse concludes with a summary from the National Institutes of Mental Health publication "Child Abuse and Neglect Programs: Practice and Theory." A valuable resource tool, it provides a positive direction for all involved in prevention, intervention and rehabilitation.

THE MALTREATED CHILDREN OF OUR TIMES

VINCENT J. FONTANA, M.D.

Medical Director and Pediatrician-in-Chief, New York Foundling Hospital Center for Parent and Child Development. Professor of Clinical Pediatrics, New York University College of Medicine. Chairman, Mayor's Task Force on Child Abuse and Neglect of the City of New York. M.D., Long Island College of Medicine, 1947.

I. INTRODUCTION

THE MALTREATED CHILD for too long has been hidden in a corner of a dark closet among our national skeletons — now his plight is out in the open. Efforts to enlighten the medical profession in the past decade have brought this problem out of its virtual blackout. The picture is an ugly one. It is extensive and it is increasing. We can ask ourselves, "Who are the maltreated children?" They are the children who are being pushed around, thrown down stairs, dropped out of windows, burned with cigarette butts, fried on stove tops, scalded in boiling water, manhandled, beaten, tortured, victims of bizarre accidents, battered to death, starved and sexually abused. They are also life starved and love starved, insidiously neglected, growing up without a sense of self-esteem and becoming future child abusers themselves. Dr. C. Henry Kempe of the University of Colorado at the Colorado General Hospital in Denver reported the results of a nationwide survey of hospitals and law enforcement agencies in 1962 indicating the high incidence of battered children within a one year period.[1] Up to this time, the syndrome of the "battered child" had for the most part been unsuspected and unrecognized by the medical profession. There was little or no information on the subject available in the standard pediatric text books. A new term was coined, namely "The Battered Child" syndrome. The battered child syndrome derived its descriptive name from the nature of the child's injuries which commonly included abrasions, bruises, lacerations, bites, hematomas, brain injury, deep body injury, fractures, dislocations, injury to the liver or kidneys, burns, scalds, and all other injuries generally resulting from battering a child.

The following year, my colleagues and I reported our observations of a large number of children who were seen at the New York Foundling Hospital Center for Parent and Child Development with no obvious signs of being "battered" but who had multiple, minor physical evidences of parental neglect and abuse. We suggested the

---

1. *See* Radbill, *A History of Child Abuse and Infanticide* in THE BATTERED CHILD 16 (R. Helfer & C. Kempe eds. 1968) [hereinafter cited as THE BATTERED CHILD].

"The Maltreated Children of Our Times," Vincent J. Fontana, *Villanova Law Review*, Vol. 23, No. 3, 1977-78, © 1978 Villanova University.

term the "maltreatment syndrome" be applied to describe this greater whole picture of child abuse, ranging from the simple — the undernourished infant categorized as a "failure to thrive" — to the battered child, oftentimes the last phase of the spectrum. In these cases, the diagnostic ability of the physician, coupled with the community treatment and preventive programs, can bring about the protection of the child from the more serious injuries resulting from inflicted battering by parents — injuries that have become significant causes of childhood deaths.[2]

II. THE MALTREATED CHILD

A. *Symptoms of Abuse*

The maltreated child is often taken to the hospital or private physician with a history of failure to thrive, poor skin hygiene, malnutrition, irritability, a repressed personality and other signs of obvious parental neglect. The more severely abused children are seen in the emergency room of hospitals with external evidences of battering. Some are seen with an unexplained ruptured stomach, bowel or liver. Some are seen with extreme symptoms of maternal deprivation syndrome where the mother allows the child to suffer the effects of deprivations that lead to physical and mental retardation. This condition is oftentimes reversible if the children are admitted to a hospital and appropriate diagnostic measures taken. Some children are seen with inability to move certain extremities because of dislocations and fractures associated with neurological signs of intracranial damage. And of course, those with the more severe maltreatment injuries arrive at the hospital's emergency room in coma, in convulsions, or dead. Actual cases of murder, battering, torture, starvation, sexual abuse and life-ruining neglect are recorded in the medical literature. The parents' accounts of how these injuries occurred range from "accidents" to "discipline."

B. *The Source of the Abuse*[3]

The maltreating parents come from all strata of society. For example, there is the drug addicted mother who was living without a husband in a ghetto basement apartment with nine children ranging from three to twelve years of age. The mother sold drugs as well as being addicted. Her twelve-year old son was also on drugs and the eleven-year old daughter was prostituting to help with the finances of the house. Another example is that of the unmarried mother who signed out of the hospital after the premature birth of a child, leaving a false address. In three days, the infant had begun to twitch, have convulsions, clutch at its face, scream and regurgitate — all symptoms of drug withdrawal. Subsequently the child was

---

2. For additional reading on the subject matter of this section, *see generally* THE BATTERED CHILD, *supra* note 1; V. FONTANA, SOMEWHERE A CHILD IS CRYING (1973); V. FONTANA, THE MALTREATED CHILD (3d ed. 1977); N.Y. STATE ASSEMBLY SELECT COMM. ON CHILD ABUSE, Report (1972) [hereinafter cited as N.Y. SELECT COMM. REP.]; Fontana, *Child Abuse: Tomorrow's Problems Begin Today*, 22 CATH. LAW. 297 (1976).

3. For additional reading, *see* Gil, *Incidence of Child Abuse and Demographic Characteristics of Persons Involved* in THE BATTERED CHILD, *supra* note 1, at 19–39; Steele & Pollock, *A Psychiatric Study of Parents Who Abuse Infants and Small Children* in THE BATTERED CHILD, *supra* note 1, at 103–45. *See generally* authorities cited note 2 *supra*.

fortunately brought to the emergency room and treated for withdrawal symptoms. Maltreatment of neonatals resulting from parental addiction is becoming more common as the epidemic of drug addiction continues to grow. From another social level we see financially comfortable parents living in a pleasant, clean house in a friendly neighborhood who are without friends. They have four teenagers who have never had visitors. One day, the oldest girl, age seventeen, went to the police and told them that she is the mother of a baby living at home and that her own father is the father of the baby; that he had been having sexual relations with her for more than four years and was now doing the same with her younger sisters. The mother, when questioned, admitted knowing about the situation for years, but had not reported it to the authorities for fear of losing her husband. Yet another example is of a family living in a low income housing project with five children. The family had been reported to the Society for the Prevention of Cruelty to Children and had a lengthy record of child abuse and neglect. The society alleged that the mother beat her children so violently that one little girl had probably died from beatings; that another was brought into the emergency room of a hospital in serious condition with a skull fracture; that another child had been brought to the emergency room, though not hospitalized, on five different occasions — once for a fracture, another time for an abscess, and on the sixth occasion she was dead on arrival from internal hemorrhages.

Maltreatment by parents may involve children of any age with a noticeably greater incidence of abuse of children under three; a large percentage of abused children are under six months of age. One parent more than the other is usually the active batterer and the other parent passively accepts the battering. The average age of the mother who inflicts the abuse on her children has been reported to be about twenty-six years. The average age of the father is thirty years.

The lives of these parents are usually marked with divorce, paramour relationships, alcoholism, financial stress, poor housing conditions, recurring mental illness, mental retardation, and drug addiction. These stress factors all play leading roles that cause the potentially abusing parent to strike out at a child during a time of crisis. As previously mentioned the problem of child abuse is not limited to any particular economical, social, or intellectual level, or to any race or religion. However, the battering parents' behavior appears to have had roots in their own childhood experiences. The parents often recall that their own childhoods lacked love, support, and protection — rendering them unable to give love, affection and the necessary "mothering" to their own children.

Unfortunately, neglectful and abusive parents with low incomes are under a somewhat greater environmental stress and usually have fewer resources and supports in coping with these stresses and strains than parents with an adequate income. Current situational stress and strain and the deleterious effects likely to result therefrom, are common among neglectful parents. The inability to cope makes them unable to care adequately for their children. This reaction to stress will probably vary with many other aspects of their lives, their circumstances and their environment.

C. *The Perpetuation of Abuse*

There is evidence to indicate that a large number of abused and neglected children will grow into adolescence and adulthood with tendencies towards committing crimes of violence. Persons who engage in violence tend to have been victims of violence.[4] This generation's battered children, if they survive, will in most cases be the next generation's battering parents. Child abuse, then, is not simply a time-limited phenomenon to be seen as an age-specific, social-medical problem, but as a dynamic phenomenon with a cyclical pattern of violence from one generation to another. In the last decade, child maltreatment has been recognized by the medical profession. However, a reluctance on the part of the physician, traditional yielding to parental authority by the courts, overlapping of investigation by the social service agencies, inadequate training of the social workers and allied personnel in the field of child abuse, and very poor communications among the various disciplines responsible for protecting the abused child have resulted in insufficient protection for the abused and neglected child. These breakdowns in the system give battering parents the opportunity to continue their abusive behavior which can lead to the death of an innocent child.[5]

III. THE ROLE OF THE PHYSICIAN

The physician is usually the first professional asked to intervene in cases of child maltreatment and he has the most difficult role to play in dealing with a case of a maltreated child. His first and foremost responsibility should be to the child and his family. All of us who have handled battered children over the years have seen rather unfortunate situations where the family physician is unable to recognize his role and oftentimes is unwilling to ask for help. It is the child who suffers.

The physician's suspicions should be aroused when an infant or child is taken to him or to a hospital and the history related by the parents is at variance with the acute clinical picture and the physical findings noted on examination. The parents in these cases often take the child to a number of different hospitals and doctors in an effort to negate any suspicion of parental abuse. The physician will often encounter difficulties in obtaining any type of history from the parents. Making the diagnosis of maltreatment is totally dependent on physical examination, x-ray findings, social service investigation, and a high degree of suspicion on the part of the physician when eliciting the medical history.

Every medical center should have a child abuse committee providing a readily available team of consultants, headed by a senior pediatrician to assist the house staff, a psychiatrist, a social worker and hospital administrator. This team must also assume the

---

4. *See* Steele & Pollock, *supra* note 3, at 111.

5. *See* N.Y. SELECT COMM. REP., *supra* note 2; Besharov, *The Legal Aspect of Reporting Known and Suspected Child Abuse and Neglect*, 23 VILL. L. REV. 458 (1978); Helfer, *The Responsibility and Role of the Physician* in THE BATTERED CHILD, *supra* note 1, at 44; Kempe, *Some Problems Encountered by Welfare Departments in the Management of the Battered Child Syndrome* in THE BATTERED CHILD, *supra* note 1, at 169–74; Redeker, *The Right of an Abused Child to Independent Counsel and the Role of the Child Advocate in Child Abuse Cases*, 23 VILL. L. REV. 521 (1978).

5. PROFESSIONAL

responsibility of educating the medical staff as well as other members of allied fields in the community.

Once the injury has occurred, the physician's first and immediate responsibility is to the child. When the parents bring their abused or neglected child to the physician, early diagnosis and treatment is essential. The main reason for admitting the child to the hospital, other than for assessing the degree of injury, is to protect him. It should be a straightforward admission for the purpose of evaluation. The medical and physical evaluation of the child must be handled thoroughly and expeditiously; emergency care is often required if the child is acutely ill.

Every child who has a serious unexplained injury should have x-rays taken of the long bones, ribs and skull. This is the physician's most important diagnostic tool. The x-ray findings often speak for the child.

X-rays of the patient's fractures may show various stages of reparative changes. On the other hand, if no fractures or dislocations are apparent on examination, the reason may be that bone injury may remain obscure during the first few days of inflicted trauma. In these cases, bone repair changes may become evident days after the specific bone trauma. For this reason, x-rays should be repeated approximately five to seven days after the suspected inflicted trauma in order to evaluate the presence of special diagnostic radiologic findings related to inflicted trauma to the bones. These unusual bone changes seen on x-rays include metaphyseal fragmentation, "squaring" of the long bones, periosteal hemorrhages, periosteal calcification, presence of bone fragments, epiphyseal separations, and periosteal shearing.

It is also most important for the physician to take photographs of the body injuries at the time of admission to the hospital. Colored photographs are most helpful in documenting findings to various law enforcement agencies and the courts after definitive diagnosis. When the medical and surgical evaluation has been completed the physician is confronted with the difficult task of gathering all the data together and making a differential diagnosis.

The physician should talk with the parents and work with the house staff. The social worker can enter the picture after the immediate medical evaluation has begun and assist in communicating with the appropriate child caring agencies. The pediatrician on the team should be responsible for completing in detail the necessary child abuse reports mandated under the state child abuse law.[6] Care must be taken not to eliminate the house staff from the care of the child. Court testimony should be given by the staff physician, not the resident, since experience in this area is essential. With this type of appropriate intervention, physicians can protect children's lives, identifying the parent or family responsible for child abuse and thereby assist in breaking the chain of abuse which is frequently perpetrated from generation to generation.

In summary, the physician's responsibility in suspected cases of child abuse and neglect should include:

---

6. *See* Besharov, *supra* note 5, at 464–69.

1. *Making a suspected diagnosis of maltreatment.*
2. *Intervention* and admission of the child to the hospital.
3. *Assessment* — including a history, physical examination, skeletal survey, and photographs.
4. *Reporting of a case* to the appropriate department of social service and child protective unit or central registry.
5. *Requesting of a social worker report* and appropriate surgical and medical consultations.
6. *Conference* within seventy-two hours with members of the medical center's child abuse committee.
7. *Arranging a program* of care for child and parent.
8. *Social service follow-up.*

Efforts have been made throughout the country to protect the abused or battered child by the enactment of child abuse laws in every state of the nation.[7] Fundamentally these child abuse laws are only the first step in the protection of the abused and neglected child. It is what happens after the reporting that is of the utmost importance. A multidisciplinary network of protection needs to be developed in each community to implement the good intention of these child abuse laws. It is the physician's duty not only to report suspected cases of child abuse but also to initiate the necessary steps to prevent further maltreatment of the patient and other siblings in the family unit. The purposes of the child abuse laws are usually threefold: 1) to protect the parents when presented with invalid evidence; 2) to protect the child by making it mandatory for physicians to report suspected cases of maltreatment; and 3) to protect the physician involved by legislation that prevents possible damage suits by the parties involved.[8]

Treating a maltreated child is totally inadequate unless it is coupled with a simultaneous concern for the parents. They must be given the benefit of therapeutic programs directed towards rehabilitation and preventive measures that will help eliminate the psychological and social environmental factors that foster the battering parent syndrome. If these parents are to be given any help they must be made to recognize their own intrinsic worth and potential as human beings. This can only be accomplished by recognition of the parents' needs and the cooperative effort by all child caring professionals and paraprofessionals.

Referrals to self-help groups, such as Parents Anonymous, group therapy programs, specialized homemaker facilities, preschool therapeutic day care centers, and foster grandparent programs assist in protecting the abused and neglected child as well as securing help for the battering parents.[9]

IV. A MULTIDISCIPLINARY INPATIENT AND OUTPATIENT PROGRAM

While other communities are doing some excellent initial work in child protection, the New York Foundling Hospital Center for Parent

---

7. *Id.* at 459.
8. Concerning protection for the parents, *see* Besharov, *supra* note 5, at 505–09, 514–15. Physicians are mandated to report suspected cases of child abuse in at least 45 states. Id. at 465 & n.36. Immunity for those persons who are required to report is provided by all 50 states. *Id.* at 475.
9. For additional reading on the subject matter of this section, *see* Besharov, *supra* note 5; Fontana, *supra* note 2; Helfer, *supra* note 5, at 43–56; Silverman,

5. PROFESSIONAL

and Child Development Program will be described here because it is the program with which I am most closely involved and also because it may well serve as a model to be shared with other communities.

While our hospital's multidisciplinary program has only been in operation for approximately five years, I would like to point out several important positive gains already achieved. First, the families are now under supervision and the team is learning constructive ways in which to help them cope with their child and their problems. We believe that a good deal of prevention has been achieved. Second, the program has developed a community awareness that there are available alternative methods of treatment as opposed to a strictly punitive approach. These gains are especially rewarding when it is realized that the clients currently being served by the Abusing Parent and Child Unit represent the most oppressed segment of the New York City population. Living in the most depressed areas of the city, they are, for the most part, isolated, lonely, poverty stricken people from completely deteriorated family situations.

Based upon our experiences, it can be concluded at this point that a multidisciplinary approach to child protection and family therapy can work to the benefit of both families and professionals involved with them. This program represents an innovative approach to the problem by combining psychiatric, medical and social approaches in the treatment of the mother (family, wherever possible) and the child. Reputed to be the only comprehensive in- and outpatient child abuse and neglect program in the United States, it opened in September 1972, with the following objectives:

1) To prevent separation of parents and child, whenever possible.
2) To prevent the placement of children in institutions.
3) To encourage the attainment of self-care status on the part of the parents.
4) To stimulate the attainment of self-sufficiency for the family unit.
5) To prevent further abuse or neglect by removing children from families who show an unwillingness or inability to profit from the treatment programs.

There are four components of the program: 1) The multidisciplinary team approach; 2) engagement of the surrogate mothers; 3) hotline service;[10] 4) inresident facility.

The *multidisciplinary* team provides comprehensive medical, psychiatric, and social services to both parents and child(ren). The psychiatrist, psychologist, psychiatric social worker, pediatrician, nurse, child care worker, house mothers and paraprofessionals (social work assistants) coordinate their skills and expertise in providing treatment, rehabilitation, and preventive measures

---

Radiologic Aspects of the Battered Child Syndrome in THE BATTERED CHILD, *supra* note 1, at 59-74.

10. For a discussion of the mechanics and legal considerations in setting up a hotline, *see* Besharov, *supra* note 5, at 489-90.

through the actual demonstration of how to "mother" while "being mothered" at the same time.

The paraprofessionals who live in the patients' community serve as the *surrogate mothers* to the parent-patients. They "mother" them to fill that very deprived need to experience how to be mothered while helping them learn mothering skills.

As an integral element of the "surrogate mother" service, a "hotline" is provided between these patients and the surrogate mothers, so that they are available to them via telephone or a home visit when the patients need someone to talk to, to ventilate their feelings, or simply someone to listen. The desired effect is achieved when, instead of projecting onto their children and taking it out on them in the form of abuse, the patients turn to the "surrogate mothers."

On a wider scale, there is a hotline at the agency manned by treatment personnel on a twenty-four hour coverage. Anybody can call directly or on behalf of a parent, and these calls are carefully monitored in order to provide instant service, which may include referral to another type of facility, or a follow-up intake interview for admission of the parent and child to the program, as outpatients or inpatients.

The *inpatient component,* as well as the outpatient, is located on the fifth floor of the New York Foundling Hospital. The patients for the inhouse facility are chosen on a very highly selective basis, as it is not our aim to uproot or break up a family unit for placement. Mothers with two to three children are able to enter the inresident program since the agency has nurseries on the seventh, eighth and ninth floors for the other children. Day care and family day care programs are also available in the agency should they be necessary. The child who has been abused remains with the mother, but provisions are made for the other children placed on the nursery to interact with them and receive appropriate services. In rare cases where a father is involved,[11] although he doesn't enter the inresident facility, he receives services as well. It is the hospital's projected goal to develop a more comprehensive program for the fathers as outpatients.

During the course of the year the program is equipped to care for forty inpatients and one hundred and twenty outpatients. Inpatients, numbering eight mothers and eight children at a time, live in the residence for at least three months. Outpatients receive services in the hospital as outpatients part of the week as well as services in their home during the remainder of the week.

The Abusing Parent and Child Unit accepts referrals from all public and private social, medical, law enforcement agencies and educational institutions in two boroughs of New York City. All cases are channelled through Protective Services of the Bureau of Child Welfare, the local child protective agency to which all cases of child abuse or neglect must be reported as mandated by New York State law.[12] In addition, the unit accepts self-referrals seven days a week, twenty-four hours a day to enable it to intervene during a crisis situation.

11. *See* Steele & Pollock, *supra* note 3, at 108.
12. N.Y. Soc. Serv. Law § 415 (McKinney 1976).

5. PROFESSIONAL

V. Conclusion

In summary, the innovative approach of the multifaceted program described above to the treatment and prevention of child maltreatment attempts to break the generational cycle of the battered child syndrome by a technique of behavior modification through corrective child care experiences, education in homeworking skills, environmental assistance and psychotherapy. This broad based concept of treating both parents and child has proven effective in providing crisis management services that not only protect the maltreated child but also simultaneously allow preventive rehabilitative treatment for the maltreated child and his family.

The results of our study with abusing and neglectful mothers clearly indicates that, because of the nature of the problem and the variety of parents involved, a coordinated effort by all disciplines is essential if we are to interrupt the generational cycle by which child abuse and neglect are perpetuated.[13]

---

13. For additional reading for this section, *see generally* authorities cited notes 2, 3 & 9 *supra*.

NEW VISTAS IN THE PREVENTION OF CHILD ABUSE

C. Henry Kempe, MD

I will discuss two kinds of advocacy: 1) the kind of personal advocacy I have done in the field of child abuse, simply to discuss the process, and 2) the advocacy that pediatricians as a group might begin to entertain on a national basis to forward the cause of the concept of the health visitor. To my mind, that is the best immediate chance for an outreach that is universal, equalitarian, not a program for the poor but for every American family, not a case finding for poor parenting but rather an aid for those who need aid, a ready standby support for all, compatible with any kind of system of medical care we care to adopt.

Let me say at the onset, so I won't repeat it throughout, that in the last 20 years I have worked closely with Brandt Steele and Ray Helfer, and lately Bart Schmitt, in predictive studies that are prospective. The two I would mention now, one in Aberdeen, Scotland, and one from Denver, Colorado, I have worked on with Jane Gray, Christy Cutler, and Janet Dean.

In the 1950s, Caffey, a pediatric radiologist, and then his associate and student, Fred Silverman, described the fractures and other lesions of child abuse in great detail. That made little impact on pediatricians, although it did impact quite considerably on radiologists. Then again in the 1950s, Paul Woolley from Pittsburgh wrote a paper on the few children who he felt clearly had been physically abused, and it made no impact either.

I saw my first abused child in 1943. I was told by my resident that this was something one saw in the county hospital quite a lot and that the cause of it was "drunken fathers or inadequate mothers." I took that quite literally and accepted it as an unusual criminal act.

I was impressed that in the late 1950s, when I came to Denver, we were seeing on the ward a veritable epidemic of failure to thrive. These infants did not have some obscure metabolic disease, there being over 200 causes of failure to thrive, most of which were ruled out assiduously, and at great expense to the child, and to the family, and to the hospital. Provided we didn't take enough x-rays and starve the child, the child proceeded to thrive in the hospital, where no child should thrive. Weight gains of 2 oz per day were common.

At the same time, we were seeing children with obscure bone diseases diagnosed by residents as "brittle bone disease" or "easy bruisers," who didn't fracture or bruise in the hospital—a whole array of children whose diagnostic label simply did not fit the reality along with a process of denial that was unequal to anything I had previously seen in pediatrics.

This offended my intellect far more than my heart, because I felt it was absolutely wrong to fail to make a correct diagnosis at any time, if you could help it. I must say I was also very much moved by the fact that there must have been good reasons why people didn't make these right diagnoses.

Silver and I published two papers on child abuse, which made no impact on

"New Vistas in the Prevention of Child Abuse," C. Henry Kempe, *Child Advocacy and Pediatrics*, Report of the Eighth Ross Roundtable on Critical Approaches to Common Pediatric Probelms. © 1978 Ross Laboratories.

anyone, and one of them didn't get on the program of a pediatric meeting because it was not interesting. But in 1961 I was happily the chairman of the Program Committee of the Academy of Pediatrics and, therefore, able to put into a plenary session a symposium that included not only a pediatrician but a radiologist, a psychiatrist, a distinguished judge, and a social worker. When we decided to name this symposium we were at a loss. I came up, late in the afternoon, with "The Battered Child Syndrome," which I thought would get everybody's attention. In that audience of over 4,000 people there were literally hundreds of pediatricians who said, "I have seen those," or "I have some of those," and there is absolutely no question, as far as that Academy meeting is concerned that a process of communication got started.

The TV show "Ben Casey" soon had an episode on a battered child. In those days we were dealing mostly with the worst child abuse cases. It wasn't for the next few years until we began to see the whole spectrum of abused children, all the way from those with the most severe, fatal disease, to those with serious sequelae in terms of brain injury, to simply bruised children, to those who had no physical injuries but severe emotional neglect or deprivation, and finally, to the child who was not fed and failed to thrive.

In retrospect it was clear that the medical diagnosis was the easiest of all, and that our first years' efforts really were to refine that diagnosis, so that any doctor could say that by the best of medical judgment the injury was inflicted. This we can now do about 92% of the time in court and under oath. That is a great change from 1960, when the gray area might have been thought to be fifty-fifty.

We were not impressed by what happened to these children when they returned home in the sense that they often came back a third of the time reinjured. The department of welfare used case work exclusively with the mother only, rarely involving the father, and never involving the child. The case work consisted of an hour, spent generally every other week. I want to be sure you understand that I am not critical of welfare departments that were working with this 1925 model, because they were so busy taking care of crises that they really had no way to begin to do anything more than address each crisis one at a time.

We, therefore, with Steele and Davoren, began to work with many of these families, began to understand better what kind of people were involved in child abuse and neglect, what outside crises precipitated the act, what made it worse, what made it better, and something about how to judge whether abuse and neglect were going to recur.

Based on this information we published the first book called "The Battered Child," with Ray Helfer, and it had, as it was written for doctors and nurses primarily, a good deal of information on diagnosis and not really much on treatment.

Over the next years, up to 1968, we experimented with lay therapists, crisis nurseries, and use of groups and other modalities of treatment, and published a second book called, "Helping the Battered Child and His Family." We thought of dropping the words "Battered Child" for that book, but decided to keep it one more time, principally because we had not yet engaged sufficiently the attention of state legislators.

We had, in 1962, gotten the Children's Bureau to convene a meeting on passing a model law on the reporting by physicians, nurses, and other citizens of suspected cases of child abuse and neglect. We felt that doctors, once having made the diagnosis, needed help and that there had to be some mechanism by which they would feel that they were obliged to share this information with someone who would be in the helping field, and that they were not to be trusted to do it automatically. The model law proposed by the Children's Bureau was accepted by all 50 states within 2 years, an absolute record of states' accepting a model law.

Nor would I say the model law was entirely "model," but it was, at least, a beginning of calling the subject to the attention of the states. But what of the next step: treatment? It is with this question that we have struggled ever since, because the response of society to the diagnosis has not been universally adequate in terms of funding of treatment and family rehabilitation.

We dropped the term *The Battered Child* in our last book, *The Abused Child*, edited by Harold Martin (Cambridge, Mass, Balinger Publishing Co, 1976) which deals with the understanding of the developmental and emotional diagnosis and treatment of the abused child, and the companion book, *Child Abuse and Neglect: The Family and the Community*, edited by Ray Helfer and myself, because we feel now that we know enough about the field and the concept is well enough accepted that the words *Battered Child* are, in fact, a harmful rather than a helpful approach, and they fail to suggest the broad spectrum of malfunction we want to address.

This leads me to say that the field is in transition. There are 3,362 counties with welfare departments in this country, each one a nation unto itself. Each county has to make an individual and political decision about what it wants to do about child abuse and neglect over the spectrum. Many of them have no concept of what it costs to provide a broad-based treatment program that is family-oriented, that addresses the needs of not just the mother, but also of the father, the abused and neglected child and the siblings, all of them, and looks at the family's needs as a whole and not just through the eye of this last injury or the last failure-to-thrive episode. That decision hasn't been made yet in many places. I think it is something we will have to face in time.

Finally, we felt that it was time for the federal government to address this matter, and we interested Senator Mondale and Pat Schroeder, our Congresswoman from Denver in her first term, in an act that was supported by a great number of people, some of whom are in this room. If anyone said they wrote the Mondale Act, I am always delighted to let them feel that, because it is great to have them believe that they have had a part, and, indeed, they have.

The Mondale Act, which went through many revisions, is an act that brought $20 million a year for 3 years, into this field for demonstration and research projects, with a fixed small amount given to the states directly, the rest to innovative programs testing newer diagnosis and treatment modalities. This bill will now be up for renewal, and we hope to improve its content. It was written very broadly, and as an aside I might say that whenever a bill is written by the Congress and is opposed by the Administration, the Administration has a way to screw it up royally.

It is helpful not to have two forces pulling apart when a given amount of money is given for a given purpose. In any event, this bill has done a great deal of good. In closing on that issue, I will say that the spin-off has been just fantastic to me. Perhaps only 5% of the major applications were funded, but I have had a chance to look at many unfunded communities that have done just about as well unfunded as they would have done funded.

There is a big lesson there, and that is, if a divided community or people who are strangers come together and spend 4 to 5 weeks writing an application for HEW, night after night after night, in the process, they discover good things about each other, and common purposes. Then their failure to get the money results in their cursing HEW, but at the same time they are saying, "Why shouldn't we go ahead and do this anyhow?" That is exactly what happened in hundreds of places. The bill isn't so important in terms of the $20 million a year it brings in, but rather in terms of the spin-off it has in many, many places. To my mind, that has been the success of the Mondale Act.

I'll close by making two remarks about prospective randomized studies on the prevention of child abuse, because pediatricians love to prevent disease; we would much rather prevent polio than invent a new artificial lung for a polio victim. If people hadn't the view of prevention that we all have, we would not be anywhere near where we are in the prevention of measles, diphtheria, whooping cough, tetanus, polio and rubella, and we would be nowhere in the field of eradication and conquest of smallpox, which has now pretty much succeeded.

I saw a very good health visitor system in a country that I shan't name where a nurse very interested in well-baby care graphed the nongaining of a child for 5 months but did nothing about it. She was, in other words, terribly good at graphing, but she wasn't any way good at doing something about it. She gave some modest advice to the mother about feeding, but she was not prepared to do much more because her basic training was that her job was "mother crafting," bathing and feeding the baby, and charting that graph. That gave me an idea that while it was good to have contact with the new baby, contact is not enough. More is needed, an intelligent response.

In Aberdeen, there has been a health visitor system for the last 75 years. Every baby born in Aberdeen, Scotland, has always had a health visitor, regardless of his family's being rich or poor.

Health visitors are registered nurses, specially trained very much like our visiting nurses in American cities. They are also very much oriented toward physical growth and development and mother crafting, and they tend to shy away, as Scots do in general, from anything to do with feelings.

We thought, however, that we were interested in what we would do if we recorded the first impression of the health visitor after the baby was born. By the way, Aberdeen had, before oil was found and the Americans came, a very stable population. Nobody left Aberdeen; nobody came to Aberdeen. Everybody was very well known.

Every baby born in Aberdeen has a health visitor visit, and we asked the health visitor to say what she thought about the mother's and the family's ability to parent. At the end of 5 years we had a chance to see what happened to all these children, since in Aberdeen all children go to one single place when they get sick. There is only one hospital for children. If a general practitioner sees a child sick enough to require hospital care, he goes there; it is a totally closed system. We wanted to see if the outcome of these children in terms of inflicted accidents and those that were not inflicted could have possibly been identified prospectively by the health visitor. We found that they were extremely good, provided you didn't read *all* they said.

If you read the typical Aberdeen health visitor's health comment about a parent she was very concerned about, she would say, "Mrs. MacDougle is distraught. I am a bit worried about her. She does not seem to like her baby. However, I know she will cope very well." And thereupon, she would do nothing further. The second part of the report always disclaimed the first. And the most interesting thing to me was that if you saw just the first part of the comment, she would turn out to be very right. Virtually all child abuse and some deaths could have been prevented if health visitors had acted on the first rather than the last part of their appraisal.

The Denver predictive study was simple and supported the health visitor concept as a mode of prevention of serious child abuse. In this instance, with the permission of both parents, 800 consecutive deliveries were included. They were videotaped. There were four modes of measurement used: a prenatal questionnaire, a prenatal set of observations, the delivery room observations, postpartum observations, and a 6-week follow-up visit. Full term, healthy first or second infants of normal pregnancy, labor and delivery, were born into 100 families thought to be in need of extra services. Fifty of these families had health visitors and 50 did not. By 2 years of age, 20% of infants in the nonvisited families had an inflicted injury requiring hospitalization, versus 0% in the visiting group at risk and in the no-risk control groups.

In this study, information gained from observations of mothers and fathers in the delivery room was most accurate in predicting potential for abnormal parenting practices. The questionnaire did not add significantly to the accuracy of prediction. If delivery room observation is not feasible and only one opportunity for evaluation exists, the early postpartum period affords the best opportunity for collection and analysis of prenatal, labor and delivery, and postpartum observations. Such observations are noninvasive and should be part of obstetrical and postpartum routine.

Immediate, effective intervention by physicians, public health nurses, and/or lay health visitors can significantly decrease many "abnormal parenting practices." In this study, such intervention prevented serious injury in a high-risk population.

Discussion

DR E. H. NEWBERGER: Dr Kempe, I would like to pose one of the questions that came from a pediatrician in practice. "How come I have been in practice for 20 years, and I have never seen a case of child abuse?"

DR C. H. KEMPE: There is no way for him to be in practice for 20 years and fail to have cared for children who have been physically or sexually abused and neglected. He has not seen it because he will not see it.

Failure to thrive is the single most common condition in our infant ward now, in children under the age of 2. I said there are 200 causes of failure to thrive, but over 50% in our hospital and 90% at the Denver General Hospital are due to maternal deprivation. It is an important medical condition. There is no way, even among the most rich patients, that you can avoid taking care of abused and failure-to-thrive children.

I am writing a paper currently entitled, "Child Abuse Among the Rich," and I am writing another paper entitled, "Incest Among the Rich." I want once and for all to lay to rest that this disease is a disease of poverty. Stresses can be internal or external or both. We see lots of child abuse and sexual abuse among very well-to-do people.

DR E. H. NEWBERGER: I have a slightly different interpretation and would give a different answer. I think the pediatrician in practice is in a very difficult bind when it comes to making the diagnosis of child abuse. It means that a given child's parent is a bad parent. Further, information shared with the pediatrician in his office in confidence, once this diagnosis is made, must be shared with a department of public welfare or a police department, depending on where he is. In many cases woefully inadequate, if not sometimes incompetent and hurtful services, can be made available to families and children as a result of his report.

For many pediatricians, mindful of the need because of the economics and ethics of practice to preserve a relationship with a family, to say a child got its injuries at the hands of or because of the neglect of a parent is a very difficult prospect. It means an onerous value judgment about a parent; it is followed by a case report that is painful to make.

DR C. H. KEMPE: But it has changed a lot, if you take a 20-year view. Twenty years ago it wasn't done at all. Now there is increasing commitment by pediatricians to child-abuse cases at every level of practice. I don't think this particular question is that representative, because I now do see referrals made to centers by pediatricians who themselves don't want to handle it, but they don't mind referring the case with some crazy diagnosis like osteogenesis imperfecta tarda or some other disease, to get it settled some other place.

DR SCHMITT: I meet pediatricians who report mild bruises and other pediatricians who don't report severe injuries. The latter physician is not blind, he just does not want to get involved with child welfare and the legal system. We need to remind him again and again to refer his case. There is always the risk that without intervention the child may be killed. It can happen in middle-class families. In a sense, by reporting early, the physician may protect parents from the criminal prosecution that follows a more serious injury.

DR LOZOFF: You made the point that one of the few times in our medical system when virtually 100% come into contact with the medical community is the newborn period. The studies that you presented, as well as the studies of Broussard,[1,2] suggest that if a mother in the postpartum period perceives her baby as better than average, the children had fewer developmental problems over the next 4 to 11 years. If the mother perceived the baby as worse than average, there was increased incidence of behavioral disturbance.

DR C. H. KEMPE: And school failures.

DR LOZOFF: Right. These studies indicate that this one time period, where everybody comes into contact, can provide valuable predictive information and is thus especially important for early preventive intervention.

DR C. H. KEMPE: The Letters to the Editor that Dr Newberger talked about addressed the question as to what right society has to enter the home, really, against the wishes of the parents. I think one has to balance rights. We are saying that in the vast majority of cases there will be no problem because health visiting is seen as a positive thing, particularly if it is not around "Are you a good mother, Mrs. Jones?", but "How are you, how are you and your husband getting along, how is your grandmother, is there anything more we can do?" There is a lot of precedent for the helping kind of person reaching out. Many communities have people who do that now. The concept that you have to be a registered nurse to be a health visitor, I would like to disagree with. RNs should select and supervise lay health visitors.

The question is: Does our care for the families stop at the hospital door when the yellow cab brings the baby and flower pot home? We say, "We will see you in school 6 years from now." And that is a very important question of policy this country must face.

Should the child be denied access to society in the case of the rare failure of parenting? Is that the penalty one has to pay? And who pays that penalty? It is the child who pays it. It is my feeling that this is not fair. People enter your home to read the gas meter, so do firemen. There are a lot of such invasions of home that are accepted.

If a parent, for example, pointedly refused health care, if they say I am going to Dr Roddey, and I think they are, I would back off. But if it turns out they are going nowhere, and nobody has seen that child for months on end, we are now able to go to our juvenile court and say, "Judge, I am worried about this baby nobody has ever seen," and then one gets a legal order for entry to "produce the child" for health evaluation.

We discussed the specific question of when do you intervene and who should intervene. It isn't the doctor's job; it isn't the social worker's job. It is ultimately society's job to look after all its people when there is a need to. The question is very simply this: the child has certain rights for survival, and basic medical care is one of those rights; basic nourishment is one of those rights. If there is any question about it, then I would intervene, regardless of what the reasons for refusal are, religious or otherwise. If the child is thriving, I couldn't care less what the parents' religion is; but if the child is not thriving, society must intervene for a short time or sometimes forever.

MS MESSENGER: It is important to differentiate the physicians who say: "I am deeply troubled because when I refer children there are no services, and I am not convinced that referring potential abuse to the court system is really any better for that child, for those who state, I haven't seen a case of child abuse in 20 years of practice. In the latter case, physician education may be needed if they are not seeing symptoms or acknowledging what they see. In the former case, pediatricians may need to become stronger advocates for improved services and options."

DR CYPRESS: There are still many states, unfortunately, where doctors aren't getting involved. They are seeing the cases, but they don't want to get involved for a lot of reasons.

DR C. H. KEMPE: I would like to refer you to the New Yorker, a medical magazine of some note, which about 2 months ago had a very beautifully written brief article about Cleveland, Tennessee. Now, Cleveland, Tennessee, is not a big city. There has been a pediatrician working on child abuse for 15 or 20 years under great handicap, and it took finally a martyred child to turn this all around. Now the State of Tennessee is addressing child abuse in a fairly major and constructive way.

This brings up the question whether society needs a martyr in each place before it will move.

DR CYPRESS: We have been working on this now for about 10 years. There is one place in Virginia where they have a hospital-based team; that is about the only place where something is being done. But in the local communities, those children go to the emergency room and they go back home. And nothing seems ever to be done.

DR VAN GELDER: In response to that issue, too, it is getting much easier for pediatricians to refer cases just by the fact that we have more child-protection agencies, so it can be done without the pediatrician feeling he is reporting the patient directly to legal authorities.

Dr Kempe has educated pediatricians. Many could not conceive that parents might act this way. Pediatricians really transferred their own feelings toward the parents with whom they were dealing.

DR C. H. KEMPE: There is no way a baby 6 months old is going to walk out the door and say, "I am having a terrible time. I am starving to death," or "I am being beaten." He cannot communicate with society.

Will a free society allow him to communicate? There are those in the civil liberties field who say: No. He is not free to communicate until he will be produced in school or somebody happens to see him starving in a Safeway Store parking lot. Those are communications that are acceptable. The communication that is not acceptable is for you to reach out and weigh him unless the parents ask you to weigh him. Now, I don't think that makes any sense at all. I would like to hear what the CDF feels about that.

DR KNITZER: The CDF is addressing the seriousness of these issues and is not taking a strict civil libertarian stand. I know we struggle with the question in relation to foster care and natural parents, and to children's rights compared to parental rights. Balancing a child's right to services and developmental opportunities with privacy requires a very difficult balancing act.

DR C. H. KEMPE: My feeling is that the issue is too polarized. When you prevent parents from hurting their child, you are doing something *for* the family; so the thrust is not against the parents or the child, but for the family.

DR KNITZER: That is how it is perceived.

DR C. H. KEMPE: Only by lawyers.

MS MESSENGER: I would like to respond as someone concerned about policy. Dr Kempe has provided a diagnosis of a problem with a potential solution. The notion of home health visitors has great relevance to an important problem in child-health policy. This has to do with bridging the schism between public health and personal health services.

On the basis solely of skills and acceptance, a health visitor need not be a trained nurse. But if one is thinking about policy and overall resource allocation, it may make sense to talk about nurses, because you can then talk about using people who are now doing other kinds of things; to revitalize public health nursing, for example, which many communities has become removed from this type of activity. One can increase and improve service effectiveness without massive new expenditures.

A home health visitor directly addresses the issue of equity of access. Dr Kempe is right in suggesting that it can be done area by area. It does not need federal legislation to begin, and it can be adopted to a variety of practicing settings. For example, a private pediatrician does not have to join a public health agency to help establish or participate in a system in which health visitors visit every newborn in his area and provide information about the pediatric resources in the community.

DR NUCKOLLS: The reason public health nursing has given up home visiting is economic. They are reimbursed for visits to the elderly. They are not reimbursed for visits to newborns. You have to swing back to the federal government to assure reimbursement in order for the agencies to be able to make the visits.

Once you have established that the health department has a reimbursement mechanism, then within the public health nursing or health department you can use other people. It does not have to be an RN; it could be an LPN or an aide.

DR C. H. KEMPE: We have a number of communities in Colorado that are doing it entirely with volunteers.

References

1. Broussard ER, Hartner MSS: Maternal perception of the neonate as related to development. *Child Psychiatry Hum Dev* 1:16, 1970.
2. Broussard ER: Neonatal prediction and outcome at 10/11 years, unpublished manuscript.

THE MEDICALIZATION AND LEGALIZATION OF CHILD ABUSE

Eli H. Newberger, M.D.,

and

Richard Bourne, Ph.D., J.D.

The Children's Hospital Medical
Center, Boston

Child abuse has emerged in the last fifteen years as a visible and important social problem. Although a humane approach to "help" for both victims of child abuse and their families has developed (and is prominently expressed in the title of one of the more influential books on the subject [29]), a theoretical framework to integrate the diverse origins and expressions of violence toward children and to inform a rational clinical practice does not exist. Furthermore, so inadequate are the "helping" services in most communities, so low the standard of professional action, and so distressing the consequences of incompetent intervention for the family that we and others have speculated that punishment is being inflicted in the guise of help.[3, 28]

What factors encourage theoretical confusion and clinical inadequacy? We propose that these consequences result, in part, from medical and legal ambiguity concerning child abuse and from two fundamental, and in some ways irreconcilable, dilemmas about social policy and the human and technical response toward families in crisis. We call these dilemmas *family autonomy versus coercive intervention* and *compassion versus control*.

This paper will consider these dilemmas in the context of a critical sociologic perspective on child abuse management. Through the cognitive lens of social labeling theory, we see symptoms of family crisis, and certain manifestations of childhood injury, "medicalized" and "legalized" and called "child abuse," to be diagnosed, reported, treated, and adjudicated by doctors and lawyers, their constituent institutions, and the professionals who depend on them for their social legitimacy and support.

We are mindful, as practitioners, of the need for prompt, effective, and creative professional responses to child abuse. Our critical analysis of the relationship of professional work to the societal context in which it is embedded is meant to stimulate attention to issues that professionals ignore to their and their clients' ultimate disadvantage. We mean not to disparage necessary efforts to help and protect children and their families.

How children's rights—as opposed to parents' rights—may be defined and protected is currently the subject of vigorous, and occasionally rancorous, debate.

The *family autonomy vs. coercive intervention* dilemma defines the conflict central to our ambiguity about *whether* society should intervene in situations of risk to children. The traditional autonomy of the family in rearing its offspring was cited by the majority of the U.S. Supreme Court in its ruling against the severely beaten appellants in the controversial "corporal punishment" case (*Ingraham vs. Wright et al*).[25] The schools, serving *in loco parentis*, are not, in effect, constrained constitutionally from any punishment, however cruel.

Yet in California, a physician seeing buttock bruises of the kind legally inflicted by the teacher in the Miami public schools risks malpractice action if he fails to report his observations as symptoms of child abuse (*Landeros vs. Flood*).[32] He and his hospital are potentially liable for the cost of the child's subsequent injury and handicap if they do not initiate protective measures.[7]

This dilemma is highlighted by the recently promulgated draft statute of the American Bar Association's Juvenile Justice Standards Project, which, citing the low prevailing quality of protective child welfare services in the U.S., would sharply *restrict* access to such services.[28] The Commission would, for example, make the reporting of child neglect discretionary rather than mandatory, and would narrowly define the bases for court jurisdiction to situations where there is clear harm to a child.

Our interpretation of this standard is that it would make matters worse, not better, for children and their families.[8] So long as we are deeply conflicted about the relation of children to the state as well as to the family, and whether children have rights independent of their parents', we shall never be able to articulate with clarity *how* to enforce them.

The *compassion vs. control* dilemma has been postulated and reviewed in a previous paper,[47] which discussed the conceptual and practical problems implicit in the expansion of the clinical and legal definitions of child abuse to include practically every physical and emotional risk to children. The dilemma addresses a conflict central to the present ambiguity about *how* to protect children from their parents.

Parental behavior that might be characterized as destructive or criminal were it directed towards an adult has come to be seen and interpreted by those involved in its identification and treatment in terms of the psychosocial economy of the family. Embracive de-

5. PROFESSIONAL

finitions reflect a change in the orientation of professional practice. To the extent to which we understand abusing parents as sad, deprived, needy human beings (rather than as cold, cruel murderers) we can sympathize with their plight and compassionately proffer supports and services to aid them in their struggle. Only with dread may we contemplate strong intervention (such as court action) on the child's behalf, for want of alienating our clients.

Notwithstanding the humane philosophy of treatment, society cannot, or will not, commit resources nearly commensurate with the exponentially increasing number of case reports that have followed the promulgation of the expanded definitions. The helping language betrays a deep conflict, and even ill will, toward children and parents in trouble, whom society and professionals might sooner punish and control.

We are forced frequently in practice to identify and choose the "least detrimental alternative" for the child [21] because the family supports that make it safe to keep children in their homes (homemakers, child care, psychiatric and medical services) are never available in sufficient amounts and quality.

That we should guide our work by a management concept named "least detrimental alternative" for children suggests at least a skepticism about the utility of these supports, just as the rational foundation for child welfare work is called into question by the title of the influential book from which the concept comes, *Beyond the Best Interests of the Child*.[21] More profoundly, the concept taps a vein of emotional confusion about our progeny, to whom we express both kindness and love with hurt.

Mounting attention to the developmental sequelae of child abuse [16, 33] stimulates an extra urgency not only to insure the physical safety of the identified victims but also to enable their adequate psychological development. The dangers of child abuse, according to Schmitt and Kempe in the latest edition of the Nelson Textbook of Pediatrics,[53] extend beyond harm to the victim:

If the child who has been physically abused is returned to his parents without intervention, 5 per cent are killed and 35 per cent are seriously reinjured. Moreover, the untreated families tend to produce children who grow up to be juvenile delinquents and murderers, as well as the batterers of the next generation.

Despite the speculative nature of such conclusions about the developmental sequelae of child abuse,[6, 10, 11] such warnings support a practice of separating children from their natural homes in the interest of their and society's protection. They focus professional concern and public wrath on "the untreated families" and may justify punitive action to save us from their children.

This professional response of control rather than of compassion furthermore generalizes mainly to poor and socially marginal families, for it is they who seem preferentially to attract the labels "abuse" and "neglect" to their problems in the public settings where they go for most health and social services.[36] Affluent families' childhood injuries appear more likely to be termed "accidents" by the private practitioners who offer them their services. The conceptual model of cause and effect implicit in the name "accident" is benign: an isolated, random event rather than a consequence of parental commission or omission.[37, 38]

CHILD ABUSE AND THE MEDICAL AND LEGAL PROFESSIONS

The importance of a technical discipline's conceptual structure in defining how it approaches a problem has been clearly stated by Mercer: [34]

Each discipline is organized around a core of basic concepts and assumptions which form the frame of reference from which persons trained in that discipline view the world and set about solving problems in their field. The concepts and assumptions which make up the perspective of each discipline give each its distinctive character and are the intellectual tools used by its practitioners. These tools are incorporated in action and problem solving and appear self-evident to persons socialized in the discipline. As a result, little consideration is likely to be given to the social consequence of applying a particular conceptual framework to problem solving.

When the issues to be resolved are clearly in the area of competence of a single discipline, the automatic application of its conceptual tools is likely to go unchallenged. However, when the problems under consideration lie in the interstices between disciplines, the disciplines concerned are likely to define the situation differently and may arrive at differing conclusions which have dissimilar implications for social action.

Table I
DILEMMAS OF SOCIAL POLICY AND PROFESSIONAL RESPONSE

RESPONSE	FAMILY AUTONOMY	*Versus*	COERCIVE INTERVENTION
Compassion ("support")	1 Voluntary child development services 2 Guaranteed family supports e.g income, housing, health services		1 Case reporting of family crisis and mandated family intervention 2 Court-ordered delivery of services
—— Versus ——			
Control ("punishment")	1 "Laissez-faire" No assured services or supports 2 Retributive response to family crisis		1 Court action to separate child from family 2 Criminal prosecution of parents

---

TABLE 1 presents a graphic display of the two dilemmas of social policy (*family autonomy vs. coercive intervention*) and professional response (*compassion vs. control*). The four-fold table illustrates possible action responses. For purposes of this discussion, it is well to think of "compassion" as signifying responses of support, such as provision of voluntary counseling and child care services, and "control" as signifying such punitive responses as "blaming the victim" for his or her reaction to social realities [49] and as the criminal prosecution of abusing parents.

What we do when children are injured in family crises is shaped also by how our professions respond to the interstitial area called "child abuse."

"MEDICALIZATION"

Though cruelty to children has occurred since documentary records of mankind have been kept,[9] it became a salient social problem in the United States only after the publication by Kempe and his colleagues describing the "battered child syndrome." [30] In the four-year period after this medical article appeared, the legislatures of all 50 states, stimulated partly by a model law developed under the aegis of the Children's Bureau of the U.S. Department of Health, Education, and Welfare, passed statutes mandating the identification and reporting of suspected victims of abuse.

Once the specific diagnostic category "battered child syndrome" was applied to integrate a set of medical symptoms, and laws were passed making the syndrome reportable, the problem was made a proper and legitimate concern for the medical profession. Conrad has discussed cogently how "hyperactivity" came officially to be known and how it became "medicalized." [5] Medicalization is defined in this paper as the perception of behavior as a medical problem or illness and the mandating or licensing of the medical profession to provide some type of treatment for it.

Pfohl [41] associated the publicity surrounding the battered child syndrome report with a phenomenon of "discovery" of child abuse. For radiologists, the potential for increased prestige, role expansion, and coalition formation (with psychodynamic psychiatry and pediatrics) may have encouraged identification and intervention in child abuse. Furthermore,

... the discovery of abuse as a new "illness" reduced drastically the intraorganizational constraints on doctors' "seeing" abuse ... Problems associated with perceiving parents as patients whose confidentiality must be protected were reconstructed by typifying them as patients who needed help. . . The maintenance of professional autonomy was assured by pairing deviance with sickness. . .

In some ways, medicine's "discovery" of abuse has benefited individual physicians and the profession.

One of the greatest ambitions of the physician is to discover or describe a "new" disease or syndrome.[24]

By such involvement the doctor becomes a moral entrepreneur defining what is normal, proper, or desirable: he becomes charged "with inquisitorial powers to discover certain wrongs to be righted." [24] New opportunities for the application of traditional methods are also found—for example, the systematic screening of suspected victims with a skeletal X-ray survey to detect previous fractures, and the recent report in the neurology literature suggesting the utility of diphenylhydantoin * treatment for child abusing par-

---

* Dilantin, a commonly-used seizure suppressant.

ents.[46]

Pfohl's provocative analysis also took note of some of the normative and structural elements within the medical profession that appear to have reinforced a *reluctance* on the part of some physicians to become involved: the norm of confidentiality between doctor and patient and the goal of professional autonomy.[41] For many physicians, child abuse is a subject to avoid.[50]

First, it is difficult to distinguish, on a theoretical level, corporal punishment that is "acceptable" from that which is "illegitimate." Abuse may be defined variably even by specialists, the definitions ranging from serious physical injury to nonfulfillment of a child's developmental needs.[13, 19, 80]

Second, it is frequently hard to diagnose child abuse clinically. What appears on casual physical examination as bruising, for example, may turn out to be a skin manifestation of an organic blood dysfunction, or what appear to be cigarette burns may in reality be infected mosquito bites. A diagnosis of abuse may require social and psychological information about the family, the acquisition and interpretation of which may be beyond the average clinician's expertise. It may be easier to characterize the clinical complaint in terms of the child's medical symptom rather than in terms of the social, familial, and psychological forces associated with its etiology. We see daily situations where the exclusive choice of medical taxonomy actively obscures the causes of the child's symptom and restricts the range of possible interventions: examples are "subdural hematoma," which frequently occurs with severe trauma to babies' heads (the medical name means collection of blood under the *dura mater* of the brain), and "enuresis" or "encopresis" in child victims of sexual assault (medical names mean incontinence of urine or feces).

Third, child abuse arouses strong emotions. To concentrate on the narrow medical issue (the broken bone) instead of the larger familial problem (the etiology of the injury) not only allows one to avoid facing the limits of one's technical adequacy, but to shield oneself from painful feelings of sadness and anger. One can thus maintain professional detachment and avert unpleasant confrontations. The potentially alienating

nature of the physician-patient interaction when the diagnosis of child abuse is made may also have a negative economic impact on the doctor, especially the physician in private practice.

"LEGALIZATION"

The legal response to child abuse was triggered by its medicalization. Child abuse reporting statutes codified a medical diagnosis into a legal framework which in many states defined official functions for courts. Immunity from civil liability was given to mandated reporters so long as reports were made in good faith; monetary penalties for failure to report were established; and familial and professional-client confidentiality privileges, except those involving attorneys, were abrogated.

Professional autonomy for lawyers was established, and status and power accrued to legal institutions. For example, the growth in the number of Care and Protection cases before the Boston Juvenile Court "has been phenomenal in recent years. . . four cases in 1968 and 99 in 1974, involving 175 different children." [44] Though these cases have burdened court dockets and personnel, they have also led to acknowledgement of the important work of the court. The need for this institution is enhanced because of its recognized expertise in handling special matters. Care and Protection cases are cited in response to recommendations by a prestigious commission charged with proposing reform and consolidation of the courts in Massachusetts. Child protection work in our own institution would proceed only with difficulty if access to the court were legally or procedurally constrained. Just as for the medical profession, however, there were normative and structural elements within law which urged restraint. Most important among them were the traditional presumptions and practices favoring family autonomy.

If individual lawyers might financially benefit from representing clients in matters pertaining to child abuse, they—like their physician counterparts—were personally uncertain whether or how to become involved.

Public concern over the scope and significance of the problem of the battered child is a comparatively new phenomenon. Participation by counsel in any significant numbers in child abuse cases in juvenile or family courts is of even more recent origin. It is small wonder that the lawyer approaches participation in these cases with trepidation.[26]

Lawyers, too, feel handicapped by a need to rely on concepts from social work and psychiatry and on data from outside the traditional domain of legal knowledge and expertise. As counsel to parents, lawyers can be torn between advocacy of their clients' positions and that which advances the "best interest" of their clients' children. As counsel to the petitioner, a lawyer may have to present a case buttressed by little tangible evidence. Risk to a child is often difficult to characterize and impossible to prove.

Further problems for lawyers concerned with child abuse involve the context of intervention: whether courts or legislatures should play the major role in shaping practice and allocating resources; how much formality is desirable in legal proceedings; and the propriety of negotiation as opposed to adversary confrontation when cases come to court.

CONFLICTS BETWEEN MEDICAL AND LEGAL PERSPECTIVES

Despite the common reasons for the "medicalization" and the "legalization" of child abuse, there are several areas where the two orientations conflict:

1. *The seriousness of the risk.* To lawyers, intervention might be warranted only when abuse results in serious harm to a child. To clinicians, however, *any* inflicted injury might justify a protective legal response, especially if the child is very young. "The trick is to prevent the abusive case from becoming the terminal case."[14] Early intervention may prevent the abuse from being repeated or from becoming more serious.

2. *The definition of the abuser.* To lawyers, the abuser might be defined as a wrongdoer who has injured a child. To clinicians, both the abuser and child might be perceived as victims influenced by sociological and psychological factors beyond their control.[17, 35]

3. *The importance of the abuser's mental state.* To lawyers, whether the abuser intentionally or accidentally inflicted injury on a child is a necessary condition of reporting or judicial action. So-called "accidents" are less likely to trigger intervention. To clinicians, however, mental state may be less relevant,

for it requires a diagnostic formulation frequently difficult or impossible to make on the basis of available data. The family dynamics associated with "accidents" in some children (*e.g.*, stress, marital conflict, and parental inattention) often resemble those linked with inflicted injury in others. They are addressed with variable clinical sensitivity and precision.

4. *The role of law.* Attorneys are proudly unwilling to accept conclusions or impressions lacking empirical corroboration. To lawyers, the law and legal institutions become involved in child abuse when certain facts fit a standard of review. To clinicians, the law may be seen as an instrument to achieve a particular therapeutic or dispositional objective (*e.g.*, the triggering of services or of social welfare involvement) even if, as is very often the case, the data to support such objectives legally are missing or ambiguous. The clinician's approach to the abuse issue is frequently subjective or intuitive (*e.g.*, a *feeling* that a family is under stress or needs help, or that a child is "at risk"), while the lawyer demands evidence.

DOCTORING AND LAWYERING THE DISEASE

These potential or actual differences in orientation notwithstanding, both medicine and law have accepted in principle the therapeutic approach to child abuse.

To physicians, defining abuse as a disease or medical syndrome makes natural the treatment alternative, since both injured child and abuser are viewed as "sick"—the one, physically, the other psychologically or socially. Therapy may, however, have retributive aspects, as pointed out with characteristic pungency by Illich:[24]

The medical label may protect the patient from punishment only to submit him to interminable instruction, treatment, and discrimination, which are inflicted on him for his professionally presumed benefit.

Lawyers adopt a therapeutic perspective for several reasons. First, the rehabilitative ideal remains in ascendance in criminal law, especially in the juvenile and family courts which handle most child abuse cases.[1]

Second, the criminal or punitive model may not protect the child. Parents may hesitate to seek help if they are fearful

of prosecution. Evidence of abuse is often insufficient to satisfy the standard of conviction "beyond all reasonable doubt" in criminal proceedings. An alleged abuser threatened with punishment and then found not guilty may feel vindicated, reinforcing the pattern of abuse. The abuser may well be legally freed from any scrutiny, and badly needed social services will not be able to be provided. Even if found guilty, the perpetrator of abuse is usually given only mild punishment, such as a short jail term or probation. If the abuser is incarcerated, the other family members may equally suffer as, for example, the relationship between spouses is undercut and child-rearing falls on one parent, or children are placed in foster home care or with relatives. Upon release from jail, the abuser may be no less violent and even more aggressive and vindictive toward the objects of abuse.

Third, the fact that child abuse was "discovered" by physicians influenced the model adopted by other professionals. As Freidson[15] noted:

Medical definitions of deviance have come to be adopted even where there is no reliable evidence that biophysical variables "cause" the deviance or that medical treatment is any more efficacious than any other kind of management.

Weber, in addition, contended that "status" groups (*e.g.*, physicians) generally determine the content of law.[45]

THE SELECTIVE IMPLEMENTATION OF TREATMENT

Medical intervention is generally encouraged by the Hippocratic ideology of treatment (the ethic that help, not harm, is given by practitioners), and by what Scheff[52] called the medical decision rule: it is better to wrongly diagnose illness and "miss" health than it is to wrongly diagnose health and "miss" illness.

Physicians, in defining aberrant behavior as a medical problem and in providing treatment, become what sociologists call agents of social control. Though the technical enterprise of the physician claims value-free power, socially marginal individuals are more likely to be defined as deviant than are others.

Characteristics frequently identified with the "battered child syndrome," such as social isolation, alcoholism, unemployment, childhood handicap, large family size, low level of parental educational achievement, and acceptance of severe physical punishment as a childhood socializing technique, are associated with social marginality and poverty.

Physicians in public settings seem, from child abuse reporting statistics, to be more likely to see and report child abuse than are those in private practice. As poor people are more likely to frequent hospital emergency wards and clinics,[36] they have much greater social visibility where child abuse is concerned than do people of means.

The fact that child abuse is neither theoretically nor clinically well defined increases the likelihood of subjective professional evaluation. In labeling theory, it is axiomatic that the greater the social distance between the typer and the person singled out for typing, the broader the type and the more quickly it may be applied.[48]

In the doctor-patient relationship, the physician is always in a superordinate position because of his or her expertise; social distance is inherent to the relationship. This distance necessarily increases once the label of abuser has been applied. Importantly, the label is less likely to be fixed if the diagnostician and possible abuser share similar characteristics, especially socioeconomic status, particularly where the injury is not serious or manifestly a consequence of maltreatment.

Once the label "abuser" is attached, it is very difficult to remove; even innocent behavior of a custodian may then be viewed with suspicion. The tenacity of a label increases in proportion to the official processing. At our own institution, until quite recently, a red star was stamped on the permanent medical record of any child who might have been abused, a process which encouraged professionals to suspect child abuse (and to act on that assumption) at any future time that the child would present with a medical problem.

Professionals thus engage in an intricate process of selection, finding facts that fit the label which has been applied, responding to a few deviant details set within a panoply of entirely acceptable conduct. Schur[55] called this phenomenon "retrospective reinterpretation." In any pathological model, "persons are likely to be studied in terms of what is 'wrong' with them," there being a "de-

cided emphasis on identifying the characteristics of abnormality;" in child abuse, it may be administratively impossible to return to health, as is shown by the extraordinary durability of case reports in state central registers.[58]

The response of the patient to the agent of social control affects the perceptions and behavior of the controller. If, for example, a child has been injured and the alleged perpetrator is repentant, a concensus can develop between abuser and labeler that a norm has been violated. In this situation, the label of "abuser" may be less firmly applied than if the abuser defends the behavior as proper. Support for this formulation is found in studies by Gusfield,[22] who noted different reactions to repentant, sick, and enemy deviants, and by Piliavin and Briar,[42] who showed that juveniles apprehended by the police receive more lenient treatment if they appear contrite and remorseful about their violations.

CONSEQUENCES OF TREATMENT FOR THE ABUSER

Once abuse is defined as a sickness, it becomes a condition construed to be beyond the actor's control.[39] Though treatment, not punishment, is warranted, the *type* of treatment depends on whether or not the abuser is "curable," "improvable," or "incurable," and on the speed with which such a state can be achieved.

To help the abuser is generally seen as a less important goal than is the need to protect the child. If the abusive behavior cannot quickly be altered, and the child remains "at risk," the type of intervention will differ accordingly (*e.g.,* the child may be more likely to be placed in a foster home). The less "curable" is the abuser, the less treatment will be offered and the more punitive will society's response appear. Ironically, even the removal of a child from his parents, a move nearly always perceived as punitive by parents, is often portrayed as helpful by the professionals doing the removing ("It will give you a chance to resolve your own problems," etc.).

Whatever the treatment, there are predictable consequences for those labeled "abusers." Prior to diagnosis, parents may be afraid of "getting caught" because of punishment and social stigma. On being told of clinicians' concerns, they may express hostility because of implicit or explicit criticism made of

them and their child-rearing practices yet feel relief because they love their children and want help in stopping their destructive behavior. The fact that they see themselves as "sick" may increase their willingness to seek help. This attitude is due at least in part to the lesser social stigma attached to the "sick," as opposed to the "criminal," label.

Socially marginal individuals are likely to accept whatever definition more powerful labelers apply. This definition, of course, has already been accepted by much of the larger community because of the definers' power. As Davis[8] noted:

The chance that a group will get community support for its definition of unacceptable deviance depends on its relative power position. The greater the group's size, resources, efficiency, unity, articulateness, prestige, coordination with other groups, and access to the mass media and to decision-makers, the more likely it is to get its preferred norms legitimated.

Acceptance of definition by child abusers, however, is not based solely on the power of the labelers. Though some might consider the process "political castration,"[43] so long as they are defined as "ill" and take on the sick role, abusers are achieving a more satisfactory label. Though afflicted with a stigmatized illness (and thus "gaining few if any privileges and taking on some especially handicapping new obligations"[15]) at least they are merely sick rather than sinful or criminal.

Effective social typing flows down rather than up the social structure. For example, when both parents induct one of their children into the family scapegoat role, this is an effective social typing because the child is forced to take their definition of him into account.[48] Sometimes it is difficult to know whether an abusive parent has actually accepted the definition or is merely "role playing" in order to please the definer. If a person receives conflicting messages from the same control agent (*e.g.,* "you are sick and criminal") or from different control agents in the treatment network (from doctors who use the sick label, and lawyers who use the criminal), confusion and upset predictably result.[56]

As an example of how social definitions are accepted by the group being defined, it is interesting to examine the basic tenets of Parents Anonymous, which began as a self-help group for abusive mothers:

5. PROFESSIONAL

A destructive, *disturbed* mother can, and often does, produce through her actions a physically or emotionally abused, or battered child. Present available *help* is limited and/or expensive, usually with a long waiting list before the person requesting help can actually receive *treatment*. . . We must understand that a problem as involved as this cannot be *cured* immediately . . . the problem is *within us* as a parent. . .[29] [emphases added]

To Parents Anonymous, child abuse appears to be a medical problem, and abusers are sick persons who must be treated.

CONSEQUENCES OF TREATMENT FOR THE SOCIAL SYSTEM

The individual and the social system are interrelated; each influences the other. Thus, if society defines abusive parents as sick, there will be few criminal prosecutions for abuse; reports will generally be sent to welfare, as opposed to police, departments.

Since victims of child abuse are frequently treated in hospitals, medical personnel become brokers for adult services and definers of children's rights. Once abuse is defined, that is, people may get services (such as counseling, child care, and homemaker services) that would be otherwise unavailable to them, and children may get care and protection impossible without institutional intervention.

If, as is customary, however, resources are in short supply, the preferred treatment of a case may not be feasible. Under this condition, less adequate treatment stratagems, or even clearly punitive alternatives, may be implemented. If day care and competent counseling are unavailable, court action and foster placement can become the only options. As Stoll[56] observed,

. . . the best therapeutic intentions may be led astray when opportunities to implement theoretical guidelines are not available.

Treating child abuse as a sickness has, ironically, made it more difficult to "cure." There are not enough therapists to handle all of the diagnosed cases. Nor do most abusive parents have the time, money, or disposition for long-term therapeutic involvement. Many, moreover, lack the introspective and conceptual abilities required for successful psychological therapy.

As Parents Anonymous emphasizes, abuse is the *abuser's* problem. Its causes and solutions are widely understood to reside in individuals rather than in the social system.[5, 17] Indeed, the strong emphasis on child abuse as an individual problem means that other equally severe problems of childhood can be ignored, and the unequal distribution of social and economic resources in society can be masked.[20] The child abuse phenomenon itself may also increase as parents and professionals are obliged to "package" their problems and diagnoses in a competitive market where services are in short supply. As Tannenbaum[57] observed in 1938:

Societal reactions to deviance can be characterized as a kind of "dramatization of evil" such that a person's deviance is made a public issue. The stronger the reaction to the evil, the more it seems to grow. The reaction itself seems to generate the very thing it sought to eliminate.

CONCLUSION

Dispelling the Myth of Child Abuse

As clinicians, we are convinced that with intelligence, humanity, and the application of appropriate interventions, we can help families in crisis.

We believe, however, that short of coming to terms with—and changing—certain social, political, and economic aspects of our society, we will never be able adequately to understand and address the origins of child abuse and neglect. Nor will the issues of labeling be adequately resolved unless we deal straightforwardly with the potentially abusive power of the helping professions. If we can bring ourselves to ask such questions as, "Can we legislate child abuse out of existence?" and, "Who benefits from child abuse?", then perhaps we can more rationally choose among the action alternatives displayed in the conceptual model (TABLE 1).

Although we would prefer to avoid coercion and punishment, and to keep families autonomous and services voluntary, we must acknowledge the realities of family life and posit some state role to assure the well-being of children. In making explicit the assumptions and values underpinning our professional actions, perhaps we can promote a more informed and humane practice.

Because it is likely that clinical interventions will continue to be class and culture-based, we propose the following five guidelines to minimize the abuse of power of the definer.

1. *Give physicians, social workers, lawyers, and other intervention agents social science perspectives and skills.* Critical intellectual tools should help clinicians to understand the implications of their work, and, especially, the functional meaning of the labels they apply in their practices.

Physicians need to be more aware of the complexity of human life, especially its social and psychological dimensions. The "medical model" is not of itself inappropriate; rather, the conceptual bases of medical practice need to be broadened, and the intellectual and scientific repertory of the practitioner expanded.[12] Diagnostic formulation is an active process that carries implicitly an anticipation of intervention and outcome. The simple elegance of concepts such as "child abuse" and "child neglect" militate for simple and radical treatments.

Lawyers might be helped to learn that, in child custody cases, they are not merely advocates of a particular position. Only the child should "win" a custody case, where, for example, allegations of "abuse" or "neglect," skillfully marshalled, may support the position of the more effectively represented parent, guardian, or social worker.

2. *Acknowledge and change the prestige hierarchy of helping professions.* The workers who seem best able to conceptualize the familial and social context of problems of violence are social workers and nurses. They are least paid, most overworked, and as a rule have minimal access to the decision prerogatives of medicine and law. We would add that social work and nursing are professions largely of and by women, and we believe we must come to terms with the many realities—including sexual dominance and subservience—that keep members of these professions from functioning with appropriate respect and support. (We have made a modest effort in this direction at our own institution, where our interdisciplinary child abuse consultation program is organized under the aegis of the administration rather than of a medical clinical department. This is to foster, to the extent possible, peer status and communication on a coequal footing among the disciplines involved—social work, nursing, law, medicine, and psychiatry.)

3. *Build theory.* We need urgently a commonly understandable dictionary of concepts that will guide and inform a rational practice. A more adequate theory base would include a more etiologic (or causal) classification scheme for children's injuries, which would acknowledge and integrate diverse origins and expressions of social, familial, child developmental, and environmental phenomena. It would conceptualize strength in families and children, as well as pathology. It would orient intervenors to the promotion of health rather than to the treatment of disease.

A unified theory would permit coming to terms with the universe of need. At present, socially marginal and poor children are virtually the only ones susceptible to being diagnosed as victims of abuse and neglect. More affluent families' offspring, whose injuries are called "accidents" and who are often unprotected, are not included in "risk" populations. We have seen examples of court defense where it was argued (successfully) that because the family was not poor, it did not fit the classic archetypes of abuse or neglect.

The needs and rights of all children need to be spelled out legally in relation to the responsibilities of parents and the state. This is easier said than done. It shall require not only a formidable effort at communication across disciplinary lines but a serious coming to terms with social and political values and realities.

4. *Change social inequality.* We share Gil's [20] view that inequality is the basic problem underlying the labeling of "abusive families" and its consequences. Just as children without defined rights are *ipso facto* vulnerable, so too does unequal access to the resources and goods of society shape a class hierarchy that leads to the individualization of social problems. Broadly-focused efforts for social change should accompany a critical review of the ethical foundations of professional practice. As part of the individual's formation as doctor, lawyer, social worker, or police officer, there could be developed for the professional a notion of public service and responsibility. This would better enable individuals to see themselves as participants in a social process and to perceive the problems addressed in their work at the social as well as the individual level of action.

5. *Assure adequate representation of class and ethnic groups in decision-making forums.* Since judgments about family competency can be affected by class and ethnic biases, they should be made in settings where prejudices can be checked and controlled. Culture-bound value judgments in child protection work are not infrequent, and a sufficient participation in case management conferences of professionals of equal rank and status and diverse ethnicity can assure both a more appropriate context for decision making and better decisions for children and their families.

REFERENCES

1. ALLEN, F. 1964. The Borderland of Criminal Justice. University of Chicago Press, Chicago.
2. BECKER, H. 1963. Outsiders: Studies in the Sociology of Deviance. Free Press, New York.
3. BOURNE, R. AND NEWBERGER, E. 1977. 'Family autonomy' or 'coercive intervention?' ambiguity and conflict in a proposed juvenile justice standard on child protection. Boston Univ. Law Rev. 57(4):670–706.
5. CONRAD, P. 1975. The discovery of hyperkinesis: notes on the medicalization of deviant behavior. Soc. Prob. 23(10): 12–21.
6. CUPOLI, J. AND NEWBERGER, E. 1977. Optimism or pessimism for the victim of child abuse? Pediatrics 59(2):311–314.
7. CURRAN, W. 1977. Failure to diagnose battered child syndrome. New England J. Med. 296(14):795–796.
8. DAVIS, F. 1975. Beliefs, values, power and public definitions of deviance. *In* The Collective Definition of Deviance, F. Davis and R. Stivers, eds. Free Press, New York.
9. DEMAUSE, L., *ed.* 1974. The History of Childhood. Free Press, New York.
10. ELMER, E. 1977. A follow-up study of traumatized children. Pediatrics 59(2): 273–279.
11. ELMER, E. 1977. Fragile Families, Troubled Children. University of Pittsburgh Press, Pittsburgh.
12. ENGEL, G. 1977. The need for a new medical model: a challenge for biomedicine. Science 196(14):129–136.
13. FONTANA, V. 1964. The Maltreated Child: The Maltreatment Syndrome in Children. Charles C Thomas, Springfield, Ill.
14. FRASER, B. 1977. Legislative status of child abuse legislation. *In* Child Abuse and Neglect: the Family and the Community, C. Kempe and R. Helfer, eds. Ballinger, Cambridge, Mass.
15. FREIDSON, E. 1970. Profession of Medicine: A Study of the Sociology of Applied Knowledge. Dodd, Mead, New York.
16. GALDSTON, R. 1971. Violence begins at home. J. Amer. Acad. Child Psychiat. 10(2):336–350.
17. GELLES, R. 1973. Child abuse as psychopathology: a sociological critique and reformulation. Amer. J. Orthopsychiat. 43(4):611–621.
18. GELLES, R. 1978. Violence toward children in the United States. Amer. J. Orthopsychiat. 48(4):580–592.
19. GIL, D. 1975. Unraveling child abuse. Amer. J. Orthopsychiat. 45(4):346–356.
20. GIL, D. 1970. Violence Against Children. Harvard University Press, Cambridge, Mass.
21. GOLDSTEIN, J., FREUD, A. AND SOLNIT, A. 1973. Beyond the Best Interests of the Child. Free Press, New York.
22. GUSFIELD, J. 1967. Moral passage: the symbolic process in public designations of deviance. Soc. Prob. 15(2):175–188.
23. HYDE, J. 1974. Uses and abuses of information in protective services contexts. *In* Fifth National Symposium on Child Abuse and Neglect. American Humane Association, Denver.
24. ILLICH, I. 1976. Medical Nemesis: The Expropriation of Health. Random House, New York.
25. *Ingraham v. Wright.* 1977. 45 LW 4364 U.S. Supreme Court.
26. ISAACS, J. 1972. The role of the lawyer in child abuse cases. *In* Helping the Battered Child and His Family, R. Helfer and C. Kempe, eds. Lippincott, Philadelphia.
27. JOINT COMMISSION ON THE MENTAL HEALTH OF CHILDREN. 1970. Crisis in Child Mental Health. Harper and Row, New York.
28. JUVENILE JUSTICE STANDARDS PROJECT. 1977. Standards Relating to Abuse and Neglect. Ballinger, Cambridge, Mass.
29. KEMPE, C. AND HELFER, R., eds. 1972. Helping the Battered Child and His Family. Lippincott, Philadelphia.
30. KEMPE, C. ET AL. 1962. The battered child syndrome. JAMA 181(1):17–24.
31. KITTRIE, N. 1971. The Right To Be Different. Johns Hopkins University Press, Baltimore.
32. *Landeros v. Flood.* 1976. 131 Calif. Rptr 69.
33. MARTIN, H., ed. 1976. The Abused Child: A Multidisciplinary Approach to Developmental Issues and Treatment. Ballinger, Cambridge, Mass.
34. MERCER, J. 1972. Who is normal? two perspectives on mild mental retardation. *In* Patients, Physicians and Illness (2nd ed.), E. Jaco, ed. Free Press, New York.
35. NEWBERGER, E. 1975. The myth of the battered child syndrome. *In* Annual Progress in Child Psychiatry and Child Development 1974, S. Chess and A. Thomas, eds. Brunner Mazel, New York.
36. NEWBERGER, E., NEWBERGER, C. AND RICHMOND, J. 1976. Child health in America: toward a rational public policy. Milbank Memorial Fund Quart./Hlth. and Society 54(3):249–298.
37. NEWBERGER, E. AND DANIEL, J. 1976. Knowledge and epidemiology of child abuse: a critical review of concepts. Pediat. Annals 5(3):15–26.
38. NEWBERGER, E. ET AL. 1977. Pediatric social illness: toward an etiologic classification. Pediatrics 60(1):178–185.
39. PARSONS, T. 1951. The Social System. Free Press, Glencoe, Ill.
40. PAULSEN, M. 1966. Juvenile courts, family courts, and the poor man. Calif. Law Rev. 54(2):694–716.
41. PFOHL, S. 1977. The 'discovery' of child abuse. Soc. Prob. 24(3):310–323.

5. PROFESSIONAL

42. PILIAVIN, I. AND BRIAR, S. 1964. Police encounters with juveniles. Amer. J. Sociol. 70(2):206–214.

43. PITTS, J. 1968. Social control: the concept. *In* The International Encyclopedia of the Social Sciences 14:391. Macmillan, New York.

44. POITRAST, F. 1976. The judicial dilemma in child abuse cases. Psychiat. Opinion 13(1):22–28.

45. RHEINSTEIN, M. 1954. Max Weber on Law in Economy and Society. Harvard University Press, Cambridge, Mass.

46. ROSENBLATT, S., SCHAEFFER, D. AND ROSENTHAL, J. 1976. Effects of diphenylhydantoin on child abusing parents: a preliminary report. Curr. Therapeut. Res. 19(3):332–336.

47. ROSENFELD, A. AND NEWBERGER, E. 1977. Compassion versus control: conceptual and practical pitfalls in the broadened definition of child abuse. JAMA 237(19):2086–2088.

48. RUBINGTON, E. AND WEINBERG, M. 1973. Deviance: The Interactionist Perspective (2nd ed.). Macmillan, New York.

49. RYAN, W. 1971. Blaming the Victim. Random House, New York.

50. SANDERS, R. 1972. Resistance to dealing with parents of battered children. Pediatrics 50(6):853–857.

51. SCHEFF, T. 1966. Being Mentally Ill: A Sociological Theory. Aldine, Chicago.

52. SCHEFF, T. 1972. Decision rules, types of error, and their consequences in medical diagnosis. *In* Medical Men and Their Work, E. Freidson and J. Lorber, eds. Aldine, Chicago.

53. SCHMITT, B. AND KEMPE, C. 1975. Neglect and abuse of children. *In* Nelson Textbook of Pediatrics (10th ed.), V. Vaughan and R. McKay, eds. W. B. Saunders, Philadelphia.

54. SCHRAG, P. 1975. The Myth of the Hyperactive Child. Random House, New York.

55. SCHUR, E. 1971. Labeling Deviant Behavior. Harper and Row, New York.

56. STOLL, C. 1968. Images of man and social control. Soc. Forces 47(2):119–127.

57. TANNENBAUM, F. 1938. Crime and the Community. Ginn and Co., Boston.

58. WHITING, L. 1977. The central registry for child abuse cases: rethinking basic assumptions. Child Welfare 56(2):761–767.

Model Child Abuse and Neglect Legislation

Judge James H. Lincoln
Juvenile Court of Wayne County
Detroit, Michigan

One of the great issues of our times is, "What role shall government play in the life of a child?" The problem is as complex and multifaceted as civilization or human nature itself.

Anyone, regardless of credentials, who claims to be an expert on this great issue, will be viewed as a charlatan a century from now. We are all alchemists when it comes to this issue, whether we are professors; psychiatrists; psychologists; social workers; attorneys; administrators; employees of the Department of Health, Education, and Welfare; judges, etc. In light of historical perspective each of us will be considered alchemists. Behavioral sciences are at least 1,000 years behind the exact sciences. I was raised by a kerosene lamp, and the plumbing was behind the lilac bush. In one lifetime I have seen man progress from a kerosene lamp to walking on the moon. That is 1,000 years of progress in the exact sciences in one short lifetime. As far as behavioral sciences are concerned, there has been a great amassing of questionable data and even more questionable theories. Much change but little progress! Of course, human behavior is much more complex than putting a man on the moon. However, those engaged in the exact sciences can disenthrall themselves, and look at their problems objectively. In the behavioral sciences (including the legal profession), we are as conditioned to certain attitudes and reflexes as Pavlov's dog. In other situations those with claimed expertise know so little about the issues that they simply follow some leader who is skilled and articulate in expounding one of the latest popular styles or fads. In the 17 years I have been on the bench, the behavioral sciences have had as many styles as women's clothing. This is also true of the legal profession.

One can classify those in this nation who write model laws, standards etc., for neglected and abused children into three groupings or classifications--right, left, and center. The behavioral and legal scientists that represent the right are largely on the West Coast and the left on the East Coast.

(1)   <u>The Right</u>: This group of eminent behavioral scientists is chaired by Michael S. Wald, professor, School of Law, Stanford University, Stanford, California. He, together with more than 50 behavioral scientists, heavily laden with credentials (with a sprinkling of attorneys and a token judge or two), has drafted model neglect and abuse laws and standards for the Institute of Judicial Administration (IJA). The work of this committee will be presented to the American Bar Association (ABA) for approval. It is an outstanding work. The West Coast proponents would severely restrict the role of government in the life of a child even to excluding thousands of neglected children needing help. They are content to help most children in need of help, but whether most means leaving out 49 or 10 percent is debatable.

(2)   <u>The Left</u>: One effective and authoritative spokesman for this group is Douglas Besharov, Director, National Center on Child Abuse and Neglect, Department of Health, Education, and Welfare, Washington, D.C. Besharov can back his views and proposals with recognized national authorities. Professors Sanford Fox and Sanford Katz, together with Besharov's committee, have credentials similar to the right or West Coast. There is no way to settle differences by weighing credentials. The East and West Coast are loaded with credentials.

"Model Child Abuse and Neglect Legislation," James H. Lincoln, *Child Abuse and Neglect: Issues on Innovation and Implementations,* © 1978 U.S. Department of Health, Education and Welfare.

5. PROFESSIONAL

HEW either has or will issue model statutes and standards on every conceivable aspect of neglect and abuse. The East Coast Group would greatly expand the role of government in the life of a child. Of course, this is done under considerable congressional direction. The Mondale Act classifies "mental injury" as child abuse. A mother yelling at her child in the backyard would be registered as a child abuser. If the East Coast (HEW) has its way, by year 2,000 there could be more social workers than any other profession in the nation.

Several examples of East Coast thinking are explained in a letter I directed to Besharov a few months ago. It was printed in the February issue of the National Council of Juvenile Court Judges' newsletter. I explained that in the proposed HEW criteria for foster homes, the children would have concerts, plays, etc. HEW set standards where the majority of parents will need a court to declare their children neglected in order for youngsters to receive these necessities of life (by HEW standards).[1]

If one could determine how the two philosophies affect specific wording in proposed model statutes or standards, it would be like fighting two tons of feathers. These documents total hundreds and hundreds of pages. I only recently found time to review the Model Act to Free Children for Permanent Placement, with commentary, developed by Professor Katz and his very "credential laden" committee. Of course, termination of parental rights is only a small fraction of the scope of neglect and abuse. However, it is not hard to choose a few parts of this proposed statute that would hardly fit the West Coast philosophy. Example: The grounds for involuntary termination are much broader than West Coast would seriously consider to adopt.

Judge Jean L. Lewis, Circuit Judge, Portland, Oregon, said, "Section 4(a) (3) (iii) indicates that the construction of a parent–child relationship will greatly diminish the child's prospects for early integration into a stable and permanent home. If the goal is to reunite a child and his parents, then it seems that every reasonable safeguard must first be found to get the child back in his home. At what point does continuation of a relationship diminish the child's prospects for early adoption?" This is one of many, many observations that could demonstrate how difference in East and West Coast philosophies would lead to different model acts and standards.

There are many factors in the development of model acts and standards that have little or no relation to philosophy. At this point there is little about which to debate. Both the East and West Coast handle these matters with equal excellence. I refer to such matters as found in section 16 of the Model Termination Act developed by Professor Katz. This requires a report within 90 days after the order of termination by the agency as to long-term placement, etc.

I, of course, highly favor the Model Termination Act drafted by the Neglected Children's Committee of the National Council of Juvenile Courts Judges (NCJCJ). Without trying to balance the merits of these various model acts, note that the NCJCJ Model Termination Act (funded by the Edna McConnell Clark Foundation) is vastly improved over the 50 termination laws now in effect in several states. It is "legal as hell" because it was drafted primarily by juvenile court judges, with heavy reliance on behavioral scientists.

We should consider section 12(b) of the act drafted under Professor Katz's direction for HEW. This proposed model act provides that in cases where the natural father's identity is unknown to the petitioner, the court may ask the mother about the natural father, but "may not compel disclosure by the mother." The juvenile court judges who developed the NCJCJ Model Termination Act would never approve such a provision. The Supreme Court, in the *Stanley* case, provides that the natural father be given notice and certainly, before publication, every effort must be made to give personal notice. Such a statutory provision will result in litigation that should be avoided. I have a petition before me in the Wayne County juvenile court to set aside an adoption. The natural father claims due diligence was not used to locate him before publication was used to give him notice. Regardless of what happens in these cases, it is best to avoid litigation over whether or not service is proper.

I do not say these things critically. I say them analytically. How can two groups of behavioral scientists and representatives of the legal profession develop such opposite views and recommendations? Let us list all possible reasons which, together, exhaust the possibilities. Remember, I have seen no minority reports from either group.

(1)   There is careful selection of those serving on each committee concerning their preconceived views;

(2)   The impact of leadership in each group determines the broad philosophical approach to the matter under consideration; and

(3)   The third possibility is that a combination of the first two account for a result that could not happen once in a billion times.

Suppose we take 70 behavioral scientists, each with impressive credentials. We randomly divide them into two groups. Then, the two groups consider the same subject and arrive at different views and philosophies. The two groups differ as much as heads and tails on a coin.

Such a result does not occur solely by chance. It would be like tossing a coin in the air and correctly predicting the outcome 70 times in a row. That is one chance in a billion. It would not happen by chance in an eternity. Thus one way or the other the conclusions reached by the East and West Coast are determined before any meeting or consultation with behavioral scientists. Why have committees in the first place except for prestige purposes!

The following exhibits[2] are for your consideration.

Exhibit One is a letter to Professor Wald, dated February 24, 1975. The 1975 draft has been changed somewhat but is essentially the same. I prepared a report to the NCJCJ last week recommending that it oppose this committee's report, and I did point out that it was useful as a counter-balance against the equally extreme views of HEW. This report is too lengthy to include here. It has not yet been approved by NCJCJ. It expressed my views, and I will be glad to furnish a copy to anyone on request.[3] Exhibit Two, relating to the East Coast position, was directed to Besharov, dated September 4, 1975.[4] Exhibit Three is a two-page excerpt from the February issue of the NCJCJ newsletter.[5] My correspondence and statement concerning HEW standards and model laws are numerous and lengthy.

We have discussed the left (East Coast) and the right (West Coast). We should clearly indicate another alternative. I labeled this the "Center" only because it is the only ground remaining. All other territory is occupied by either the right or the left.

It is, however, misleading to label this position the Center. The position of this large but ignored group expounds no philosophy that would lead us into either of the other two positions. The group labeled (or mislabeled) the "Center", believes we should rise above principle and be practical. This group is well aware that with perfect logic one can proceed to the grand fallacy.

Thus, in the development of model acts, standards, regulations, etc., there should be a massive injection of the views of several juvenile court judges.

(1) These judges should help draft the project, and should also be present at the discussion stage. It is not worth a damn to be called in after the project has jelled. Having experienced this, I know very well that my presence at one meeting only constitutes "tokenism." It can then be said that NCJCJ was included. Nonsense!

The failure to include a massive injection of the thinking of juvenile court judges is an old and respected abuse. Perhaps the most flagrant example of this occurs in the "Task Force Report on Juvenile Delinquency and Youth Crime" printed in 1967 and issued under the names of Katzenback and Vorenberg. To lend authenticity to the report, five juvenile court judges are listed as advisors. My name is one of those. Four of the five judges listed were never consulted concerning this document. The Supreme Court has quoted this report as the Bible of authority in no less than three decisions. Much of the report is unmitigated nonsense. Much of the task force staff came from HEW.

Vorenberg was the executive director, and if he did not know juvenile court judges were completely excluded from the project, then he did not know what the hell went on in the project. That is what I think happened. His staff wrote and/or assembled the report, and then added names to impress everyone.

I want to clarify that no one has misused judges' names in relation to any neglect and abuse project. The East and West Coast may not desire massive injection of judicial thinking in their projects, but they have not misrepresented or claimed support they did not have. However, I want to strongly stress that the Center has been, with a number of exceptions, either ignored or given only token representation.

(2) How many judges should serve on the committees responsible for drafting model acts, regulations, etc.? When Professor Katz was good enough to invite me to one of his committee meetings in New York, there were several judges and behavioral scientists, etc., present. The same situation existed when I visited Professor Wald's committee in California. I received lengthly material from Mr. Besharov after it was drafted, and I knew by merely thumbing through it that he excluded any extensive judicial input from the draft. Frankly, the situation should be reversed, and all these committees should contain ten judges to every behavioral scientist instead of ten behavioral scientists to every judge.

(3) How should judges be selected to participate in these projects for writing model acts, standards, etc.? The few judges who have been asked to serve on these committees by either the East or West Coast have been well-qualified and

experienced. Their views should certainly be heard. However, the judges selected have seldom represented the views of a vast majority of juvenile court judges. This indicates the very skilled way in which these committees are set up and composed. It also may account for the strong division between the East and West Coast.

Ideally, the president of the NCJCJ should nominate five or ten judges for these committees in addition to those selected by the chairman or director of the project. As a matter of fact, the judges who served on these committees for the East and West Coast are as intelligent and well-informed as any of the 3,000 juvenile court judges in the nation. I have had several on the committees I have chaired, and their contributions were second to none. There is no question of the ability of the East and West Coast to select intelligent, experienced, and highly capable judges. However, if the president of the NCJCJ had been permitted to inject the massive thinking of a considerable number of perhaps less gifted judges into the development of these model acts and standards, we might not have such fractured and fragmented recommendations that will surely confuse state legislators and everyone else. HEW and IJA-ABA are a million miles apart, and NCJCJ is somewhere in the middle.

Both the East and West Coast either have or will have a very legitimate complaint should they try to massively infuse judicial thinking into their projects. I do not want to suggest judges are busier than professors or others in the behavioral sciences, but sometimes it is damned hard to get judges to take time from court to work on a project. I know this because I am a former president of the NCJCJ, and have been a member of at least 75-100 judges' committees in the past 16 years. Recruiting judges to work on these projects is frustrating. No committee that I ever served on or chaired worked harder than the NCJCJ Neglected Children Committee. I have chaired this committee for two and one-half years, and we have developed an excellent model terminating act. It has a good chance of being adopted without changes by the Michigan Legislature this year. The Edna McConnell Clark Foundation financed the project. It takes judges only a small fraction of funds to produce excellent model legislation as compared to the East or West Coast projects. A camel is a horse designed by a committee. After reaching a certain point, the larger the committee, the more likely the end product will have several "humps."

The East (HEW) presents the greatest concern. Legislatures and state governments follow the federal dollar like a hound dog follows a rabbit. I personally believe HEW should not issue model legislation and standards. The injection of the federal government in this role is a two-edged sword. Neither IJA-ABA or NCJCJ can use federal grants as bait to impose undesirable uniformity in the 50 states. The federal government should stay out of this business.

Two weeks ago the casework services director of the Wayne County juvenile court came to me with a case where the baby was found dead after being released from a hospital that had a grant to treat drug and alcohol addicts. It is not unusual for heroin-addicted women to be admitted to the hospital, give birth to a child, and both be treated because of heroin addiction. This hospital fears to report abuse cases that Michigan law mandated be reported prior to release of the child. But the experts in Washington decided to delve into the very complex business of confidentiality, and through law and regulation make it a violation for the hospital to report these cases. We are going into federal court hoping to receive a declaratory judgment to have these cases reported. This is not the first child that has died that could have been saved if reported under the state statute, but was not reported because the federal government stuck its nose into something better left to the states.

The state can complicate the very complex problem of confidentiality without receiving any help from Washington. There is no special wisdom in Washington, and all states had laws on this subject. There was no valid reason for the federal government to be involved unless to make more jobs for a larger bureaucracy.

The business of promulgating standards, model acts, etc., by HEW has a far different result than when accomplished by IJA-ABA or NCJCJ. The states can take it or leave it when these organizations get involved. But Congress and HEW have clout. Many states have taken the bait on the Mondale Reporting Act in order to receive federal funds. The states should decide whether "mental injury" or "yelling at a child in the back yard" is a proper act to be subject for a reporting system under child abuse. The end result may be a monolithic system imposed on the 50 states as a result of enforcing uniformity through the bait or requirement of federal grants.

We have not come that far down the road. Much that was good when I went on the bench in 1960, both in behavioral sciences and law, is now considered bad, and much that was considered bad is now viewed as good. We need another two or three decades of variety, experimentation, diversity, and massive noninterference by HEW. After we finish writing all the laws, model statutes, and regulations, the social worker will be the most important factor in handling neglect and abuse cases. I say this in all due respect to the rest of us who work in the system.

When the year 2,000 rolls around some of you here today will still be debating the role government should play in the life of a child. Maybe if you keep a copy of this statement in your files, you will find that much of what I have said will remain relevant in the twenty-first century.

If the East Coast (HEW) has its way, over a period of decades the social worker will present as big a threat to our way of life as the atomic bomb. If the West Coast gets its way, tens of thousands of abused and neglected children will not receive protection. In the meantime, whether you are a caseworker, a judge, or whatever, just keep on handling your caseload. The greatest sense of achievement I have received from hearing a multitude of abuse and neglect cases is that in applying my very best thinking and efforts, I am convinced that life for these children has been improved because I have been allowed to serve in this time and place. A judge must have gray hair to look distinguished, and hemorrhoids to look concerned. But most important, he should realize he is not infallible. I view myself as a concerned, inquisitive, and learning alchemist.

My personal wish for each of you is that when you approach retirement, as I do now, that you will have some measure of my sense of fulfillment that comes from working in one of the most demanding of all professions. I refer to anyone whose work concerns troubled children. Neither you nor I must depend on the East or West Coast, or the Center, in order to make our own unique, exceptional contribution to our time and place.

FOOTNOTES

[1] Louis W. McHardy, "Lincoln Speaks Out On Proposed Standards," *Juvenile Court Newsletter*, 1977, 48 (1), 10.

[2] Exhibits have been omitted here because of space limitations. Interested readers may contact Judge Lincoln directly (ed.).

[3] James H. Lincoln, Letter to Professor Michael S. Wald, (February 24, 1975).

[4] James H. Lincoln, Letter to Douglas Besharov (September 4, 1975).

[5] McHardy, "Lincoln Speaks Out" p. 10.

CHILD ABUSE AND NEGLECT PROGRAMS:

Practice and Theory

Summary, Conclusions, and Recommendations

Our review of the literature and our site visits to the eight programs, as well as to public social service agencies, mental health centers, hospitals, schools, day care centers, juvenile courts, and attorneys in the eight communities served by these programs, have left us with specific observations and recommendations relating to child abuse and neglect and to the services designed to help parents and children.

In this chapter, we highlight and summarize those issues discussed at various points in the report which we feel are of particular importance and offer recommendations for policy and practice.

DEFINITIONS

- Programs should develop operating definitions of abuse and neglect which take into account the child's age and the location and severity of the injury. In addition, such definitions should provide a clear statement as to what comprises a minimal level of acceptable care in the areas of health, nutrition, housing, education, and supervision, and the extent of bruising which will be regarded as nonabusive.

- Such operational definitions should be incorporated into State laws so that they can serve as the basis of a clear statement to parents and to other caretakers as to what is and what is not against the law. At present, the laws tend to be vague, not providing sufficient clarity as to what are

and what are not acceptable "omissions" and "commissions" in child care. For instance, while many State laws mention health practices, they do not specifically state whether parental refusal to allow immunization of children 0-5 years (on other than religious grounds) constitutes neglect of the children's health care or not.

REPORTING AND INCIDENCE

- Reporting by professionals increases when they have ready access to a team which provides them with consultation and support and which has provided them with an initial orientation to the importance of reporting.

- Reporting increases when the community feels that something positive and appropriate will be done and when the mechanisms for reporting are clearly understood and well publicized.

- Incidence studies are fraught with methodological problems which include problems of definition, sampling base, and under-reporting. Thus, current estimates of incidence are likely to be grossly misleading.

CHARACTERISTICS OF ABUSIVE/ NEGLECTFUL PARENTS

- Demographic variables tend to be so confounded that there is little sense which can be made of the interrelationships among income, single parent status, occupation, education, family size, age of mother

From *Child Abuse and Neglect Programs: Practice and Theory*, National Institute of Mental Health, Alcohol, Drug Abuse, and Mental Health Administraiton, U.S. Department of Health, Education and Welfare.

at first birth, and ethnic status. Even a very large-scale study which could partial out the contribution of each of these variables would be vulnerable to sampling error, as low-income families are more likely than high-income families to come to the attention of both service providers and researchers.

- Sufficient data exist to support the view that child abuse occurs in middle- as well as in low-income families, in intact as well as single parent families, in caucasian as well as in ethnic minority families, in small as well as in large families, in older as well as in younger families. Neglect seems to be more clearly related to income and factors associated with income than does abuse.

- Abuse is the result of an interplay between psychological, social, and chance factors. There seems to be considerable consensus among practitioners regarding the dynamics of abuse. Parents who have unrealistic expectations of the child based on their own needs and who lack knowledge of child development and child-rearing skills, parents who have themselves been abused or who have experienced only criticism and lack of nurturance in their own childhood, parents who have a low sense of self-worth and a feeling of overall helplessness in terms of getting their needs met or in terms of coping with day-to-day living, parents who live under conditions of acute relationship tensions, and parents who are isolated and lack a supportive network, are prime candidates for the role of abuser. Abusive parents are not detached from their children, rather they tend to be overly attached to their children or to at least one child in a manner which does not allow them to see that child as a separate individual with legitimate needs. In the context of a history of frustration and an inability to gratify dependency needs, the child becomes a need-gratifying object who is doomed to fail in this role not only because this is inherently not a role that infants can fill but also because the child as an extension of the parent is also seen as bad and unworthy.

- It is important to understand that the dynamics of abuse as summarized above are derived from the experience of practitioners and are not well documented by research. The primary reason for this is that most of the studies to date have been poorly designed and lack a comparison group. It is simply not enough to make statements about the proportion of abusive parents who exhibit this or that characteristic without comparable statements about the proportion of parents in a non-abusive demographically comparable population who exhibit the characteristic in question.

- The *dynamics* of abuse have received more attention than have *structural* variables. Given a crisis, and the dynamic conditions necessary for abuse, it is unclear whether abuse would occur in the absence of certain structural ego defects. That is, poor impulse control and a deficit in object relationships may well be necessary conditions of abuse. In addition, impairments in reality testing, in the thinking processes, and in the executive and planning functions of the ego seem to be characteristic of many abusive individuals.

- Most of the abuse literature focuses on the characteristics of the parents or of the children, there is relatively little work on parent-child interaction. It may well be that abuse lies neither in the parent nor in the child, but rather in the relationship between them.

CHARACTERISTICS OF ABUSED/ NEGLECTED CHILDREN

- There is no solid evidence to suggest that abused children are more likely than other children to have physical or emotional problems which precede the abuse and act as a triggering mechanism. In a large proportion of cases, the abused child was not premature, colicky, hyperactive, or either physically or mentally deviant.

- The theory of the "identified" child is largely unproven and potentially dangerous. Cases are common in which more than one child in the family has been abused or in which the child who is most disliked is spared and another child is abused or killed. The danger of the identified child theory is that protective services workers do not routinely require a physical examination of all the children in the family where one child has been abused because they have been taught that "usually" only one child is abused. In a family in which one child has been abused, all of the children should have a complete physical examination.

5. PROFESSIONAL

- The consensus seems to be that abused/neglected children are severely damaged in terms of their ability to function adaptively and that if intervention does not occur at a very young age, the damage may well be permanent.

- These children are most often characterized as unable to relate to others, unable to experience pleasure, aggressive, fearful, and delayed in reaching their developmental milestones.

IDENTIFICATION, CASE MANAGEMENT, AND TREATMENT

- Abusive parents are most likely to accept services and to form a positive therapeutic relationship at the point of crisis. Therefore, it is often particularly important that the worker assigned to a case continue with that case throughout the treatment process. Program models in which the responsibility for intake, case management, and treatment are each vested in a different staff member may appear functionally efficient; however, they do not seem to be as effective in terms of treatment outcomes as are programs in which one person fulfills all three functions.

- If transfer from one person to another is unavoidable within the design of the program, there should be adequate time for overlap so that the worker who has already established a relationship with the parents can assist in the transfer of that relationship to the next worker. For instance, if a protective services worker makes a referral to a mental health agency and if the new therapist is to be the primary source of contact, the protective services worker should effect the transfer of the client in person and should participate in the first few sessions between the client and the mental health worker.

- In the first contact between client and worker, the worker should be absolutely honest and straightforward about his/her role and about the changes that have to occur which affect the parenting of the child, supportive of the parents' desire to do well by the child through concrete reference to those aspects of the parenting which are sound, and able to recognize the parents' feelings of fear and needs for assistance.

- In many cases, confrontation over the issue of abuse itself is counterproductive and only serves to strengthen the parents' denial. Rather, the focus should be on the difficulties the parent is having in her/his life and the difficulties which the child presents and what the worker can do to help improve the situation.

- A plan should be devised with the parent in terms of services which can be made available. Every effort should be made to inform the parent of the purpose of each of the services and of what the parent can expect. Resistance to use of any particular service which is felt to be beneficial should be handled by requesting that the parents "try" on a short-term basis and then discuss the merits or nonmerits of the service.

- In programs which rely on a variety of services in the community and which do not have these services under one roof, every effort should be made to personally introduce the parent to each service provider. The worker's participation in the parents' first contact with day care, with public health nurse, and with homemaker, can mean the difference between acceptance and rejection of the service.

- So long as the parent continues to use a service which is part of a treatment plan and so long as the parent has not been discharged from the program as stabilized, the worker should maintain at least monthly contact with other service providers in order to monitor the progress of the parent in the use of the services. The issue is not only whether the parent is or is not using the service, but also *how* she/he is using it. Day care staff, public health nurses, and homemakers can all share important observations with the worker as to how the family is functioning and what further goals need to be accomplished.

- If the children are removed from the home as part of a voluntary agreement between the parents and the social service agency, there should be a very specific agreement as to what work the parents need to do in order to prepare for the children's return and the timeframe in which this is to occur. If, when the agreed-upon time comes the parent is still not ready, the social service agency should take the case to juvenile court and should invoke the authority of the court to assist in the development of a new therapeutic contract and timeframe for achievement of goals. If this new contract is also not honored, termination of parental rights should be seriously considered and pursued. Regardless of the needs of the parents, children should not be placed in long-term storage in the blind hope that the parents may one day, in the distant future, provide an adequate home.

- If the children are removed against the parents' wishes, the conditions of their return should be clearly spelled out in operational terms so that when the case is reviewed the court will have an informed base from which to make a judgment as to whether the changes have or have not been made. The contract between the program and the parent(s) should be made with the juvenile court and should be referred to frequently during the treatment process. Besides allowing for a therapeutic use of the authority of the juvenile court, this joint planning helps the parent to achieve a sense of mastery over her/his own destiny, promotes the use of the organizing and planning functions of the ego, promotes a therapeutic alliance between parent and worker, and provides the parent with the opportunity to enjoy recognition of real gains.

- It should be apparent from the above that removal of children from their families should in no way end program treatment efforts with respect to the parents. If the parents are so hopeless that no one can work with them, then there is no reason to expect things to get better and the only solution is termination of parental rights.

- Transfer of placement cases to a child welfare worker is counterproductive and serious thought should be given to program organization which allows protective services workers to continue with all family members even when a child has been placed, rather than to transfer the family or the child in placement to another worker.

- Visits with children in out-of-home care and eventual returns should be planned and executed with great care. The return of a child to his home requires not only that the parents have made agreed-upon changes and progress, but that there has been a systematic plan for visits of longer and longer duration and that the parents' feelings in terms of their own abilities to cope have been carefully explored. The return of children, who have been inadequately prepared for their return and who regard the parent(s) as a stranger, is harmful and sometimes dangerous.

- Whenever possible, visits between children and their natural parents should be in the company of the primary worker as these visits should be part of the therapeutic process. When the worker takes part in the visit, she/he is able to discuss specific incidents and feelings around them and to model alternate forms of behavior. Participation in these visits allows for therapeutic discussion of specifics rather than of vague generalities to which many parents cannot relate.

- While the timing of the removal of a child from his home is often not under anyone's control, in the sense that it reflects an emergency situation, the return of a child to her/his home can be planned and should be carried out with great care. In addition to considerations about the parents and their positive movement, the developmental age of the child should be very carefully considered. Separation of the child from a foster home in which he is thriving, during the period of maximal separation anxiety (approximately 6 months to 2 years of age), may very well not be in the child's best interest.

- The therapeutic relationship with the family should not be terminated as soon as the child is returned to his home. This is likely to be a period of considerable strain for the parents, of very active testing by the child, and of very great stress for the child. If anything, the worker's active involvement should be increased for at least 3 months following a successful return.

- During the time that a child is in foster care, the primary worker who is known to that child and to his natural parents should meet with him weekly to allow him to discuss his feelings and concerns. This weekly visit should include time with the foster parents to talk with them and to provide them with the support which is necessary to protect the placement. It is not enough to ask generally how things are going and to be told "fine." Rather, problems particular to the child should be probed and discussed and alternative ways of handling difficult behavior should be explored.

- Children of elementary school age and older should not be excluded from problem-solving sessions. Children who are told to "run and play" while grownups plan their lives are only made anxious and mistrustful. Children also need the opportunity to work on their feelings and their behavior and should be seen in a regular weekly session.

- People working in abuse and neglect programs need training, direction, and support if they are expected to work with children and with families. Many workers in this field have received no training in child development and have had no therapeutic experience with children, with adolescents, or with families. Yet, this is a field which demands work with children and with families and not with individual adults.

- Many abusive parents can derive considerable benefit from participation in a group. The group serves an energizing and supportive function and should be led by an individual who has had training and experience in group therapy. If this individual is not the primary worker, the primary worker should participate in group sessions so that there is a flow of information and a sense of continuity between individual and group sessions.

- Parents of average intelligence, who are not massively resistant or hostile, and who are not so needy that they monopolize all attention, can benefit from a group experience. A group can be for couples, for single parents, or be mixed without impairment of its effectiveness. Socializing among members and development of a mutual support system seems to be an important feature. Optimal group size seems to be between 8-10 clients.

- Differences in impact between a Parents Anonymous group and a professionally led group are not clear; many of the benefits ascribed to each are overlapping. Ideally, a community should have both available but, if this is impossible, every effort should be made to develop one or the other.

- For parents of more limited intelligence or for those who are unable to share in a group setting, an activity group can be of great value. Emphasis on completion of simple projects, sharing meals and recipes, and household management and child care issues can be very helpful. Such a group does not replace a group therapy experience and is intended for a different set of clients.

- A family therapy approach to abusive families has not yet been developed. Within mental health in general, family therapy is relatively new; therefore, most communities do not yet have anyone who is well trained in the use of this modality. Because the dynamic tensions in abusive families are often so extreme and because so many abusive families are characterized by destructive relationships between parents and grandparents, it seems that use of a family therapy approach to abusive families could represent a very significant contribution. If the primary caseworker is not skilled in family therapy, she/he should participate in family therapy sessions conducted by the family therapist.

- Husbands/boyfriends should not be left out of the therapeutic work; when they are left out they often sabotage the treatment. Moreover, their exclusion from therapy does little to promote their own improvement or significant change. Because relationship stress is one of the root dynamics of child abuse, it seems clear that every effort should be made to include both psychological partners in the treatment.

- Individual casework should be used as a sole treatment modality only for those individuals who are living totally alone with very young children and who cannot make use of any group experience. In most cases, the individual casework relationship should be one key aspect of the treatment plan in addition to ongoing participation in group, family, or couple therapy.

- Individuals working with abusive/neglectful families should have the opportunity for weekly supervision in the form of case conferences designed to constantly upgrade the level of treatment skills and techniques. At group supervisory meetings, there should be a continual collegeal questioning of treatment interventions, interpretations, and approaches. Alternative approaches and interpretations and their possible consequences should be explored so that the therapeutic work with a client is based on informed choice rather than on lack of knowledge of alternatives.

- The majority of abusive parents, if they exhibit the major dynamics of abuse, need not only concrete services but also therapeutic intervention. Services alone will not help them work through their sense of low self-esteem and their pathological fusion with the child.

- In most abuse cases, treatment can be viewed as a two-phase process. The first phase involves linking the family to services and establishing an initial therapeutic relationship with the primary worker. The focus of this early phase in the relationship is to establish a sense of trust and of support. The worker should serve the parents as the good parent she/he never had and provide gratification of dependency needs. As soon as this basic alliance is established, the parent is ready for the second phase: participation in additional treatment modalities and new learning about her/himself, about child development and childrearing, and about relationships with others.

- In general, problem-focused goal-oriented therapy addressed to changes in behavior seems to be more effective than is a general exploration of feelings and underlying attitudes. This does not mean that feelings are to be ignored but rather that they are to be grounded in specific experiences. Modeling and demonstration of behavior by the workers appear to be particularly effective. For example, parents can be taught to look for alternative means of discipline if the worker models this kind of problem-solving behavior in interactions with the parent and with the parent and child.

- Positive reinforcement for small gains is especially important and should never be understated. That is, a worker should never assume that a parent does not need to have small gains explicitly acknowledged and praised.

- Neglectful parents who exhibit the dynamics of abuse should be treated within the same treatment modalities as are abusive parents. Neglectful parents whose neglect is borne of ignorance, low intelligence, and/or extreme apathy should be helped to achieve their optimal level of functioning by means of concrete services. Highly specific step-by-step instruction in budgeting and household management can be especially effective.

- In the case of abuse, the consensus seems to be that active treatment should involve at least weekly contact, continued for 6 months to 2 years. Neglect cases usually take far longer; most workers agree that some families require support and ongoing supervision for a period of many years.

- Caseloads should be no greater than 15-20 families if the worker is to have adequate time with clients and with service providers and for supervision and upgrading of technical skills.

- Treatment can be successfully carried out by mental health professionals, by lay therapists, or by protective services workers. Relevant training, ongoing clinical supervision, caseload size, frequency of client-worker contacts, and responsiveness to client needs are more important than is professional training. A well-trained lay therapist who has ongoing supervision, sees each family at least weekly, and is able to visit in the home and provide access to concrete services is likely to be more effective than is the psychiatrist who sees the family only once and then rejects in-office visits, or the protective services worker who sees families monthly, responds primarily to crisis situations, and provides very little ongoing clinical supervision.

- Treatment services for children are underdeveloped. Every abused and/or severely neglected child should have the opportunity to express his/her concerns on a regular basis. In most cases, such contact should be weekly and should not be left to chance encounters or occasional visits to the family home.

- In the case of school age children, there should be ongoing regular bimonthly contact between the child's worker and the school social worker or guidance counselor.

- Preschool abused and severely neglected children should be placed in developmental day care programs which have a strongly therapeutic and stimulation-oriented approach. High quality therapeutic day care can do much to overcome many of the problems with which the child initially enters. All too often day care is viewed primarily as a relief for the parent without adequate consideration for the quality of day care required by the child and his developmental needs.

5. PROFESSIONAL

- Day care for abused children can also play an important role in the treatment of the parents. The parent learns that the fusion between her and the child can be replaced with a healthier experience of herself as a separate individual who can engage in activities which are fulfilling so that the child becomes less of a need-gratifying object.

- Adolescent children who have been abused or who live in a home in which their siblings are abused should be offered a special group experience in which the focus is on undoing the effects of the experience and on providing more benign and appropriate models for later parenting.

SERVICE DELIVERY SYSTEMS

The Public Welfare or Social Service Agencies

- Every public welfare agency which is responsible for protective services should either be able to deliver the case management and treatment services discussed or to contract for these services with other agencies in the community.

- In addition to traditional income maintenance and child welfare services, every public agency should have available to it the services of public health nurses, day care centers, and homemaker agencies. These services not only provide relief for parents and protection for children, they can also be used dynamically as key features of a treatment plan designed to produce real changes in the functioning of the family.

- Every public social service agency should have a specialized child protection unit or worker; protective services work requires a particular set of services and training. Eligibility workers or generic child welfare workers do not have this necessary training or experience.

- As no single agency can have under one roof all of the necessary services and professional expertise, the public social service agency should take the lead in organizing a child abuse and neglect team which participates in case planning and case review and which assists in the task of community education. The individuals who represent their agencies on this team should have sufficient authority to commit their agencies in terms of policy, planning, and the delivery of services.

- The public social service agency needs to develop systematic procedures for creating, maintaining, and updating resource files, for maintaining linkages with other service providers, and for monitoring quality of purchased services.

- Public social service agencies need to devise mechanisms by which to reduce worker turnover and "emotional burnout." The maintenance of an abuse unit which provides peer support, which maintains caseloads of no more than 15-20, and which provides for active supervision, and activities other than direct work with abusive families, e.g., working with resources, participating in a speaker's bureau, will enhance worker satisfaction and effectiveness.

Hospitals

- Any hospital which admits children should have at least one physician and one social worker or nurse who take responsibility for educating and alerting others to possible signs of abuse, who are versed in appropriate procedures, who provide consultation and support to other professionals, and who maintain a liaison with the public social service agency.

- Hospitals which have no such team are very likely to be underreporting cases of abuse and neglect. In virtually all hospitals which have implemented such a team, the rise in reporting has been sharp and dramatic.

- Hospitals with a psychiatric department have the capability of going beyond case identification and should give serious consideration to the development of a treatment unit, so that severely abused children and their families can have continuity of physical and mental health treatment.

Mental Health Agencies/Child Guidance Clinics

- While in most communities there is considerable expertise within these agencies regarding child therapy, group, family, and couple therapy, this expertise is not used on behalf of abusive families.

- Mental health service delivery, which typically includes fixed, in-office, 50-minute appointments and which offers no concrete services and no followup in relation to missed sessions, is not compatible with the treatment needs of most abusive families.

- In most cases, referrals to a mental health agency which has no abuse unit and no staff training in work with abusive parents are simply nonproductive.

- Mental health staff and protective services workers in the public agencies could work together to the mutual benefit and training of staff at both agencies. Group and family co-therapy modalities represent an excellent vehicle for such collaboration and joint development. Through such a co-therapy approach protective services caseworkers can upgrade their therapeutic skills and techniques and mental health workers can gain experience in working with difficult, demanding, and often hostile families.

- Case investigation and case management seem clearly to be within the domain of the public social service agency with input and cooperation from many other agencies. There is considerable controversy over whether treatment of abusive families should be the responsibility of the public social service agencies or of the mental health centers. Those who advocate treatment by the public social service agencies point to the mental health centers' lack of responsiveness, unwillingness to provide outreach services, and the negative effects of the therapeutic alliance between therapist and parent which sometimes leads to a dangerous overestimation of the parent's ability to parent. The best argument in favor of these advocates against referral to the mental health centers is that, by and large, because of the way in which they deliver services the mental health centers are not effective in helping abusive families. Those who advocate treatment by the mental health centers point to the expertise in treatment techniques and to the high caseloads and low frequency of contacts between clients and public social service workers. The best argument in favor of these advocates against treatment by the public agency is the fact that in most agencies the caseloads are too high and the staff is untrained in treatment techniques.

Thus, we are confronted with a situation in which, in most communities, no agency provides the treatment which is necessary and effective.

- There needs to be a coherent national policy as to where the treatment of abusive families belongs. If the consensus is that such treatment is the responsibility of the mental health centers, then the National Institute of Mental Health should issue guidelines as to effective practice, should make available case materials descriptive of different treatment processes, and should provide opportunities for training. Every mental health center should be encouraged to develop a child abuse treatment unit. The members of such a unit would receive training, would provide treatment, and would work closely with the public agency.

Day Care Centers/Schools

- All such institutions should have at least one person trained in identification who can provide support and consultation to others in the system.

- Day care centers and schools should have a relationship with protective services so that they can plan jointly with respect to certain cases. Abused and neglected children require a great deal of nurturance, support, and understanding; the school can respond to these needs if included in case planning. Day care, Head Start, and school nurses can be particularly supportive of a protective services effort to monitor and improve the health of the children in a family.

Law Enforcement Systems

- Regardless of whether or not the police represent the only agency which has the legal authority to remove an endangered child from his home, they play a central role in most communities. In many cases of intrafamily violence which result in child abuse, the police are the first to be called. A high level of training and awareness on the part of the police can mean the difference between life and death for a child; similarly their attitude toward the parents can mean the difference between the parents' willingness to accept help and their view of all outsiders as the enemy.

5. PROFESSIONAL

- Juvenile court judges play a central role in abuse and neglect cases. An informed judge understands the points of view and professional biases represented by all of the key actors and is able to provide the leadership which is necessary for a therapeutic use of the court. The court can monitor whether all of the agencies and the parents have carried out the conditions of an agreement and ultimately the court decides the fate of the child. Informed judges who have received training in child abuse and neglect cases are a major resource in any community in which they exist. All too often, juvenile court judges have not had any training in this area, are parents' rights oriented, and have no understanding of the therapeutic value of the court.

- Any abuse program, no matter what the auspice, should maintain close collaborative ties with the police and the juvenile court. This collaboration should include joint training and discussions to ensure mutual understanding of objectives and intentions. An atmosphere of mutual respect and confidence can be engendered if representatives from each agency understand the responsibilities and work of those in the other agencies. This means, for instance, that the abuse program has to know how to present cases in court in order to ensure relevance and adequacy of data, while the juvenile court has to be informed about abusive families in order to make decisions which are maximally productive.

All of the agencies discussed in the preceding section have a role to play in the delivery and provision of services to abusive and neglectful families. Every community should have a child abuse and neglect council or committee which seeks to coordinate and upgrade existing services, which advocates for the development of new services, and which takes responsibility for public and professional education. Such committees can effectively bring problems to the attention of participating agencies, can alert administrators within these agencies to areas of poor practice and to areas of needed improvement, and can advocate for a child abuse team, and for training within each agency.

In rural areas, if the service agencies cover several communities or even counties, then the council should follow the catchment area of the agencies in deciding on its area of responsibility. Agencies serving abusive and neglectful families in rural areas are subject to the same problems which are endemic to health and social service agencies in rural areas: distance, difficulty recruiting qualified staff, and scarcity of resources. The scarcity of resources and difficulty of recruiting trained staff make the team approach especially important in rural areas. When all of the agencies pool their resources, there may be an adequate case management and treatment capability in the team itself. The team can also ensure that several members get training which they are then responsible for bringing back to the rest of the team. In this way scarce resources can be shared effectively. Scarcity of staff makes a lay therapy, parent aide, or volunteer program especially attractive. The need to drive long distances to see families imposes a requirement of smaller caseloads and this, too, suggests the importance of volunteers in rural areas.

In large urban centers, the complexity and variety of resources available may require regionalization of the child abuse and neglect committee within the city if the community is to avoid the diffusion borne of large size and nonarea specific problems. Each area of the city should have its own committee with representation from those public social service and public health agencies, hospitals, school districts, and police precincts which serve that area.

The central issue is one of ensuring that every relevant agency is alert to the possibility of abuse and neglect, is clear about the mechanisms of reporting cases and of dealing honestly and sensitively with families to be reported, and delivers the services which the community has assigned to it in a responsible and effective manner. As we have discussed, staff in all relevant agencies need training and an identifiable person(s) with primary responsibility in this area. Reporting increases and outcomes, as measured by recidivism rates, improve when all of the agencies are doing their job.

RECOMMENDATIONS TO NIMH

Of all the agencies, perhaps the greatest discrepancy between the potential to provide help to these families and actual practice lies in the community mental health centers. Every mental health center should have a specialized capability for treating abusive families which includes certain essential elements.

- Each mental health center should have at least two staff members who have received intensive training in the problems and treatment of abuse; one of these should be an individual who works primarily with adults and who has experience as a group and family therapist and one should be an individual who works primarily with children. It should be apparent that in larger mental health centers the size of the special abuse staff should be increased.

- Each center should have at least one on-going therapy group for adults for which the mental health center has primary responsibility but which includes a protective services worker and at least one ongoing therapy group for abused adolescents which, through linkages with day care or Head Start, includes opportunities to practice a different kind of parenting.

- Each center should have a demonstrated capability for working with clients in their own homes, at least in the first few months of treatment, and a demonstrated capability of following up on every missed appointment by an abusive parent.

- The child abuse team within the mental health center should hold a weekly case conference for the purpose of sharing cases and treatment skills with colleagues, for the purpose of providing training to colleagues within the mental health center who might be encouraged to work with abusive families, and for the purpose of providing training and sharing information with protective services staff. Participants in these case conferences should include the team within the mental health center, other interested mental health staff, several protective services workers who may be assigned on a 1-year basis as a training experience, and the protective services worker whose particular case is being addressed.

- Finally, one of the members of the team should participate on the community child abuse and neglect committee and should bring back the concerns of the committee regarding improvements in services to the mental health center and it administrative staff.

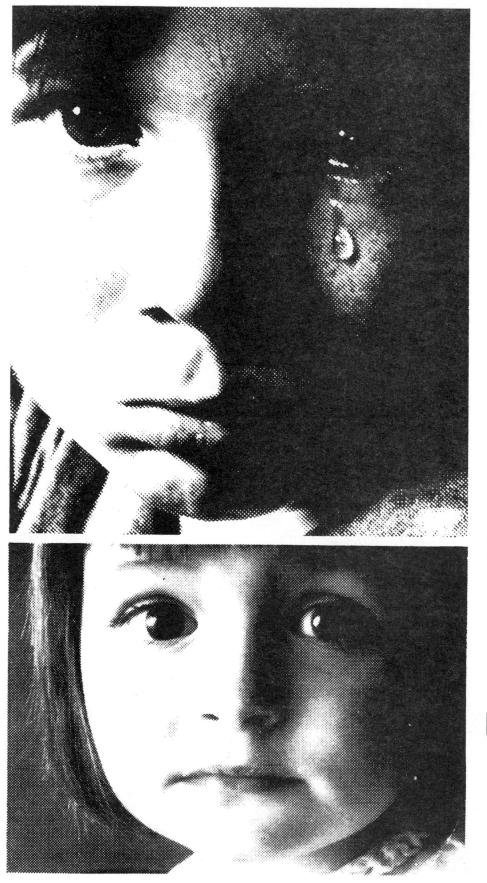

It shouldn't hurt to be a child

APPENDIX

The appendix is a list of state protective services and agencies organized especially for child abuse and maltreatment services, or have a branch for that purpose. The last page is a list of national agencies and the regional division offices provided for in the Child Abuse Prevention and Treatment Act of 1974. It is impossible to include all local and private agencies, and services provided by hospitals and universities. Those listed should be able to assist in contacting the nearest and most appropriate facilities.

ALABAMA
Bureau of Family and Children's Services
Department of Pensions and Security
Administrative Building
64 North Union Street
Montgomery, Alabama 36104

ALASKA
Alaska Children's Service
4600 Abbott Road
Anchorage, Alaska 99507

ARIZONA
Family & Child Welfare Services Division
Arizona State Department of Public Welfare
1624 West Adams Street
Phoenix, Arizona 85007

ARKANSAS
Division of Child Welfare
Arkansas State Department of Public Welfare
Box 1437
Little Rock, Arkansas 72203

CALIFORNIA
Department of Social Welfare
State of California Health and Welfare Agency
744 P Street
Sacramento, California 95814

Los Angeles Department of Public Social Services
Family and Children's Services
1801 West Valley Boulevard
Alhambra, California 91803

Pasadena Welfare Bureau
238 East Union Street
Pasadena, California 91101

Parents Anonymous
2009 Farrell Avenue
Redondo Beach, California 90278

COLORADO
Family & Children's Services
Division of Public Welfare
1575 Sherman Street
Denver, Colorado 80203

Colorado University Medical Center
Denver, Colorado 80910

Jewish Family & Children's Service of Denver
1375 Delaware Street
Denver, Colorado 80204

CONNECTICUT
Connecticut Welfare Department
1000 Asylum Avenue
Hartford, Connecticut 06115

Connecticut Child Welfare Association
P.O. Box 3007
New Haven, Connecticut 06515

DART Committee
Department of Pediatrics
Yale-New Haven Hospital
789 Howard Avenue
New Haven, Connecticut 06504

DELAWARE
State Department of Health & Social Services
Division of Social Services
3000 Newport Gap Pike
Wilmington, Delaware 19808

FLORIDA
The Division of Family Services
5920 Arlington Expressway
Jacksonville, Florida 32211

GEORGIA
Division of Family and Children Services
Georgia Department of Human Resources
State Office Building
Atlanta, Georgia 30334

HAWAII
Public Welfare Division
Department of Social Services and Housing
P.O. Box 339
Honolulu, Hawaii 96809

IDAHO
Family & Children's Services
State Department of Social and Rehabilitation Services
P.O. Box 1189
Boise, Idaho 83701

ILLINOIS
Illinois Department of Children and Family Services
524 South Second Street
Springfield, Illinois 62706

Juvenile Protective Association
12 East Grand
Chicago, Illinois 60619

Chicago Child Care Society
5467 South University
Chicago, Illinois 60615

Illinois Children's Home and Aid Society
1122 North Dearborn Street
Chicago, Illinois 60610

INDIANA
Division of Social Services
Department of Public Welfare
100 North Senate Avenue—Room 701
Indianapolis, Indiana 46204

Lutheran Social Services, Inc.
330 Madison Street
Fort Wayne, Indiana 46802

IOWA
Department of Social Services
Lucas State Office Building
Des Moines, Iowa 50319

Black Hawk County Department of Social Service
Court House
Waterloo, Iowa 50703

Cerro Gordo County Department of Social Service
Court House
Mason City, Iowa 50401

Dubuque County Department of Social Service
Conlin Building—3rd Floor
1472 Central Avenue
Dubuque, Iowa 52001

Johnson County Department of Social Service
538 Central Avenue
Iowa City, Iowa 52240

Linn County Department of Social Service
400—3rd Ave. S.E.
Cedar Rapids, Iowa 52401

Polk County Department of Social Services
112—116 Eleventh Street
Des Moines, Iowa 50309

Pottawattamie County Department of Social Services
231 Pearl Street
Council Bluffs, Iowa 51502

Scott County Department of Social Services
808 West River Drive
Davenport, Iowa 52801

Wapello County Department of Social Services
Court House
Ottumwa, Iowa 52501

Woodbury County Department of Social Services
411 Seventh Street
Sioux City, Iowa 51101

Child Abuse and Severe Neglect Committee
Court House
Waterloo, Iowa 50703

Child Abuse Committee
Department of Pediatrics
University Hospitals
Iowa City, Iowa 52240

KANSAS
Division of Services to Children, Youth & Their Families
State Department of Social Welfare
State Office Building
Topeka, Kansas 66612

Kansas Child Protective Services, Inc.
P.O. Box 16105
Wichita, Kansas 67202

KENTUCKY
Department of Child Welfare
403 Wapping Street
Frankfort, Kentucky 40601

Metropolitan Social Services Department
522 West Jefferson
Louisville, Kentucky 40203

Fayette County Children's Bureau
115 Cisco Road
Lexington, Kentucky 40504

LOUISIANA
Department of Public Welfare
P.O. Box 44065
Baton Rouge, Louisiana 70804

MAINE
Department of Health and Welfare
Augusta, Maine 04330

MARYLAND
Social Services Administration
1315 St. Paul Street
Baltimore, Maryland 21202

MASSACHUSETTS
Massachusetts Department of Public Welfare
600 Washington Street
Boston, Massachusetts 02111

Jewish Family and Children's Service
31 North Chardon Street
Boston, Massachusetts 02114

Massachusetts Society for the Prevention of Cruelty to Children
43 Mt. Vernon Street.
Boston, Massachusetts 02108

Children's Advocates
21 James Street
Boston, Massachusetts 02118

Children's Hospital
Trauma X Committee
295 Longwood Avenue
Boston, Massachusetts 02115

Trauma X Committee
Boston City Hospital
Harrison Avenue
Boston, Massachusetts 02111

MICHIGAN
State Department of Social Services
Bureau of Family and Children's Services
Lewis Cass Building
Lansing, Michigan 48913

Jewish Family and Children's Services
10801 Curtis
Detroit, Michigan 48221

Catholic Social Services of the Diocese of Grand Rapids
300 Commerce Building
Grand Rapids, Michigan 49502

D. A. Blodgett Homes for Children
805 Leonard N.E.
Grand Rapids, Michigan 49503

Catholic Social Services of St. Clair County
2601—13th Street
Port Huron, Michigan 48060

Child and Family Service of Saginaw County
1110 Howard Street
Saginaw, Michigan 46801

MINNESOTA
Minnesota Department of Public Welfare
Centennial Building
St. Paul, Minnesota 55108

MISSISSIPPI
Family and Children's Services
Mississippi State Department of Public Welfare
P.O. Box 4321, Fondren Station
Jackson, Mississippi 39216

MISSOURI
Family and Children's Services
State Department of Public Health and Welfare
State Office Building
Jefferson City, Missouri 65101

Social Service Department
Cardinal Glennon Hospital
1465 South Grand Boulevard
St. Louis, Missouri 63104

MONTANA
Social and Rehabilitation Services
Social Services Division
P.O. Box 1723
Helena, Montana 59601

NEBRASKA
Division of Social Services
Nebraska Department of Public Welfare
1526 K Street—Fourth Floor
Lincoln, Nebraska 68508

Nebraska Committee for Children and Youth
State House—Eleventh Floor, N.W.
Lincoln, Nebraska 68501

NEVADA
Nevada State Welfare Division
201 South Fall Street
Carson City, Nevada 89701

Washoe County Welfare Department
1205 Mill Street
Reno, Nevada 89502

Clark County Juvenile Court Services
East Bonanza Road and Pecos Drive
Las Vegas, Nevada 89107

NEW HAMPSHIRE
Bureau of Child and Family Services
Department of Health and Welfare
1 Pillsbury Street
Concord, New Hampshire 03301

NEW JERSEY
New Jersey Bureau of Children's Services
Department of Institutions and Agencies
163 West Hanover Street

Trenton, New Jersey 08625
Child Service Association
284 Broadway
Newark, New Jersey 07104

NEW MEXICO
New Mexico Health and Social Services Department
Social Services Division
P.O. Box 2348
Santa Fe, New Mexico 87501

NEW YORK
Protective Services Unit
Bureau of Community Services
State Department of Social Services
1450 Western Avenue
Albany, New York 12203

Select Committee on Child Abuse
270 Broadway
New York, New York 10007

Mayor's Task Force on Child Abuse
St. Vincent's Hospital
Seventh Avenue and West 11th Street
New York, New York 10003

Brooklyn Society for the Prevention of Cruelty to Children
67 Schermerhorn Street
Brooklyn, New York 11201

Manhattan Society for the Prevention of Cruelty to Children
110 East 71st Street
New York, New York 10021

Bronx Society for the Prevention of Cruelty to Children
370 East 149 Street
Bronx, New York 10455

Queensboro Society for the Prevention of Cruelty to Children
105-16 Union Hall Street
Jamaica, New York 11433

Monroe County Committee on Child Abuse
260 Crittenden Boulevard
Rochester, New York 14620

Onondaga County Child Abuse Committee
c/o United Community Chest and Council
107 James Street
Syracuse, New York 13202

Children's Aid & the Society for the Prevention of Cruelty to Children of Erie County, New York
330 Delaware Avenue
Buffalo, New York 14202

Jewish Family Service of Erie County
775 Main Street
Buffalo, New York 14203

Louise Wise Services
12 East 94th Street
New York, New York 10028

NORTH CAROLINA
Family & Children's Services Section
Department of Social Services
P.O. Box 2599
Raleigh, North Carolina 27602

NORTH DAKOTA
Department of Social Services
Capitol Building
Bismarck, North Dakota 58501

Catholic Family Services
Box 686
Fargo, North Dakota 58102

Lutheran Social Services of North Dakota
1325 11th Street South
Box 389
Fargo, North Dakota 58102

Children's Village
1721 South University Drive
Box 528
Fargo, North Dakota 58102

OHIO
Division of Social Services
Department of Public Welfare
Oak Street at Ninth
Columbus, Ohio 43215

Geauga County Department of Welfare
13281 Ravenna Road
Chardon, Ohio 44024

Montgomery County Children Services Board
3501 Merrimac Avenue
Dayton, Ohio 45405

Children Services of Richland County
50 Park Avenue East—4th Floor
Mansfield, Ohio 44902

Summit County Children Services Board
264 South Arlington Street
Akron, Ohio 44306

Children's Protective Service
Ohio Humane Society
2400 Reading Road
Cincinnati, Ohio 45215

Catholic Charities of Dayton
922 West Riverview Avenue
Dayton, Ohio 45407

Jewish Family Service
1175 College Avenue
Columbus, Ohio 43209

OKLAHOMA
Department of Institutions
Social and Rehabilitative Services
Sequoyah Memorial Office Building
Oklahoma City, Oklahoma 73125

OREGON
Children's Services Division
Department of Human Resources
Public Service Building
Salem, Oregon 97310

Battered Child Committee
Department of Pediatrics
University of Oregon Medical School
3181 S.W. Sam Jackson Park Road
Portland, Oregon 97201

PENNSYLVANIA
Bureau of Child Welfare
Office of Children and Youth
State Department of Public Welfare
Harrisburg, Pennsylvania 17120

RHODE ISLAND
Rhode Island Department of Social and Rehabilitative Services
Child Welfare Services
600 New London Avenue
Cranston, Rhode Island 02920

SOUTH CAROLINA
State Department of Social Services

Box 1520
Columbia, South Carolina 29202

Connie Maxwell Children's Home
P.O. Box 1178
Greenwood, South Carolina 29646

SOUTH DAKOTA
Service Administration
State Department of Public Welfare
State Office Building
Pierre, South Dakota 57501

TENNESSEE
Department of Public Welfare
State Office Building
Nashville, Tennessee 37219

Children's Protective Agency
Humane Educational Society
212 North Highland Park Avenue
Chattanooga, Tennessee 37404

TEXAS
Texas State Department of Public Welfare
Division of Special Services
John H. Reagan Building
Austin, Texas 78701

UTAH
Bureau of Family and Children's Services
State Division of Family Services
231 East 4th South
Salt Lake City, Utah 84111

VERMONT
Division of Child Services
Department of Social Welfare
Montpelier, Vermont 05602

VIRGINIA
Bureau of Family and Children's Services
Division of General Welfare
State Department of Welfare and Institutions
429 South Belvidere Street
Richmond, Virginia 23220

WASHINGTON
Social Services Division
Department of Social and Health Services
P.O. Box 1788
Olympia, Washington 98504

WEST VIRGINIA
Division of Social Services
Department of Welfare
Charleston, West Virginia 25305

WISCONSIN
Division of Family Services
Department of Health and Social Service
1 West Wilson Street
Madison, Wisconsin 53702

WYOMING
Division of Public Assistance and Social Services
Department of Health and Social Services
State Office Building
Cheyenne, Wyoming 82001

NATIONAL

American Public Welfare Association
1155 16th Street, N.W.
Washington, D.C. 20036

Center for Studies of Child and Family Mental
Health
National Institute of Mental Health
5600 Fishers Lane, Room 512
Rockville, Maryland 20857

Child Abuse Listening Medication (CALM)
P.O. Box 718
Santa Barbara, California 93102

Child Protective Service Training and Research
Project
Health Sciences Learning Resource Center
T252 Health Sciences
University of Washington
Seattle, Washington 98195

Council for Exceptional Children
1920 Association Drive
Reston, Virginia 22091

Education Commission of the States
300 Lincoln Tower
1860 Lincoln Street
Denver, Colorado 80203

Family Development Study
Children's Hospital Medical Center
300 Longwood Avenue
Boston, Massachusetts 02115

MANCO (Mexican-American Neighborhood Civic
Organization)
2811 Guadalupe
San Antonio, Texas 78207

National Alliance for Prevention and Treatment of
Child Abuse and Maltreatment
41-27 169th Street
Flushing, New York 11358

National Association of Social Workers
Child Abuse and Neglect Training Project
1425 H Street, N.W., Suite 600
Washington, D.C. 20005

National Center for Comprehensive Emergency
Services for Children
Urban Observatory
Metro Howard Ofice Building, Room 231
25 Middleton Street
Nashville, Tennessee 37210

National Committee for Prevention of Child Abuse
111 East Wacker Drive
Chicago, Illinois 60601

National Center for the Prevention and Treatment
of Child Abuse and Neglect
1205 Oneida Street
Denver, Colorado 80220

National Center on Child Abuse and Neglect
Children's Bureau
Office of Child Development, DHEW
P.O. Box 1182
Washington, D.C. 20013

Regional Offices:

Region I (Connecticut, Maine, Massachusetts,
New Hampshire, Rhode Island, Vermont)
Judge Baker Guidance Center
295 Longwood Ave.
Boston, Massachusets 02115

Region II (New Jersey, Puerto Rico, Virgin Islands)
Protective Services Resource Center
Rutgers Medical School
P.O. Box 101
Piscataway, New Jersey 08854

Region III (Pennsylvania, Virginia, Delaware, West
Virginia, District of Columbia)
Institute for Urban Affairs and Research
Howard University
2935 Upton St., N.W.
Washington, D.C. 20008

Region IV (Alabama, Florida, Georgia, Kentucky,
Mississippi, South Carolina, Tennessee)
Regional Institute of Social Welfare Research
P.O. Box152
Heritage Building
468 N. Milledge Ave.
Athens, Georgia 30601

Region V (Illinois, Indiana, Michigan, Minnesota,
Ohio, Wisconsin)
Midwest Parent-Child Welfare Resource Center
Center for Advanced Studies in Human Services
School of Social Welfare
University of Wisconsin-Milwaukee
Milwaukee, Wisconsin 53201

Region VI (Arkansas, Louisiana, New Mexico,
Oklahoma, Texas)
Center for Social Work Research
School of Social Work
University of Texas at Austin
Austin, Texas 78712

Region VII (Iowa, Kansas, Missouri, Nebraska)
Institute of Child Behavior and Development
University of Iowa
Oakdale, Iowa 53219

Region VIII (Colorado, Montana, North Dakota,
South Dakota, Utah, Wyoming)
National Center for the Prevention and Treatment
of Child Abuse and Neglect
University of Colorado Medical Center
1205 Oneida St.
Denver, Colorado 80220

Region IX (California, Hawaii, Nevada, Guam,
Trust Territorities of the Pacific, American Samoa)
Department of Special Education
California State Universtiy
5151 State University Dr.
Los Angeles, California 90033

Region X (Alaska, Idaho, Oregon, Washington)
Northwest Federation for Human Services
P.O. Box 2526
Boise, Idaho 83720

National Center for the Study of Corporal
Punishment and Alternatives in the Schools
823 Ritter Hall South
Temple University
Philadelphia, Pennsylvania 01922

National Center for Voluntary Action
1214 Sixteenth Street, N.W.
Washington, D.C. 20036

National Coalition for Children's Justice
66 Witherspoon Street
Princeton, New Jersey 08540

National Juvenile Law Center
3642 Lindell Boulevard
St. Louis University
St. Louis, Missouri 63108

National Organization of Victim Assistance
University of Southern Mississippi
McClesky Hall, Room 230
Southern Station Box 5127
Hattiesburg, Mississippi 29401

Parents Anonymous
see California

The Panel for Family Living
1115 S. 4th Street
Tacoma, Washington 98405

Project CARE
Brooke Army Medical Center
P.O. Box 66
Fort Sam Houston, Texas 78234

Suspected Child Abuse and Neglect (SCAN)
Hendrix Hall
4313 W. Markham
Little Rock, Arkansas 72201

U.S. Committee for UNICEF
331 East 38th Street
New York, New York 10016

International

National Advisory Center on the Battered Child
Denver House, The Drive
Bounds Green Road
London N. 11, England

STAFF

Publisher	John Quirk
Editor	Roberta Garland
Editorial Ass't.	Carol Carr
Director of Production	Richard Pawlikowski
Director of Design	Donald Burns
Customer Service	Cindy Finocchio
Sales Service	Dianne Hubbard
Administration	Linda Calano

Cover Design	Donald Burns
Cover Photo	Richard Pawlikowski